getting started

on research

The Academic's Support Kit

Building your Academic Career
Rebecca Boden, Debbie Epstein and Jane Kenway

Getting Started on Research
Rebecca Boden, Jane Kenway and Debbie Epstein

Writing for Publication
Debbie Epstein, Jane Kenway and Rebecca Boden

Teaching and Supervision
Debbie Epstein, Rebecca Boden and Jane Kenway

Winning and Managing Research Funding
Jane Kenway, Rebecca Boden and Debbie Epstein

Building Networks
Jane Kenway, Debbie Epstein and Rebecca Boden

getting started

on research

Rebecca **Boden**

Jane **Kenway**

Debbie **Epstein**

⑤SAGE Publications
London • Thousand Oaks • New Delhi

First published 2005

SAGE Publications Ltd
1 Oliver's Yard
55 City Road
London EC1Y 1SP

SAGE Publications Inc.
2455 Teller Road
Thousand Oaks, California 91320

SAGE Publications India Pvt Ltd
B-42, Panchsheel Enclave
Post Box 4109
New Delhi 110 017

British Library Cataloguing in Publication data

A catalogue record for this book is available from the British Library

ISBN 978 1 4129 0696 8

Library of Congress control number available

Typeset by C&M Digitals (P) Ltd, Chennai, India
Printed in Great Britain by Cromwell Press Ltd, Trowbridge, Wiltshire

Contents

Acknowledgements

Books such as these are, inevitably, the product of the labours, wisdom and expertise of a cast of actors that would rival that of a Hollywood epic.

Our biggest thanks go to our publishers, Sage, and especially Julia Hall and Jamilah Ahmed for unswerving enthusiastic support from the very beginning and for their careful and constructive advice throughout.

We would like to thank the authors of *Publishing in Refereed Academic Journals: A Pocket Guide* and especially Miranda Hughs for her hard work and insights which led the way conceptually.

Many people reviewed the initial proposal for the *Academic's Support Kit* at Sage's request and gave it a very supportive reception. We are grateful for their early faith in us and promise to use them as referees again!

The annotated Further Reading was excellently crafted by Penny Jane Burke, Geeta Lakshmi and Simon Robb. In addition, Elizabeth Bullen gave enormous help on issues of research funding and William Spurlin helped us unravel the complexities of US universities. All are valued friends and colleagues and we appreciate their efforts.

Much of the material in the *Kit* was 'road-tested' in sessions for our postgraduate students, colleagues and others. Many other people kindly gave their time to read and comment on drafts. We are very grateful to these human guinea pigs for their hard work and can assure our readers that, as far as we are aware, none of them was harmed in the experiment.

Chris Staff of the University of Malta devised the title the *Academic's Support Kit*, and he and Brenda Murphy provided glorious Mediterranean conditions in which to write. Malmesbury, Morwell and Gozo were splendid writing localities, although Dox 'added value' at Malmesbury with his soothing yet sonorous snoring.

We are grateful to our universities – Cardiff, Monash, South Australia and the West of England – for the material support and encouragement they gave the project.

Many people in many different universities around the world inspired the books and unwittingly provided the material for our vignettes. They are too many to mention by name and besides we have had to tell their stories under other names. We are deeply indebted to our colleagues, ex-colleagues, friends, enemies, students and past students, old lovers, past and present combatants and allies and all the managers that we have ever worked with for being such a rich source of illustration and inspiration!

We particularly thank that small and select band of people who have acted as a constant source of succour and support, wise guidance and true friendship at various crucial stages of our careers: Michael Apple, Richard Johnson, Diana Leonard, Alison Mackinnon, Fazal Rizvi, Gaby Weiner, Roger Williams and Sue Willis.

Finally, as ever, our greatest thanks go to our nearest and dearest, without whose tolerance, love and hard work these books would not be in your hands today.

R.B.
J.K.
D.E.

Introducing the *Academic's Support Kit*

Before you really get into this book, you might like to know a bit more about the authors.

Rebecca Boden, from England, is professor of accounting at the University of the West of England. She did her PhD in politics immediately after graduating from her first degree (which was in history and politics). She worked as a contract researcher in a university before the shortage of academic jobs in 1980s Britain forced her into the civil service as a tax inspector. She subsequently launched herself on to the unsuspecting world of business schools as an accounting academic.

Debbie Epstein, a South African, is a professor in the School of Social Sciences at Cardiff University. She did her first degree in history and then worked briefly as a research assistant on the philosopher Jeremy Bentham's papers. Unable to read his handwriting, she went on to teach children in a variety of schools for seventeen years. She returned to university to start her PhD in her forties and has been an academic ever since.

Jane Kenway, an Australian, is professor of education at Monash University with particular responsibility for developing the field of global cultural studies in education. She was a schoolteacher and outrageous hedonist before she became an academic. But since becoming an academic she has also become a workaholic, which has done wonders for her social life, because, fortunately, all her friends are similarly inclined. Nonetheless she is interested in helping next-generation academics to be differently pleasured with regard to their work and their lives.

As you can see, we have all had chequered careers which are far from the stereotype of the lifelong academic but that are actually fairly typical. What we have all had to do is to retread ourselves, acquire new skills and learn to cope in very different environments. In our current jobs we all spend a lot of time helping and supporting people who are learning to be or developing themselves as academics. Being an accountant, Rebecca felt that there had to be a much more efficient way of helping people to get the support they need than one-to-one conversations. This book and the other five in the *Academic's Support Kit* are for all these people, and for their mentors and advisers.

We have tried to write in an accessible and friendly style. The books contain the kind of advice that we have frequently proffered our research students and colleagues, often over a cup of coffee or a meal. We suggest that you consume their contents in a similar ambience: read the whole thing through in a relaxed way first and then dip into it where and when you feel the need.

Throughout the *ASK* books we tell the stories of anonymised individuals drawn from real life to illustrate how the particular points we are making might be experienced. While you may not see a precise picture of yourself, we hope that you will be able to identify things that you have in common with one or more of our characters to help you see how you might use the book.

Pragmatic principles/principled pragmatism

In writing these books, as in all our other work, we share a number of common perceptions and beliefs.

1. Globally, universities are reliant on public funding. Downward pressure on public expenditure means that universities' financial resources are tightly squeezed. Consequently mantras such as 'budgeting', 'cost cutting', 'accountability' and 'performance indicators' have become ubiquitous, powerful drivers of institutional behaviour and academic work.

2. As a result, universities are run as corporate enterprises selling education and research knowledge. They need 'management', which is essential to running a complex organisation such as a university, as distinct from 'managerialism' – the attempted application of 'scientific management techniques' borrowed from, though often discarded by, industry and commerce. What marks managerialism out from good management is the belief that there is a one-size-fits-all suite of management solutions that can be applied to any organisation. This can lead to a situation in which research and teaching, the *raison d'etre* of universities, take second place to managerialist fads, initiatives, strategic plans, performance

indicators and so on. Thus the management tail may wag the university dog, with the imperatives of managerialism conflicting with those of academics, who usually just want to research and teach well.

3. Increasingly, universities are divided into two cultures with conflicting sets of values. On the one hand there are managerialist doctrines; on the other are more traditional notions of education, scholarship and research. But these two cultures do not map neatly on to the two job groups of 'managers' and 'academics'. Many managers in universities hold educational and scholarly values dear and fight for them in and beyond their institutions. By the same token, some academics are thoroughly and unreservedly managerialist in their approach.

4. A bit like McDonald's, higher education is a global business. Like McDonald's branches, individual universities seem independent, but are surprisingly uniform in their structures, employment practices and management strategies. Academics are part of a globalised labour force and may move from country to (better paying) country.

5. Academics' intellectual recognition comes from their academic peers rather than their employing institutions. They are part of wider national and international peer networks distinct from their employing institutions and may have academic colleagues across continents as well as nearer home. The combination of the homogeneity of higher education and academics' own networks make it possible for them to develop local identities and survival strategies based on global alliances. The very fact of this globalisation makes it possible for us to write a *Kit* that is relevant to being an academic in many different countries, despite important local variations.

6. In order to thrive in a tough environment academics need a range of skills. Very often acquiring them is left to chance, made deliberately difficult or the subject of managerialist ideology. In this *Kit* our aim is to talk straight. We want to speak clearly about what some people just 'know', but others struggle to find out. Academia is a game with unwritten and written rules. We aim to write down the unwritten rules in order to help level an uneven playing field. The slope of the playing field favours 'developed' countries and, within these, more experienced academics in more prestigious institutions. Unsurprisingly, women and some ethnic groups often suffer marginalisation.

7. Most of the skills that academics need are common across social sciences and humanities. This reflects the standardisation of working practices that has accompanied the increasing managerialisation of universities, but also the growing (and welcome) tendency to work across old disciplinary divides. The *Academic's Support Kit* is meant for social scientists, those in the humanities and those in more applied or vocational fields such as education, health sciences, accounting, business and management.

8. We are all too aware that most academics have a constant feeling of either drowning in work or running ahead of a fire or both. Indeed, we often share these feelings. Nevertheless, we think that there *are* ways of being an academic that are potentially less stressful and more personally rewarding. Academics need to find ways of playing the game in ethical and professional ways and winning. We do not advise you to accept unreasonable demands supinely. Instead, we are looking for strategies that help people retain their integrity, the ability to produce knowledge and teach well.

9. University management teams are often concerned to avoid risk. This may lead to them taking over the whole notion of 'ethical behaviour' in teaching and research and subjecting it to their own rules, which are more to do with their worries than good professional academic practice. In writing these books, we have tried to emphasise that there are richer ethical and professional ways of being in the academic world: ways of being a public intellectual, accepting your responsibilities and applying those with colleagues, students and the wider community.

And finally . . .

We like the way that Colin Bundy, Principal of the School of Oriental and African Studies in London and previously Vice-Chancellor of the University of the Witwatersrand in Johannesburg, so pithily describes the differences and similarities between universities in such very different parts of the world. Interviewed for the *Times Higher Education Supplement* (27 January 2004) by John Crace, he explains:

> The difference is one of nuance. In South Africa, universities had become too much of an ivory tower and needed a reintroduction to the pressures

of the real world. In the UK, we have perhaps gone too far down the line of seeing universities as pit-stops for national economies. It's partly a response to thirty years of underfunding: universities have had to adopt the neo-utilitarian line of asserting their usefulness to justify more money. But we run the risk of losing sight of some of our other important functions. We should not just be a mirror to society, but a critical lens: we have a far more important role to play in democracy and the body politic than merely turning out graduates for the job market.

Our hope is that the *Academic's Support Kit* will help its readers develop the kind of approach exemplified by Bundy – playing in the real world but always in a principled manner.

Books in the *Academic's Support Kit*

The *Kit* comprises six books. There is no strict order in which they should be read, but this one is probably as good as any – except that you might read *Building your Academic Career* both first and last.

Building your Academic Career encourages you to take a proactive approach to getting what you want out of academic work whilst being a good colleague. We discuss the advantages and disadvantages of such a career, the routes in and the various elements that shape current academic working lives. In the second half of the book we deal in considerable detail with how to write a really good CV (résumé) and how best to approach securing an academic job or promotion.

Getting Started on Research is for people in the earlier stages of development as a researcher. In contrast to the many books available on techniques of data collection and analysis, this volume deals with the many other practical considerations around actually doing research – such as good ways to frame research questions, how to plan research projects effectively and how to undertake the various necessary tasks.

Writing for Publication deals with a number of generic issues around academic writing (including intellectual property rights) and then considers writing refereed journal articles, books and book chapters in detail as well as other, less common, forms of publication for academics. The aim is to demystify the process and to help you to become a confident, competent, successful and published writer.

Teaching and Supervision looks at issues you may face both in teaching undergraduates and in the supervision of graduate research students. This book is not a pedagogical instruction manual – there are plenty of those around, good and bad. Rather, the focus is on presenting explanations and possible strategies designed to make your teaching and supervision work less burdensome, more rewarding (for you and your students) and manageable.

Winning and Managing Research Funding explains how generic university research funding mechanisms work so that you will be better equipped to navigate your way through the financial maze associated with various funding sources. The pressure to win funding to do research is felt by nearly all academics worldwide. This book details strategies that you might adopt to get your research projects funded. It also explains how to manage your research projects once they are funded.

Building Networks addresses perhaps the most slippery of topics, but also one of the most fundamental. Despite the frequent isolation of academic work, it is done in the context of complex, multi-layered global, national, regional and local teaching or research networks. Having good networks is key to achieving what you want in academia. This book describes the kinds of networks that you might build across a range of settings, talks about the pros and cons and gives practical guidance on networking activities.

1 Who should Use this Book and How?

The purpose of this book is to help you know enough about the research process to get you going and to establish a research career. If this is the first book in the *Academic's Support Kit* that you are reading, then you may find it useful to read 'Introducing the *Academic's Support Kit*' before you read any further.

This book will be especially useful for you if you are in any of the following categories. Someone who:

- Is a research student of some sort.
- Has had an academic job for a while but who has not yet managed to get going on research.
- Is in their first academic job (with or without a research degree).
- Has made a career change and has recently become an academic.
- Is a casual (sessionally or hourly paid) teacher in a university who would like to develop an academic career in the fuller sense.
- Has already done some research but who is not entirely confident that they have got the hang of things yet.
- Is a more experienced academic who is mentoring someone in one or more of these categories.

This book is not meant for contract researchers, who will, inevitably, be working to someone else's agenda, though they may also be wanting to do their own work and would find the book useful for that purpose.

You may:

- Want to develop a successful academic career as a researcher or a teacher-researcher.
- Feel and/or actually be under tremendous institutional pressures to develop a research profile.
- Be someone who is genuinely inquisitive, self-driven, and who really wants to do research for its own sake.

Whatever, you are likely to be ready to go but may not be confident about how to set about it. Many good academics are compulsive over-achievers who nonetheless feel surprisingly insecure and ambivalent about their own achievements. Anxiety about research is therefore an extremely common phenomenon. We have lost count of the number of highly successful academics who constantly feel as if someone is going to 'find them out' for being 'inadequate'. This book should help you to acquire some good basic knowledge and to cope better with these common feelings of inadequacy.

In many disciplines it is common for people to become academics as a second career after time spent working in a profession of one kind or another. In others, it is more likely that you will have progressed directly, or with a very short break, from undergraduate studies to a postgraduate degree and then an academic job. Whatever your background, you may be surprised to find that you already have many of the skills and personal attributes that you need to become a successful researcher. If you have become an academic after a period as a professional, many of the skills and competences that you have had to develop and deploy in your everyday working life will be incredibly important and useful. If you are a continuing student, with no professional work experience, you will have recent and relevant study/research skills.

Some of the relevant skills for successful research that you might already have acquired in whole or in part are:

- Curiosity and an enquiring mind.
- The ability to read, digest, summarise and synthesise complex material.
- The capacity to work with others to achieve your goals.
- The competence to grapple with complex technical issues and techniques.
- Enthusiasm for seeking out new challenges without feeling (too) intimidated.
- The ability to organise yourself and manage your own work.
- Good problem-solving, observational and communication skills.

In any case, successfully developing your research will require some strong personal motivational forces. These can include:

- Working on something that can sustain your interest over a long period.

- Doing research on something about which you feel passionately.
- Feeling that your research work can really make a difference in whatever way is important to you.

If you can't identify any of these forces, or any like them, then think again about what you want to research or indeed whether you *really* want to do research. For many academics, research is *the* thing that really makes their job worthwhile. Conversely, doing research that you do not enjoy can make you extremely miserable.

Finally, we'd like to introduce you to some people who are in the kind of position we think would lead them to find this book useful.

Sasha's first career was as a senior nurse and she had been very successful in her work. She had enjoyed her part-time masters degree, for which she had received a distinction. Consequently, when she was approached to apply for a post in health sciences at the university where she had done her masters, she leapt at the chance to become an academic. Soon after her appointment, the government audited research activity and she was not deemed to be acceptably research-active. At that point, this was not a particular problem as she was such a new academic. Over the next few years she found that she had little time and less support to become research-active. In her department there was a clear line drawn between the higher-status researchers and the lower-status vocational teachers. Although she kept trying to do research, she gradually gave up hope that she would ever be able to achieve the standard required. As you can imagine, by this time her confidence was shattered.

John had worked successfully as a lawyer for a number of years before his wife died, leaving him with sole care of his young children. He took on a teaching post at a local university because it enabled him to combine working with his childcare commitments. He joined a department with quite strict divisions between those who taught and those who did research. The then head of department told him that he should concentrate on teaching and 'not bother his head with ▶

▶ research'. He did as instructed and, for ten years, was an exemplary teacher. The policy of the university then changed and John came under increasing implied and overt pressure to become research-active. However, he had so completely excluded himself and been excluded from the research culture that he simply didn't know where to begin. His sense of personal well-being and happiness at work were severely disrupted.

Mukesh had been a teacher of French in a university for a few years when the head of department gave him a project and forcefully suggested that he should do a PhD in the area. At the same time, he advised Mukesh never to do research in anything you were not interested in because you would never finish it. Mukesh did indeed complete his PhD, but the exercise left him with little passion for or real skill in research. This, combined with the arrival of two children in swift succession, meant that he failed to pursue a research career after completing his PhD. As the higher education climate changed, Mukesh found himself under increasing pressure to commence research again, but found it psychologically difficult because of his previous experience.

2 Getting Going: Developing Research Ideas

In this chapter we discuss the question of what academic research is and how to begin to establish your own identity as a researcher. In particular, we look at the thorny question of what you can research and how you can choose, formulate and move on from your research questions.

What do you mean, 'research'?

All kinds of people do 'research', either in their private lives or as part of their work. Journalists, police officers, teachers, travellers and tour guides all need to find things out. For instance, the tourist or the tour guide may want to find out about a local church. They might ask local people, the priest, or consult history books, travel guides, parish records, the internet or simply go and look around the church itself. What they probably want is some interesting factual information to be entertained by or to entertain with. This is all research in the general sense, but it is not academic research.

An academic researching the same church would have very different objectives, depending on their own disciplinary perspectives. For example, an ecclesiastical historian might be interested in the role of this particular church in the history of Catholicism in the region, or its role in sustaining religious beliefs and observances in a local area. A sociologist might be interested in the social functions of the church, or its role and power in local culture and everyday life. An economist might be interested in the system of local tithes that sustain church finances and in how it impacts on the local economy. An education academic might want to explore the role of the church in local schooling and the curriculum and churches as pedagogic agents. An English scholar might be interested in the ways in which local churches, congregants and priests feature in the literature of the area, while an art historian might want to study the artworks in the church or the role of Church patronage of artists in developing particular genres or tastes. What all these academic researchers are seeking is much more than the factual information sought by the tourist or the tour guide. The academics want some deeper understanding or knowledge of social, economic, political, cultural or aesthetic life. Their interests are broad and deep and tackle fundamental questions.

So the type of research that we're talking about is done in order to gain deeper understandings or knowledge, rather than just to acquire information or facts, unlike Charles in the following vignette.

> Charles was a non-research-active teacher at a university. He had to go and see his Director of Research for an interview. She asked him for an explanation as to why he wasn't doing research. He protested that he was doing research. He explained that he ran a business consultancy business in his 'spare' time and that this frequently involved him making quite complex research investigations in order to solve his clients' individual business problems. The Director of Research explained, patiently but through gritted teeth, that such research was not academic research because it only provided individual answers rather than more comprehensive explanations.

In order to get to grips with what research in your own academic field means, you should aim to participate as much as possible in the research culture of your department, university or wider academic community. Read your colleagues' work, go to research seminars in your department and others, go and talk to people whom you know to be active researchers and read widely. In this way, you will begin to get a feel not only for what is going on, but also for what is interesting in your area and for what it means to be a researcher.

What *can* I research then?

Almost any social, political, cultural, economic or aesthetic phenomenon, issue or problem can be the subject of academic research in the wider social sciences and humanities. The key thing is not what it's about, but the way that you approach the issue. If you are looking for a subject for your research the best thing to do is to develop a real sense of curiosity about how the world around you works or let yourself be open to ideas, objects, experiences or events (current or historical).

Sometimes you might read something or hear something that you disagree with so profoundly that you decide to research the area yourself. At other times, you might hear or read something that sparks your interest and catches your imagination. One of Rebecca's colleagues recently railed to her about students who came to see him asking, 'What should we research?' He had been in the supermarket that morning and noticed that a cleaning product called 'Jif' had been renamed 'Cif' as part of a global rebranding exercise. He argued that something as simple as this brand name change could be used as the starting point of research on all aspects of globalisation, including global capitalism, branding and marketing.

Some people will have an area of technical or professional expertise that they can build on to develop their research interests. But your initial interest in something is likely to result in a research project that is sustained by your own curiosity and passion for it. Once you have identified a broad area, think about how you can use your technical or disciplinary knowledge to focus on this subject to develop real understandings.

An important part of the process of developing your research topics and ideas is your reading of the available literature. Starting to dip into it at this stage should provoke your interest and curiosity, help you formulate your ideas further and start to engage you in argument in your area.

Vivienne was registered for a PhD in history at an Ivy League university in the USA. Her original proposal was to do with the historical development of ethnic identities in the American south. Her reading in her first year showed her that she was much more interested in the literatures of women's history and the history of slavery than in that of the history of the south. Sparked by her interest in these topics, she changed her research proposal completely and did her thesis on the gendered history of slavery.

It sounds straightforward: find something in your everyday world that catches your interest and then ask big and deep questions about it. However, in our experience the single most difficult task for any new researcher is to move from a general curiosity or even a specific interest in something to being able to frame it as a subject for academic research.

The best question to ask yourself to ensure that you have made this shift is 'If I do this investigation and somebody then asks me, "So what?" will I be able to give a credible answer?' That is, will the answers you reach be of interest beyond the information you have collected itself and to anyone other than yourself? You must be able to frame your subject in such a way that you move from description to explaining what the data you have found means. In other words, you must be able to *theorise* your subject.

> Roger started his research on a particular UK factory at the University of Ambridge. His supervisor, an economic historian, had persuaded him to collect reams of facts and figures about output, finances and markets, etc. Roger did not enjoy this research and had little passion for how the subject was developing. He then moved to another university, where a new supervisor persuaded him to use theories of how social and cultural capital are formed to examine the socio-economic and cultural impacts on community formation of the development of the particular factory. Suddenly, the minutiae of the money value extracted from the business by the owners and how it was spent extravagantly in fancy London stores became a way of explaining how social classes sought to distinguish themselves and ensure their social positions.

How do I define what I'm going to research?

We can think about people's research as nested, as shown in Figure 1. There are three principal levels:

- *Personal intellectual projects.* These are the overarching themes and areas that you really want to know about and will spend years,

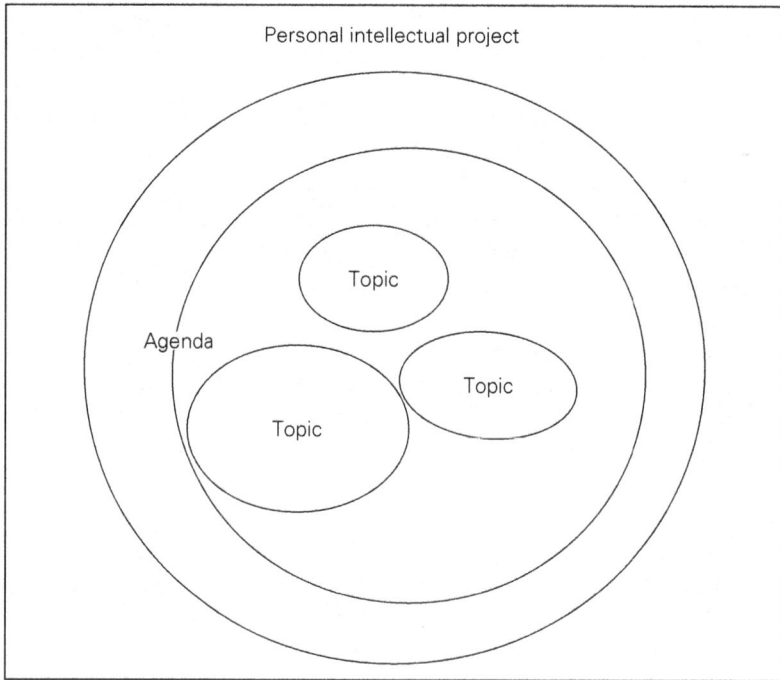

Personal intellectual project

Agenda

Topic

Topic

Topic

FIGURE 1   Nesting your research

possibly your whole career, developing. For instance, Sigmund Freud was interested in the workings of the subconscious and the influence of early experience on later emotional and psychological development. Of course, few academics will ever have the status and long-term impact of Freud. Nonetheless, having their own personal intellectual project will substantially enhance their work.

- *Research agendas.* These encapsulate clusters of research topics that hang together in the here and now. One of Freud's agendas was to understand the particular dynamics that contribute to the formation of adult sexuality.

- *Research topics.* These are specific, individual foci that should fit within your broader research agenda and personal intellectual project. Within his agenda on the formation of sexuality, Freud investigated such topics as hysteria, melancholia and dreams through his clinical practice. Individual research projects are formulated to investigate one or more specific research topics.

You can't do good research unless and until you identify your research topic. People with an established research identity tend also to have personal intellectual projects and research agendas and choose research topics within them. The level of abstraction and theorisation tends to increase as you move from individual topics towards your personal intellectual project. This is to be expected as you begin to get a more comprehensive grasp of the whole area. You can expect an iterative relationship between these three levels as work at each impacts on your thinking, the research you do and the direction you want to go in next.

Researchers tend to start with a topic and the whole enterprise subsequently grows into an agenda and a personal intellectual project. If you start in this way, you will need to have some kind of feel for or notion of what the bigger picture is and how your personal intellectual project might eventually develop. This is part of ensuring that the work you start on has a long shelf life and is capable of sustaining not only your interest but the interest of others. It needs to be capable of a greater level of theorisation and abstraction than you may start with. Ideally, it will also be capable of becoming a field which is demonstrably 'yours' or in which you are a major researcher.

Miguel became fascinated with the governance structures of his own university and started to investigate them systematically. After discussing this with his mentor, he realised that there was a wider research agenda here: what his university did reflected the state of higher education in the country generally. A whole stream of related topics concerning higher education suggested themselves. This research agenda soon grew into a personal intellectual project to investigate notions of governance in the not-for-profit sector inhabited by universities.

On a career note, if you really want to make a name for yourself, try to identify topics, agendas and personal intellectual projects that you can make very much your own territory. Conversely, never believe that the fact that there is no research in a particular area is sufficient justification for you to do it.

> Madhur, a well established researcher with an international reputation, was told by a group of feminist doctoral students that they felt exposed because their research topics were risky, endangering their chances of getting academic jobs in the future. They asked Madhur how she felt about the fact that her research was in a very contentious area. Madhur said that when she had started her work in this area, just after her PhD, she had a strong sense that it would be politically important and valuable as a contribution to theory. The fact that she was one of only very few people who were doing research in her area meant that her first book was one of the first two or three such books in the world. Strategies that felt risky could also therefore bring high rewards. She might have ended up being unable to get a job, but she was confident when she started that what she was beginning to work on was worthwhile. On the other hand, working a well-trodden field carried different consequences. Had she continued with her doctoral research area, the work might have been just as good, but she would have been one of many people doing good stuff in her field and therefore may have had a lower profile.

There are a number of issues to bear in mind here.

- First, whilst being innovative and imaginative are all well and good, it doesn't excuse you from the necessity of making sure that what you are doing passes the 'so what?' test and can make a sustained and valuable contribution.
- Second, breaking new ground can appear and feel risky, even foolhardy, but if you have done your homework in defining your research topic, this is not necessarily the case.
- Third, keeping to the mainstream and going over fields that have already been well ploughed may appear less risky, but in fact carry the danger of never getting the recognition you may deserve as you struggle to compete with many others in the same area.

What should I read?

There is a whole range of different sorts of literature that you will need to read as a researcher. We define these as follows:

- *Research literature.* This is the body of academic work produced by researchers working within or affiliated to academic institutions. Such work will normally be published in academic, refereed journals and books published by recognised academic publishers. If you look at *Writing for Publication* you will find a more detailed description of what constitutes 'academic literature'. In brief, the crucial test is whether the publication has been refereed by other academics – this is called 'peer review'.
- *The 'grey' literature.* This term is often used to describe research reports published by and/or for policy-oriented organisations such as governments, supranational organisations such as the World Bank or the OECD, non-governmental organisations, trade unions and so on.
- *Professional literature.* Professional bodies worldwide usually produce publications, above and beyond their newsletters, which aim to facilitate detailed discussion of professional practice between practitioners. Sometimes academics use these journals to disseminate research findings to practitioners. You should bear in mind that such articles will be written in a style different from their more usual academic publications and will usually refer to the latter.
- *Other publications.* These include newspapers, newsletters of organisations, popular books and magazines, and so on.

A problem that researchers frequently encounter is how to identify the research literatures relevant to their project and which to exclude. There are two sorts of difficulties people find.

First, they think they have to read absolutely everything that might possibly have a bearing on their research. This is because they do not yet have a strong sense of belonging to a particular community of scholars with whom they are, in their thinking at least, in conversation. Whilst reading widely is good, there does come a point at which you have to put some boundaries in place and get on with your own work rather than endlessly seek to keep up with the plethora of other people's work. Often people have a primary affiliation to a particular field of study and most of their reading will be in that discipline or in a particular inter-disciplinary space. By and large, having such identifications will eventually help you put some boundaries around the literature you decide to use. If you are a novice researcher, it's a good idea to take advice from your doctoral supervisor or a research mentor on where to start and stop reading.

Second, people think that there is 'nothing to read' in their field because they are looking too specifically. As Keiko's story demonstrates, there will always be something relevant, though it may not be on your specific topic.

Keiko was an architect who had taught the technical aspects of building design for many years. She started her PhD looking at the role of architecture in the construction of 'disability' and particularly the impact of building design on people with short-term memory loss. She went to her supervisor and complained that there was no literature relevant to her interests because no-one had ever written anything about such issues. Her supervisor despatched her to the library to read the extensive sociological and cultural studies literature on disability. Engaging with this sophisticated literature assisted her in developing the theoretical and conceptual basis of her thesis.

You shouldn't cling desperately to your own narrow subject area. Explore other literatures and take some risks in spreading your net wider. This will usually enrich your study conceptually. What you are looking for are areas of literature that help you to think deeply and imaginatively about your own topic.

Eventually you will be able to locate yourself and your personal intellectual project in a particular area of literature and this will become what people call your 'epistemic community' (more on epistemology later). Once you know what this space is, you should know:

- Who the key thinkers are currently and have been over time.
- What the central debates in the area are, both historically and contemporaneously.
- The difference between various research methodologies.
- How to distinguish between key innovative thinkers and those who have made use of and developed their work in more specific ways. This will allow you to be more discerning in your reading.
- Who is at the cutting edge in your areas, and you should be able to distinguish between short-term fads and more lasting influences.

In other words, you need to know your way around your intellectual home and be able to rearrange the furniture in ways that please you.

Here are some good ways to start identifying and locating your literatures:

- Try an electronic key-word search of on-line databases. When you do this you need to be thoughtful and selective about your words.
- When you get your search results, work out what it is immediately possible to exclude. You will be able to decide this on the basis of your disciplinary affinities and your reading of the abstracts.
- Take note of which authors and journals come up frequently in the search results.
- Follow up on authors and texts that appear with regularity in the bibliographies, seem important, particularly interesting or contentious. This is called 'chaining' and will help you to map the field.
- Talk to other people in similar and related fields and find out which authors they find particularly useful.
- Go to the library (yes, actually go) and browse along the shelves next to the books you know you are interested in. Stephen Kemmis, a well known Australian academic, calls this 'grazing in the groves of academe'.
- Go to the current issues of journals in your disciplinary area. You can sign up to such electronic journal alerts as SARA and EMERALD, which belong to the big publishing houses and will automatically notify you by email of the contents pages of the latest issues of your selected journals.

Having done all this, you will clearly need to be highly selective in your eventual choices and develop the capacity to synthesise the literature you use. One useful way to think about the sorts of things you do as you immerse yourself in the research literature comes from a well known taxonomy developed by Bloom, as illustrated in Table 1. In our experience, many novice researchers stop at stage two from Bloom's taxonomy: understanding.

Another possible approach to sorting out the literature is to ask yourself (and make notes on) the following questions as you read.

- Who is talking?
- What standpoints or personal histories are they bringing with them?
- Whom are they talking for and to?
- Who benefits (i.e. in whose interests do they speak)?
- What is the impact of what they say?

TABLE 1   Bloom's taxonomy of reading

Knowledge	Know who the characters are and recognise their voices
Understanding	Comprehend what people are saying
Analysis	Think critically about what they are saying
Evaluation	Apply your judgement about the merit or otherwise of what is being said
Synthesis	Pull together those parts of the literature useful for your own work (that is, be very selective) and map this literature in ways that will help you think through your own work

Bertram, B.S., Messia, B.B. and Krathwohl, D.R. (1964) *Taxonomy of Educational Objectives* (two vols: 'The Affective Domain' and 'The Cognitive Domain'), New York: David McKay.

How big should a project be?

In our experience, most people who want to get started on research try to bite off more than they can chew in picking a research topic. They don't yet know what their personal intellectual project will become, as this is something that usually grows with time. However, they may have a research agenda, which they confuse with an immediately researchable topic. Supervisors and mentors, therefore, frequently spend a good deal of time and effort in persuading and helping people to define their topics more closely and focus on something achievable in a known and limited time span. Don't be worried or concerned if your resulting research topic appears too narrow. If you have worked things through and thought about the bigger picture, you should have a reasonable degree of confidence about how your topic fits into wider contexts, as Thabo's experience shows.

Thabo arrived to meet his prospective PhD supervisor wanting to do 'something about post-colonialism and literature'. After discussion, he developed a research proposal that was near enough to being do-able for him to be accepted on to the PhD programme, but he still needed to define more closely precisely what it was that he would do. In the event, his topic was about how Southern African post-colonial writers had, so far, responded to the AIDS pandemic.

People often want to know how big their project should be. This is a bit like asking 'How long is a piece of string?' and you won't actually know the precise answer straight away. However, in certain situations, you will be given a specific external constraint. For example a doctoral student will have a maximum and minimum period of time during which she will be expected to produce a thesis with a prescribed maximum word length. Apart from such situations, you will generally be much freer to define the parameters of your project yourself or sometimes in conjunction with collaborators or a mentor.

The question then becomes 'How do I decide how big to make this project?' Think very carefully about the practical constraints under which you have to work. They include time, money, skills and access to sources of data and help and advice. For instance, it is no good deciding that you want to do research on a literary manuscript held in a private collection in another country if you have a heavy teaching load, no funds for travel and cannot be sure that the owners of the manuscript will allow you access to it. If you are a totally novice researcher and are unsure about whether you will like, or be any good at, research you may want to deliberately pick a very small and contained first project. Getting something successful under your belt can be a major confidence booster. Some people get this by doing a dissertation on a masters degree course, but not all.

Where are the pitfalls?

Mind the gap. When you think about your research topic or agenda, it is tempting to start off by looking for 'gaps' in the research literature. This is a real chimera. It makes us think of the image of a British dry-stone wall; these are built from unevenly sized rocks, carefully fitted together without mortar and so riddled with tiny gaps. These walls last for many years but need maintenance, and parts have to be rebuilt from time to time. In our image the wall is the metaphorical body of research and researchers are anxiously examining it in microscopic detail to find the tiny gaps so that they can quickly plug them. It does not occur to them that the holes may have been left to allow for drainage, or because it simply isn't worth filling them in. And, of course, at the same time as they are looking for holes to plug there may be another bit of the wall crying out for attention. Rather than look for holes and gaps in existing knowledge, you need to think about what's really engaging your interest and what's really worth doing. Doing it may involve rebuilding bits of the wall, or even laying the foundations of a new one.

Avoid the totally parochial and truly trivial. It may sound contradictory for us to say, at this point, that you should avoid doing parochial research. After all, we have been pressing you to look to the world around you for your research ideas. What we mean, here, is that you need to avoid doing research that is of interest only to you and your immediate colleagues and which is not capable of broader theorisation and conceptualisation. Every year academia presents to itself awards for improbable research. Some of it is quite valuable: other stuff just shouldn't have been done. We think it best to avoid this type of publicity for your research. Here are details of the 2002 winners.

The 2002 IgNobel Prize Winners

Biology

Norma E. Bubier, Charles G.M. Paxton, Phil Bowers, and D. Charles Deeming of the United Kingdom, for their report 'Courtship Behaviour of Ostriches towards Humans under Farming Conditions in Britain.' [REFERENCE: 'Courtship Behaviour of Ostriches (Struthio camelus) Towards Humans Under Farming Conditions in Britain,' Norma E. Bubier, Charles G.M. Paxton, P. Bowers, D.C. Deeming, *British Poultry Science*, vol. 39, no. 4, September 1998, pp. 477–481.]

Physics

Arnd Leike of the University of Munich, for demonstrating that beer froth obeys the mathematical Law of Exponential Decay. [REFERENCE: 'Demonstration of the Exponential Decay Law Using Beer Froth,' Arnd Leike, *European Journal of Physics*, vol. 23, January 2002, pp. 21–26.]

Interdisciplinary research

Karl Kruszelnicki of the University of Sydney, for performing a comprehensive survey of human belly button lint – who gets it, when, what color, and how much.

▶ *Chemistry*

Theodore Gray of Wolfram Research, in Champaign, Illinois, for gathering many elements of the periodic table, and assembling them into the form of a four-legged periodic table table.

Mathematics

K.P. Sreekumar and the late G. Nirmalan of Kerala Agricultural University, India, for their analytical report 'Estimation of the Total Surface Area in Indian Elephants.' [REFERENCE: 'Estimation of the Total Surface Area in Indian Elephants (Elephas maximus indicus)', K.P. Sreekumar and G. Nirmalan, *Veterinary Research Communications*, vol. 14, no. 1, 1990, pp. 5–17.]

Literature

Vicki L. Silvers of the University of Nevada-Reno and David S. Kreiner of Central Missouri State University, for their colorful report 'The Effects of Pre-existing Inappropriate Highlighting on Reading Comprehension.' [PUBLISHED IN: *Reading Research and Instruction*, vol. 36, no. 3, 1997, pp. 217–23.]

Peace

Keita Sato, President of Takara Co., Dr Matsumi Suzuki, President of Japan Acoustic Lab, and Dr Norio Kogure, Executive Director, Kogure Veterinary Hospital, for promoting peace and harmony between the species by inventing Bow-lingual, a computer-based automatic dog-to-human language translation device.

Hygiene

Eduardo Segura, of Lavakan de Aste, in Tarragona, Spain, for inventing a washing machine for cats and dogs.

▶

▶ *Economics*

The executives, corporate directors, and auditors of Enron, Lernaut & Hauspie [Belgium], Adelphia, Bank of Commerce and Credit International [Pakistan], Cendant, CMS Energy, Duke Energy, Dynegy, Gazprom [Russia], Global Crossing, HIH Insurance [Australia], Informix, Kmart, Maxwell Communications [UK], McKessonHBOC, Merrill Lynch, Merck, Peregrine Systems, Qwest Communications, Reliant Resources, Rent-Way, Rite Aid, Sunbeam, Tyco, Waste Management, WorldCom, Xerox, and Arthur Andersen, for adapting the mathematical concept of imaginary numbers for use in the business world. [NOTE: all companies are US-based unless otherwise noted.]

Medicine

Chris McManus of University College London, for his excruciatingly balanced report, 'Scrotal Asymmetry in Man and in Ancient Sculpture.' [PUBLISHED IN: *Nature*, vol. 259, February 5, 1976, p. 426.]

Source: http://www.improb.com/ig/ig-top.html

A little bit of exercise ...

We think that at this point in the book it is probably a good time for you to do some retail therapy. Most serious academics like good stationery. Go to a good stationery store and buy yourself one or two large-format hardback notebooks. These may have lined, squared or plain paper, as you prefer, but must be of good quality. We will return to the question of these notebooks later. You will also need some nice pens that you enjoy using. (We like to have fibre-tip pens in as many different hues as possible as this suits our note-taking styles.) Once you have your notebooks, you might like to write yourself some notes in response to the following queries:

• What are my motivations for doing research at all? Are they positive and will they sustain me in the enterprise?

- Where do my research ideas come from? Are they things that I genuinely find fascinating and absorbing and that will sustain me through all the hard work? Are they subjects that will get me out of bed in the morning (or even in the middle of the night if I wake up with a good idea)?
- Is my proposed research idea capable of passing the 'So what?' test? Can it lead to theorisation? Is it part of a big picture? Can I begin to see where agendas and personal intellectual projects will develop?
- Is my topic sufficiently focused, given all the constraints under which I must work?
- Above all, is this a topic that I can really get passionate and enthusiastic about?

If you can do this exercise and write more or less positive answers, then you are taking the first steps towards good reflexive practice as an academic researcher. Indeed, these sorts of notes can eventually end up as the starting point of formal research proposals, which we discuss in detail below.

Framing research questions

Having successfully identified your research topic, the next step is to develop a set of specific questions that your research project will set out to answer. The one golden rule is that you must have at least one research question and possibly more.

But why do I have to have research questions?

In the previous section we talked about finding and defining your research topic. This will have enabled you to understand and explain what you are interested in and why it's worth looking at. Going a step further, and defining one or more research questions within that topic, enables you to say exactly what you are looking for as well as why you are looking at it. Having a question focuses our analysis and forces us to have an argument that runs through our work. This is important because it protects us from the temptation of indulging in pure description without trying to achieve the deeper understanding reached by theorising what we are doing. Figure 2 shows the part that research questions can play in a virtuous cycle of knowledge creation.

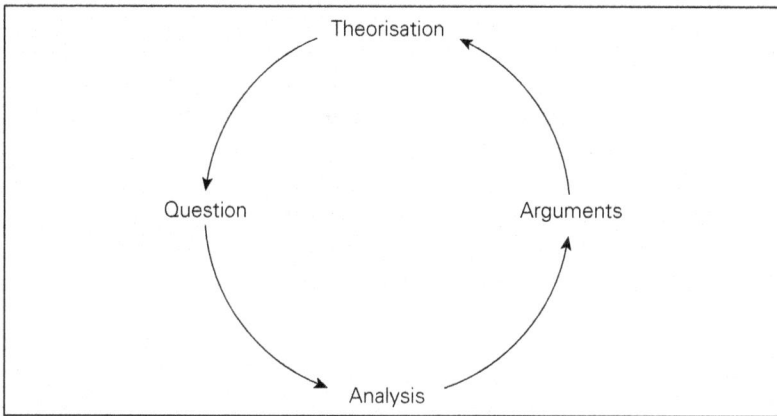

FIGURE 2   The circuit of question, theory and argument
production

Other reasons why we start with research questions are that
developing them makes us delimit what we are going to do and become
very focused in our research. This may sound pedantic, but a research
project that is never finished or that spreads out uncontrollably in every
direction is really of no use to anybody.

It is also kinder to readers, users and/or beneficiaries of your research
to start with specific questions. That way they can see what you have
attempted to do and how far you have got in achieving it.

Finally, having clearly set out questions avoids the perils of the
pugilistic, or even friendly or well intentioned, questioner at conferences
or vivas who takes great delight in asking why you haven't looked at *x* or
whatever their particular hobby horse is. If you have well worked out
questions, you will always be able to respond to such questioners by
saying, 'My questions were [such and such], and what you suggest is/may
be extremely interesting but was not the focus of this project.' In
summary, one of the purposes that research questions serve is an
authoritative defining statement about what the research focus actually is.

But don't you have to have hypotheses?

Some people, especially in the social sciences and some aspects of the
humanities, may be encouraged to frame their research questions as
formal 'hypotheses'. Even if you've never heard of the idea of a
hypothesis in research, you should read this section because it will help
you to understand what follows.

The notion of a 'hypothesis' comes from the natural sciences. The classical scientific method of research, as described by Karl Popper in his book *The Logic of Scientific Discovery* published in 1934, commences with the development of hypotheses. A hypothesis is a formal statement, usually grounded in observation – for example 'living creatures can fly only if they have feathers'. Using the scientific method, the objective is to test such hypotheses. By their nature, they cannot be proven because there always might be other effects that explain a phenomenon. But whilst hypotheses cannot ever be proven with absolute certainty, they can be disproved. For instance, to use the example above, the scientist might discover flying insects (which of course don't have feathers). This process of disproving hypotheses is known as 'falsification'. All hypotheses must be falsifiable; that is, capable of being tested. Just one example that disproves a hypothesis destroys it. This type of research is known 'deductive' and in the social sciences the tag most often attached to it is 'positivist'.

Early social scientists sought to present sociology and psychology as 'scientific' in the same sense as physics or chemistry. This was partly because of the higher status given to knowledge produced as part of a 'scientific' process, which led to what one might term 'physics envy'. The equivalent in literary studies was the notion that every text (especially classical ones) has a fixed meaning, and the task of the researcher was to find out what the meaning 'really' was. In legal studies, the equivalent is what's known as 'black-letter law': the detailed study of what legislation says rather than looking at law as a social, economic or political phenomenon. There are many other such examples in all branches of humanities and social sciences.

In all these areas, these approaches are underpinned by a belief that the 'truth is out there' and there is an objective answer that can be discovered by research. Yet, even in the natural sciences, this classical approach to knowledge building is being questioned and problematised. Despite this, it can sometimes feel uncomfortable for new researchers to accept and give voice to the idea that knowledge can only ever be partial and is always subjective.

Examples of (loosely worded) hypotheses in social sciences might be:

- Stock markets efficiently process information from company annual reports such that the resulting stock prices accurately reflect the real market value of the companies.

- Boys achieve higher marks in school tests when they are taught to read by male teachers.
- Capital punishment reduces the murder rate.

It is likely that a number of our readers will work within this tradition and find it to be a productive approach. We think that there are a number of problems with such positivist approaches.

- The process isn't as objective as you may think at first. The very selection and formulation of hypotheses imply a subjective view of the world. Few researchers would formulate a hypothesis and then spend a lot of time and effort testing it if they did not have a good subjective hunch that the answer would be interesting.
- People don't usually formulate hypotheses that they expect to be easily falsifiable. Formulating a hypothesis implies that you think it is likely to be 'true' and creates that impression among others, including the people you are researching (if you tell them what your hypothesis is) in ways that may well affect the outcomes of the research.
- Starting from hypotheses tends to lead to answers to questions about 'what' but not about 'why' something is as it is.
- Because the investigation of hypotheses is reliant on the investigation of observable phenomena, we can only explore that which we can see. This creates problems when the phenomenon or process you want to investigate is not directly observable. If, for example, you formulated a hypothesis that women do the bulk of child care because they want to, you would not be able to observe the operation of gendered power or unconscious motivations that might explain why they express such a desire.
- Because hypotheses must be falsifiable (that is, you can test them), they will always be rather simplistic. Complex social processes are not the subject of simple hypotheses and cannot be captured in this way.

Despite these reservations, which you will find amply expressed elsewhere in the research literature, this type of positivist research is still carried out in certain areas of the social sciences and humanities. You may find that the dominant way of doing things in your disciplinary area or university department is positivist. Remember that, as long as you do your work well, you do have the option of breaking away from such practices or of sticking with them. If you feel that such methods of investigation are the best for what you want to do, then be aware of the pitfalls and problems outlined above.

So what is a good research question?

We have already argued that you need research questions to frame and guide your research. So this section is really about what constitutes a good research question. It is, unfortunately, much easier to come up with poor or problematic questions than with good ones. The characteristics of good research questions are as follows.

- They don't invite true/false testing in the way that a hypothesis would.
- They don't have the answer contained or implied within them.
- They don't invite 'yes' or 'no' answers. Instead, the answers are likely to be complex and richly nuanced.
- They do facilitate a closely focused investigation, helping to keep the researcher on track. That is, they are not so broad that they allow the researcher to wander all over the place looking for answers.
- They are questions that are answerable through investigation and do not rely on belief or faith. For instance, 'Does God exist?' is not answerable other than through belief or faith. It is not, therefore, a research question, even for theologians (who may well do research into what drives religious belief, or the historical nature of particular holy texts).
- For relatively inexperienced or novice researchers, having a research question framed in such a way that it has a question mark at the end can be a wonderful way of ensuring that your question is really tightly formulated and focused.
- Research questions should be brief.
- Research questions should be able to be coherently grouped within a project, such that you have one or two principal questions with, perhaps, a *few* subsidiary sub-questions for each main one. Save surplus questions for future projects or you may find yourself trying to find out the answer to life, the universe and everything.
- Good research questions are the result of a rigorous process of developing and refining one's ideas.
- They have a demonstrable relationship with the existing literature in the area. This means that you will have had to begin to read the

literature more closely in order to develop a good feel for the shape of debates in your area and are reasonably confident that your answers will make some new contribution to knowledge.

- Good research questions lead to projects that are achievable within the time and other constraints under which you must work.
- Good research questions are amenable to constant revisiting and adjustment where necessary as the research progresses.
- In any research, you will have to be selective about what you look at. Good research questions will make transparent, to yourself and others, the basis of your selection.

In sum, good research questions are do-able and answerable. They focus the mind, the enquiry and the product. The consequence of not having good research questions to start with are evident in Douglas Adams's writing.

In the late Douglas Adams's excellent 'trilogy with four books' (*The Hitchhiker's Guide to the Galaxy, Life, the Universe and Everything, The Restaurant at the End of the Universe and Goodbye* and *Thanks for all the Fish*) a central theme was that the world had been created as a giant experiment by mice in order to determine the answer to 'life, the universe and everything'. In the first volume the answer emerged as '42'. This prompted a mere Earthling, and part of the experiment, 'Dent, Arthur Dent', to ask what the question was. The whole of the next book was the search for the question, which turned out to be 'What do you get if you multiply six by nine?'

Apart from having written a very amusing comment on many aspects of life in late modernity, Douglas Adams illustrates beautifully the need to start with good, answerable questions. Because the question of 'life, the universe and everything' is unanswerable, the solution found doesn't make sense and turns out to be the answer to quite another question.

A very important reason for ensuring that you have good research questions to start with is that otherwise the whole process of research can become unmanageable. If you are trying to answer the riddle of

TABLE 2 Research questions and hypotheses

Hypotheses	Principal research questions	Subsidiary research questions
Stock markets efficiently process information from company annual reports such that the resulting stock prices accurately reflect the real market value of the companies.	How do stock markets process the information they receive from company annual reports? By what means, and to what extent, does such information processing impact on share prices?	What are the regulations, processes and structures that shape the way information is processed? Do stock markets actively promote the belief that share prices accurately reflect the real market value of the companies listed? If they do, by what means?
Boys achieve higher marks in school tests when they are taught to read by a male teacher.	Is there a relationship between boys' measured achievement in reading and the gender of their teacher? If so, how can it be explained?	How do boys in classes with similar demographic characteristics taught by women and men differ in scores on a standard reading test at the end of their first year of compulsory schooling? Is there a difference in the way boys construct their identities at this age when taught by men and by women? What are the implications for boys' school-based reading achievement?
Capital punishment reduces the murder rate.	Is there a demonstrable relationship, and if so what, between perceptions of punishment and murder rates?	What are the different motivations that murderers have or express? In cases of premeditated murder, do the murderers say that they actively considered the likely punishment and what effect, if any, did this have on their actions? Is there a perceptible difference between murder rates in comparable countries/states and how can we account for them?

'life, the universe and everything', you have no basis for deciding what to do or how to set about doing it. In the vignette below we see the panic that can set in if there is no good research question in place (or if the researcher doesn't focus on the research question).

Giacoma advised one of her students who had just started some fieldwork where they were observing children in a classroom. The student was beginning to panic because she was totally unable to make a note of all that happened in the class and was worried that this would compromise her research. Giacoma pointed out that you are not expected to make a note of every single thing that happens. A bird flying past a window will not appear in your field notes, for example, unless it causes some kind of major disruption relevant to your research. What you note is dependent on what your question is.

In Table 2, we have taken the examples of hypotheses we gave you earlier and recast the research questions in the same areas, so that you can see the significant differences between the two approaches.

How do I write my research questions then?

Before you frame your questions, you must have your topic clear in your mind. At this point, it is useful to write about what really engages your interest and why. Writing in this way often helps people to clarify their questions. This happened to Alexandre.

Alexandre was exploring the dualistic nature of the working lives of dentists working in small country practices, who have to be both dental professionals and business people who make a profit. He had been working for some time on this doctoral research but had never clearly articulated what his research questions were. As a practising dentist himself, working in a small practice, he had a very personal and intuitive sense of what the important research issues were. However, this was not sufficient to enable him to make sense of his ▶

▶ considerable data and shape it into a thesis likely to be awarded a doctorate. He was really struggling with writing the thesis and did not know which way to turn. A new supervisor asked him what his research questions were and he was unable to state them clearly, even though he was nearly at the end of his maximum registration period. After a stiff drink and much cursing (*sotto voce*), the new supervisor made Alexandre write a diary of his day at the office. Together they analysed the activities he had undertaken and used this as a means of explicating the key questions that had implicitly driven Alexandre's fieldwork. Once he had done this, Alexandre was able to formulate clear questions and to begin the real work of writing his thesis. His key question was 'How do small dental practices deal with the dual imperatives of making money from a business and simultaneously acting in a professional capacity for their clients?' An added benefit of this exercise was that his diary, the analysis of it, and the writing he had done on the questions, formed a strong, engaging and convincing introductory chapter for his thesis. Alexandre achieved his PhD with flying colours, but he would have saved himself much time and anxiety had he undertaken a similar exercise at the very beginning of his work.

In parallel with clarifying what exactly is engaging your interest, a good step is to visualise what you want to know about your topic and what you or others want to do with that knowledge or what impact you want it to have. You may want to do one or more of the following things:

- Satisfy your own intellectual curiosity.
- Make an intervention in or contribution to intellectual and theoretical debates.
- Influence policy makers.
- Raise others' consciousness around particular issues.
- Get your PhD in the shortest possible time.
- Get issues on to agendas.
- Meet publication targets that have been imposed on you.

You need to think about what you want the finished product to look like and do, as this will be largely determined by the nature of the questions you ask. As Rebecca's old boss used to say, 'Never ask a question if you don't know what you are going to do with the answer.' That is, there is an important and synergistic link between questions and final products.

> Once your questions begin to take some sort of shape in your head, it is time to return to your hardback notebook and your word processor and write an exercise that Jane Miller, a well known British academic, has called 'the autobiography of the question'. She suggests to students that they tell the story of how they became interested in the research question that they plan to address. Once they have written this story, they can move on from their own interest in the question to thinking about wider contexts and where their question sits in relation to the existing literature in the field.

This is something that we get all our students to do when they are starting a research project. The beauty of the exercise is that it forces you to do many of the things we have been urging on you up to now:

- It makes you think about where you are coming from on the topic and why it is interesting or important to you.
- It makes you think about the origins of the question.
- It encourages you to articulate the 'so what?'-ness of the question.
- But, most important, it forces you to have a question (or two).

A really good suggestion that we've heard is to write your research questions on a nice piece of coloured card and pin it above your work space so that it is clearly visible. This should have the advantages of directly and immediately reminding you what your question is and of encouraging you to keep it short enough to fit on the card.

3   The Research Process

If you've started to formulate research questions, you have gone a good way towards beginning a research project. The next stage is to write a plan of your intended work to act as a guide and to make sure that you think through the major issues before you begin. In this chapter we will guide you through the process of writing research plans, or proposals, stage by stage. At each stage, we detail what you need to think about.

What is a research proposal?

Once you know what you want do your research about and have formulated some research questions, you need to think about how you will actually carry out the research. Doing a research project always involves several different activities and sorts of thinking, some sequential, some running in parallel and some iterative.

Because research is a complex process, it's always a good idea to write yourself a good plan of where you are going and what you are going to do along the way. In this way, you will have a kind of route map to guide you as you travel the research path. However, this path is a little like the roads in *Alice through the Looking Glass*: it sometimes changes direction when you are not looking. So it's important to remember that you can't rely on the map completely. You must keep revisiting it and adjusting it to your changing needs and directions.

These route maps are usually called research proposals. There are some situations in which you may well be required to write a research proposal. For example:

- If you want a place on a research degree programme.
- If you want a bursary to do a research degree.
- In some universities it will form part of a progression exam on a research degree programme.

- If you are looking for funding for your research, however small, from your own university or some external funding body.
- In some cases, especially when the research is in collaboration with or investigating an external body, that body will need to see the proposal in order to decide whether or not to give you access and assistance to do your research.
- If you want your employer to give you time to do the research; for example, you may want a reduced teaching load or a sabbatical or paid time off from a non-university job to allow you to do the research.
- You may need to get formal approval from your university that your proposed research conforms to certain ethical guidelines. In order to gain this approval, you will need to present a proposal.

In any case, even if you are not required to write a research proposal, it's a really good idea to do one for your own benefit. Writing a research proposal will:

- Help you to be sure that you have a viable research project.
- Provide a clear 'route map' for the research.
- Enable you to identify any possible problems and issues with the proposed project.
- Assist you in choosing an appropriate supervisor or mentor who knows the area in which you are interested. (More on choosing mentors later.)
- Help your mentor or supervisor support you, as they will know what it is you are trying to do.
- Give a project a momentum of its own, almost a material form.
- Give you a reference point to monitor your progress as the project develops. This can give you a lot of confidence and a big boost to your morale.

Writing research proposals

What we will do now is take you through the generic stages and sections of a research proposal. Whatever your discipline or research area, you will need to give consideration to the matters we are about to describe. However, the language you use to address these may differ according to your disciplinary home, as will the relative weightings you give to the various aspects. Also, your proposal will need to be tailored to the specific expectations of its various audiences, such as research funding bodies, PhD committees and so on. This is discussed further in *Winning and Managing Research Funding*. For your own purposes, your research proposal is likely to include a section on each of the following areas:

- Background and rationale: the 'so what?' -ness of the research topic.
- Research questions: what, precisely, are you trying to find out?
- Available literature: the public story so far.
- Theoretical frameworks: the e-word and the o-word.
- Methods: your investigative and analytical techniques.
- Ethical considerations: will your research do harm?
- Time scales: establishing phases and deadlines.
- Dissemination: getting it out and about.

Writing your proposal will be an iterative process, especially in relation to your reading and framing of questions, but remember that, like a lot of academic writing, proposals tend to read best if they are presented in a linear way. The order in which we have outlined the sections is not the only logical order possible and you will have to decide what works for your proposal, always remembering that what you present must be clear, coherent and cogent. Remember, also, that in an actual research process the various stages of research run concurrently, iteratively and sequentially.

Background and rationale: the 'so what?' -ness of the research topic

Now is the time to go back to your hardback notebook, as the notes that you made on your research topic and the 'so what?' -ness of it are about to come into their own.

This section needs to explain the background, issues and the 'so what?' -ness of your proposed research. As we explained before, the best research issues usually start because someone has been curious about the world immediately around them or has had their interest stimulated by something they have seen, heard or read. You might care to start with your own experiences, describing how it is that you came to be interested in the subject – a brief 'autobiography of the question'.

The importance or 'so what?' -ness of the proposed research will lie in the contribution you think it can make to knowledge, to intellectual and theoretical debates, to policy and practice in particular areas – in sum, to our understanding of the world. You need to use this section to convince the readers of the proposal (and yourself) that your project is worth the time and trouble.

Research questions: what, precisely, are you trying to find out?

It is essential to formulate your research questions very clearly and explicitly in your proposal. If you have more than one principal question, you may want to number them. If you have subsidiary questions, they should come immediately after the principal question they relate to. It is necessary to have an answerable question that is clear and sufficiently well defined/focused for you to do the research implied within an appropriate time-frame and the available resources.

If you work in an area in which you are required to put your questions in the form of formal hypotheses, these need to be very clearly stated and numbered. The usual convention is to number them as H_1, H_2, H_3 and so on.

Available literature: the public story so far

In developing your research topic and questions you will already have engaged with the literature sufficiently to be able to give a good account of what is known about the answers to your questions and which theories and concepts you expect to find particularly useful. The proposal itself will contain only a relatively short section on the existing literature, but what you write there will need to demonstrate that you know what you are doing and have a good idea of what has been done before.

To reiterate, this is *not* the same as reviewing the literature to find a gap, which, as we explained above, is a bit of a trap for unwary researchers. You will already have a fairly clear idea of what sort of thing you want to look at and therefore your visit to the literature isn't to find a topic. Rather, the proposal needs to make two points clear on the subject of literature.

- First, you need to talk about the work of others that provides empirical data and/or creative insights that contribute to answering your questions. This will demonstrate that you have refined your questions, and that the answers you eventually produce are likely be a real contribution to knowledge. You will be able to show what further evidence you need to collect to answer your research questions more fully.
- Second, reference to the literature will enable you to pinpoint those theories and concepts useful to you in trying to make sense of your own research.

Most important, you must make a convincing case as to why your research would create valuable and useful knowledge that builds upon or challenges existing work in the field.

Theoretical frameworks: the e-word and the o-word

One of the problems we frequently see in research proposals is the absence of any explicit theoretical framework. Research without a theoretical framework is description and does not qualify as academic research or as a contribution to knowledge. We cannot say it too often or too loudly.

Don't forget the theory.

One of the biggest reasons why people avoid talking or writing about theory is that they feel excluded by the language which people use. In particular, it may take a long time to be confident in the use of commonly used words in academic writing (but not in the rest of the world) such as 'epistemology' and 'ontology'.

Debbie, Rebecca and Jane all admit, to each other and now to you, that when they were novice researchers they had to return to the dictionary many times to clarify their understanding of 'epistemology' and 'ontology'. Here is our best attempt to explain them in readily understandable ways.

Epistemology

Here's one of the many dictionary definitions that we find useful:

'The philosophical theory of knowledge, which seeks to define it, distinguish its principal varieties, identify its sources, and establish its limits'

(from *The New Fontana Dictionary of Modern Thought*)

What this means to us is that epistemology is a theoretical framework for making sense of how the world works or some aspect of how the world works. It's about what counts as knowledge in your world view. For example, all three of us are feminists and we see feminism as an epistemology. What this means, in practice, is that the lens through which we view the world is shaped by certain understandings about gender, power and the position of women. So an epistemology may be defined as a particular sort of lens that allows you to make sense of some aspect of the world around you in a particular way. Different lenses (different epistemologies) will obviously give different views. No epistemology can give you a total view of the world, because they only allow you to see from particular perspectives. So it's useful to have a whole range of epistemologies available. Foucault conceptualised this as a theory toolbox.

Everybody, in daily life, no matter what they do, makes sense of the world according to their understandings and theories about it. These may take the form of religious beliefs or common sense or cultural values or social norms and they may not be explicit or apparent even to the person themselves. What distinguishes academic research epistemologies from these everyday epistemologies is that they are expected to be explicit, rigorously defined and robust. That is why we call them theories. You cannot make sense of your data without an epistemology/theory.

▶

▶ ***Ontology***

If 'epistemology' is about what counts as knowledge, 'ontology' is concerned with the nature of the knower. It is about how our place in the world, identity and embodied experiences impact on the way in which we see the world and, consequentially, the epistemologies that we find meaningful and useful. It follows that our ontological perspective will have a significant impact on which epistemologies we are drawn to and how we use them. We've noticed that the early authors in new fields of enquiry such as gender, race, sexuality and disability are often ontologically steeped in the issues they are investigating: they are women, ethnic minority people, lesbian or gay people, or people with mental or physical impairments.

In your 'autobiography of the question' you will have begun, either implicitly or possibly explicitly, to make connections between your own ontology and epistemology.

We do not believe that any knowledge is 'objective' or that researchers can take a god-like stance as knowers. It is therefore important to be clear, up-front and honest about your ontology and epistemology in your research. This will enable your readers to understand where you are coming from and to make a judgement on the quality of your work based on that understanding. Saying who you are and where you are coming from will not stop people who genuinely believe in the possibility of 'objective truth' from criticising you for being partial and subjective. But at least, in contrast to them, you will have been honest about your subjectivity and partiality. And remember, subjectivity is not and should never be synonymous with lack of rigour. Being clear about your frameworks is part of that rigour.

You should therefore use your proposal to clarify what theoretical resources you will be drawing on and why. There should, therefore, be clear linkages between this discussion and your discussion of the literature. In particular, you need to explain the relevance and usefulness of your theoretical framework to your proposed project. You need to give particular consideration, at this point, to the issues that loom large within your chosen theoretical framework and how they will affect the research process.

Methodology and methods: your investigative and analytical techniques

Definitions of methodology differ confusingly and vary greatly between disciplines. However, a reasonable definition is that it is the package of epistemology, ontology and method that shapes and informs your research project. People in different disciplines have different methodological approaches:

Methods are the ways in which you go about collecting, locating or creating the material you are going to analyse and the associated practical techniques. For example:

- A cultural theorist might use auto/biography, stories and myths, novels, poetry and plays, visual images, films and television programmes, newspapers and so on.
- People in the creative arts often produce a work of art, a play or an exhibition and write an exegesis of it.
- An art historian might use both cultural artefacts and archival material about the people who created and consumed them.
- An economist might garner government statistical data and use this to construct a model to generate research results.
- A sociologist might go out and interview people, participate in some aspect of their lives or distribute survey questionnaires.

It's difficult to find a collective name for all the different kinds of material mentioned here. In the social sciences, it tends to be called 'data' and, for convenience, we will use this term. But remember that we are using the term inclusively.

Finally, there are research traditions that don't rely on data, even as broadly defined. These are the types of research – such as pure mathematics, logic and some branches of philosophy and theology – which are purely conceptual and directed at the resolution of abstract problems.

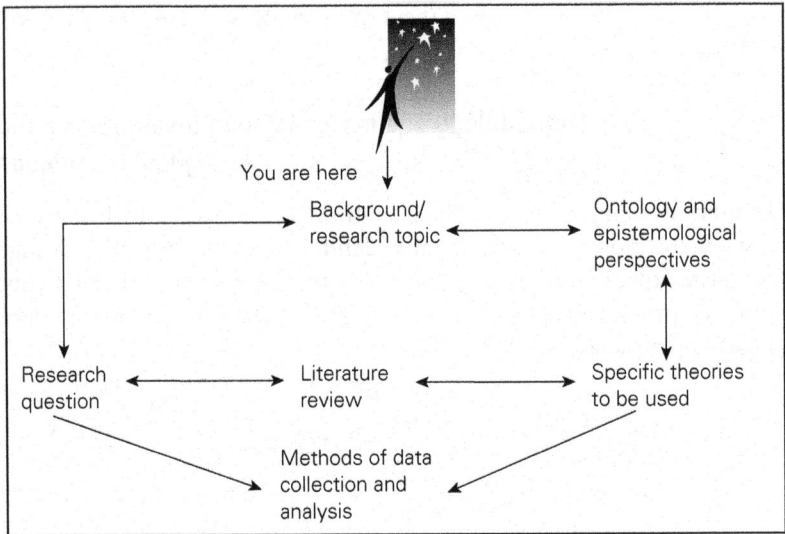

FIGURE 3   Processes and linkages in research proposals

We've already explained that the proposal mirrors the research process itself and therefore, like research, your proposal must represent a coherent and integrated process. The questions you are seeking to address, together with your epistemological perspectives, will inform the methods you choose. The methods you decide to use should enable you collect and analyse the data that you need in order to answer your questions using your chosen epistemological perspectives. Figure 3 gives a visual image of the kinds of processes and linkages discussed so far that should be explicit in your proposal.

To summarise, this section of a research proposal should consist of a detailed description and justification of how you will actually go about collecting and analysing your data. That is, what data will you collect, how will you collect it and how will it be analysed? You need to justify why these are the best methods for your question(s).

Use your imagination in solving the problem of how to collect the data that you need. People often resort to what seems like the simplest, easiest and even the most 'objective' method of data collection. This is not necessarily the best method for answering the questions you are trying to ask. Methods such as questionnaires, for example, may evoke feelings of fatigue and *ennui* among the target recipients, especially if those recipients have no empathy with, or particular interest in, what you are researching. On the other hand, where people feel strongly about an issue a questionnaire may be a very good source of data. At Rebecca's university, for example, a long and detailed questionnaire survey to all staff about the research culture in the institution produced a very healthy and very rapid response rate. Rebecca attributes this to the fact that staff were either antithetical to research or deeply committed to it. Either way, everyone was very keen to have their say.

Helen and James demonstrated admirable ingenuity and imagination in designing their data collection methods.

> Helen, a marketing academic, was researching people's food shopping and consumption habits. She needed to know what they bought and how they used it. Rather than simply send out a questionnaire or carry out an interview based on memory, she asked her respondents to write a list of the foodstuffs in their fridges and cupboards. She used the list as the basis of a guided discussion with the respondents.

> James was doing research in cultural studies/sociology on how children form their identities, including how they see 'home' and the part it plays in who they think they are. As a starting point, he gave the children a disposable camera and asked them to take photographs of 'home' (that is, whatever 'home' meant to them). When he had developed the photographs (including several of front doors and pets) he used them to discuss with the children why those particular images meant 'home' to them.

Practical matters such as whether or not you will get physical access to the data you need or whether you have the practical skills you need to access it are real considerations in research design. Will you have enough time to collect the data required? Will your data collection requirements stretch the goodwill of those on whom you depend for access?

> In 1945 the border between Germany and Poland was redrawn and some formerly German territory became part of Poland. As a result, many of the regional government records relating to the formerly German territories passed into Polish archives and were often catalogued in Polish. Cathy ▶

▶ was a fluent German-speaker but her Polish was non-existent. Access to these crucial records was therefore dependent not only on obtaining funding for research trips to Poland, but also on learning enough Polish to interrogate the catalogues and negotiate with Polish archivists.

In this section, it is absolutely essential to describe not only how you will collect your data but also how you will analyse it. Data analysis is often scantily done or left out completely. This seriously weakens many proposals.

Data analysis needs two things: first, an appropriate theoretical lens through which to view and make sense of the material collected; second, appropriate tools and techniques to organise, categorise, sift and manage it. You will need to refer back to your theoretical framework and your research questions to be absolutely sure that you explain how you will use and address them in your analysis of your data.

Explain what skills you will need and whether you have them or how you will acquire them. Think about the particular software or other tools available (see later in this book), and how you will acquire the skills to use them. It's a good idea to visualise yourself sitting down with your carefully collected data and asking 'What do I do now? How do I make sense of all of this?'

Ethical considerations: will your research do harm?

Later in this book we will give detailed consideration to ethical practice in research. For the proposal, you will need to ensure that your reader is confident that you have thought carefully about the ethical dimensions of your proposed research and, where appropriate, that you intend to comply with all relevant ethical guidelines and procedures. Sometimes research may have no obvious ethical issues attached to it. However, we think that research completely devoid of any ethical considerations or consequences whatsoever is a virtual impossibility.

Time scales: establishing phases and deadlines

It is important to map out a reasonable schedule of your work so that you can monitor your progress and manage your project effectively. If your project is externally funded, bear in mind that your funders may also ask for a time schedule and even ask you to report against it. Start with your intended finishing date and do not underestimate the amount of time that it takes to polish your draft writing into a finished product.

In Table 3, we show the timeline of a real project involving a number of researchers. On this project the researchers had to juggle a number of conflicting time constraints. These included the time scale that the organisation under investigation imposed, the need to use research assistants and also the proposers' own busy schedules. Note that many of the activities are concurrent.

Making an impact: getting it out and about

You need to make a clear statement in your proposal about how you intend your work to have an impact. We deal with this issue in much more detail in *Building Networks*. Making an impact may involve three different sorts of dissemination of your research output.

To other academics

A key indicator of the worth of much research is whether it is publishable in refereed academic journals, as an academic book or as a chapter in an academic book. You may like to give some consideration at this stage to what sorts of things may be publishable and where you would like them to appear.

Also think about which conferences you may wish to give papers at. This may involve conferences that will give you high academic visibility, which can help with your career prospects, but just as important is to find smaller conferences where you can have a good and detailed discussion about your work and get constructive feedback that will help you improve your papers and other writing. If you are seeking funding for your project, you may be able to ask for money to go to these conferences as part of the research funds.

This kind of dissemination is especially important if you wish to pursue a career as an academic in a university.

To relevant non-academic users and beneficiaries of your research

These may include people who were involved in the research process as gatekeepers and/or respondents, possibly the people who funded your

TABLE 3 Women's participation in research activities

Date	Task	Responsibilities
2002 May	Advertise researcher posts internally Submission of proposal and consent procedures to university ethics committee	PMG
25 June	Interviews for researcher posts	
1 September	Project starts	RA
September–December	Initial literature review (reading of the literature continues throughout the project)	RA
September–December	Analysis of secondary data on women in science	RA
September–October	Design of research instruments	RA, PMG
October	Advisory group meeting to advise on research design and access	
End October	Submission of survey questionnaire and interview schedule to ethics committee	RA, PMG
November	Distribution of survey questionnaire	RA
December–Early January 2003	Survey data entry	Casual employee(s)
December–January 2003	Interview recruitment	RA
January	Survey data analysis	RA, PMG
February–June	Interviews	RA
May–July	Interview data analysis	RA, PMG
July–September	Preparation of report	RA, PMG
September	Draft report to advisory group	PMG
October	Dissemination of report Seminar to present findings	RA, PMG
2003–4	Conference attendance Preparation/submission of papers for publication	RA, PMG

PMG Project Management Group. *RA* Research Associate.

research and, indeed, anyone else or any other groups who might find your work of use or interest.

The form of such dissemination may include a workshop for policy users, articles in appropriate professional journals or newspapers, a popular book, magazine articles or public lectures. For instance, if you were conducting research into children and young people, you might want to hold a special conference for such groups of people and include it in the costings and dissemination strategy.

Through the popular media

This means of dissemination can reach wider audiences and, if well done, can be effective and very beneficial to your personal research profile and that of your university. However, media exposure is fraught with dangers and we would strongly advise you to seek professional help, support and training in how to deal with journalists. Your institution's press office should be able to help in this regard. A good way of attracting media attention is by producing good press releases. Again, your institution's press office, if there is one, should be able to guide you in this. If you anticipate that your research will attract media interest, make sure that there are plans for dealing with it in your proposal, especially if that interest is likely to be hostile.

And finally ...

When you have done all this and have a complete draft research proposal, get other people, your peers as well as those more experienced than you, to read it and comment. This will help you to revise the proposal before you proceed further. That way, you will ensure that you start off on a firm footing.

4   Doing your Project

This is a very practical chapter. In it we include practical advice and handy hints, tools of the trade, writing, coping with uncertainty and dealing with problems.

Now that my proposal is done, what next?

If you've prepared a good proposal, you've already started your research project. This planning phase is a bit like planning a big vacation trip abroad. So what have you done so far?

- You've identified where you want to go – or rather, you have a topic.
- You've started to familiarise yourself with the place you are going to by reading the tour guides and novels about the area – in other words, you've started to engage with the literature.
- You've decided precisely where you're going to stay and why – that is, you have framed your research questions.
- You've packed your bags with everything that you think you might need at this point – just like your suitcase, your theory toolbox is full of useful stuff for making sense of your work.
- You've decided what you are going to do when you are there – that is, what data you need and how you will collect and analyse it.
- You've thought about your impact as a tourist on the environment you're visiting – in other words, what the ethical dimensions of your research are and how you will deal with them.
- You have your dates for your holiday and all your bookings are made for going away and returning – in other words, you've established a sensible schedule for getting all the work done.

A bit like being very well planned for your holidays, having a good proposal makes you feel confident and relaxed and lets you enjoy yourself more, but plans don't have to be rigidly kept to if there are good reasons for changing them. If you arrive at your hotel and you don't like it, it's better to find one you do like than to have a miserable time. Or you might go on holiday and find that there's a much more interesting place to stay than the one you had planned, possibly one with fewer tourists and more surprises. Inexperienced tourists are more likely to have to adapt their plans as they go along; they don't know the good places or the perils of distant locations. In the same way, less experienced researchers should expect to have to modify and adapt their plans as they gain knowledge, experience and confidence in their areas.

What all this means is that you will need to return at regular intervals to your research proposal in order to think about whether you are still on track and whether you need to adapt your plans in the light of what you have done so far, the knowledge you have gained, the additional reading you've done and other events. A very short project, such as a masters dissertation, may not need you to do this. There is a direct correlation between the length and size of a project and the extent to which the proposal will need to be adapted during the course of the research.

Practical points for budding researchers

Research journals

We usually call our hardback notebooks research journals. Other people call them research diaries or research notebooks. What you call them is your own business. The important thing is to have them and to use them sensibly. They are the single most important tool of your research career.

Many academics seem to be obsessed with using the latest technology. Students often ask if they can keep their research journals on their computers. We don't think this is a good idea. The whole point about the hardback notebook is that you can: take it to fieldwork sites and into libraries and archives; take it on the bus or train; keep it by the side of your bed; leaf through it in the bath; take it on holiday; staple things into it; easily draw pictures or diagrams; and easily show it to your mentors or supervisors.

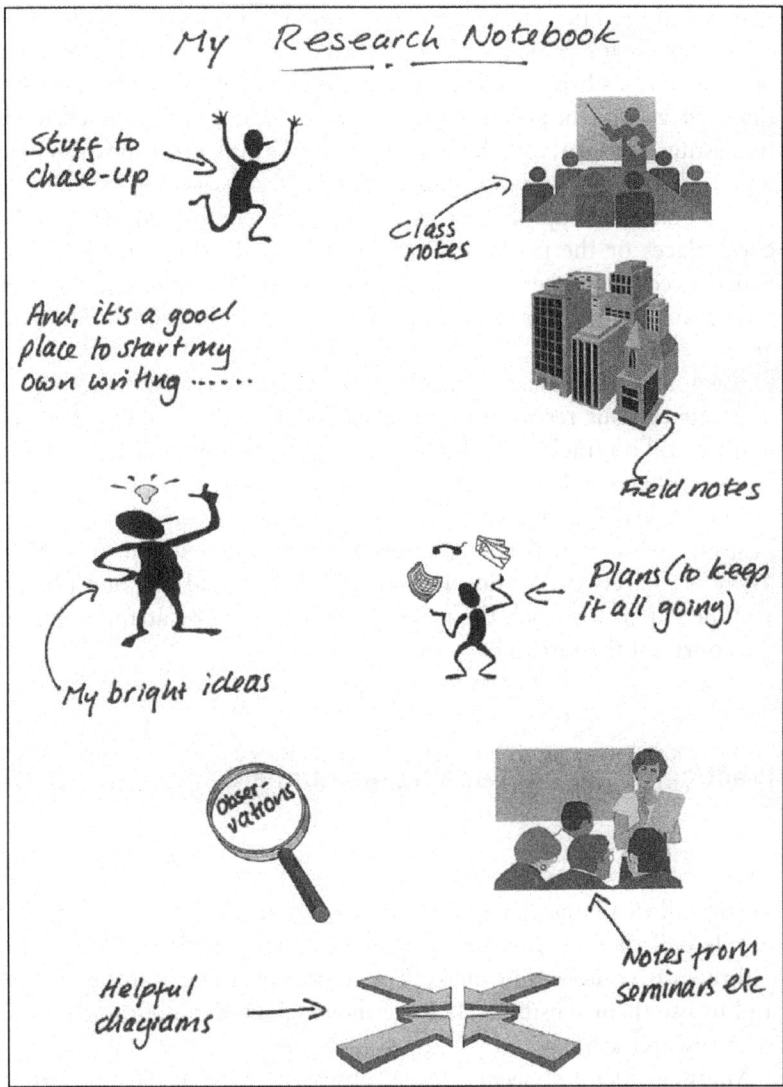

FIGURE 4   What to write in your research journal

People also often ask us what they should write in their research journal. Our answer is that, like any diary or journal, it's personal to you and should contain what you find useful. Figure 4 is a picture of the sorts of things that we keep in our research journals and the vignette below illustrates one way of using them.

When Miranda was doing her PhD she started her first research journal in a big red hardback book. She took it into the school where she was collecting her data and the children very quickly took to calling it 'your big red book'. Even when she had filled up her first notebook and gone on to the second, which was not red, the children continued to refer to it as 'your big red book'. She used the journal to make notes of her observations in the playground and classrooms, to write down snippets of conversation that she overheard and to draw maps of how the children were using the space, and diagrams of how she was thinking. The children regularly used to ask her to show them what she had written about them, which she did. As they got to know her better, and became more confident with her, they would ask if they could write or draw in her book from time to time. The notebook thus contained children's writing and drawing as well as Miranda's.

Look after yourself

Research is hard work. Don't make it harder by failing to take good care of your mental and physical well-being. Sleep, rest and relaxation are not unwarranted time-out from research but essential ways of keeping yourself going. Obsessive overwork is bad not only for you but also for your colleagues and your family. And it doesn't necessarily lead to the best research.

It may sound obvious, but don't put yourself in dangerous situations if you can possibly avoid it. Build in safety routes and mechanisms to protect yourself. If you are going to do fieldwork, make sure that somebody knows where you are going and when you should be coming back. In this day and age of mobile phones, it's a very good idea to carry one at all times and keep it on, with the ringer set on silent so that it doesn't disturb your research. Don't be neglectful of little things that can become big problems. It's okay to make decisions based on personal safety considerations about what research you will and won't do.

Trupti was a young South African Indian researcher. She was doing an ethnographic study of several different kinds of school in post-apartheid South Africa. Because of the high level of violence in certain ▶

▶ parts of the country and in particular schools, she and her supervisor discussed in detail where she should go, and she avoided going to schools (and types of schools) where she might be in danger of being raped or suffering other serious violence. Even though this meant that she did not explore every possible type of school, she completed an excellent PhD that made a significant contribution to knowledge.

On a much lighter note, it's crucially important to build in treats for yourself to ensure that sometimes you do things just because they're nice for you. Treats can be as big or little as seems appropriate. They might include: eating more chocolate than is good for you, taking the dog for a walk; stopping work to watch a soap on TV, going on holiday, going to the theatre, reading a trashy novel, chatting to friends on the phone or cooking a nice meal. Choose your own poison, but we would avoid making tobacco, alcohol or other drugs your principal rewards or coping strategies.

File it!

It's important to develop a good hard copy and computer filing system for your research project because it helps you to:

- Keep track of all of the materials relating to your research project.
- Keep valuable things safe.
- Establish a complete history or audit trail of your project that complements your research notebooks.
- Work efficiently and find things that you need when you need them.
- Know what materials you have.
- Manage the project.
- Develop a personal archive of research materials that you and your research collaborators and students may use in the future.

The types of materials you may accumulate include:

- Photocopies of papers.
- Newspaper cuttings.

- Your project proposal.
- Old notebooks.
- Letters and other correspondence.
- Drafts of pieces of writing. Old drafts can be very useful if you lose all your electronic copies of work – at least you can scan in an older version to help you recover from the loss.
- Drafts with comments written on them by others. You will find most people unwilling to repeat the exercise if you carelessly lose their notes.
- Official forms.
- Details of monies spent or expenses claimed. University accounts systems, worldwide, are inherently fallible – so keep your own records.
- Books, pamphlets, reports, etc.
- Photographs.
- Audio and video-tapes or mini-disks.
- CDs, computer diskettes or memory sticks with back-ups of electronic material. Such back-ups of current work should be made at least once a day when you are writing intensively and at least once a week at other times.

You will acquire a lot of things that really need to be kept safe. This means not just filing them carefully but also protecting them from the extremes of temperature and the ravages of children and family pets. If something like copies of computer files are irreplaceable then keep copies in different locations.

Eiko, a student at Kobe in Japan, was finalising her masters dissertation at the very moment when the massive and destructive earthquake of 1995 occurred. As the earthquake developed momentum, she quickly saved her dissertation on a diskette and ran out into the street clutching it to her chest. It was her only copy.

You have to devise your own system for keeping these materials in an accessible and methodical way appropriate to your project and way of working. Possible methods include:

- A series of box files.
- Putting things in plastic pockets (we like plastic pockets a lot) and filing them in lever-arch files.
- Plastic crates.
- A special place on your bookshelves.
- A drawer(s) in a filing cabinet.

Don't wait until things get in a mess and you have a huge and dispiriting pile of what looks like rubbish in the middle of your office floor. Neither should your computer desktop be in chaos – you also need to develop systems for electronic filing and labelling. It might be a good idea to set a regular time, maybe when you know that your mental energy tends to be quite low, to do your filing. On the other hand, don't run away with the notion that endless hours spent devising ever more sophisticated filing systems constitute research work.

Save it and keep it safe
Save it and keep it safe
Save it and keep it safe

Work avoidance and security zones

Work avoidance is something that everybody does and everybody beats themselves up about. If anyone tells you that they don't do it, then they are lying, probably to undermine your confidence. Take no notice.

Reasonable amounts of 'work avoidance' activity are perfectly normal and acceptable, even desirable. We will come back to this later. So don't worry if, when you get stuck doing a piece of writing, or when you mean to make a start early in the morning on something difficult, you end up making yourself endless cups of coffee, reading the newspaper, cleaning the house, doing the crossword or taking the dog for an extra-long walk. You probably need this time and space to get yourself and your brain into gear. Remember that good research is, at least in part, a creative process and most people can't be creative 'to order'.

Avoidance becomes a problem only when these activities squeeze out time for work and you end up not doing it at all or being so late that you miss important, immovable deadlines.

Some activities that look like work avoidance are actually important ways of giving ourselves a comfort and security zone that enables us to work. As the following vignettes demonstrate, particular rituals may be an important part of the working day, especially when what you are doing is done on your own and is difficult and/or intensive and intimidating, as the stories below show.

Ng is a social psychologist who also trains other academics in the use of software for data handling and analysis. Despite his advanced computing skills, he confesses that he cannot start a piece of academic writing unless he is sitting at his desk in his comfortable study, wearing his 'white writing shirt' and using his 'nice fountain pen'.

Helen, now sadly dead, made her own bread. When asked how she found the time to do it, she said, 'Whenever I've got a really busy day at home, working on my research, I make a loaf of bread.' She explained that the various physical activities, which need to be done at different times throughout the day, of mixing and kneading the dough were important ways of pacing herself and giving herself a bit of a break and a structure. She also said that the sensual pleasure of the smell and taste of the freshly baked bread were a major treat at the end of her day's work.

Time and motion

It's important to think about how you will organise, protect and use your research time. Very few people are in the fortunate position of being genuinely full-time researchers. Even full-time doctoral students usually have to do some teaching or other paid work and full-time contract researchers often get dragged into administrative work in their organisations.

If you are a university teacher or part-time research student, your research time is likely to be quite constrained and very precious. It is treacherously easy for your research to become the part of your work that slips off the edge of your over-full in-tray – destined to disappear into oblivion. You need, therefore, to think and act proactively about strategies for ensuring that your precious time is ring-fenced, safeguarded and used well.

Diana Leonard, a well known British academic, uses a modified version of Parkinson's Law to explain what happens to research time. She says that there are four different kinds of work that research students and academics have to do:

urgent and trivial,	non-urgent and trivial
urgent and important	non-urgent and important

She maintains that the urgent and trivial invariably drives out the non-urgent but important. Of course, research work is usually non-urgent but important. The trick is to forget about the trivial, whether urgent or not, and concentrate on the important.

The best sort of research time is that which is 'joined up'. That is, it comes in significant chunks, where you can really bury yourself in what you are doing without the interruption of teaching, other work, family, meetings, etc. Never underestimate the amount of time it takes to get back into a project that you have had to put on one side, even for a few days. You will not work effectively if you try to do your research in the 'odd hour' here and there. It just won't work like that. If you teach, you must try to ensure that your teaching timetable is compacted into the smallest possible space so that you have consecutive, whole days to spend on your research.

Another good way of protecting time is to spend your research time away from places where you will be interrupted. For many academics, this means staying at home, though if you have young children or other responsibilities it may not. It may mean, if you really need some headspace, renting a cottage on a remote island away from the phone, your family and the email. Less expensively, it may mean having a study at home well away from the other inhabitants of the house.

Margaret is a political scientist. She was desperately trying to finish her first book, but had a time-devouring family. She resolved this situation, on her limited budget, by buying a kit garden shed and erecting it in the backyard. She fitted it out so that it was homely and spent her research time in there.

For most busy academics the real time-vulture is pointless bureaucracy that seems to engulf us at an ever-increasing rate. People in more junior posts and those on marginalised forms of employment contracts (fixed-term or untenured) are in a difficult position here, as they may feel obliged or even coerced into doing this sort of work. There are two strategies that you can employ to help you. First, you can do what you have to do but don't get sucked into it and never believe that it is truly important. The second is with care and good grace, to 'just say no'. That is, don't go to meetings unless you really need to be there. Give your apologies and explain that you are (1) in an archive, (2) conducting an interview, (3) giving a research presentation at another university, (4) trying desperately to finish a book/chapter/paper that will attract prestige to your institution/department, (5) ill or (6, a favourite among some) 'at another meeting'. If you are an academic and you are giving your students a good deal and doing your research well, then you justify your salary without getting bogged down in what is usually bureaucracy invented by people who can neither teach nor research well but who are trying to justify their salaries. Have confidence on this.

> Fiona is a busy Australian academic and successful researcher. Her university funded her to go to an overseas conference to deliver a research paper. On her return she was pestered with a series of increasingly imperative demands from her 'line manager' to submit a report on the conference. In fact she was busy running a research centre and writing her next paper. Eventually she relented and wrote her report. It read, in its Caesarean entirety,' I went, I delivered, I returned.' The report was accepted and filed, in the right folder, in the right file and on the right shelf, where no-one ever looked at it again. We think Fiona got the balance just right.

In describing how to write a research proposal we urged you to include a time schedule for the completion of the research project. The reason was that it is very useful to have deadlines and to try to stick to them. Schedules help you to manage your time.

Try to define your schedules by setting regular milestones for achievement – small packages of work that together, and cumulatively, constitute the whole project. This not only boosts your morale as you can tick them off, but also gives you a sense of climbing a series of small hillocks rather than scaling Mount Everest in one go. Milestones also help your mentors to gain a sense of what progress you are making with the work.

In setting yourself a timetable, particularly for writing, you should always estimate how long you think something will take and then build in a comfortable margin for the inevitable slippages that occur.

When writing something specific, set yourself a daily timetable. If you finish your allotted work early, take the rest of the day off and go and treat yourself.

Don't mess about

Doing any research requires the tolerance, co-operation and assistance of other people. Such people include: mentors and supervisors; research respondents; your employer; your family; your research collaborators; other students if you are on a course; librarians and archivists; publishers; funders; etc.

Conducting research is inherently problematic in that it's not always possible to do what you've said you will do, or to stick to the schedules and deadlines that you set yourself or that others have imposed on you. Sometimes failure to keep to your commitments and delays is really unavoidable. You may have to work around such issues as serious illness, bereavement, having to cover for a colleague at work or unexpected problems with the planned research.

Despite these facts of life, it is incumbent upon you, as the researcher, to make every reasonable effort to do what you say you will do in an efficient and timely way. For example, if you agree to meet someone whom you are going to interview and you have agreed a time, a place and the length of the meeting, you should honour that agreement.

If you can't keep to your commitments you must, at the earliest opportunity, explain the problems to those affected and develop a strategy for rectifying them. Most people are very understanding if you keep them informed of what's happening. This kind of honesty will help you develop good relations with all those people who are essential to your research.

Take note(s)

You need to take notes on your reading, and some people like to keep these separate from their research journals. You will use the notes for many projects and for many years to come. You don't want to have to try desperately to remember which project you were doing when you read a particular article or book in order to find your notes. Try to develop a system that suits you.

Tools of the trade

So far, our discussion of research equipment has been quite low-tech and confined to the joys of nice stationery. It's time to get technical. We take it as axiomatic that researchers will be able to use popular word-processing packages. By the way, it is well worth getting yourself a typing tutor program and spending the time learning to touch-type. This may slow you down for a while if you are a fast two-finger typist but will bring its rewards in the medium and long term. There are other standard software tools, such as Excel and PowerPoint, which it may be well worth learning to use.

In addition to these standard tools, there exist a number of software packages designed for, and some designed by, academics. These fall into two broad camps: those that help us organise our research materials and those that are analytical tools.

We find that you really learn how to use a software package only when you need to use it. Software training courses that are unconnected with reasonably immediate use get consigned to your mental dustbin unless they are of the brief 'taster' sort designed to show you the capabilities of the software and give you enough confidence to get going on your own.

Bibliographic databases

The one software device that we regard as absolutely essential for all researchers, no matter what their topic, and regardless of their discipline, is a bibliographic database program. There are many different software packages that do this job, the most common of which are EndNote, Reference Manager and ProCite (all pretty similar). What can you do with a bibliographic database?

- You can input the complete bibliographic details of anything that you may wish to use or cite in your work. This includes: books, journal articles, websites, book chapters, manuscripts and other archival material, statutes, films, newspaper articles, television programmes, maps, theses, scores, letters, works of art and many more. The program will have a pre-set way of recording most of these and it will also be possible to customise your recording method and the type of thing you record according to your needs or the conventions in your discipline.
- You can make notes on the individual database records. This can vary from key words and short abstracts to extensive and detailed note taking.
- You can use the database, once you have compiled it, to search for material that you have recorded by author, subject, title, key words, medium and so on. You can then generate specific bibliographies for your own use or for others.
- Best of all, these packages have dynamic links with many word-processing programs. This means that you can insert citations as you write, using a special command. When you have finished your work, another command results in the automatic generation of a list of references at the end of your document. Using this facility is likely to save you hours of heartache and hard work at the end of a major project. We think it is like magic.

These programs also have the facility to allow you to choose the style of the referencing to suit the journal or publisher or university regulations that you have to comply with; they also have many built-in reference styles as well as the facility to add your own. It is worth checking, however, how suitable the particular program is for your discipline, as some of them are more oriented towards scientific disciplines.

- If you are working collaboratively, you can store the database on a networked system so that all the researchers in your team have common access to it.
- The Internet access functions of these databases allow you to access and download publications databases and also to launch URLs from your own database.

These software packages are extremely powerful tools, with many different functions. You may only use a few of them – but those few will be a lifeline.

It is likely that your university will have site licences for one or more of these packages. If it hasn't, you should lobby hard for one to be adopted and for the kind of licence to be bought that allows members of the university to put it on to their machine at home. Stress to your administrators that most academics do most of their academic writing at home and therefore a licence that allows people to use the program only at work is virtually useless. Because most of these databases are very similar, you don't need to worry if you move to a new job where they have a licence for a different program. You are likely to be able to import your library from your old program to your new one quite easily.

Carmen was doing her PhD in Spanish literature and had to use archives in several different countries. She put EndNote on her laptop and took it to the archives. She used EndNote not only for bibliographic purposes, but also to make notes on each manuscript that she examined as she was doing it. This database was crucially useful both in her analysis of the data and in writing and referencing her thesis.

Data handling and analysis packages

There are a number of sophisticated software packages written specifically to assist researchers with data handling and analysis. Some of them are for qualitative material and some for quantitative. Some of the qualitative packages allow the use of 'mixed methods'. That is, they will handle both qualitative and quantitative data.

Why do you need help handling data? If you have qualitative data, then it is likely that you have reams and reams of transcripts or notes or documents. The sheer physical difficulty of searching through these to identify themes pertinent to your analysis, or of finding particular passages or quotes, or of simply keeping track of what you have got and where, cannot be underestimated. Traditionally this task was undertaken manually. Rebecca is used to using coloured pens on the back of old rolls of wallpaper. Debbie also likes coloured pens, with different colours for each theme on the left-hand side of her text, and writes comments on the right-hand side. She also does things like cutting up paper and putting it in different places. Jane uses text highlighting on her computer screen. We know of people who cut up their interview transcripts and peg bits that they might want to quote on a washing line strung across their office.

Software packages promise some help in handling data. The best known qualitative data handling package on the market so far is NVivo, which is a close cousin of NUD*IST. It is said that NUD*IST and NVivo were developed by an Australian sociologist and her partner when she became frustrated at the sheer difficulty of analysing a very large quantity of qualitative interview data – particularly when her young child disrupted all her carefully arranged piles of cut-up interview transcripts.

Software data handling packages allow you to do two principal things. First, you can input any written or visual material in an electronic format. You can catalogue this, code it and search it. Second, within the program you can establish the themes through which you are analysing your data. Using these, you can then search your inputted data for material relevant to that particular theme or themes. Data handling packages do not analyse your data for you, but can take the tedium and risk out of more manual methods of data analysis. Saying you will use NVivo, or any similar package, in a research proposal is not synonymous with explaining how you will analyse the data.

Perhaps the reasons why people need software to help them with analysing quantitative data are more obvious. No-one really wants to sit and crunch through vast numbers of calculations, only to find that the answer wasn't that useful after all. Software packages for quantitative analysis have been around for a good time and there are many of them. The most common ones are SPSS (Statistical Package for Social Scientists) and Microdata. There are many training courses and written training materials available to help people become acquainted with these packages.

Web tools and skills

Another essential skill is the ability to work effectively on the Internet. You need to be confident searching the Web, at the very least, and should experiment with different search engines to find one that suits your needs best. The Web can be a useful source of secondary data, literature and information crucial to your research. It is also a great way of searching libraries and you must be able to use the electronic databases to be found there. You will need a password for some of these, which can be obtained via your own university library. In addition, most major journal publishers now make articles in their journals available electronically, and there are some journals available only on-line. In order to access journal articles you, or your library, may well need to have a print and/or electronic subscription to that journal.

Some people are now making the Internet a major data-gathering tool. For example, you could:

- Set up a Web-based conference for your respondents to talk together.
- Ask respondents to send you email diaries and maintain a correspondence with them.
- Analyse conversations in Internet chat rooms.
- Read newspaper articles from around the world on a particular event.

If you do not feel confident using Web-based resources, do go and get help. Everybody had to learn some time. Librarians are often an excellent source of support and assistance in using the Internet in a whole variety of ways.

We offer you plenty of advice about writing styles, practices and publication in *Writing for Publication*. But it is worth making a few points here, if only to impress on you the real importance of starting to develop good writing habits and skills early in your research career.

Writing is often something that inexperienced researchers (and sometimes more experienced ones too) feel very anxious about. Having other people read your work can make you feel exposed and vulnerable. This fear can often make people put off writing for as long as possible. Often inexperienced researchers feel that, a bit like having all their ducks in a row before they shoot, they have to have accumulated every scrap of evidence, read every book and conceived of every idea before they put pen to paper or finger to keyboard. This is dangerous for two reasons.

First, there are remarkably few people who naturally write fluently, clearly and elegantly. Writing, like bricklaying or plastering, is an apparently prosaic skill that can actually be developed only by frequent and regular practice. The more writing you do, and the more constructive criticism you take note of, the better your writing will become. It is no good being precious or defensive about it. If you show your writing, as you should, to your supervisor, mentor and peers, you should expect to have it returned to you, especially in the early stages, covered in comments and suggestions. The only time when you are entitled to get upset about this is if they use a red pen (any other colour is fine) or if the comments are rude, unhelpful or both.

Second, in the social sciences and humanities especially, writing is an integral part of the research process. Even in laboratory-based scientific research, the process of articulating the work in its final written form is often a rewriting of the researcher's laboratory notebooks. Writing is the means by which you achieve real unity with your data, sort out your ideas, articulate your thoughts, decide where you've gone wrong, discover the holes in your theory, work out what you really think and so on.

We share Karen Locke and Karen Golden-Biddle's (see Further Reading for details) serious pet hate for the notion of someone completing their research and then sitting down to 'write it up'. The image that this phrase calls to mind is of an athlete deciding to run a marathon but to delay breathing until they pass the finishing line.

Your first attempts at writing will probably be schematic and eventually subject to substantial change. No-one can produce brilliant first drafts, and you should not be expected to do so either. One of Rebecca's students told her that he had been surprised when he looked at the log of his MBA dissertation file: he had redrafted the entire document thirty-seven times. His MBA dissertation was awarded a distinction – the highest possible mark. Most people don't redraft quite as often as that, but all successful academics redraft many, many times. The longer the piece of work the more redrafting will take place.

It's never too soon to start writing. Having stuff on paper gives you a real and justified sense of making progress. It develops your essential writing skills. It makes the task of completing your final written work far less onerous and daunting. It means you have something to show for your hours of work, and that can be important if you are accountable for your time. If you need to talk about your work with others, you have something to give them that will form the concrete basis for a discussion.

Ultimately you need to become your own most effective critic so that you are not dependent on supervisors, mentors or other critical friends. This doesn't mean you stop using them, but it does mean that you will be able to present them with a good-quality draft. This will avoid imposing on busy people's time and goodwill and will help them to give you better advice.

When is enough 'enough'?

There are two problems here: those people who are over-confident with no good reason and those who are under-confident with no good reason.

Over-confident researchers stop thinking and rush to publish before they have anything of interest to say. They are often very unreflexive about their research projects and their work tends to be un- or under-theorised. If you are reading this book it is not at all likely that you are in this category, but you do need to be able to recognise such people, particularly when they try to undermine you and your confidence. They are usually wearing the Emperor's New Clothes.

Conversely, we've talked previously about how some academics suffer from compulsive over-achievement combined with lack of confidence. The fear of being exposed as an academic fraud or inter-loper is often particularly intense among inexperienced researchers. But even established researchers may continue to feel that way in certain circumstances. These common feelings, especially (but not only) among women, can make finishing a project quite difficult. It takes a long time and a lot of experience to get over such feelings, and they may well continue to lurk under the surface. They tend to inhibit us from feeling that we have 'done enough' on a project and, at their worst, can lead to a kind of paralysis.

We can only advise you that many people feel the same. You need to develop a realistic assessment of the quality of your own work and trust the judgement of those who are helping you. If you have good sources of advice (and we'll be talking about how to access this in the next section) you should believe them if they say that you have done enough. Remember that no piece of work is ever perfect and the best is the enemy of the good. Seeking perfection is a fool's errand. Our mottoes are:

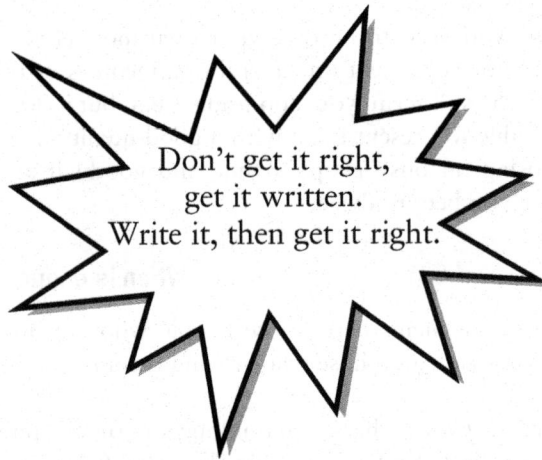

> Don't get it right,
> get it written.
> Write it, then get it right.

There's a second feeling that stops us from stopping. This is where we continue to see interesting and unexplored corners in our research topic. We think that we have to keep going to cover every base and every theoretical eventuality. This is an inability to recognise when a research project has reached the stage where it possesses academic integrity and coherence, and can assume its rightful place as part of a body of knowledge. A good proposal and tightly focused research questions will all help to keep you on track here.

Grainne was at the end of her doctoral studies and close to submitting her thesis. Her work was on the consumption of Guinness and Irish national identity. Part of her argument was that Guinness did not advertise itself as particularly Irish in the UK or the USA. However, just as she was finalising her thesis the company produced a new advertising campaign that made explicit reference to the Irishness of Guinness. Grainne was thrown into a state of panic, thinking that she should revisit her entire argument and rewrite her thesis taking account of this latest advertising campaign. Her supervisor advised her to do no such thing. The work stood as an original contribution to knowledge by examining the phenomenon up to the company's change of advertising strategy. Looking at the new campaign, Grainne was advised, would make an interesting subsequent piece of work after her PhD. Grainne passed her viva and got her doctorate.

A third reason why people have difficulty realising when enough is enough is that they simply can't bear to let go. For such people, concluding a stage in their research is a bit like giving their precious baby away. For doctoral students, in particular, the period of their studies has often been very intense and personally formative and there can be a kind of terror that once you are no longer a student you will not know who you are. Debbie calls this 'fear of finishing'.

The best way of overcoming this psychological hurdle is to think of concluding one piece or stage of a research project as something that will lead seamlessly to the next interesting thing to do. If you feel yourself suffering from these feelings, sit down and plan what you would like to do next in your research, taking care to see it as the development of a research agenda, or even a personal intellectual project.

Muddling through: fixing things when they go wrong

We're very much aware that, up to this point, we have been counselling perfection. Paradoxically, we've also been advising you against self-flagellation. We appreciate the irony and hope you do too. The truth is that the research process is always messy and one of muddling through. Things can, and under Sods' Law therefore always do, go wrong. Research projects are usually planned and the final results presented as a seamless, neat and linear process. This is a snare and a delusion.

Unfortunately, inexperienced researchers are rarely made aware of this sad truth. Therefore when they encounter muddle, confusion, mistakes, obstacles and errors it enhances their own feelings of failure and inadequacy. Afraid of looking like the failures they feel they are, they don't tell others of their trials and travails. That leaves everyone feeling and thinking that they are the only ones to be having difficulties.

To our mind, the mark of a really good academic is someone who can work their way through all these issues and is brave enough to tell others how they did it. In medical science, Alexander Fleming is a famous example of this. He discovered penicillin because he allowed the medium used for growing bacterial cultures to become contaminated through sloppy laboratory practice. His genius was in noticing that what had gone wrong was actually much more interesting and important than the experiment he had set out to do.

So what are the sorts of things that are likely to go wrong on your research project? It's unpredictable, but we can tell you about the sorts of things that have gone wrong for some people we know.

Rachel and several colleagues were conducting a research project within their own institution which relied on the distribution of a questionnaire survey to all members of academic staff. The Personnel Department agreed to distribute the questionnaire with individuals' salary advice statements to achieve proper coverage.

In fact, the Personnel Department failed to do so. Instead, it sent out bundles of the questionnaires with the pay slips to the various university faculties. It did not give faculty administrators any advice on the distribution of the questionnaires. Nor did they send enough questionnaires for all members of academic staff. Furthermore, they failed to inform the researchers that casual hourly paid academic teaching staff received their pay slip by mail at home rather than in their pigeonholes at work. Administrators in the faculties had placed the questionnaires in staff pigeonholes along with the pay slips. Where there was no pay slip they did not distribute the questionnaires. The

▶ instructions on the questionnaire asked respondents to return it in the 'enclosed pre-addressed envelope'. The harassed research assistant had forgotten to have these envelopes printed and attached to the questionnaires.

The research team met after this debacle to decide how to rectify the situation. They contacted named administrators of known competence in each faculty to establish how many members of regular staff had not received questionnaires, had further copies printed and distributed them to the faculties. They contacted Personnel regarding the casual hourly paid staff. Personnel declined to give the researchers the home addresses of such staff, but suggested that the Payroll Department would send out copies of the questionnaire with the pay advice slips the following month. The researchers contacted the Payroll Department, which declined to do the work.

The researchers then ascertained the number of casual teaching staff in each faculty and distributed hard copies of the questionnaire to each dean, with the request that they be placed in individuals' pigeonholes. One obstructive dean declined to have this done for self-evidently spurious reasons. The project leader wrote back to him, copying the letter to the dean's superior, pointing out the spurious nature of his objections and the fact that the university Ethics Committee had approved the project.

The survey was successfully conducted – eventually – with a good response rate from all the targeted respondent groups.

The lesson from this vignette is that excrement happens (to paraphrase politely). The skill comes in keeping a cool head and finding pragmatic solutions to obstacles and difficulties. In situations like this, it's really important to call on all your resources, human, financial and otherwise, to solve the problem creatively. Remember that the published output of research is the polished version for public consumption. Real research processes go round in circles, up blind alleys, and fall over with alarming regularity. It's like the swan swimming serenely across the calm lake, while simultaneously paddling furiously and invisibly under water.

5 Moving on: Developing Yourself as a Researcher

By the time you've got your first proper research project well under way, you've already begun to develop yourself as a researcher. In this chapter we want to look at two issues that will help you to continue that developmental process. These are: getting help and good ethical practice. These are more generic issues, but ones that should inform or shape every aspect of every research project that you undertake, and, indeed, your way of being in the world.

What is a professional researcher?

We would like to think that what you want is to become a professional research practitioner. So what is such a person like?

- They have a toolbox of personal attributes and skills that allow them to undertake academic research at an appropriate level in a professional and competent manner. The aim of this book, thus far, has been to give you some insight into what those attributes and skills are.
- They are capable of independent thought. They engage actively with the world and think creatively and innovatively about it. Good academics have a real buzz about them, interesting ideas and as much curiosity as killed the cat. They constantly ask questions. In this sense, they are a lot like young children who constantly, and often irritatingly, ask 'Why?'

  The actress Jodie Foster, who had been a star student at Yale, once made an alumni speech in which she told graduating students that 'it's not good enough to put change in the [parking] meter without questioning what the meter is doing there in the first place'

(*Guardian,* 19 December 1998). In similar vein, one of Rebecca's old mentors, and a senior academic, once told her that 'the job description of an academic is to ask difficult questions.' Even in these times of ever-increasing managerialisation, it is important to take your role as a public intellectual, who asks difficult questions, very seriously.

- At the same time as being self-reliant, you have to be self-reflexive and know your own limits. A good academic knows what they are good at and when they need to find others to compensate for their weaker areas or complement their expertise.

- Given what we've said about the need for good academics to be independent, critical and creative thinkers, it may sound paradoxical, but they also have to be capable of making a real contribution to a team. Being a good team member is about bringing your strengths to the team and about letting (and helping) other team members contribute theirs. In other words, you should neither dominate nor become a dogsbody. In a good team, the sum is greater than the parts and all members of the team recognise both the strengths and the weaknesses that they and others bring to it.

- Collegiality comes into teamwork but goes beyond it. Good researchers also need to be good colleagues. Ideally, this is about being part of a co-operative, self-directed community where you have a sense of belonging, mutuality and shared values. While it is important to look after yourself and protect your own interests, it is equally important not to become selfish and look *only* after yourself and your research.

Getting help but not being helpless

Becoming a good academic is a process of development, not an innate set of characteristics. Academics are not born, like Athena, fully formed from Zeus's head, or like supermarket chickens, oven-ready. Like any developmental process, people need help in getting there. Sadly, a lot of academics don't get the help they need. It's useful for mentors to ask themselves the question posed by an Australian academic, 'What sort of help helps?' Our primary motivation for writing the *Academic's Support Kit* is our perception that there are a lot of people in universities who do not receive the kind of mentoring they should. That said, we can't emphasise enough that ultimately you are responsible for your own research career. You will frequently need to take the initiative and be a self-starter rather than waiting for other people to do it for you. A good mentor helps you to develop a strong sense of agency, as the following vignette illustrates.

> Cynthia was encouraging her doctoral students to become involved in academic publishing in various ways. She was particularly keen for them to get a good practical understanding of the publishing process and its different stages and practices. She therefore suggested to some of her students that they should offer to edit a special issue of a journal. In the process of doing this they learnt a lot about putting together a coherent set of papers around a common theme, the editing and refereeing process, negotiating with managing editors of journals, the time it takes to do such work and dealing with referees' feedback. The resulting special issue was accepted in its entirety by a respectable refereed academic journal and has now been published.

Why don't people get the help they need?

The reasons why people don't get the help they need are threefold. First, sometimes they are too proud, too shy or too scared to ask for help. These feelings are, in part, created and sustained by an academic environment in which there can be a perceived expectation that people will 'just be able to get on with it'. The fear of being 'found out' contributes to reluctance to ask for help. If you are someone who is quite capable and intelligent, others, who could help you, may not realise that you feel you need help.

Second, some of the more experienced and senior people who should be providing such help simply don't do their job. There are a variety of reasons. It may be because they are selfish with their time and energies or because they had to 'just get on with it' themselves and see this as a kind of rite of passage for becoming an academic. Equally, they may simply not have the know-how that you need – they may even be ill equipped to do the job they have been promoted into. They may have poor social or communication skills and simply don't realise that others need their help or they don't know how to offer help. They might be judgemental or prejudiced – thinking, for example, that it's not worth the effort to help women with young families to develop a research career. Or they may be going through a period where they are, themselves, under considerable personal or professional stress and simply have no reserves of time or energy to help others. Those in the last group, will, however, come round when they get control of their lives and when times are better.

Third, some institutions simply don't take the formal training needs of staff seriously. Training courses can be useful ways of plugging specific skill gaps. Some institutions in some countries have got better at putting resources into the continuing professional development of academics, but it isn't general. The best training is an extension, or formalisation, of the help provided by good experienced academics. However, some staff training is provided by people who don't really understand what it is to be an academic. Consequently, they may put on courses that suffer from poor pedagogy or inadequate content. However, it has to be said that the very worst training, in our experience, is for management, appraisal or teaching rather than for research. Certainly you should lobby your university to provide the training you need but sometimes you may have to resort to putting on courses yourself. The following vignette shows that this can sometimes shame your university into attending to your and your colleagues' needs.

Jenny and four of her colleagues wanted to be trained in the use of NVivo. Using her contacts, she located a suitable external trainer. The trainer was expensive, unless a full complement of participants could be recruited on to the course and the cost shared between them all. Jenny advertised the availability of the three surplus places around the faculty. She was inundated with requests for places. She eventually organised training for sixty-four people. All the trainees were positive and enthusiastic about the training they had received and most are now planning to use NVivo in their research. The university has, as a consequence of the demand created by this training, bought a site licence for the software.

Can I really ask for help?

We think that getting help, advice and support in your academic research is a reasonable entitlement, especially given the pressures to 'perform' that you are likely to be under. But, like any entitlement, it also brings with it certain obligations.

Because the sorts of help, advice and support you are likely to need will be particular to you, and because we live in the real world, it is likely that you will have to be proactive in identifying what you need and seeking it out. Don't expect others to automatically divine what it is you need help with and freely offer it unrequested. Your colleagues are not mind-readers and are also busy with their own research and other work.

If you are at the very beginning of your research career, it is unlikely that you will be able to specify what your needs are, beyond saying that you need help in getting started. We hope that this book has gone some way towards helping you identify what you don't know and can't do as well as what you do know and can do. If you are at the very beginning, what you need is a friendly face, someone who will take an interest in your plans and take the time to chat with you and, metaphorically, hold your hand in the early stages. They may be able to give you the help you need at this stage themselves, or they may be able to point you in the direction of alternative sources of assistance. Often what you need is someone to give you enough confidence to feel that you can make a start, no matter how small your first step is.

Josie was a recently appointed lecturer who had successfully completed her MA but had not yet begun to establish herself as a researcher. The department she worked in had a tradition of getting more junior academics to join the research teams of those more experienced, but not of supporting them to do their own research. Josie wanted to do her own research and to register for a PhD in order to give her work some structure. The problem was that she didn't really know what it was that she wanted to do for her PhD project and didn't feel that anyone in her own department would be willing or able to help her define it, as that simply was not their way of working.

▶

▶ She became friendly with a new professor in another department whom she met at a management meeting. They met socially and she discussed her ambition to become a researcher and the problems of doing so in her own department. The professor encouraged her to continue in this vein and suggested that she write a brief research proposal outlining her interests. Josie did so, and the professor read it and suggested that it still needed to be focused. She also said that she was not really the best person to help Josie develop the proposal further and sent her to another senior woman in her (the professor's) department. Josie had several meetings with this other woman, and eventually narrowed her focus sufficiently to be able to write an excellent research proposal. She was accepted to do her PhD in one of the most prestigious departments in the country at another university and her own department agreed to pay half her fees.

By now perhaps you have embarked on an initial research project based on a well worked-through project proposal. If so, you should have a sense of the sorts of help, advice and support you need. The types of things you might need help with include:

- Library skills.
- Understanding or 'getting into' theory and theoretical debates.
- Locating and joining suitable networks of like-minded researchers.
- Particular data collection and analysis techniques and tools.
- Writing.
- Finding conference venues to present your work and preparing for those presentations.
- Finding suitable journals to send your papers to.
- Organising your research.
- Thinking about how you might move on from one topic to a research agenda or a personal intellectual project.
- Finding ways of gaining access to research respondents, archives and other sources of data.

Always remember that you are perfectly within your rights to ask for help on such topics. What's more, you would be foolish if you decided to struggle on miserably on your own.

Conversely, it is not okay to expect anyone or any system to carry you, to do your work for you, to mother you or to generally accept responsibility for your own personal professional development as a researcher. It is perfectly okay to have needs. It is not okay to be an over-dependent complete pain in the behind: this is unlikely to endear you to those people whom you most need to help you.

Sue's early academic experiences had, through no fault of her own, severely affected her confidence in her ability to do research. A new head of department established a new mentoring system. The head of department and the person responsible for the mentoring scheme took care to ensure that Sue got a mentor who would be sympathetic to her problems and patient with her because her previous experience had made her distrustful and lacking in confidence. Sue worked hard with her new mentor, who in turn devoted enormous amounts of time and energy to her – seeing her once or twice a week in the early stages. Over the ensuing six months, with consistent support, Sue was able to analyse some data that she had previously collected but hadn't known what to do with, write a conference paper, deliver it at the conference and submit it for publication in an international journal. During the summer vacation, when her mentor was away, Sue was notified that her paper had been accepted, subject to minor revisions. On her own she made the changes, resubmitted the paper and it was accepted for publication. Sue has now registered for a PhD – something that she would never have countenanced before this confidence-building mentoring process.

What Sue's story shows is that, with help, even people who have had the worst of experiences can grow into being capable of taking responsibility for their work, defining a project and developing their own research career. Sue will continue to need advice and support – as all doctoral students and emergent researchers do – but she now does so as an confident and self-knowing person who is making reasonable demands of a system that has a duty to provide care and support if it wants her to do research.

As people who regularly have to provide support and help to colleagues, we would ask you to make strenuous efforts to avoid the following behaviours:

- Always assuming that those helping you are available 24/7 to deal with your problems, or that your problems are the most important thing in their lives.
- Dominating groups, meetings, etc., with your requirements and needs.
- Giving someone something to read and then getting upset if they can't turn it round and give you feedback immediately. They will have many other competing demands on their time.
- Ignoring advice and feedback on your writing without good reason.

On the whole, our experience is that people don't always have a sense that it is okay to ask for support and help. At the other extreme, some people become time and emotion vultures. The best way to get balance is to sit down with the person or people helping you and agree about the basis on which you are going to get help. There will be an implicit/tacit contract in any such support relationship anyway, and it is better to make it explicit. Those who provide help and support are human beings with their own lives, needs and pressures. You need to achieve a certain level of reciprocity: the relationship should not be all one way.

How do I avoid bad advice and how do I know it when I get it?

This is a tough question. It's a bit like when your car breaks down. You take it to a garage you don't know and the mechanic takes one look underneath and comes up for air shaking his head, muttering, and talks about expensive parts and big labour bills. You know nothing about cars. What do you do? Is his advice good or is he incompetent or trying to take advantage of your credit card? There are a number of strategies that you might take to avoid the risk of bad advice – with your car or with your research:

- Take your car to a garage you know and trust. Similarly, seek help from sources that you know and trust. Look for people who are successful researchers themselves and who have a reputation among colleagues for being helpful, supportive and collegial. Pick your source with care.
- If you don't know any garages, or any good sources of research help, ask around among people like yourself.
- If the mechanic makes you feel stupid and undermined there is a fair chance that they are trying to deceive you. Similarly, if the person helping you isn't building your confidence but instead is bullying you, making you feel awful about yourself or is trying to get you to do their work instead of your own, then find another source of help.
- If the mechanic disparages the garage down the road, trying to get you to stick with them, it is reasonable to assume that they don't want to be exposed for having given the wrong information. Similarly, if the person or people trying to help you try to prevent you from speaking to anyone except themselves they may be trying to exploit you, make you their own 'little helper' or otherwise prevent you from developing your own academic research identity and independence. The idea is that you get help to become an independent free-thinking academic, not that you are caught in someone's shadow, doing their bidding.

By implication, if your help and advice are the inverse of all this, then it's probably pretty good.

What are my potential sources of advice and support?

Advice, support and help tend to have two principal dimensions: the formal/informal and the obligatory/discretionary. In our experience, the utilisation and provision of formal sources is to some extent or another obligatory whilst informal sources are more likely to be taken up and offered on a discretionary basis. As with everything, how well all these things works is dependent not only on having good systems but on the individuals involved, how they choose to make them work (or not) and their interpersonal dynamics.

We set out below a range of sources of help, advice and assistance that you might choose to access and to offer others.

Research degree supervisors or advisers

This is at the far end of the scale in terms of formality. If you are registered for a research degree your university will have regulations that require you to have at least one supervisor/adviser. For the supervisor, this is formally allocated work for which they are accountable to the university. They should have clearly set out responsibilities and duties with regard to being your supervisor. This should ease the pain of getting them to help you: in a very formal sense, they are simply doing their job.

Every supervisory relationship is different, and the expectations of supervisors/advisers will, to some extent, differ from department to department, from university to university and even from country to country. Broadly, you should expect the following sorts of things from your supervisor/adviser:

- They should know enough about your research topic to be able to start you off in a good direction and keep you on track. Inevitably, the culmination of a successful research degree programme is distinguished by your becoming more expert than your supervisor and probably *the* expert in that particular field.
- They will engage with you on an intellectual level around your research topic. They should suggest readings and be able to challenge you in constructive ways on your ideas.
- They should be able to provide practical advice on matters such as organising your research, data collection and data analysis. It's no good trying to be supervised by someone who has never done your type of research before.
- They should be someone with whom you can engage critically on ethical issues.
- They can and do help you develop your writing skills, not only for the thesis but also for publication of your research.
- They put you in contact with wider academic networks and help you develop your own.
- They can and will help you develop your wider and long-term academic career profile and think about that proactively. In short, they should also act as a sort of career mentor, not just a research adviser.
- They treat you with respect, courtesy and consideration, but at the same time are sufficiently demanding to keep you going when you are feeling demotivated and demoralised.

Unfortunately, bad supervisory practice abounds. The reasons why it doesn't work are numerous. Sometimes, the interpersonal dynamics in what should be a very close intellectual and academic friendship simply aren't right. This may not be anyone's fault. It may just be that the chemistry is wrong. In that case, you should discuss the problem with your supervisor and, if it can't be resolved, request a change of supervisor.

Sometimes the relationship doesn't work because the supervisor fails to take his/her responsibilities seriously enough or does not even know what they are. On other occasions the supervisor simply may know enough about your area of research. Sadly, few universities provide proper training on how to supervise research students well and supervisors have only their own, sometimes very bad, experience to guide them. Sometimes students have to 'manage upwards': seeking to define the relationship in such a way that they get what they need. Your relationship with your supervisor/adviser is a partnership in which both sides have responsibilities and you are entitled to have reasonable expectations about the other party's behaviour. If there is not a good match between their expertise and your topic then you should discuss with your supervisor whether to change supervisors or to add someone with complementary expertise to your advisory team.

How can you avoid some, or all, of these problems? As with any prospective long-term, significant relationship, don't get into bed with someone you don't know. Beware of universities that simply tell you that you will be 'assigned' a supervisor or adviser. Departments with good research degree programmes and good supervisory arrangements would never accept students for whom they did not have an entirely appropriate supervisor.

For such a significant person, or people, you need to do your homework: check out their academic and personal reputation; discuss your proposed topic with them; read what they have written; see if they are willing to give you helpful and constructive advice on your draft proposal before you have registered. If you are applying to do a research degree in another country, it is particularly important to find out about your prospective supervisor before you accept a place on a programme. If at all possible, arrange to meet your prospective supervisor or, at the very least, have an email and/or telephone conversation with them. Overall, you have to judge whether this is a person you like, can work closely with and who can help you in ways that are appropriate and good for you.

Increasingly, universities are willing to support members of staff who do not have a doctorate in obtaining one. In such circumstances, and

TABLE 4   Where to do your PhD

Factor	Own institution	Other institution
Finance	Usually no fee payable	A fee may be payable
Supervision	May not have a supervisor with the right expertise who is also sufficiently distanced from you	Choice of supervisor will be far less constrained
Institutional care	May have a greater vested interest in you succeeding at your PhD as part of their staff development. Conversely, may want to extract the maximum amount of teaching and administrative work from you	May have less commitment to you as an individual as a part-time student rather than a full-time colleague. Conversely their imperatives and demands may be a useful lever to help you manage your workload downwards in your own institution
Geography	Your supervisor may be more readily accessible	You may have to travel long distances to meet your supervisor and regular informal contact may be quite problematic
Widening perspectives	May promote parochialism in intellectual thought and even when it doesn't it's less likely to surprise you as you already know these people	More likely to challenge your thinking and widen your perspectives and you can bring something back to your own institution. Increases your knowledge of how other institutions organise things

for understandable reasons to do with financial and other resources, they are likely to encourage their staff to do a research degree within their own department or institution. This may or may not be the best course to follow. Each case needs to be carefully evaluated on its own merits. Table 4 may help you think/argue this matter through.

Formal/informal mentoring schemes

Much of what we have said about supervisors/advisers applies equally to research mentors, whether formal or informal. So if you skipped that section because you are not a research degree student and don't intend to become one, you might like to go back and read it.

By mentoring, what we mean is someone who takes an interest in you, your research and your career and is in a position which enables them to help you develop them. They will, therefore, be more experienced than you are.

When Roxanne was coming towards the end of her PhD she was fortunate to meet Ludmilla, a senior academic prominent in the field of gender and education. Roxanne was working in an administrative capacity to earn some money at a summer school for distance learners. Ludmilla was a very inclusive course director and made sure that Roxanne was included in all meetings and in as many of the academic activities as was practical and appropriate. Following the summer school, Ludmilla invited Roxanne to join a symposium she was organising at a major international conference – Roxanne's first-ever conference paper. Since then, Ludmilla has helped Roxanne to shape her research agenda, offered her significant opportunities for publication, ensured that she was invited to take part in seminars where other significant academics in her field would be present and acted as a referee and informal career adviser.

Some universities or departments have established formal research mentoring schemes. This means that better established researchers in the department are formally matched with their less experienced colleagues on a one-to-one basis. Done properly, these schemes can be invaluable, as can be seen from the vignette of Sue and her research mentor. The reason they are valuable is that they can make sure that everyone who needs it has a port of call when they need help with their research. When they work well, no-one should slip through the net of research support and advice. An advantage of formal mentoring schemes is that they signal the willingness of those acting as mentors to give their time and effort to such work. This can make the mentees feel a bit better about 'bothering' their mentors and consequently more likely to use them.

Conversely, formal schemes can work badly. In some schemes, mentors are assigned without any consultation or agreement and often with little care. Mentors may regard their position as giving them *carte blanche* to become bossy or controlling with their mentees. Sometimes these schemes are honoured more in the breach than in the observance. At their best they work something like, albeit probably less intensively, a doctoral supervisory relationship.

Whether or not you have a formal mentoring scheme in your department, you can also seek out informal mentors. Sometimes concerned senior academics will seek you out. These informal mentors may be in your own department, elsewhere in your institution or even at another university. They may be people you have met at conferences, through your own wider research community, journal editors or through teaching or committees as in the case of Roxanne, above. They may also be your ex-teachers for your first or master's degree.

Inexperienced researchers often seem quite surprised that anyone should take a genuine interest in their research well-being. In fact, most good academics regard this kind of work as integral to, and one of the most rewarding aspects of, their professional practice. Many of them will be genuinely delighted if they find an early career researcher who is interested in the same stuff that they are and will derive pleasure from working with you and in watching you grow and succeed as a researcher. Many of these people will have benefited from just this sort of help when they were in your position, and should see this work as payback time. Alternatively, they may have received no such help and wish they had – their efforts represent an attempt to help you avoid the difficulties that they encountered.

You will have to rely on your judgement in deciding whether to accept proffered help or who to approach yourself. Be aware that some unscrupulous characters may just be keen to get their grubby hands on your data or your good ideas. However, fear of this shouldn't deter you from accepting genuine offers. In seeking out a mentor the same kinds of considerations apply as in seeking a good research degree supervisor or adviser. They are most likely to be a work colleague, so you should be able to have a pretty good feel for what kind of person they are.

Julie had been a teaching member of staff for many years. She became increasingly anxious as, simultaneously, the university wound down the specialist subjects that she taught and she came under pressure to become research-active. The Director of Research in her department made a practice of having a 'fireside chat' with all members of staff at least once a year, just to see how they were getting on and whether the department could offer any further support and assistance. ▶

▶   During this chat, Julie and the Director of Research realised that they had a very strong mutual interest in the subject of taxation. Julie had excellent technical expertise and the Director of Research was able to frame the issues in a more theoretical way. The Director of Research suggested that Julie should conduct some research on this issue, gave her some ideas about how to approach it and suggested that she could come back for further help whenever she needed it.

Julie has proven herself to be a good independent worker. At each stage in her subsequent research she went off and tackled the task, returning to her mentor when she needed feedback on how she had done and advice as to what the next stage was. Within six months of their initial chat, Julie had written a paper and presented it at a major conference.

Staff appraisal

As part of what an English academic calls the 'creeping cancer of managerialism' most universities around the world have some sort of formal staff performance review or appraisal. This can be a formal system for grading academics' performance in order to make decisions about tenure, promotion or levels of pay. Alternatively, it can be a system designed as more akin to a formal mentoring system with the added advantage that any developmental needs identified as a result of the appraisal process are formally notified to the university to action. (However, don't hold your breath that anything will actually happen.) The worst sort of scheme fraudulently attempts to marry these two approaches, pretending to be helpful and supportive whilst really evaluating your performance the better to control you as an employee. Here we are talking only about those systems designed to act as types of mentoring schemes.

Such schemes can be extremely helpful, for two reasons. First, they make the university pay individual attention and consideration to each employee on a regular and individual basis. Second, they give the individual a formal opening to discuss what is concerning them, how they feel they're getting on and what the university can do to further their research efforts. Such appraisals will take quite a long time and, to use it properly, both you and your appraiser need to prepare well. We think it important that such meetings are completely confidential, apart from an agreed record of what the university should be providing for you, and should be addressing to help its academic staff. In other words, the record should not be about your performance but about that of the university. To paraphrase John F. Kennedy, in appraisal, but especially in records of appraisal, you should ask not what you can do for the university but what the university can and should do for you.

As with any other form of mentoring help that you get, in appraisal processes you should be treated with dignity, courtesy and respect, and you should make sure that you get positive help and guidance from your appraiser. Sometimes the management of universities attempt to impose schemes that are not regarded by academics themselves as optimal for these purposes. There's many a slip betwixt cup and lip, and many academic departments, in such circumstances, freely adapt the scheme to something that is good for them while maintaining the fiction to the university administrators that the scheme is operating entirely as designed. We could not possibly condone such behaviour ...

Ken's anxieties about not doing research had reached crisis point when he had to have a formal staff appraisal. The professors in his department had objected to the university appraisal scheme because they saw it as insufficiently supportive and had 'tweaked' it so that it would be genuinely helpful to colleagues.

Ken carefully identified one of the professors, a well known and enthusiastic researcher, as likely to understand his dilemma over research. In a nerve-racking interview Ken confessed that he felt under awful pressure to do research but didn't know how to do it. It was evident to his appraiser that he was extremely stressed and unhappy.

During the course of the appraisal interview, the sympathetic appraiser helped Ken to decide that he wanted to explore whether or not he could do research and identify an outline research topic about which he was enthusiastic. Subsequently, the professor acted as his mentor and research partner and Ken is now regarded as an active emerging researcher in his department.

He subsequently admitted to the professor and other colleagues that he had fully expected his appraisal to result in dismissal from his post. This confession was an object lesson to his appraiser, who had previously failed to appreciate the very serious stresses that some colleagues felt under with regard to research.

Research training courses

We have already written briefly about research training. Most institutions, these days, provide access to training for their research students, at least, and usually extend this availability to all academic staff. They may also provide research training specifically for staff, particularly in the use of IT. Training courses may also be offered by disciplinary associations, by other universities which open them up 'for sale' or by analogous professional bodies.

You will need to make a judgement about whether you need these and will benefit from them. Don't become a training junkie and don't go on courses where you can't see any short or medium-term use for them. That is just research work avoidance. On the other hand, if you identify a need for a particular piece of training, don't be afraid to ask for it, perhaps justifying the running of a course by demonstrating that others in your department, faculty or university would also benefit. As with mentors and supervisors/advisers there are good and bad trainers. If you can, it is worth asking around to find the good courses on the topics or issues that you need help with.

Research teams

By research team we mean a combination of any number of researchers (more than one) who are working together on a project or series of projects which may or may not be externally funded. Teams can be formally constituted or be just two or more people who have decided to work together.

Being a member of a research team can bring mixed blessings. Being in a good team can give you support, teach you new skills, overcome isolation and help you to get good access, a good reputation and publications. Conversely, in poor research teams the inexperienced or novice researchers are thoroughly exploited: they do the dogsbody footwork, are 'invisible' professionally in that they are not credited with the work they have done (especially in any publications) and can have poor security of employment. If you work with a good team it can be one of the best research experiences ever. If you work with a bad one, it can make you very unhappy indeed and/or seriously prejudice your career prospects. If in the early stages, for example when the proposal is being drawn up, you are excluded, bullied or 'put upon' you should not hesitate to withdraw from the team. A team that starts in that way will carry on that way. They never mend their ways.

Before you join any team, it is a good idea to thoroughly check out your prospective colleagues in much the same way as you would a supervisor/adviser or mentor. Make sure that your expected contribution to the endeavour and the *modus operandi* of the team are clearly articulated. In particular, get prior agreement on matters such as who gets named on publications and in what order.

Don't forget that, even as a 'junior' partner, you will have something useful to bring to the party. Don't underestimate the real value of someone who will do basic and often routine work such as searching the literature, gathering data or keeping the project archive. You aren't necessarily being exploited if that is your contribution: you are probably learning and rehearsing valuable skills and also learning how larger projects function. You should also be able, in a good team, and in time, to develop into a more 'senior' member, contributing your own ideas and suggestions for ways of moving the work forward. We have more to say on research teams and funded research in *Winning and Managing Research Funding*.

Research centres

Often, academics in particular universities come together in different sorts of combinations than the regular departments or faculties. These may be constituted as research centres. The main reason why people set up centres is to give a better profile to the particular area of research that they are working in (and thereby attract more external funding). They also aim to provide a focal point for collegiate research activities around particular research agendas.

Centres can be good places for the emergent researcher to hang out: they are often interdisciplinary; provide a lively intellectual environment in a specific area; have plenty of on-going projects and research teams; and can attract prestigious visiting speakers and fellows, enabling emergent researchers to meet inspiring people who are the leaders in their field. They are sometimes quite well resourced financially. A good research centre will be a warm and welcoming place for beginning researchers.

Robyn was director of a very successful research centre in Australia. She made a point of involving doctoral students, postdoctoral fellows and early career researchers in all centre activities. A representative of each of these groups was included on the centre steering committee. They were encouraged to invite their own visiting scholars, to run their own seminars, initiate reading and writing groups and, where possible, were involved in externally funded research projects.

Reading groups

A reading group is an informal collection of people who are interested in similar sorts of literature or areas of research. They agree to meet regularly to discuss a prearranged paper, book or report. The purpose is to help people in the group get to grips with difficult theory or keep on top of new developments in the literature in that area. The group can be a very enjoyable and non-threatening way of doing this. In time, they may well become research teams as people start to coalesce around particular topics of mutual interest.

If no reading group exists for you to join, you might think about collecting some of your colleagues together and setting one up. Debbie has found that joining or setting up reading groups has been one of the most productive and supportive aspects of her academic career. She has made new academic friends, enjoyed a mutually supportive environment and read much more widely than she might otherwise have.

Research networks and associations

These are discussed at length in *Building Networks*, but it is pertinent to make some brief points here. Many academic discipline areas have associations of researchers, such as the American Accounting Association, the International Sociological Association, the Australian Association for Research in Education, the Modern Languages Association (in the USA) and the American Historical Association. These provide a focal point for communities of like-minded researchers. They usually engage in activities such as running conferences, publishing their own journals, staging doctoral colloquia, organising research training or setting up special sub-groupings for doctoral students. In addition, these associations usually facilitate the organisation of special interest groups (SIGs): sub-groups of people with more specific interests.

It is worth joining the appropriate association in your country, other countries and possibly some international ones. This will give you access to a community of scholars outside your institution, conferences, special workshops and so on. They can be good places to start to develop a wider network of support and help.

Outside such organisations, or if one doesn't exist, from time to time academics set up an informal network or grouping to help keep in touch and give each other support and share information. The Internet and email present an excellent way of doing this: both for identifying potential members and for staying in touch.

Peers and academic friends

The most important and long-lasting support that you can get will come from your peers and academic friends. Academia is a global community with relatively few inhabitants. This, combined with our propensity to move jobs and travel a lot, means that we often have quite a close-knit but geographically spread group of friends. It is this kind of friendship network that led Debbie and Rebecca in the UK to be writing this *Kit* with Jane in Australia. These sorts of friendships go well beyond the sorts of workplace friendships that people in other occupations tend to form. We think that it is a big compensation for what can otherwise be very hard work.

Is it okay to use such friendship networks as a source of help? We think so: friendships are, by definition, mutually supportive and everyone benefits over the long term. While one person may be more in need of support at one time, someone else will receive it at others. These networks are like help banks. Sometimes you pay in and sometimes you withdraw. We can't tell you how to find your friends, obviously, but participating in the research culture of your department, university or general disciplinary field is an obvious first step.

Jo and Hilary met because they were doing their PhDs with the same supervisor. They quickly discovered that they shared theoretical interests and enjoyed each other's company in a variety of ways. They ▶

▶ have subsequently published papers, developed conference symposia and research proposals together. Having completed their PhDs and gone on to academic appointments at different universities they remain in close contact and regularly give each other support and academic feedback for their teaching and research.

Everyone has to form their own relationships, but here are some of the ways in which we have benefited from our friendship networks in terms of:

- Kicking around new and half-baked ideas in a safe space where we know we won't be laughed at, thought stupid or ripped off.
- Reading of papers in early drafts by supportive but critical friends.
- Notification of and invitations to participate in interesting conferences, seminar series or research projects.
- Joint research and writing projects.
- Interesting and inspiring conversations.
- Knowing people at conferences whom you can hang around and have fun with.
- Telling us about interesting things that they've read which we should be reading too.

Librarians

University librarians are brilliant. We have found, with the utmost consistency, that whilst they are usually not researchers in their own right, they are very good scholars who take pleasure in having a comprehensive knowledge of the literature of the area in which they specialise and helping academics to access it. Even in times of straitened resources, they will usually do their utmost to help you. They also tend to be enormously patient as they take you, again and again, through the processes by which you can do literature searches, use the Web, and access international databases of literature. Cultivate good relations with them and respect their expertise. They will rarely let you down.

Books on research techniques

There are lots of books out there on how to do research and you may want to read some of them. Some are better than others, and we have picked the ones we like in our Further Reading suggestions. Ironically, whilst one of the objects of research activity is to write and publish, academics rarely write and publish well on how to do research. Ultimately, learning how to do research is an experiential process, which requires a period of 'apprenticeship' either through doctoral studies or through active engagement in research and using such help and advice as are available. Books can help to some extent, but they provide a far from complete answer.

Ethical practice in research

We've already touched on the question of ethics in this book and now want to deal with it in more detail. We first of all want to draw a distinction between the structures for ethical approval for research which risk-averse universities and funding or research commissioning bodies establish and the notion of ethical practice as a research professional. We deal with each in turn.

Research governance is becoming a very trendy term. It basically means universities ensuring that they have in place formal procedures for 'ensuring' that 'good practice' is always followed. A major aspect of research governance arrangements is the establishment of procedures for scrutinising ethical aspects of proposed work and granting approval for it to proceed. The most common manifestations of these systems are university ethics committees and formal guidelines for the conduct of research.

We have mixed feelings about such formal systems. On the one hand, we find it hard to criticise the notion that researchers should always seek to apply the highest possible ethical standards in their research work. On the other, our experience tells us that all too often ethics committees represent the triumph of form over content. They may punctiliously insist that researchers keep to strict research protocols to avoid risk to the university regarding, for instance, the storage of data, but remain blind to issues such as the wider socio-economic consequences for marginalised groups of the release of that data. They may also insist on researchers following particular rules, regardless of their adverse impact on the research or the participants in it. Ethics committees are gatekeepers who can effectively stop your research going ahead if they are in some way prejudiced against it, as George's story shows.

George wanted to do his masters research, a substantial undertaking in Australia, on the masculinities of young men who identified as gay whilst still at school. The Ethics Committee of his prestigious university insisted that he could not interview school students without the informed consent and written permission of their parents. Obtaining this would have necessitated informing the parents that the young men identified as gay. However, the potential research respondents themselves, with few exceptions, had kept their sexuality a closely guarded secret from their parents and did not want them to know. Indeed, many of them felt that their family relationships would be seriously damaged, that they might be thrown out of their homes and even that they might suffer physical harm should their sexuality become known within their families. In the event, George changed his research proposal so that he interviewed older men about their experiences when they were at school. This resulted in a successful masters dissertation, but did not – and could not – capture the kind of fresh experience that George had hoped for.

Of course, you will have to ensure that your research projects comply with the formal requirements of your institution and/or funder. Reference to the relevant ethical guidelines of your research association may prove helpful in demonstrating to ethics committees that your proposed research is of a satisfactory ethical standard. However, far more important in our view is that you develop a good sense of what it means to be a good ethical practitioner in your research.

Key to ethical practice is that you think carefully, deeply and reflexively about the power relationships in the research process. What sorts of power relationships do we mean?

Consequences

When people agree to act as respondents in research it is important to respect them, and to understand the consequences that your intervention in their life may have. Speaking with you might bring to the surface difficult feelings, memories or emotions – only for you to leave their lives almost immediately, carrying your data (their lives) with you. We see this as tantamount to the researcher acting as vampire. Moreover, our dissemination and publication of respondents' stories may expose them individually or as a community in many undesirable ways. Anonymity for an individual may be ineffective if the published research leads to the vilification of the group of which that person is a member. We therefore have to be both respectful and caring of respondents whilst we are engaging with them, but also mindful of the consequences of our findings for them and their wider group.

In a project that Debbie was involved in on how schools deal with violence, the team was very exercised about how to maintain the confidentiality of the schools which eventually took part in the research. The researchers realised that it had taken a great deal of courage on the part of the management teams of these schools, particularly where the schools were having considerable difficulty in handling the levels of violence within them. The researchers therefore made a number of decisions early in the project. They decided on pseudonyms for the schools before gathering any data and scrupulously referred to the schools in all their notes and transcripts by these. This meant that even if some of the data accidentally got lost or left on someone's desk so that anyone who came into the room, such as a cleaner, might see, the school would not be identifiable by name. They also agreed, and wrote it into their contracts with the schools, that at no time would they do more than identify London as the city within which the schools were located and they would never mention where in London the schools were situated. This meant that they were limited in the way they wrote about the schools and their neighbourhoods and had to be very careful about their descriptions. However, they feel that the price was well worth paying in order to undertake the research.

Blast from the past

In some cases, researchers make use of historical data. The fact that the data may be about, or produced by, people who are long dead does not exempt the researchers from their ethical obligations. It can also raise some interesting ethical dilemmas. For instance, if you are doing research that involves the use of diaries or private papers, you should give serious consideration to whether the individuals who wrote them intended them for public consumption. We are not saying that you shouldn't use such material, but you should engage with the on-going debates about the ethics of such uses. Often, the descendants or other keepers of such papers may have concerns about the impact of your use of such material, as these two vignettes show.

In Australia there is an on-going debate about the use by historians of material describing Aboriginal culture written and collected by white colonialists (who subjected Aboriginal people to genocidal acts in the nineteenth and twentieth centuries). Aboriginal communities are concerned about the indiscriminate use of material produced by their oppressors that purports to describe their cultures and communities. One response to this by some state archivists has been to place access to such material under the control of the relevant indigenous groups. More broadly, a number of institutions have developed specific ethical guidelines for any research project that involves indigenous people or artefacts.

Asha's doctoral research included biographical work on some nineteenth- and twentieth-century collectors of Chinese art and artefacts. She needed access to the private papers of these individuals, some of which were in archives and some in the hands of their descendants. She found that the keepers of the papers were generally extremely generous in allowing her access and, in some cases, opening their homes to her. As she wrote about the collectors, she became concerned that some of her more negative judgements might make her gatekeepers feel betrayed. While she did not wish to compromise her academic judgement, she was, nevertheless, careful in her expression so that she felt that she would be able to send the material to their descendants with a clear conscience and without causing them undue offence or pain.

Be generous

A further area of ethical practice is in our relations and working practices with colleagues. In essence, this is about being a good colleague. Most aspects of unethical behaviour are perfectly obvious: plagiarism and other ways of not respecting the intellectual property of others such as stealing their research ideas; stymieing others' research efforts and careers in an attempt to further your own interests or out of plain jealousy; not acknowledging the contribution of other people to your research; promoting research on the basis of favouritism rather than merit; and not giving people proper credit in the authorship of publications. We believe in the old adage 'what goes round comes round': that if you are mean now it will just come back to haunt you. Be generous, and others will generally be generous with you.

The good citizen

Researchers have a responsibility to the wider communities in which they live. We have already noted that one of the marks of a 'good academic' is that they take seriously their role as public intellectuals. What does this mean in practice? It means being aware of the impact that your research may have on how people think, what they believe and how they act. It means being prepared to talk to people who are not academics about your research without talking down to them – recognising that they are a legitimate audience for what you have to say, for their own reasons. Above all, you should never regard yourself as the producer of 'objective knowledge' the use of which you can or should dissociate yourself from.

And finally ...

What we've done in this book is suggest to you ways in which you might take the first steps towards becoming a researcher. We have looked at the generation of research topics, the refining of research questions, how to write a research proposal to act as a route map through the process, some practical points about actually doing your research and, finally, some thoughts about moving on and developing as a researcher. Reading this whole book in one go may make the process of undertaking a research project appear quite intimidating. But you should bear in mind that the process we've described may take place over a prolonged period of months or even years, giving you time to reflect and learn as you go. Remember, also, that we've been trying to give you the kind of advice in one small book that we give to people we work with as and when they need it.

The reality of most researchers' lives is that this process of undertaking research projects is repeated iteratively. Everyone learns as they go along, and we haven't stopped yet.

Cumulatively, research projects should develop into research agendas, and eventually they should reflect the personal intellectual projects of individual researchers. Most people's research eventually runs in a series of parallel streams. But those streams aren't self-contained: there are points at which they meet, run together and then sometimes separate again.

As such, it's important to regard your research from the very beginning as the start of a life's work. You need to put in place all the practical things that will help you. This includes developing your skills, building your library and accumulating data, evidence and other materials that will sustain subsequent and continuing research projects.

Through all this, you need to think about achieving an identity as a researcher. The nature of academic research work is such that it isn't usually constrained by fixed working hours or a set place of work. As such it becomes an integral, rather than a discrete, part of our everyday lives.

Although these sorts of work practices can be stressful, there is a beneficial aspect. It can be nice to do the kind of work which has a lot of flexibility and which becomes an enjoyable aspect of our everyday existence.

Further Reading

Coffey, A. and Atkinson, P. (1996) *Making Sense of Qualitative Data*, Thousand Oaks CA, London and New Delhi: Sage. This book introduces new researchers to the many different ways of analysing qualitative data. It is written in accessible language and provides a practical resource for thinking about the range of analytic approaches available to the qualitative researcher. It avoids a narrow 'how to' approach and is constructed as a tool to think through and make choices about data analysis, emphasising that there is no one way to do it. The book offers practical examples of the stages of analysis of 'real' data, from coding to narrative analysis, from theorising the data to using computer software as an aid to analysis. This gives the reader a valuable understanding of the processes of data analysis while avoiding an over-practical 'guide' that distorts data analysis as a mechanical set of linear steps.

Creswell, J.W. (2003) *Research Design: Qualitative, Quantitative, and Mixed Methods Approaches*. Thousand Oaks CA, London and New Delhi: Sage. This book is aimed at research students or academics who are working on developing an academic paper. The book breaks down the processes involved in writing a research paper into a set of steps, although this may suggest to the reader that research is a neat process made up of predictable stages. The strength of the book is that it considers the use of mixed methods, as well as separate qualitative and/or quantitative methods, and examines the ethical issues that may arise from these different research approaches. The book usefully includes many exercises to help engage the reader in making connections between their own research and the discussion in the book.

Golden-Biddle, K. and Locke, K.D. (1997) *Composing Qualitative Research*, Thousand Oaks CA, London and New Delhi: Sage. This book is immensely refreshing because it adopts a vehemently anti-'writing-up' stance, choosing instead to see writing as an integral part of the qualitative research process. The book carefully takes readers through the theoretical underpinnings of this approach and then delineates the various stages in the writing process. It is richly illustrated with examples of cogent and successful academic writing and is very well written itself.

Hollway, W. and Jefferson, T. (2000) *Doing Qualitative Research Differently: Free Association, Narrative and the Interview Method*, Thousand Oaks CA, London and Delhi: Sage. This is not designed as a manual but rather as a substantive exploration of using psychoanalytic approaches in qualitative research. It uses the case of research on fear of crime to argue for such approaches when asking 'why' questions – particularly those related to identity. It is worth reading, whether or not you do this kind of research, because of the important points it makes about method and, in particular, its excellent discussion of ethical issues in research.

Marshall, C. and Rossman, G.B. (1999) *Designing Qualitative Research*, 3rd edn, Thousand Oaks CA, London and New Delhi: Sage. This is a valuable book for those writing a research proposal for the first time. Marshall and Rossman identify two main aspects of the research proposal: the conceptual framework and the design soundness. The chapters then provide detailed and in-depth accounts of the ways to write a proposal that meets the challenges of these two aspects. The book engages the reader in thinking through the connections between the 'what' of the research, or the conceptual framework, and the 'do-ability' of the research, linking the methods with theoretical, epistemological and methodological underpinnings. The vignettes that are used to illustrate the process of constructing an argument in a proposal, giving examples of how others have approached the research proposal and have been able to convince the reviewer(s) that the researcher is worthwhile, 'do-able' and methodologically sound. The variety of vignettes offered helps the reader to think through his or her own research approaches.

May, T. (ed.) (2002) *Qualitative Research in Action*, London, Thousand Oaks CA and New Delhi: Sage. This collection considers the theoretical, methodological and epistemological complexities of contemporary qualitative research practices. It focuses on the connections between research theory and practice. The book is divided up into thematic sections, with the aim of providing coherence as well as highlighting links between research process and product. The central theme running through the book is 'issues in practice' and this is approached in a critical way to interrogate current social research practices through the examination of specific examples. Although it is suggested that the book may be used for advanced undergraduate levels, some chapters may be inaccessible to those unfamiliar with contemporary debates within qualitative methodology. There are some highly accessible chapters, though, for those new to qualitative research, and the whole book is very useful to those who want to deepen their understanding of and engage with contemporary debates in the field of qualitative research.

Potter, S. (ed.) (2002) *Doing Postgraduate Research*, London, Thousand Oaks CA and New Delhi: Sage. This book is of particular interest to postgraduate students and new researchers. It is clearly laid out, readable and easy to use. It starts by explaining that research is not experienced as a smooth, linear process as many guidebooks would suggest. Drawing on accounts of a PhD student, the editor points out that research is not straightforward, and that coping with change and problems is part of the research process. The structure of the book reflects this insight and the reader is able to dip in and out as needed. Each chapter begins with a clear set of aims and has a series of activities designed to get the reader to engage with the issues raised by research, and to get her or him to start writing.

Punch, K.F. (2000) *Developing Effective Research Proposals*, London, Thousand Oaks CA and New Delhi: Sage. Aimed at postgraduate students preparing a research proposal in the social sciences, this book covers issues including the function and purpose of research proposals, the processes of developing and writing research proposals, issues in identifying approaches and frameworks, research design and ideas for getting started. The book includes some examples of successful research proposals, as well as a summary checklist of guiding questions to help develop and write a proposal. The chapters are concise and the book could be dipped into according to need.

Rudestam, K.E. and Newton, R.R. (2001) *Surviving your Dissertation*, London, Thousand Oaks CA and New Delhi: Sage. This book is aimed at doctoral students in the social sciences. The authors explain that the research phases can be thought of as 'a research wheel ... a recursive cycle of steps that are repeated over time'. Part I concentrates on getting started, including issues involved in finding a research focus, generating research questions and getting to grips with the different methods of inquiry available. Part II moves to a focus on the dissertation chapters, including literature review, method and different ways of presenting the analysis of the data in writing. Part III shifts from product to issues of process including overcoming barriers, writing processes, using the computer effectively and ethical issues.

Walliman, N. (2001) *Your Research Project: a Step-by-step Guide for the First-time Researcher*, London, Thousand Oaks CA and New Delhi: Sage. This book is aimed at novice researchers and focuses on the writing of a strong research proposal. It addresses both practical and theoretical issues involved in research. It is clearly laid out and relatively easy to use. Each chapter begins by setting out its aims. The book is interactive, with cartoons to make it visual and lively, key terms clearly defined and various exercises aimed at engaging the reader in an active learning process. The eight chapters include: research and the research problem, information and how to deal with it, types of research, the nature and use of argument, more about the nature of research, research quality and planning, research methods, preparing the research, proposal and starting to write. This provides an overview of some of the theoretical perspectives in research and a guide to the stages involved in the research process, but is of particular value at the beginning of a research project when developing a proposal.

Index

Lightning Source UK Ltd.
Milton Keynes UK
UKOW01f1427180917
309410UK00001B/32/P

Jörg Schildknecht · Rebecca Dickey ·
Martin Fink · Lisa Ferris
Editors

Operational Law in International Straits and Current Maritime Security Challenges

Springer

Editors
Jörg Schildknecht
NATO Centre of Excellence for
Operations in Confined and Shallow
Waters
Kiel, Germany

Rebecca Dickey
United States Navy
Jacksonville, FL, USA

Martin Fink
CDC/DOPD/JDV
Netherlands Ministry of Defence
Utrecht, The Netherlands

Lisa Ferris
Defence Legal Services
New Zealand Defence Force
Wellington, New Zealand

ISSN 2523-806X   ISSN 2523-8078   (electronic)
Operational Maritime Law
ISBN 978-3-319-72717-2   ISBN 978-3-319-72718-9   (eBook)
https://doi.org/10.1007/978-3-319-72718-9

Library of Congress Control Number: 2018935285

Printed on acid-free paper

This Springer imprint is published by the registered company Springer International Publishing AG part of Springer Nature.
The registered company address is: Gewerbestrasse 11, 6330 Cham, Switzerland

Contents

Introduction: Challenges in Operational Maritime Law

Martin Fink, Rebecca Dickey, Jörg Schildknecht, and Lisa Ferris

Abstract
This book is the first volume of the Operational Maritime Law series. The series provides a platform for practitioners and scholars with specific interest in current operational maritime law issues, to publish research advancing legal discourse, as well as analysing current issues. The theme of the first volume is *Operational Law in International Straits and Current Maritime Security Challenges*. This volume is broken down into three parts. Part I explores international straits in an operational law context, Part II discusses current subjects on maritime security and maritime safety and Part III offers some thoughts on the law of armed conflict at sea. This introduction highlights today's maritime challenges in naval operations and provides an explanation of the relevance of each section of the publication. In regard to operational maritime law, three strands, in particular, stand out: maritime security, focus on persons and non-international armed conflict. Furthermore, in terms of positioning the law applicable for naval operations within the context of international law, it is argued that this area may be seen as a sub-regime of the international law of military operations.

M. Fink (✉)
Royal Netherlands Navy, University of Amsterdam, Amsterdam, Netherlands
e-mail: finkmd@hotmail.com

R. Dickey
United States Navy, Jacksonville, FL, USA

J. Schildknecht
Centre of Excellence for Operations in Confined and Shallow Waters, Kiel, Germany

L. Ferris
New Zealand Defence Force, Wellington, New Zealand

J. Schildknecht et al. (eds.), *Operational Law in International Straits and Current Maritime Security Challenges*, Operational Maritime Law 1, https://doi.org/10.1007/978-3-319-72718-9_1

1

1   Introduction

What are today's legal challenges for States and their defence forces in the maritime domain? How do naval operations adapt to modern conflict to confront the changing nature of legal challenges while operating at sea? These questions are central to this, first-in-a-series, publication on operational maritime law. It provides a platform for practitioners and scholars with specific expertise in current operational maritime law to publish research advancing legal discourse, as well as analysing current issues on these matters. The initiative of this series is driven by the Centre of Excellence for Operations in Confined and Shallow Waters (COE CSW) in Kiel, Germany.[1] It is born out of an understanding that the combination of broad tasking and an array of growing mission sets for naval assets today and the increasing complexity of international law at sea create a necessity to further study current international law applicable to the maritime domain. The first volume's theme is *Operational Law in International Straits and Current Maritime Security Challenges.* To present this first volume, some introductory remarks are made here with regard to today's legal challenges in the maritime dimension.

2   Today's Maritime Challenges

There is little debate over the existence and relevance of the maritime domain in modern conflict. But what does 'modern conflict' actually mean in a maritime context? Perhaps one important overarching evolution in conflict from the last two decades has been the gradual decline of the 'statist approach'. The rise of non-State actors and non-international armed conflict developed as one of the main challenges inherent to today's conflict. An abundance of legal questions also emerged from this evolution. These questions spring from issues that originate from trying to fit or adapt the *ius ad bellum* and *ius in bello* to this changing situation and have also included debates from other sources of international law, such as human rights law. The maritime domain did not lag in this evolution of the decline of the statist approach. Although the legal debates, arguably, have not been as vigorous as in the land dimension, it has not felt the changing face of conflict any less. The recent focus within the maritime dimension may, arguably, be captured in three distinct themes: the rise of the importance of the concept of maritime security, the focus on persons during naval operations and the participation of naval forces in non-international armed conflict (NIAC). These three themes can be discussed as separate issues but are clearly related to each other.

---

[1]See the website of the CEO CSW at: http://www.coecsw.org/.

2.1   Maritime Security

States analyse the maritime dimension in terms of possible threats that may come from or arise from the sea and aim to enhance security against those threats. Maritime security is the enhancement of a State's security interests in the maritime dimension. Interestingly, the concept of maritime security takes on a broad under-standing, and it can be perceived that the sharp classic divide between war and peace has completely melted away. Threats to a State in the maritime dimension can exist at all levels and types of conflict. The scope of the threat is broad and is difficult to concretely define. More often maritime security is defined as a set of pressing security issues, which may include topics such as illegal fisheries, security and safety in ports and on board vessels, piracy, boat refugees, terrorism at sea and weapons of mass destruction at sea.

Today, States generally accept that naval forces play a role in enhancing maritime security. The military and the more traditional military security issues are, however, not central to maritime security. The military is one of the many different instruments to help enhance maritime security. Still, what is interesting to note is that organisations such as NATO and the EU have through their recent maritime strategies bound themselves to this idea of a role for naval forces in maritime security.[2] NATO, as a classic collective defence organisation, assumed a role in counter-piracy operations, became active in the Aegean Sea in relation to refugees, and recently changed its Article-V Operation *Active Endeavour* into Operation *Sea Guardian,* which aims to build on maritime situational awareness, counter-terrorism and support to capacity building.[3] Oliver Clark, in his chapter on piracy, is exposing some legal challenges that arise from the involvement of traditional naval forces in maritime security operations in the context of piracy. Jouko Lehti's contribution explains the EU's legal ventures into helping boat refugees and battling refugee smuggling and trafficking operations.

What also emerged in this context is the issue of private military companies (PMCs) at sea to protect merchant vessels and maritime trade. After we have seen much (legal) discussion in the land dimension with regard to PMCs in Iraq and Afghanistan, the piracy threat that emerged in the last 10 years in and around the Indian Ocean has fired this practice also in the maritime dimension, with accompanying legal debates. Are they a welcome alternative for sea-trade protection by naval forces? Should they exist next to, or instead of the military? And how will they meet the legal thresholds for using force? In this volume, Ian Ralby discusses some of these challenges of regulating the use of PMCs.

Apart from operational level consequences and legal challenges that focus on the importance of enhancing maritime security, on a strategic-political level maritime security arguably advances a different point of departure than the classic 'Grotian'

---

[2]NATO has adopted its Alliance Maritime Strategy (AMS) in 2011. The EU adopted its EU-Maritime Security Strategy (EUMSS) in 2015.
[3]NATO (2016).

view of the freedom of the seas. In order to enhance security at sea and act in a timely manner against threats, one must understand the maritime environment, gain a sufficient level of awareness of the operating environment and reach a certain level of control. Often used terms like 'policing the seas' and the general acceptance of so-called 'maritime security operations' may have, arguably, caused a silent evolution in which the strategic-political thinking has changed from freedom of the seas to controlling the seas. The question is whether this way of thinking is also trickling through legal concepts and thinking or whether the legal fundamental point of departure of the freedom of the seas still stands.

2.2   Persons

The importance of enhancing maritime security has also brought about a focus on persons. Traditional naval warfare and naval operations conducted within the UN collective security system, such as maritime embargo operations, always had a primary focus on goods and vessels. Today's challenge for naval forces in the maritime dimension is mainly focused on human beings. Warships are tasked to confront pirates, boat refugees, slave and drug traffickers, mercenaries and terrorists. Naval operations moved from its traditional goods/vessel focus to person-focused operations.

This focus also provides a new dimension to legal challenges at sea. To name two of these challenges in particular, firstly, in the past decade, the application of human rights law in the maritime environment has emerged as an important and well-discussed legal issue.[4] It ranges from issues with regard to fundamental human rights in relation to piracy and arresting persons for drug trafficking, such as fair trial and detention rights, to *non-refoulement* in the context of boat refugees. Some of these legal challenges that apply human rights law in the maritime dimension have reached the European Court of Human Rights (ECtHR). In this context of applying human rights law at sea, the challenges between the interrelationship of human rights law and the international law of the sea are on different subjects not yet crystallised. Rick Button, for instance, highlights the challenges of the difference between search and rescue (SAR) and law enforcement operations. The same question examining the interrelationship that exists may be present between the provisions on the rescue of persons in the law of naval warfare, the law of the sea and human rights law.

The second example of a legal challenge that can be mentioned here is the so-called 'legal finish' during naval operations. Interestingly, this issue of the legal finish appeals back to the way traditional, but unused, prize law is organised, namely in a 'wet' dimension and a 'dry' dimension. The wet dimension is the actual action and legal issues at sea in which a good, a vessel or—today—a person is captured. The dry dimension is the subsequent actions that need to be considered in the aftermath of the action. The smooth connection between both dimensions is challenging in itself. Transferring the person to a State or to another State that is willing

---

[4]See e.g. Treves (2010), Guilfoyle (2010) and Papastavridis (2013).

to start legal procedures and ensuring that sufficient evidence is produced that holds in a court of law are examples of this. Apart from the non-use of prize law, during the '1990s of the former century, maritime embargo operations that had been the primary focus in naval operations arguably pushed the notion of a dry dimension in naval operations further to the background. Today, however, law enforcement types of operations that naval forces are confronted with have renewed the understanding that efforts must be put also into the dry dimension and that a successful 'legal finish' to what happens at sea urges for a whole government approach.

2.3 Non-international Armed Conflict

If conflict rises to the level of an armed conflict, then current conflicts can often be characterised as non-international. Fighting against non-State actors has given States a plethora of legal issues to debate, ranging from detention issues to an expanding set of conflict types beyond international and non-international, to complex issues on the legal boundaries of the battlefield. Obviously, these debates also have an impact in the maritime dimension. At the same time, recent years have seen armed conflicts erupt in coastal States in which naval forces were part of the military campaign. Examples are Libya, Yemen, Iraq Gaza and Lebanon. These conflicts confronted maritime lawyers with interesting legal questions, such as whether the law of naval warfare, and the law of blockade in particular, actually applies to conflicts in the Gaza or off the coast of Yemen. How must the right of belligerent visit and search be understood in the fight against non-State actors? What are the legal possibilities to detain persons on a foreign-flagged vessel from a State that has nothing to do with the underlying conflict? These are all questions that surface when having to deal with non-State actors during a non-international armed conflict at sea.

3 Traditional Conflict Is Not a Thing of the Past

Having noted above the focus in the maritime dimension during the last 15 years through three strands that have emerged as a consequence of the decline of the statist approach, it is something completely different to state that traditional international armed conflict is a thing of the past. The current situation is, in fact, quite the contrary. Much on the foreground, for instance, is the tension between States in the South China Sea, which is an issue that cannot be forgotten in this context. David Letts, in his chapter, searches for options on how to scale down tensions between States. Re-emerging tensions between Russia and other States may also develop beyond the cyber-dimension or a situation where Russia's military involvement is kept in the grey zone of conflict. What must, therefore, be underlined is that the above-mentioned strands have resulted in a certain focus, rather than concluding that other types of warfare belong to history. The challenge for naval operators (and the military as a whole) is that they have to deal with the complete spectrum of conflict and crises from peacetime crises to 'grey-on-grey' war fighting and from law enforcement operations to restoring international peace. It merits, therefore, also to keep in mind that certain aspects of international law may have been snowed under but still exist, like the forgotten basics of prize law, to which Marcel Schulz devotes a chapter. This volume also includes multiple authors' analyses on the use of international straits and maritime areas. Another forward-leaning analysis in this context is Tassilo Singer's chapter on the legal possibilities of occupational law applied at sea.

4 Operational Maritime Law

One can take different approaches to study the relationship between international law and the maritime dimension. Broadly seen, there are two approaches that have emerged. The first is the increasingly generally accepted approach to centralise military operations and consider what aspects of international law apply and how they interrelate to each other during military operations. This approach, usually termed the *International Law of Military Operations*, has become a well-accepted approach and term. The term underlines the influence of and the interrelationship between various branches of international law that regulate military operations.[5] The maritime dimension is an essential aspect of military operations with particular legal challenges of its own. Similar to international law of military operations, the law that applies to maritime operations consists of various branches of international law. Arguably, the particularities and challenges of the maritime dimension and applicable laws make *Operational Maritime Law* a specific sub-discipline of its own within the general international law of military operations.[6]

The second is the approach that centralises around the term of maritime security, which logically flows from the focus on the strands mentioned above and is reflected in a legal sub-discipline that is termed *Maritime Security Law*. Although these terms may overlap in terms of content, the difference between operational maritime law and maritime security law lies with the view that the first focuses on security and military operations, and the second contains a broader scope of issues in which the military may play a role within security and safety challenges in the maritime dimension. In the latter, for instance, port security measures, merchant vessel safety measures and maritime environmental issues belong to this broader legal discipline. *Maritime Security Law*, therefore, includes both security and safety issues that emerge out of the maritime community as a whole. There is merit in combining security and safety, as Kraska and Pedrozo mention, 'In many respects the fusion of

---

[5] Gill and Fleck (2015), p. 5.

[6] Arguably the term operational maritime law encompasses a broader term than the law of naval operations, because the 'naval' emphases the military, where maritime includes all maritime activities of a State.

maritime security and maritime safety is unavoidable. The legal regimes that regulate each activity are less distinct today than in the past and now share common and mutually reinforcing objectives.'[7] However, as this series is primarily aiming to unlock the current legal challenges that are connected to the use of naval assets, the term *Operational Maritime Law* will be used as the more on point approach and term for this particular purpose.

This introduction has touched upon only a few challenges that are emerging in the maritime dimension and has not even scratched the surface of the legal issues that come with these challenges. For sure, scholars and practitioners will have many more analyses, findings and debates on their minds that need sharing and a platform in order to enhance our understanding of international law in the maritime dimension. Let this be your invitation.

References

Centre of Excellence Confined and Shallow Waters CEO CSW at: http://www.coecsw.org/. Accessed 7 July 2017

Gill TD, Fleck D (2015) Concept and sources of the international law of military operations. In: Gill TD, Fleck D (eds) The handbook of the international law of military operations, 2nd edn. Oxford University Press, Oxford, pp 3–13

Guilfoyle D (2010) Counter piracy law enforcement and human rights. Int Comp Law Q 59:141–169

Kraska J, Pedrozo R (2013) International maritime security law. Nijhoff publishers, Martinus

NATO (2016) Operation active endeavour. http://www.nato.int/cps/en/natohq/topics_7932.htm. Accessed 5 July 2017

Papastavridis E (2013) European convention on human rights and the law of the Sea: the Strasbourg court in unchartered waters. In: Fitzmaurice M, Merkouris P (eds) The interpretation and application of the European -convention of human rights: legal and practical implications. Martinus Nijhoff, Leiden, pp 117–146

Treves T (2010) Human rights and the law of the sea. Berkely J Int Law 28(1):1–13

Martin Fink is a Commander in the Royal Netherlands Navy. He has served in several national and international legal postings as a military legal advisor, among which were the Netherlands Maritime Force (NLMARFOR) and the NATO Joint Force Command Naples, and a brief spell at the Netherlands Ministry of Defence. He has been on several operational tours as a legal advisor, among which were Iraq, Afghanistan and South Sudan. He has been a lecturer of international law at the Netherlands Defence Academy and is a researcher at the University of Amsterdam, at the Amsterdam Centre of International Law (ACIL), and holds a doctor iuris at the same university.

Rebecca Dickey is a Lieutenant in the United States Navy. She has served in operational positions on board multiple naval vessels and has served internationally as a Legal Advisor at the NATO Centre of Excellence for Operations in Confined and Shallow Waters (COE CSW). Her operational tours include Humanitarian Aid missions to Central and South America, as well as deployments to the South China Sea, East China Sea and Yellow Sea.

---

[7]Kraska and Pedrozo (2013), p. 5.

Jörg Schildknecht is a Commander (res.) of the German Navy. He is currently stationed as the Legal Advisor of the NATO Centre of Excellence for Operations in Confined and Shallow Waters (COE CSW) in Kiel, Germany. He is a civil servant of the German Navy and has been deployed in several military missions in his military reserve rank. He has worked for, inter alia, EU NAVFOR Northwood and Rome, the Mürwik Naval Academy, German Fleet Command Flensburg and the International Law Department of the German Ministry of Defense in Berlin. He is a specialist in international law and holds a doctor iuris at the University of Hamburg.

Lisa Ferris is the Director of New Zealand Defence Legal Services. In 2008, she was deployed to the Arabian Gulf as the Legal Officer aboard the frigate HMNZS TE MANA where she provided legal advice to the Commanding Officer. In late 2009, Lisa Ferris was deployed to Afghanistan as the legal officer advising the New Zealand senior national officer on rules of engagement, law of armed conflict, and general military law issues. Lisa Ferris was deployed to Afghanistan again in 2012 as counsel assisting a Court of Inquiry, and to Iraq in 2015 to support the planning for the deployment of NZ force elements. In 2013, she was appointed as the Deputy Director Operations Law and the Chief of Staff for Defence Legal Services. In 2017, Lisa Ferris was promoted to Colonel and appointed as the Director of Defence Legal Services. On 23 January 2018, Lisa Ferris was appointed to her present rank. Lisa Ferris holds a Master of Laws with Honours and a Bachelor of Commerce and Administration from Victoria University and completed United States Marine Corps Staff College (Extramural) in 2014.

Part I

International Straits

Minelaying and the Impediment of Passage Rights

Wolff Heintschel von Heinegg

Abstract

Naval mines are considered to pose a serious threat to international shipping. This certainly holds true for free-floating submarine contact mines but not necessarily for modern naval mines that are highly discriminating weapons. Be that as it may, the mere fact that naval mines have been laid in a given sea area will impede upon freedom of navigation. The only international treaty dealing with naval mines is the 1907 Hague Convention VIII, whose scope is limited to automatic submarine contact mines and which was concluded at a time when the breadth of the territorial sea did not exceed 3 nautical miles and other concepts, such as the EEZ, were unknown. The first part of the present chapter deals with the question whether and to what extent belligerents are entitled to lay mines in international straits overlapped by their territorial sea, their archipelagic waters, or in the high seas. The second part deals with the legality of naval minelaying in times of peace, which is to be determined in the light of the Corfu Channel judgment, the international law of the sea, and the positions taken by States in military manuals.

1   Introduction

Naval mines are an extreme threat to innocent shipping. Indeed, not just during armed conflicts but also in times of peace (e.g., in the Red Sea in 1984) that international shipping has suffered considerable losses by hitting naval mines, whose presence had

This article was originally published in International Law Studies, 90 Int'L. Stud 544 (2014).

W. Heintschel von Heinegg (✉)
Europa-Universität Viadrina, Frankfurt (Oder), Germany
e-mail: heintschelvonheinegg@europa-uni.de

not been notified or which were "free-floating" mines. In view of the importance of the freedom of navigation to the world economy and international security, the naval mine threat the "hidden menace"[1] seems to be intolerable. Therefore, the question arises whether international law principles and rules provide effective protection of international shipping by prohibiting or restricting the use of these means of warfare.

It must not be forgotten, however, that today's naval mines, which can be programmed to hit only certain categories of ships or, if sufficient data are available, even an individual ship, are highly discriminating weapons.[2] The use of unanchored automatic submarine contact mines that do not become harmless within 1 h after they have been laid, and anchored contact mines that do not become harmless as soon as they have broken loose, is prohibited. However, even then, such mines do not necessarily pose an indiscriminate danger to innocent shipping because the "bow wave brushes the mine clear of the ship."[3] Still, the fact that naval mines have been laid in a given sea area or even reasonable grounds for suspicion that they may be present will always have an impact on innocent shipping. Such shipping will either refrain from using the area or proceed with utmost caution, thus extending the duration of the voyage. Because minesweeping and countermine operations are a very challenging, costly, and time-consuming task, even the availability of the necessary assets to undertake those operations does not mean that the mine threat can be quickly and effectively eliminated.

This article focuses on two questions. The first concerns the exercise of the belligerent right of minelaying and its impact on the freedom of navigation enjoyed by innocent, in particular neutral, shipping. In this context, a brief discussion of the term "passage rights" is necessary. In the contemporary international law of the sea, the term is usually used for the rights of innocent passage, transit passage, and archipelagic sea-lane passage. During international armed conflicts, the belligerents will often not limit their operations to their national waters but employ methods and means of naval warfare, including naval mines, in high seas areas. Therefore, the term "passage rights" is understood here in a broad sense, not including just those rights but also including the freedom of navigation in sea areas beyond the outer limits of the territorial sea. The starting point will be 1907 Hague Convention VIII.[4] In a second step, the subsequent practice of States will be analyzed with a view to establishing the contemporary law on belligerent minelaying in the light of passage rights/freedom of navigation. The law of neutrality, in particular the right of neutral States to lay mines in their national waters, will be dealt with only marginally.

The second question concerns the laying of naval mines in times of peace. Operations to lay mines are not easy but rather are a time-consuming task unless

---

[1]This quote is borrowed from Griffith (1981).

[2]For a short overview of the technology currently in use, *see* Levie (1992), pp. 97–115. For further details, *see* Fuller and Ewing (2013), p. 115. *See also* Rios (2005), pp. 11–15.

[3]Levie (1992), p. 141, quoting a Report of Experts submitted to the International Court of Justice (ICJ) in the *Corfu Channel* case. *See also* Cowie (1949), pp. 188–189.

[4]1907 Hague Convention VIII, 36 Stat. 2332, T.S. No. 541. Although the Convention is limited to automatic contact mines, there is wide agreement that it is applicable to modern naval mines that are based on a different technology. *See* Heintschel von Heinegg (1994).

they are intended to hit vessels indiscriminately. A State may therefore plan to lay mines well before the outbreak of an international armed conflict in order to be prepared to counter a threat. Moreover, it may wish to pursue its national security goals by denying others the use of its territorial sea, including that overlapped by international straits, and its archipelagic waters, including those within archipelagic sea lanes. Seemingly, such minelaying might be considered as clearly illegal because of the international law of the sea, which, certainly during times of peace, guarantees freedom of navigation not only in high seas areas but also in the territorial sea, international straits, and archipelagic waters while recognizing that these sea areas are subject to the territorial sovereignty of the coastal or archipelagic State. A closer examination shows that international law provides no absolute prohibition on minelaying during peacetime.

2 The Law of International Armed Conflict on Naval Mines and Passage Rights

2.1 The 1907 Hague Convention VIII and the Freedom of Navigation

One of the most difficult and contentious issues faced by the 1907 Hague Peace Conference was the regulation of mine warfare at sea. In view of the experience of the Russo–Japanese War (1904–1905),[5] the delegates were prepared to assure "to pacific commerce an effectual protection"[6] against the effects of naval mines both during and in the aftermath of an international armed conflict.[7] There was, however, no agreement as to how such protection should be accomplished.

Some delegations proposed far-reaching restrictions that would have resulted in an almost absolute prohibition on minelaying in high seas areas to safeguard the freedom of navigation of innocent, in particular neutral, shipping.[8] While some of those proposals were too ambitious to have a realistic chance of being accepted by a

---

[5] The Russo-Japanese War was the first international armed conflict during which naval mines were used extensively and which had long-lasting detrimental effects on shipping after the end of hostilities. *See* Lauterpacht H (ed) Oppenheim L (1952), p. 471; Hoffmann (1977), p. 145; Colombos (1968), p. 531 and Castrén (1954), p. 275.

[6] 1907 Hague Proceedings Vol. III, p. 3:399.

[7] For the various proposals, see id., Annexes 9–37, at 662–682. Worth mentioning is the British proposal (Annex 9) according to which the use of automatic contact mines would have been limited to the territorial seas of the belligerents. Only when laid off military ports could the distance be extended to 10 nautical miles.

[8] *Id.* It may be added that some of those proposals were far from altruistic or motivated by the wish to protect innocent shipping. In particular, States with large navies were afraid that the use of naval mines could jeopardize their naval supremacy. "Behind the proposals of the Conference stood the politics of force." Reed (1984), p. 294.

sufficient number of delegations,[9] there was a short period during which it seemed possible to arrive at a compromise between those who were in favor of limiting the use of naval mines to certain sea areas and those who wished to prevent such geographical limitations. The Committee of Examination, in its report to the Third Commission, proposed four draft articles defining the sea areas in which naval mines could be laid.[10] The committee was guided by the wish to protect as far as possible innocent shipping without unduly depriving belligerents of the use of an effective, inexpensive means of naval warfare.[11]

Eventually, the draft articles that dealt with the sea areas in which minelaying was to be limited did not obtain the necessary majority. The Third Commission in its Report to the Conference emphasized:

> By thus overturning, through the suppression of Articles 2 to 5, the decision which had seemed to obtain unanimous support in the committee and according to which a restriction as to area in the use of anchored mines ought to be expressly set forth in the regulations, there has been no intention to swerve from the conviction that a restriction as to area also is imposed upon the employment of such mines. The very weighty responsibility towards peaceful shipping assumed by the belligerent that lays mines beyond his coastal waters has been several times placed in evidence, and it has been unanimously recognized that only "absolute urgent military reasons" can justify such a usage with respect to anchored mines. "Conscience, good sense, and the sentiment of duty imposed by the principle of humanity" will be the surest guide for the conduct of mariners of all civilized nations; even without any written stipulation, there will surely not be lacking in the minds of all the knowledge that the

---

[9]For instance, the Colombian delegation proposed the following:

> The employment of anchored automatic mines is absolutely forbidden except as a means of defense. Belligerents may not employ such mines except for the protection of their own coasts and only within a distance of the greatest range of a cannon. In the case of arms of the sea or navigable channels leading exclusively to the shores of a single Power, that Power may bar the entrance for its own protection by laying automatic contact mines. Belligerents are absolutely forbidden to lay anchored automatic contact mines in the open sea or in the waters of the enemy.

1907 Hague Proceedings Vol. III, Annex 36, at 682.

[10]*Id.*, Annex 31, at 677. Articles 2 to 5 would have limited the right to lay mines to the three-nautical mile territorial seas of the belligerents unless laid off military ports. In the latter case the distance would extend up to 10 nautical miles. There was, however, no absolute prohibition of employing naval mines in high seas areas. According to Article 5, the belligerents would have been entitled to lay automatic contact mines "within the sphere of their immediate activity," provided they became harmless "within 2 h at most after the person using them has abandoned them."

[11]On the other hand, we must take into account the incontestable fact that submarine mines are a means of warfare the absolute prohibition of which can neither be hoped for nor perhaps desired even in the interest of peace: they are, above all, a means of defense, not costly but very effective, extremely useful to protect extended coasts, and adapted to saving the considerable expense that the maintenance of great navies requires. ... This means that automatic contact mines are an indispensable weapon. Now to ask an absolute prohibition of this weapon would consequently be demanding the impossible; it is necessary confine ourselves with regulating its use. 1907 Hague Proceedings Vol. III, p. 399.

principle of the liberty of the seas, with the obligations that it carries for those who make use of this means of communication open to all peoples, is definitively dedicated to humanity.[12]

This statement probably correctly reflected the general attitude of the delegations present in The Hague. However, the 1907 Hague Convention VIII contains no specific provision that prohibits or considerably restricts the laying of mines in certain sea areas.[13] Therefore, the general view is that "Article 3 ... allows the implication that, within the terms of the Convention, belligerents may sew [sic] anchored automatic contact mines anywhere upon the high seas."[14] However, the preamble should be considered in a systematic interpretation of the operative provisions. The preamble indicates that the parties were "inspired by the principle of the freedom of sea routes, the common highway of all nations" and wished "to restrict and regulate [the] employment [of automatic submarine contact mines] in order to mitigate the severity of war and to ensure, as far as possible, to peaceful navigation the security to which it is entitled, despite the existence of war." In view of this stated purpose, Article 3(1) can be interpreted as prohibiting vast minefields in high seas areas if they disproportionally interfere with freedom of navigation.[15] The preamble is, however, subsidiary to the operative provisions, in particular Articles 1 and 3(2). In those, peaceful shipping is protected only against anchored and unanchored mines that do not become harmless in accordance with Article 1 (1) and (2). And the State's obligation to render anchored mines harmless "should they cease to be under surveillance" is far from absolute in character; Article 3 qualifies the obligation by requiring only that they "undertake to do their utmost." The same holds true for the obligation to notify shipowners of danger zones, the requirement being subject to "military exigencies." Moreover, the preamble itself reveals that Hague Convention VIII does not provide "all the guarantees desirable." Therefore, and in view of the drafting history, the provisions of the Convention cannot be interpreted as limiting the right of belligerents to use naval mines to certain sea areas or as prohibiting their use if they unduly interfere with the freedom of navigation, in particular with certain passage rights.

During the 1907 deliberations, the Netherlands delegation exerted considerable effort to obtain agreement to a prohibition on the laying of mines in international straits. Originally, the Dutch delegation had proposed the following provision: "In all cases straits uniting two open seas cannot be barred."[16] Later, the Dutch delegation modified its proposal: "In any case, the communication between two open seas

---

[12] 1907 Hague Proceedings Vol. I, p. 282.

[13] Article 2 prohibits the laying of mines off the enemy's coats and ports only if it serves the "sole object of intercepting commercial shipping."

[14] Tucker (1955), p. 303.

[15] *See, e.g.*, Reed who maintains that 1907 Hague Convention VIII created a standard for the protection of neutral shipping that "should be interpreted from the viewpoint of a neutral shipper." Reed (1984), p. 301. However, he ignores the fact that the obligations of belligerents under Article 3 (2) of the Convention are subject to feasibility and military exigencies.

[16] 1907 Hague Proceedings Vol. III, Annex 12, p. 663.

cannot be barred entirely, and passage will be permitted only on conditions which are indicated by the competent authorities."[17] Those proposals were rejected because "the proposal of the Netherlands met objections drawn from rights of territorial sovereignty as well as from conventional stipulations existing on the subject of certain straits."[18]

It follows from the text and drafting history that those delegates who were opposed to an establishment of fixed limits within which mines could be employed and who advocated the right of belligerents to make use of anchored mines without restrictions as to place, even on the high seas, eventually prevailed. Accordingly, under the 1907 Convention, minelaying could impede the customary right of innocent passage, even if exercised in an international strait and on the freedom of navigation in high seas areas.[19]

Interestingly, the British delegate emphasized that "the right of the neutral to security of navigation on the high seas ought to come before the transitory right of the belligerent to employ these seas as a scene of operations of war," and he considered the Convention as constituting "only a partial and inadequate solution of the problem."[20] Since the Convention could not "be regarded as a complete exposition of the international law on this subject," it would "not be permissible to presume the legitimacy of an action for the mere reason that this Convention has not prohibited it."[21]

The German delegate responded by emphasizing that "a belligerent who lays mines assumes a heavy responsibility towards neutrals and to-wards peaceful shipping" and that "no one will resort to this instrument of warfare unless for military reasons of an absolutely urgent character," but it would be a great mistake to issue rules the strict observance of which might be rendered impossible by the law of facts. It is of the first importance that the international maritime law "... contain only clauses the execution of which is possible from a military point of view and is possible even in exceptional circumstances. Otherwise, the respect for law would be lessened and its authority undermined."[22]

Despite the obvious disagreement regarding the right to use naval mines in high seas areas, seemingly both delegates agreed that the laying of mines that interfered with innocent, in particular neutral, shipping is subject to considerations of military necessity "of an absolutely urgent character." In other words, minelaying in high seas areas would, according to both delegates, clearly be unlawful if not justified by a

---

[17]*Id.*, Annex 22, p. 671.

[18]*Id.*, p. 408.

[19]For further discussion of the Convention, see Haines (2014).

[20]Statement by Sir Ernest Satow, Delegate of Great Britain, at the Eighth Plenary Meeting (Oct. 9, 1907). 1907 Hague Proceedings Vol. I, p. 275.

[21]*Id.*

[22]Statement by Baron Marschall von Bieberstein, Delegate of Germany. *Id.* p. 275, 76. He added that "military acts are not solely governed by stipulations of international law. There are other factors: Conscience, good sense, and the sentiment of duty imposed by principles of humanity will be the surest guides for the conduct of sailors and will constitute the most effective guaranty against abuses."

significant military advantage.[23] Unfortunately, the words of the German delegate were vitiated by the German practice of the First and Second World Wars.

2.2   Subsequent Practice and Developments

2.2.1   The Two World Wars

The belligerents of the two world wars resorted to a practice of almost unrestricted mine warfare at sea.[24] The disregard of the 1907 Hague Convention VIII and the legitimate interests of neutral shipping was partially justified as a reprisal to allegedly prior unlawful conduct by the enemy.[25] Therefore, the practice does not establish that the Convention had fallen into desuetude.[26] Rather, it proves that the belligerents accepted the obligation to issue appropriate warnings and to provide notifications of danger areas.[27] Moreover, the practice of the Second World War, at least in its beginning, seems to support the view that, despite the lack of geographical limitations on the use of naval mines in the Convention, belligerents were prepared to either refrain from mining international straits or, if they had mined such straits, provide for piloting services in order to ensure a safe passage.[28] That practice conformed to the second Dutch proposal at the 1907 Hague Conference under which international straits could be mined if provision is made for safe passage.[29]

2.2.2   Post-1945 Mining During International Armed Conflicts

In the post-Second World War era, naval mines have been employed in several instances. The first was the mining of the Corfu Channel in 1946. Because Great Britain and Albania were not parties to an international armed conflict, we will return to it, and the International Court of Justice judgment that addressed it, later.[30]

---

[23]*But see* Tucker (1955), p. 303, who states that "it is only mine laying of an openly indiscriminate character that is prohibited i.e., mines sewn [sic] without regard to any definite military operation save that of endangering all peaceful shipping, and without any reasonable assurance of control or surveillance."

[24]*See* Lauterpacht H (ed) Oppenheim L (1952), p. 473; Colombos (1968), pp. 533–534; Castrén (1954), p. 277; Tucker (1955), p. 303–305; Levie (1992), pp. 65–89 and Cowie (1949), pp. 43–87, 119–165.

[25]Mallison (1968), p. 68.

[26]For the contrary view, *see* Baxter (1970), p. 97.

[27]Levie (1992), pp. 78–83. *See also* Reed (1984), p. 306 (who maintains that the practice of the two world wars has contributed to a customary rule according to which minefields in high seas areas must always be notified).

[28]On April 9, 1940 the German government provided notification of a "mine warning area" in the Skagerrak between Lindesnes, Lodbjerg and Flekkeröy, Sandnäs Hage; on September 3, 1939 regarding the Southern entrance of the Sound and the Great Belt; and on April 29, 1940 regarding the Kattegat. The British government allowed passage through the Strait of Dover and the Firth of Forth.

[29]*Supra* note 17 and accompanying text.

[30]Corfu Channel (U.K. v. Alb.), 1949 I.C.J. 4 (Apr. 9).

Similarly, the mining of the Red Sea in 1984[31] is not relevant to this analysis as it did not occur during an armed conflict.

Since the armed conflicts during which naval mines were used have been addressed extensively elsewhere,[32] it suffices here to highlight only those aspects of the conflicts relevant to the examination of the relationship between the belligerent right to employ naval mines and the passage rights of innocent neutral shipping. Hence, the Korean War (1950–1953)[33] need not be addressed because the mines laid off Wonsan to prevent an amphibious landing operation resulted in no lasting impediment to passage rights. The same holds true for the mining in 1972 of three North Vietnamese ports during the Vietnam War[34] (although it is worth mentioning that neutral ships were given a period of grace to leave[35]) and of the approaches to Port Stanley during the Falklands/Malvinas conflict (1982).[36] During the 2011 conflict in Libya, Quaddafi's forces laid mines off the port of Misurata, probably in order to prevent food and other supplies from reaching the city.[37] This conduct was considered unlawful, not because of its impact on the freedom of navigation but because of its disregard for humanitarian considerations and for UN Security Council Resolution 1973, which obliged Libyan authorities to "ensure the rapid and unimpeded pas-sage of humanitarian assistance."[38]

The mining of the Suez Canal during the Arab–Israeli Wars (1967 and 1973) also need not be considered here because the Suez Canal is subject to a special treaty regime[39] and its passage is not governed by the law of the sea. However, the 1973 conflict is notable in that both the Gulf of Suez and the Gulf of Aqaba were closed by minefields.[40] Interestingly, their closure attracted considerably less attention than did the closure of the Suez Canal.

The use of naval mines during the 1971 India–Pakistan conflict still remains widely unnoticed even though at least five neutral merchant vessels were sunk by mines.[41] The mining of the Bay of Bengal by India and of the delta of the Ganges River by Pakistan did not extend beyond the territorial seas of the belligerents and had no broader impact on passage rights or on the freedom of navigation.

---

[31]See Truver (1985), pp. 115–117.

[32]See authorities cited *infra* notes 33–48.

[33]See Cagle and Manson (1957), pp. 121–122.

[34]See Levie (1992), pp. 144–157 and Swayze (1977).

[35]Mallison and Mallison (1976), p. 102.

[36]See Levie (1992), p. 159 and Fenrick (1985).

[37]See Heintschel von Heinegg (2012), pp. 211, 217.

[38]S.C. Res. 1973, 6, U.N. Doc. S/RES/1973 (Mar. 17, 2011).

[39]Convention Respecting the Free Navigation of the Suez Maritime Canal, Gr. Brit.-Ger.-Austria-Hung.-Spain-Fr.-It.-Neth.-Russ.-Turk., Oct. 29, 1888, *reprinted in* (1909) AJIL Supplement 3:123.

[40]See Levie (1992), pp. 157–158.

[41]See Rohwer (1974), pp. 24–26.

The India–Pakistan conflict and the use of naval mines against Nicaraguan ports in 1984[42] support the position that the laying of mines in the enemy's territorial sea and internal waters is permissible under the law of armed conflict. As has been rightly stated by Judge Schwebel in his dissent to the Nicaragua judgment, a "belligerent is entitled . . . to take reasonable measures (a fortiori, within the internal waters of the opposing belligerent) to restrict shipping, including third flag shipping, from using the ports of its opponent. Thus the use of mines in hostilities is not of itself unlawful."[43] Judge Schwebel also emphasized, however, that as against third States whose shipping was damaged or whose nationals were injured by mines laid by or on behalf of the United States, the international responsibility of the United States may arise. Third States were and are entitled to carry on commerce with Nicaragua, and their ships are entitled to make use of Nicaraguan ports. If the United States were to be justified in taking blockade-like measures against Nicaraguan ports, as by mining, it could only be so if its mining . . . were publically and officially announced by it and if international shipping was duly warned by it about the fact that mines would be or had been laid in specified waters.[44]

The use of naval mines during the Iran–Iraq War (1980–1988)[45] is the most important post-Second World War armed conflict in which the question of the legality of belligerent interference with the freedom of navigation of neutral shipping has arisen. In response to the laying of naval mines in the Persian Gulf, the international community made use of a variety of measures to enforce the right of freedom of navigation, ranging from convoying their merchant vessels[46] and mine-sweeping operations[47] to the use of force against Iranian vessels that had been caught laying unanchored mines and two oil platforms that had been used as bases for operations.[48] These enforcement measures were considered lawful as either self-defense actions or countermeasures in response to the illegal use by Iran of unanchored mines and of nonnotified anchored mines. It may be concluded, therefore, that had Iran refrained from the use of unanchored mines and had it properly provided notification of the minefields, the international community's response to the mining activities would not have been based on the illegality of the Iranian

---

[42]For the facts established by the ICJ, see Military and Paramilitary Activities in and against Nicaragua (Nicar. v. U.S.), 1986 I.C.J. 14, 76–80 (June 27) [hereinafter *Nicaragua*]. *See also* Levie (1992), pp. 162–166.

[43]*Nicaragua*, *supra* note 42, 236 (Schwebel J dissenting opinion).

[44]*Id.*, 238.

[45]For a comprehensive analytical assessment of the legal issues of the Iran-Iraq War, see the contributions in de Guttry and Ronzitti (1993). The Iran-Iraq War (1980–1988) and the Law of Naval Warfare. Cambridge University Press, Cambridge; Dekker and Post (1992). The Gulf War of 1980–1988. Kluwer Academic Publishers, Dordrecht.

[46]Nordquist and Wachenfeld (1988).

[47]Ronzitti (1987).

[48]For the facts established by the ICJ, see Oil Platforms (Iran v. U.S.), 2003 I.C.J. 161, 23–25 (Nov. 6). *See also* Levie (1992), pp. 166–70.

conduct. Thus, the international community's rationale for the actions taken does not support a conclusion that the mining of the Persian Gulf was unlawful per se.

An important facet of the Iran–Iraq conflict concerns the status of the Strait of Hormuz and the question of whether during an international armed conflict mines may be laid in international straits. In October 1982, the Iranian government, in a letter to the UN Security Council, declared:

> As certain rumours have been spread concerning the Straits of Hormuz, which might disturb international navigation in that area, the Ministry of Foreign Affairs of the Islamic Republic of Iran reaffirms that Iran is committed to keeping the Straits open to navigation and will not spare any effort for the purpose of achieving this end.[49]

This statement is remarkable in that Iran has consistently taken the position that the regime of transit passage set forth in Article 38 of the 1982 United Nations Convention on the Law of the Sea[50] does not apply to the Strait of Hormuz because Iran has merely signed, not ratified, the Convention.[51] At the same time, the

---

[49]U.N. Security Council, Charge D'Affaires of the Permanent Mission of Iran, Letter dated Oct. 21, 1980 from the Charge D'Affaires of the Permanent Mission of Iran to the United Nations to the Secretary General. U.N. Doc. S/14226 (Oct. 22, 1980).

[50]United Nations Convention on the Law of the Sea, Dec. 10, 1982, U.N.T.S. 1833:397 [hereinafter UNCLOS]. The Convention entered into force on November 16, 1994. As of November 12, 2014, 166 States, including the Holy See, are parties to it.

[51]Upon signature, Iran made the following declaration:

Notwithstanding the intended character of the Convention being one of general application and of law making nature, certain of its provisions are merely product of *quid pro quo* which do not necessarily purport to codify the existing customs or established usage (practice) regarded as having an obligatory character. Therefore, it seems natural and in harmony with article 34 of the 1969 Vienna Convention on the Law of Treaties, that only states parties to the Law of the Sea Convention shall be entitled to benefit from the contractual rights created therein.

The above considerations pertain specifically (but not exclusively) to the following:
The right of Transit passage through straits used for international navigation (Part III, Section 2, article 38).
Declarations and Statements, Oceans & Law of the Sea. http://www.un.org/Depts/los/convention_agreements/convention_declarations.htm (than follow Iran hyperlink). Accessed 8 June 2017.
It should also be noted that Oman, which borders the Strait of Hormuz as well, neither explicitly accepts nor rejects the applicability of the transit passage regime. Upon signature, Oman declared:
It is the understanding of the Government of the Sultanate of Oman that the application of the provisions of articles 19, 25, 34, 38 and 45 of the Convention does not preclude a coastal State from taking such appropriate measures as are necessary to protect its interest of peace and security.
Id. (then follow Oman upon signature hyperlink).
Upon ratification on August 17, 1989, Oman declared that the
Sultanate of Oman exercises full sovereignty over its territorial sea, the space above the territorial sea and its bed and subsoil, pursuant to the relevant laws and regulations of the Sultanate and in conformity with the provisions of this Convention concerning the principle of innocent passage.
Id. (then follow Oman upon ratification/accession hyperlink).

statement does not necessarily establish that Iran will not take belligerent (or peacetime) measures that would prevent or impede passage through the Strait of Hormuz and, thus, Iran's acceptance of a legal obligation to refrain from such actions.

2.2.3 Some Preliminary Conclusions

Subject to further matters that will be considered in the following section, the 1907 Hague Convention VIII and State practice seem to indicate that during an international armed conflict, the belligerents are entitled to lay naval mines in all sea areas beyond the national waters (i.e., internal waters, territorial sea, and archipelagic waters) of neutral States. Accordingly, there is no prohibition on impeding innocent passage in the territorial seas of the belligerents as long as the closure has been properly notified in advance.

While there is no State practice involving archipelagic States, it is safe to conclude that the same holds true for those parts of belligerent archipelagic waters in which only the right of innocent passage (as distinct from the right of archipelagic sea-lane passage) applies.[52]

International straits overlapped by the territorial seas of the belligerents are not absolutely excluded from mining. Hence, naval mines may be laid in belligerent international straits as long as the belligerent has given prior notice and ensures a means of safe passage, e.g., by providing piloting services or by temporarily disarming the mines. It remains to be seen whether the provisions of UNCLOS Article 38 on transit passage have contributed to an extended protection of such straits.

Minelaying in high seas areas (i.e., sea areas beyond the outer limit of the territorial sea) is not prohibited, again as long as the belligerent has notified the minefield in a timely and appropriate manner.[53] However, in view of the continuing right of neutral shipping to use the high seas for legitimate purposes, the legality of any employment of naval mines depends upon its justification by military necessity considerations. The laying of extensive minefields or their maintenance over a long period of time will not be in compliance with the law of naval warfare if there is no legitimate military necessity that justifies depriving neutral shipping of the freedom of navigation given its importance to international trade and the world economy.

Finally, and for the sake of completeness, it should be added that neutral States are entitled to lay mines off their coasts to defend their national waters and territories against belligerent interference.[54] Such mining must be limited to the territorial sea and may not extend to international straits or archipelagic sea lanes unless it does not suspend, hamper, or otherwise impede the rights of transit passage or archipelagic

---

[52]See UNCLOS, supra note 50, art. 52.

[53]For a similar assessment of the prior notification requirement, see Reed (1984), pp. 306–307 (who rightly maintains that during the two world wars all "war zones," including those enforced by the use of naval mines, had been notified by the belligerents.).

[54]1907 Hague Convention VIII, supra note 4, art. 4.

sea-lane passage.[55] Notification of the laying of armed mines and the arming of prelaid mines in neutral national waters is required.

2.3   Belligerent Minelaying and Passage Rights: Contemporary Law

The 1907 Hague Convention VIII does not provide a comprehensive legal framework on minelaying during an international armed conflict since its scope of applicability *ratione materiae* is limited to "automatic submarine contact mines." Although it is possible to deduce from the Convention a number of principles that also apply to modern naval mines,[56] an identification of contemporary international law is not limited to a dynamic interpretation of the Convention. Rather, it is indispensable to also consider those publications that shed light on what States are willing to accept as the current state of the law applicable to minelaying during international armed conflicts. These include the San Remo Manual,[57] as well as the military manuals of the U.S. Navy,[58] Canada,[59] the United Kingdom,[60] and Germany.[61] While the manuals selected for examination is rather limited, there are two reasons why they may still serve as reference points. First, the U.S. Navy manual (NWP, 1-14) has been adopted by a number of other States, which consider its provisions to correctly reflect the current state of the law. Second, these manuals are the most current statements on the international law applicable to mine warfare.

2.3.1   Access to and from Neutral Waters

In accordance with the law of maritime neutrality prohibiting the conduct of hostilities in neutral waters, there is a clear prohibition on laying naval mines in waters subject to national sovereignty, i.e., the internal waters, territorial sea, and archipelagic waters of neutral States.[62] Although it is lawful to conduct hostilities, including minelaying, in the sea areas beyond the outer limits of the territorial sea, that is, in neutral exclusive economic zones (EEZ) and the high seas, access to and exit from neutral waters may not be barred. As stated in three of the manuals, mining of those sea areas "shall not have the practical effect of preventing passage between neutral waters and international waters."[63] Accordingly, the belligerent that lays

---

[55]SRM (1995), p. 29.

[56]*See* Heintschel von Heinegg (1994), pp. 59–70.

[57]SRM (1995), *supra* note 55. *See also* the related Explanation, which provides additional detail concerning each of the *Manual's* basic rules.

[58]NWP 1-14M (2007).

[59]Canadian Manual (2001).

[60]UK Manual (2004).

[61]German Manual (2013).

[62]SRM (1995), pp. 15, 16, 86; NWP 1-14M (2007), 7.3, 9.2.3; Canadian Manual (2001), 805, 806; UK Manual (2004), 13.8, 13.9, 13.58 and German Manual (2013), 1205, 1214, 1216.

[63]SRM (1995), p. 87; Canadian Manual (2001), 839 and UK Manual (2004), 13.59.

mines off a neutral's coast is obliged to provide for safe routes through the minefield, e.g., by leaving open convenient channels or by providing piloting services. It must be emphasized, however, that the laying of mines in close proximity to a neutral territorial sea will be lawful only in exceptional circumstances, for example, in a confined sea area that is used by the enemy.

2.3.2 Belligerent National Waters and the Right of Innocent Passage

According to all the manuals, belligerent national waters, which are its internal waters, archipelagic waters, and territorial sea, are "areas of naval war-fare."[64] Hence, there is no prohibition on mining a State's own or enemy national waters. This right was acknowledged at the 1907 Hague Peace Conference. The impact of mining these waters on the right of innocent passage is a deplorable but necessary consequence of an international armed conflict. Neutral shipping's only protection is to avoid belligerent national waters. It may be added that UNCLOS Article 25(3) provides that in times of peace, States are entitled to suspend innocent passage "if such suspension is essential for its security." This right, which only the coastal State concerned may exercise, is limited to specified areas of the territorial sea. During an international armed conflict, it is modified by the law of naval warfare that supersedes the peacetime rules of the law of the sea. However, the minelaying State is obliged, "when the mining is first executed," to provide "for free exit of shipping of neutral States."[65] This, by necessity, implies that there is an obligation on the minelaying State to notify "the laying of armed mines or the arming of pre-laid mines, unless the mines can only detonate against vessels which are military objectives."[66] Hence, the presence of highly sophisticated and discriminating modern mines need not be notified because, by their design, they do not pose a risk to innocent shipping and thus do not impede the exercise of the right of innocent passage.

---

[64]SRM (1995), *supra* note 55, 10; Canadian Manual (2001), *supra* note 59, 703(1); UK Manual (2004), *supra* note 60, 13.6; German Manual (2013), *supra* note 61, 1011.

[65]SRM (1995), *supra* note 55, 85; Canadian Manual (2001), *supra* note 59, 836 and UK Manual (2004), *supra* note 60, 13.57.

[66]SRM (1995), *supra* note 55, 83; Canadian Manual (2001), *supra* note 59, 838 and UK Manual (2004), *supra* note 60, 13.55. According to NWP 1-14M (2007), 9.2.3, international notification must be made only, "as soon as military exigencies permit." It is unclear whether the United States believes the safety of neutral shipping is subsidiary to considerations of military necessity. However, a minefield most often serves the purpose of "modifying geography" and of preventing other vessels from using a certain area of the seas. This can be accomplished only, if the respective minefield is notified in advance. The German Manual does not expressly mention notification. However, according to paragraph 1046, any minelaying is subject to the principles of effective surveillance, risk control and warning. The latter implies an obligation to notify the laying of armed mines or the arming of prelaid mines.

2.3.3 Transit Passage and Archipelagic Sea-Lane Passage Through Belligerent Waters

As has been seen, the 1907 Hague Convention VIII does not contain a prohibition on laying mines in international straits. With the acceptance in UNCLOS of a 12-nautical-mile territorial sea, many international straits that had contained high seas corridors when the maximum breadth of the territorial sea was 3 nautical miles are today overlapped by the territorial seas of the States bordering the strait. Similarly, sea lanes through an archipelagic State, which were located in international waters prior to the adoption of UNCLOS, are now in archipelagic waters over which the archipelagic State enjoys sovereignty. In order to preserve the freedoms of navigation and overflight, UNCLOS provides for the rights of transit passage, archipelagic sea-lane passage, and nonsuspendable innocent passage.[67] Although UNCLOS is a peacetime instrument, these provisions have had a remarkable impact on the law of naval warfare. This, however, does not mean that the peacetime rules have made their way into the law of naval warfare in an unmodified fashion.[68]

Before elaborating on the rules of naval warfare on the mining of international straits and archipelagic sea lanes, it is important to stress that the right to extend the breadth of the territorial sea to a maximum width of 12 nautical miles was part and parcel of a "package deal."[69] In other words, a coastal State that extends its territorial sea to 12 nautical miles is under a clear obligation to grant other States the right of transit passage through now overlapped international straits. The same holds true for archipelagic waters, whose recognition was subject to an archipelagic State's acceptance of the right of archipelagic sea-lane passage. Therefore, States bordering an international State and archipelagic States are bound by these special regimes,[70] and any declaration reducing the rights of other States to innocent passage, which may be suspended, is unlawful under UNCLOS.

The main characteristics of the rights of transit passage and archipelagic sea-lane passage are that they may not be suspended or impeded and that the coastal or archipelagic State is under an obligation not to hamper passage and to give appropriate publicity to any danger.[71] During an international armed conflict, these

---

[67]UNCLOS, *supra* note 50, arts. 38, 45, 53. In archipelagic waters that are not subject to the regime of archipelagic sea lanes passage, other States enjoy the right of innocent passage, which, according to UNCLOS Article 52(2), may be suspended temporarily in specified areas.

[68]SRM (1995), p. 27, provides "[t]he rights of transit passage and archipelagic sea lanes passage applicable to international straits and archipelagic waters in peacetime continue to apply in times of armed conflict." While this statement is correct insofar as neutral sea areas are concerned, it is highly questionable whether it also holds true for belligerent international straits and archipelagic sea lanes because there is no obligation of a belligerent to grant the enemy those passage rights.

[69]For a discussion of the "package deal" reached during the negotiations that produced UNCLOS, *see* Kraska (2014), pp. 354–357. Its intent was to balance the interests of flag, port and coastal States.

[70]The declarations by Iran and Oman concerning the Strait of Hormuz, *supra* note 51, have, therefore, not prevented an application of the transit passage regime to that international strait.

[71]UNCLOS, *supra* note 50, arts. 38, 44, 53, 54.

provisions apply to belligerent international straits and archipelagic waters, but only in a modified manner.

Under the law of naval warfare, belligerent international straits and archipelagic sea lanes are within "areas of warfare."[72] Thus, despite their importance to international shipping, there is no prohibition on laying mines in those areas. While the prohibition on impeding the rights of transit and archipelagic sea-lane passage continues to apply during international armed conflicts, the belligerents are entitled to mine international straits and archipelagic sea lanes if they provide for "safe and convenient alternative routes."[73]

The provisions of the UK Manual and NWP 1-14M do not fully reflect that position. According to the UK Manual, the safe and convenient rule only applies to archipelagic sea lanes.[74] As regards international straits, the prohibition of impeding the right of transit passage is absolute in character.[75] NWP 1-14M provides: "[n]aval mines may be employed to channelize neutral shipping but not in a manner to deny transit passage of international straits or archipelagic sea lanes passage of archipelagic waters by such shipping."[76] The term "impede" means "to delay or block the progress or action of."[77] The term "deny" means "to refuse to give."[78] Obviously, the NWP 1-14M provision is less limiting with regard to the right of a belligerent to mine its international straits than the UK Manual provision. Although not using the same language, it seems to reach the same result as the San Remo Manual and German and Canadian manuals, that is, a denial of passage rights to neutral shipping will be unlawful but that impeding those rights, while simultaneously providing safe and convenient alternative routes, would be lawful.

The UK Manual provision concerning transit passage cannot be reconciled with that of the other manuals. It introduces the strict peacetime standards for international straits while providing no exception for belligerent actions during international armed conflicts. It is doubtful that this standard is part of the law of naval warfare. Applied to the United Kingdom, for example, it would mean that, as a party to an international armed conflict, the United Kingdom would be obliged to permit unimpeded passage through the Strait of Dover and to refrain from channelizing neutral shipping by the laying of mines. In practice, however, since the UK Manual

---

[72] See authorities cited *supra* note 65. For the status of neutral international straits and archipelagic sea lanes, *see* SRM (1995), pp. 23–30.

[73] SRM (1995), p. 89 and Canadian Manual (2001), p. 841. According to the German Manual (2013), p. 1046, there seems to be no prohibition of mining international straits and archipelagic sea lanes either. The obligation of belligerents to take all feasible precautionary measures for the protection of peaceful shipping seems to suggest that it includes the provision of safe and convenient alternative routes.

[74] UK Manual (2004), 13.61 ("Passage through waters subject to the right of archipelagic sea lanes passage shall not be impeded unless safe and convenient alternative routes are provided.").

[75] *Id.*, 13.61 ("Transit passage shall not be impeded.").

[76] NWP 1-14M (2007), 9.2.3(6).

[77] Stevenson and Waite (2011), p. 713.

[78] *Id.* at 383.

provides for exceptions in the case of mines that "can only detonate against vessels which are military objectives,"[79] it is safe to conclude that the United Kingdom is prepared to use these highly sophisticated weapons in both its own and enemy international straits because they will not "impede" transit passage.

Finally, while the law of naval warfare establishes the basic framework for the conduct of war at sea, individual States are, of course, free to deliberately apply stricter standards to their belligerent activities than those provided for by international law. Thus, a State could refrain from laying mines in its own international straits or that of its enemy as a matter of policy even though safe and convenient alternative routes are available.

2.3.4 Neutral Navigation in International Waters

As stated above, high sea freedom of navigation is not a "passage right" in the strict sense. Still, in view of its importance to the world economy and international security, it is necessary to briefly touch upon the legality of mining operations in international waters (i.e., sea areas beyond the outer limits of the territorial sea) in light of the rights that neutral States enjoy in those waters. In doing so, it is important to distinguish between the high seas in the technical sense (which are those areas not included in an EEZ or in the territorial, internal, or archipelagic waters of a State) and those parts of international waters that are subject to EEZ and continental shelf rights of neutral States.

The conduct of hostilities within the EEZ or on the continental shelf of neutral States is not prohibited[80]; however, the belligerents are under an obligation to pay due regard to the rights that coastal States enjoy in those areas.[81] If a belligerent considers it necessary to lay mines in the EEZ or on the continental shelf of a neutral State, it is obligated not to "interfere with access" to artificial islands, installations, and structures.[82] Moreover, the "size of the minefield and the type of mines used [shall] not endanger" such installations.[83] Accordingly, the minelaying State is under an affirmative obligation to provide for free access routes to and from such installations and to refrain from all activities that may have a detrimental effect on such structures.

The due regard principle for neutral States engaged in the exploration and exploitation of natural resources also applies in sea and seabed areas beyond national

---

[79]UK Manual (2004), *supra* note 60, 13.55.

[80]SRM (1995), pp. 10(c), 34, 35; NWP 1-14M (2007), 7.3.8; Canadian Manual (2001), 804 (1)(c), 821, 822; UK Manual (2004), 13.6(b), 13.21 and German Manual (2013), 1011, 1014, 1016. For an analysis of the relationship between the law of the sea and the law of naval warfare, *see* Heintschel von Heinegg (2005).

[81]SRM (1995), p. 34; NWP 1-14M (2007), 7.3.8; Canadian Manual (2001), 821; UK Manual (2004), 12.21 and German Manual (2013), 1014.

[82]SRM (1995), p. 35; Canadian Manual (2001), 822 and UK Manual (2004), 13.21.

[83]SRM (1995), p. 35.

jurisdiction, i.e., the high seas and the seabed thereunder.[84] Since neutral States continue to enjoy the freedom of navigation in high seas areas (including the EEZ and over the continental shelf) and in view of the importance of that right, a mining of high seas areas not justified by reasons of military necessity will certainly be in violation of the contemporary law of naval warfare. Hence, expansive minefields of the kind established during the two world wars would clearly be unlawful. As stated in NWP 1-14M, under the current law of naval warfare, the "mining of areas of indefinite extent in international waters is prohibited. Reasonably limited barred areas may be established by naval mines, provided neutral shipping retains an alternate route around or through such an area with reasonable assurance of safety."[85] Any mining of high seas areas that does not conform to these standards will certainly no longer be tolerated by the international community.

2.4   Notification

One of the preconditions that a State engaged in minelaying must fulfill for it to be lawful is providing notification.[86] The obligation to notify is no longer limited to situations in which the mines "cease to be under surveillance," and it is no longer subject to "military exigencies."[87] Although NWP 1-14M provides that "international notification of the location of emplaced mines must be made as soon as military exigencies permit,"[88] it is hard to conceive of exigencies that would permit a belligerent to refrain from providing notice of the laying of mines. Additionally, since publicity is necessary in order to achieve the aims of a minefield, i.e., denying the enemy the use of the mined sea area, it is in the belligerent's interest to provide notification. It is important to note that the obligation to notify is limited to the laying of armed mines and to the arming of prelaid mines.[89] Hence, the laying of unarmed mines need not be notified. This is also the rule for highly sophisticated naval mines that "can only detonate against vessels which are military objectives."[90] Finally, the communication of the notification "to the Governments through the diplomatic channel"[91] is no longer required under the contemporary law; today it suffices to use a Notice to Mariners.

---

[84]SRM (1995), p. 36; Canadian Manual (2001), 823; UK Manual (2004), 13.22 and German Manual (2013), 1015.

[85]NWP 1-14M (2007), 9.2.3(8).

[86]*See supra* note 27 and accompanying text. *See also* Reed (1984), pp. 306–307.

[87]1907 Hague Convention VIII, *supra* note 4, art. 3.

[88]NWP 1-14M (2007), 9.2.3(1).

[89]*See* SRM (1995), p. 83.

[90]*Id.*

[91]1907 Hague Convention VIII, *supra* note 4, art. 3.

2.5   Demining Operations by Neutral States

Finally, while to this point the analysis has focused on a belligerent's minelaying, the response of neutral States to that mining also merits discussion. Neutral States will no longer tolerate mining operations that pose an intolerable threat to the freedom of navigation in sea areas beyond the outer limit of the territorial seas of the parties to the conflict if the mines have been laid in violation of the law of naval warfare. The demining operations conducted by neutral States in the Persian Gulf[92] have generally been considered as in compliance with international law, in particular with the law of maritime neutrality.[93] The San Remo Manual provides: "[n]eutral States do not commit an act inconsistent with the laws of neutrality by clearing mines laid in violation of international law."[94] States have adopted this rule in their military manuals.[95] Accordingly, neutral States are entitled to enforce the freedom of navigation, including passage rights, if a belligerent unduly interferes with those rights, e.g., by mining areas of indefinite extent. However, a word of caution is necessary. A demining operation by neutral States will most certainly be regarded as assisting the opposing belligerent or even an act of "direct participation in hostilities"[96] because it would deprive the minelaying State of the military advantage linked to the mining. Therefore, any demining operation based upon the alleged unlawfulness of a minefield must be approached cautiously and preferably conducted in a multinational context vice unilaterally to establish international legitimacy.

3   Peacetime Mining

Two States, the United States and Germany, which have officially stated their policy, have taken the position that mining operations are not absolutely prohibited in peacetime, particularly when in pursuit of national security interests. Moreover, an analysis of the *Corfu Channel* case reveals that, according to the International Court of Justice, a coastal State may indeed lay mines in its territorial sea in peacetime.

Notwithstanding this interpretation, the employment of naval mines in times of peace seems to be contrary to the international law of the sea because their presence or the mere suspicion of their presence in a sea area will necessarily have an impeding effect on the exercise of passage rights and the freedom of navigation. Furthermore, developments of the international law of the sea since the Court's 1949 judgment make it questionable whether the use of mines in times of peace can still be considered lawful.

---

[92]*See supra* note 47 and accompanying text.

[93]*See* Ronzitti (1987) and Gioia and Ronzitti (1992), pp. 237–38.

[94]SRM (1995), *supra* note 55, 92.

[95]Canadian Manual (2001), 843; UK Manual (2004), 13.64 and German Manual (2013), 1245.

[96]*See* International Committee of the Red Cross (2009), pp. 41–68.

In addressing this issue, only situations that involve a conduct attributable to a State will be considered. Incidents such as the mining of the Red Sea in 1984, which could not be attributed with sufficient certainty to a State,[97] will not be addressed.

3.1   National Positions on Peacetime Mining Operations

The German Manual, by adopting NATO doctrine, distinguishes between protective, defensive, and offensive minelaying.[98] A "protective minefield" is defined as "a minefield laid in friendly territorial waters to protect ports, harbours, anchorages, coasts and coastal routes."[99] A "defensive minefield" is a "minefield laid in international waters or international straits with the declared intention of controlling shipping in defence of sea communications."[100] An "offensive minefield" is defined as a "minefield laid in enemy territorial water or waters under enemy control."[101] According to the German Manual, a resort to protective minelaying prior to the outbreak of an international armed conflict is permitted if the right of foreign ships to innocent passage is observed and as long as the minelaying State exercises sufficient control over the mines. The German Manual continues by repeating almost verbatim UNCLOS Article 25(3) in stating that the coastal State may suspend temporarily in specified parts of its territorial sea the innocent passage of foreign ships if that is essential for the protection of its security and only after international shipping has been duly warned.[102] According to the Manual, protective mining of international straits is explicitly prohibited in times of peace; defensive and offensive minelaying is not permissible in situations other than armed conflict.[103]

The United States has given a more detailed statement of its policy on peacetime mining, which is quoted in its entirety as follows:

> Consistent with the safety of its own citizenry, a nation may emplace both armed and controlled mines in its own internal waters at any time with or without notification. A nation may also mine its own archipelagic waters and territorial sea during peacetime when deemed necessary for national security purposes. If armed mines are emplaced in archipelagic waters or the territorial sea, appropriate international notification of the existence and location of such mines is required. Because the right of innocent passage can be suspended only temporarily, armed mines must be removed or rendered harmless as soon as the security threat that prompted their emplacement has terminated. Armed mines may not be emplaced in international straits or archipelagic sea lanes during peacetime. Emplacement of

---

[97]There were allegations that the mines had been laid by Libya, although the terrorist group of the Islamic Jihad had claimed it laid the mines. *See* Levie (1992), pp. 159–162 and the authorities he cites.

[98]German Manual (2013), 1045.

[99]NATO Standardization Agency (2014), 2-P-10.

[100]*Id.* at 2-D-3.

[101]*Id.* at 2-O-1.

[102]German Manual (2013), 1047.

[103]*Id.*, 1049, 1050.

controlled mines in a nation's own archipelagic waters or territorial sea is not subject to such notification or removal requirements.

Naval mines may not be emplaced in internal waters, territorial seas, or archipelagic waters of another nation in peacetime without that nation's consent. Controlled mines may, however, be emplaced in international waters (i.e., beyond the territorial sea) if they do not unreasonably interfere with other lawful uses of the oceans. The determination of what constitutes an "unreasonable interference" involves a balancing of a number of factors, including the rationale for their emplacement (i.e., the self-defense requirements of the emplacing nation), the extent of the area to be mined, the hazard (if any) to other lawful ocean uses, and the duration of their emplacement. Because controlled mines do not constitute a hazard to navigation, international notice of their emplacement is not required.

Armed mines may not be emplaced in international waters prior to the outbreak of armed conflict, except under the most demanding requirements of individual or collective self-defense. Should armed mines be emplaced in international waters under such circumstances, prior notification of their location must be provided. A nation emplacing armed mines in international waters during peacetime must maintain an onscene presence in the area sufficient to ensure that appropriate warning is provided to ships approaching the danger area. All armed mines must be expeditiously removed or rendered harmless when the imminent danger that prompted their emplacement has passed.[104]

Germany and the United States agree that it is permissible, if essential or necessary for national security purposes, to mine its own national waters. In principle, prior notification is required unless the mines can be sufficiently controlled so as not to pose a threat to innocent shipping. Although the German Manual does not distinguish between armed and controlled mines, its reference to an exercise of "sufficient control"[105] leads to the conclusion that notification is unnecessary in the case of controlled mines. The manuals differ, however, with regard to the mining of international straits and archipelagic sea lanes. Whereas the German Manual prohibits the laying of any mines in those areas, NWP 1-14M appears to accept that controlled mines (as distinguished from armed mines) may be laid in both international straits and archipelagic sea lanes.

Both States agree that offensive minelaying during peacetime is prohibited. The United States provides for an exception if the State in whose waters the mines will be laid has given its consent; the German Manual does not contain this exception. The German Manual, however, obviously starts from the premise that offensive mining is characterized by the lack of consent. Hence, if the State concerned consents, the mining will not be "offensive" and, taking into account "circumstance precluding wrongfulness," will not be considered a violation of the State's territorial sovereignty and integrity.

---

[104]NWP 1-14M (2007), 9.2.2.
[105]German Manual (2013), 1047.

There also seems to be a significant difference between the manuals with regard to mining in international waters. According to the German Manual, the mining of sea areas beyond the outer limit of Germany's territorial sea is impermissible in peacetime, whether with armed or controlled mines. According to the U.S. position, it is permissible to lay controlled mines at all times and to lay armed mines if "demanding requirements of individual or collective self-defense" justify such conduct and the mines are notified and are sufficiently controlled. However, this apparent difference is less significant when it is realized that the applicability of the German Manual, despite its reference to peacetime mining, is limited to times of armed conflict. There are no indications that the German government has intended to limit its options under the right of individual or collective self-defense, i.e., under the *jus ad bellum*. It may be concluded, therefore, that both States generally share a common position on the legality of peacetime mining operations, subject to the difference on the issue of the peacetime mining of international straits. But even that distinction is a minor one if the right of self-defense comes into play. Insofar as highly sophisticated and discriminating naval mines are concerned, it is quite improbable that the German government would be willing to waive its right to counter an armed attack or imminent armed attack solely because the only effective response is to employ mines in an international strait.

3.2   The *Corfu Channel* Judgment

The U.S. and German positions on peacetime mining are reconcilable with the *Corfu Channel* case.[106] The Court did not rule that the mining of the Albanian territorial waters as such was in violation of international law. It may be added that, for obvious reasons, the Court was unaware of the regime of transit passage. Although it indicated that the North Corfu Channel belonged to that class of "international highways" through which passage could not be prohibited during peacetime,[107] the judgment is not necessarily significant with regard to the special legal status of international straits as established by UNCLOS.

Albania was held responsible for the damage inflicted on the British warships only because it had positive or constructive knowledge of the presence of mines that were armed, thus posing a considerable hazard to international shipping.[108] Because of that knowledge, Albania was obliged to notify "for the benefit of shipping in general, the existence of a mine field in Albanian territorial waters" and to warn "the approaching British warships of the imminent danger to which the minefield exposed them."[109] According to the Court, such obligations are based, not on the Hague Convention of 1907, No. VIII, which is applicable in time of war, but on

---

[106]*Corfu Channel, supra* note 30.

[107]*Id.* at 29.

[108]*Id.* at 18–22.

[109]*Id.* at 22.

certain general and well-established principles, namely, elementary considerations of humanity, even more exacting in peace than in war; the principle of the freedom of maritime communication; and every State's obligation not to allow knowingly its territory to be used for acts contrary to the rights of other States.[110]

Had the Albanian authorities lacked positive or constructive knowledge, there would have been no obligation to warn international shipping. Moreover, the Court started from the premise that the mines were indeed dangerous. It did not need to address the issue of controlled mines that, if not armed, do not pose a danger to international shipping. The approach taken by both the United States and Germany on peacetime mining of the territorial sea is consistent with the Court's holdings because both States agree that they are obliged to issue warnings if the mines pose a threat to international shipping.

3.3   Peacetime Mining and UNCLOS Navigational Provisions

In a final step, it is necessary to measure the United States and German positions against the provisions of UNCLOS. Although the United States is not a party, it considers that the provisions on passage rights and freedom of navigation reflect customary international law,[111] which is binding on all States.

3.3.1   Innocent Passage

According to UNCLOS Article 24(2), a "coastal State shall give appropriate public-ity to any danger to navigation, of which it has knowledge, within its territorial sea." This obligation is identical with the judgment in the Corfu Channel case, but the legal basis is no longer the "general and well-established principles" upon which the Court relied. Rather, the basis as applied to naval mines is found in UNCLOS Article 25(3), under which a coastal State may, without discrimination in form or in fact among foreign ships, suspend temporarily in specified areas of its territorial sea the innocent passage of foreign ships if such suspension is essential for the protection of its security, including weapon exercises. Such suspension shall take effect only after having been duly published.

The U.S. and German positions on peacetime mining of a State's own territorial seas are in accord with the provisions of the two articles. While Article 25(3) refers only to weapon exercises, that reference is not exclusive, and both countries agree that the laying of armed mines is a danger to navigation that will result in a suspension of the right of innocent passage in the area concerned and that such minelaying must be notified. Since the laying of controlled mines does not result in a

---

[110]*Id.*

[111]NWP 1-14M (2007), 1.2. This position is illustrated in specific NWP 1–14 provisions addressing passage rights and freedom of navigation. *See id.*, 2.5.2.1 (innocent passage), 2.5.3.1 (transit passage), 2.5.4.1 (archipelagic sea lanes passage), 2.6.3 (freedom of navigation in international waters).

suspension of the right of innocent passage and since they do not pose a danger to navigation, their existence need not be notified under either UNCLOS Article 25 (3) or Article 24(2). While stating that there is a right to lay mines in a State's own sovereign sea areas, both agree that the right to lay armed mines arises only when necessary to protect national security.

Unfortunately, both manuals are silent on the right of nonsuspendable innocent passage provided by Article 45. Given their countries' acceptance of the navigational provisions of UNCLOS as either treaty law (Germany) or customary law (United States), it can be concluded, however, that neither is prepared to interfere with that right.

Finally, UNCLOS Article 52 provides the same rights to an archipelagic State to suspend innocent passage in its archipelagic waters as those permitting suspension of innocent passage in the territorial sea. The U.S. position on the mining of territorial seas is equally applicable in archipelagic waters and is consistent with Article 52.

3.3.2 Transit Passage and Archipelagic Sea-Lane Passage

Under UNCLOS Articles 38(1) and 44, the right of transit passage and archipelagic sea-lane passage, respectively, may not be impeded, hampered, or suspended. The United States and Germany consider the laying of armed mines within international straits and archipelagic sea lanes as irreconcilable with these obligations. Although not stated directly, the United States appears to take the position that controlled mines may be laid in an international strait and within an archipelagic sea lane. While it is conceded that controlled mines do not pose a hazard to innocent shipping as long as they are not armed, international shipping may refrain from navigating through an international strait or utilize an archipelagic sea lane merely because it is suspected that mines are present. Or even if proceeding through the strait or sea lane, they may do so with extreme caution. If that were to occur, transit and archipelagic passage could be delayed, thus "impeded"[112] in contravention of Articles 38(1) and 44.

3.3.3 Freedom of Navigation in High Seas Areas

The international law of the sea does not prohibit military uses of the high seas, including the EEZ and continental shelf of other States.[113] Hence, States are allowed to lay mines in those areas if they do not pose a danger to international shipping.

As with the placement of mines in the territorial sea and archipelagic waters, the United States distinguishes between armed and controlled mines in the mining of international waters, approving the latter if there is no unreasonable interference with other lawful uses of the oceans. With regard to armed mines, the United States does not assert that there is authority to lay armed mines in international waters to further general national security interests, nor does it base that authority on the law of the sea, but it cites the inherent right of individual or collective self-defense as now set

---

[112]For the meaning of the term "impede," see *supra* note 77 and accompanying text.

[113]*See* Heintschel von Heinegg (2005).

forth in Article 51 of the UN Charter as providing the legal authority. Because UNCLOS was drafted with the intent of regulating uses of the sea in peacetime, it does not address the exercise of the right of self-defense. Moreover, the conditions under which the United States is prepared to lay armed mines in international waters (prior notification, onscene presence, expeditious removal when the imminent threat has passed) conform to the requirements of necessity, proportionality, and immediacy and are, therefore, in accordance with the limitations on the right of self-defense. There are good reasons to believe that Germany is prepared to share that approach if naval mines are the only effective means to counter an imminent threat.

4   Concluding Remarks

The contemporary law of naval warfare and maritime neutrality has considerably strengthened the position of neutral States regarding their right to continue to exercise freedom of navigation in general and transit and archipelagic sea-lane passage rights in particular. The law has done so by restricting the circumstances under which a belligerent State may employ naval mines and providing enhanced authority to neutral States to enforce navigational rights.

Although there is no prohibition on the mining of sea areas other than those covered by the territorial sovereignty of neutral States, belligerents are no longer entitled to unduly interfere with the freedom of navigation enjoyed by neutral States in the high seas or with their rights of transit and archipelagic sea-lane passage. While that is true as a general statement of the law, the issue of mining of belligerent international straits and archipelagic sea lanes is not entirely settled.

In addition to restrictions placed on the laying of mines, contemporary practice has established that neutral States may undertake self-help measures in response to unlawful employment of mines. Thus, if a belligerent lays mines in violation of the restrictions provided for by the law of naval warfare, aggrieved neutral States are entitled to remove the unlawfully laid mines in order to enforce their navigational rights. The right of removing illegally laid mines is not limited to international waters but also applies in international straits and archipelagic waters even if the areas concerned are part of the sovereign territory of the delinquent belligerent.

While the laws of naval warfare and maritime neutrality provide comparatively clear rules on the protection of innocent shipping against the threats posed by naval mines during international armed conflicts, the situation is less clear when it comes to the legality of mining operations in peacetime. So far, only two States have indicated under what conditions they consider such operations to be in accordance with international law. According to both, peacetime mining is an exceptional right; they also agree on the law applicable to mining a State's own national waters. While the United States has set forth the circumstances under which it believes mining of international waters is permitted, the German position is not as clear and may, in fact, differ from that of the United States. It cannot, therefore, be currently claimed that international law provides established and specific rules on the issue.

Rather, the legal yardstick to be applied in order to determine the legality of such operations is and shall remain the international law of the sea because this is the best approach to ensure continuing and effective protection of international shipping that is so important to the world economy. This, of course, does not preclude an application of the *jus ad bellum*, in particular the right of individual or collective self-defense, in specific circumstances. Clearly, a State need not wait until it has been subjected to an armed attack to respond; it may respond to an imminent armed attack by laying mines, whether controlled or not, in international waters in the exercise of its inherent right of self-defense.

Finally, the law applicable to naval mines recognizes how far mining technology has advanced beyond that addressed in the 1907 Hague Convention VIII and accepts the distinction between armed and controlled mines. Armed mines are indeed a "hidden menace," both during international armed conflicts and in peacetime, and as such the rules and principles regulating their use recognize the danger presented to international shipping and prohibit or restrict their use to alleviate this danger. Controlled mines, particularly in peacetime and also when programmed during armed conflict to hit only military objects, do not pose the same hazard to international shipping. There are no restrictions on their use other than those protecting the territorial sovereignty or certain well-established sovereign rights of other States.

Wolff Heintschel von Heinegg is Professor of Public Law, European University Viadrina, Frankfurt (Oder), Germany. He previously served as the Dean of the Law Faculty of Europa-Universität and as the University's Vice President. Prior to his association with Europa-Universität, he served as Professor of Public International Law at the University of Augsburg. Professor Heintschel von Heinegg was the Charles H. Stockton Professor of International Law at the U.S. Naval War College in the academic years 2003–2004 and 2012–2013.

References

[1907 Hague Proceedings Vol. I] Third Commission (1907) The laying of automatic submarine contact mines: report to the conference (Presented at Eighth Plenary Meeting, Oct. 9, 1907). reprinted In: Scott JB (ed) (1920) The proceedings of the Hague peace conferences: translations of the official texts. Oxford University Press, New York

[1907 Hague Proceedings Vol. III] Committee of Examination (1907) The laying of automatic contact mines: report to the commission (Fifth Meeting, Sept. 17, 1907). reprinted In: Scott JB (ed) (1921) The proceedings of the hague peace conferences: translations of the official texts. Oxford University Press, New York

Baxter RR (1970) Treaties and custom. Recueil des Cours 129:25

Cagle M, Manson FA (1957) The sea war in Korea. Naval Institute Press, Annapolis

[Canadian Manual] Chief of the General Staff (Canada) (2001) B-GJ-005-104/FP-021, Law of armed conflict at the operational and tactical level

Castrén E (1954) The present law of war and neutrality. Helsinki, Suomalainev Tiedeakemia

Colombos CJ (1968) The international law of the Sea, 6th edn. Longmans, London

Cowie JS (1949) Mines, minelayers and minelaying. Oxford University Press, Oxford

de Guttry A, Ronzitti N (eds) (1993) The Iran-Iraq war (1980–1988) and the law of Naval warfare. Cambridge University Press, Cambridge

Dekker IF, Post HHG (eds) (1992) The Gulf War of 1980–1988. Kluwer Academic Publishers, Dordrecht

Fenrick WJ (1985) Legal aspects of the falklands naval conflict. Mil Law Rev 24:241

Fuller M, Ewing D (eds) (2013) IHS Jane's weapons: naval, 57th edn. London, Janes Information Group

[German Manual] Bundesministerium der Verteidigung (2013) ZDv 15/2, Humanitäres Völkerrecht in bewaffneten Konflikten. English edition: U.S. Naval War College (2013) Stockton e-Portal, http://usnwc.libguides.com/ld.php?content_id=5616055. Accessed 8 June 2017

Gioia A, Ronzitti N (1992) The law of neutrality: third states' commercial rights and duties. In: Dekker IF, Post HHG (eds) The Gulf war of 1980–1988. Kluwer Academic Publishers, Dordrecht

Griffith M (1981) Hiden Menace: mine warfare – past, present and future. HarperCollins, New York

Haines S (2014) 1907 Hague Convention VIII relative to the laying of automatic submarine contact mines. Int Law Stud 90:412

Heintschel von Heinegg W (1994) The international law of mine warfare at Sea. Israel yearbook on human rights 23:53 (1994). reprinted In: Schmitt MN, Heintschel von Heinegg W (eds) (2012) The conduct of hostilities in International Humanitarian Law 1:53

Heintschel von Heinegg W (2005) UNCLOS and maritime security operations. Ger Yearb Int Law 48:151

Heintschel von Heinegg W (2012) Methods and means of naval warfare in non-international armed conflicts. In: Watkin K, Norris AJ (eds) Non-international armed conflict in the twenty-first century (U.S. Naval War College International Law Studies, vol 88). U.S. Naval War College, Newport

Hoffmann RF (1977) Offensive mine warfare: a forgotten strategy?. In: U.S. Naval Institute Proceedings 143, 145 Annapolis (MD)

International Committee of the Red Cross (2009) Interpretive guidance on the notion of direct participation in hostilities under International Humanitarian Law. ICRC, Geneva

Kraska J (2014) Legal vortex in the strait of hormuz. Va J Int Law 54:323. 354-57

Lauterpacht H (ed) Oppenheim L (1952) International law: a treatise, vol. 2: disputes, war and neutrality, 7th rev edn. Longmans, London

Levie HS (1992) Mine warfare at sea. Martinus Nijhoff, Dordrecht

Mallison WT Jr (1968) Studies in the law of naval warfare: submarines in general and limited wars (U.S. Naval War College International Law Studies, vol 56). U.S. Naval War College, Newport

Mallison SV, Mallison WT Jr (1976) A survey of the international law of naval blockade. In: U.S. Naval Institute Proceedings 43, 51, Annapolis (Feb 1976)

NATO Standardization Agency (2014) AAP-06, NATO glossary of terms and definitions

Nordquist MH, Wachenfeld MG (1988) Legal aspects of reflagging Kuwaiti tankers and laying of mines in the Persian Gulf. Ger Yearb Int Law 31:138

[NWP 1-14M] U.S. Navy, U.S. Marine Corps & U.S. Coast Guard (2007) NWP 1-14M/MCWP 5-12/COMDTPUB P5800.7A, The commander's handbook on the law of naval operations

Reed JJ (1984) "Damn the Torpedoes!": international standards regarding the use of automatic submarine mines. Fordham Int Law J 8:286

Rios JJ (2005) Naval mines in the 21st century: can NATO navies meet the challenge? 11–15, unpublished M.A. thesis, Naval Postgraduate school, https://calhoun.nps.edu/bitstream/handle/10945/10018/05Jun%255FRios.pdf?sequence=1. Accessed 6 June 2017

Rohwer J (1974) Der indisch-pakistanische Konflikt 1971. Marine Rundschau 71:7

Ronzitti N (1987) La Guerre du Golfe, le Déminage at la Circulation des Navires. Annuaire Français de Droit International 33:647

[SRM] Doswald Beck L (1995) San Remo manual on International law applicable to armed conflict at sea. Cambridge University Press, Cambridge

Stevenson A, Waite M (eds) (2011) Concise oxford english dictionary, 12th edn. Oxford University Press, Oxford

Swayze FB (1977) Traditional principles of blockade in modern practice: United States mining of internal and territorial waters of North Vietnam. JAG J 29:143

Truver SC (1985) Mines of August: an international whodunit. In: U.S. Naval Institute Proceedings, vol 111, no 95. Annapolis, May 1985, pp 115–17

Tucker RW (1955) The law of war and neutrality at Sea (U.S. Naval War College International Law Studies, vol 50). U.S. Naval War College, Newport

[UK Manual] United Kingdom Ministry of Defence (2004) The manual of the law of armed conflict

Professor Dr. Wolff Heintschel von Heinegg holds the Chair of Public Law, especially Public International Law, European Law and Foreign Constitutional Law at the Europa-Universität Viadrina in Frankfurt (Oder), Germany. In the academic years 2003–2004 and 2012–2013, he was the Charles H. Stockton Professor of International Law at the U.S. Naval War College. From October 2004 until October 2008, he was the Dean of the Law Faculty of the Europa-Universität. Since May 2012, he has been the Vice-President of the International Society for Military Law and the Law of War. Professor Heintschel von Heinegg was among a group of international lawyers and naval experts who produced the San Remo Manual on International Law Applicable to Armed Conflicts at Sea. He has been a member of several groups of experts working on the current state and progressive development of international humanitarian law. Professor Heintschel von Heinegg is a widely published author of articles and books on public international law, in particular international humanitarian law and European and German constitutional laws. For more detailed information, see https://www.rewi.europa-uni.de/de/lehrstuhl/or/voelkerrecht/index.html.

"Left of Splash" Legal Issues Related to the Use of Force to Counter Mining in the Strait of Hormuz

Sean P. Henseler

Abstract

Since late 2011, Iranian officials on more than one occasion have suggested that Iran would consider "closing" the Strait of Hormuz (SOH) in response to economic sanctions or an attack on its nuclear facilities. Moreover, many experts believe that in the event of an armed conflict, naval mining would likely be part of an Iranian anti-access, area denial (A2AD) strategy. As a result, policy makers and military commanders must consider options required to maintain freedom of navigation (FON) through this vital chokepoint. A thorough understanding of the legal issues related to mining is essential to formulating courses of action that will be perceived as legitimate. This article addresses the most significant legal issues and reaches three conclusions for consideration by decision makers during course of action development. Firstly, nations can lawfully conduct intelligence, surveillance, and reconnaissance (ISR); maintain a "fires" presence; and conduct mine warfare information-gathering activities in the SOH during peacetime. Secondly, nations may use proportionate force against assets about to mine, or in the act of mining, the SOH either in self-defense or to ensure the freedom of maritime commerce depending on the circumstances. Lastly, nations may use proportionate force in self-defense to protect assets engaged in mine hunting and sweeping, to possibly include attacking targets ashore that represent an imminent threat to the MCM forces.

S. P. Henseler (✉)
United States Naval War College, Newport, RI, USA
e-mail: sean.henseler@usnwc.edu

This is a U.S. government work and its text is not subject to copyright protection in the United States; however, its text may be subject to foreign copyright protection 2018
J. Schildknecht et al. (eds.), *Operational Law in International Straits and Current Maritime Security Challenges*, Operational Maritime Law 1,
https://doi.org/10.1007/978-3-319-72718-9_3

39

1   Foreword by Rear Admiral (Ret.). Kenneth M. Perry, U.S. Navy, Former Vice Commander of Naval Mine and Anti-Submarine Warfare Command, and Commander International Mine Countermeasure Task Force, U.S. 5th Fleet

The US Navy has stepped up fleet readiness, capability, and investments against maritime mines. The 2012 International Mine Counter Measures Exercise (IMCMEX 12) hosted by US Naval Forces Central Command saw over 30 countries participate in a fruitful symposium in Bahrain and successful at-sea maneuvers across 1000 miles of the Gulf region. Navies and nations from every continent came together to strengthen relationships, improve understanding of mine-countermeasure capabilities, and harvest ideas about international MCM interoperability. The engagement proved fertile.

Sparked by informative presentations from a range of experts from international navies, industry, and academia, senior naval commanders at IMCMEX engaged candidly on how navies can work together to protect the global maritime commons from a persistent mine threat. Among the symposium speakers was Professor Sean Henseler from the US Naval War College, who presented an insightful history of international legal conventions and thoughts on how nations might choose to act in defending against mining in international straits. Consistent with the framework of IMCMEX, Professor Henseler's briefing in Bahrain focused not on any one chokepoint or country but rather on providing a perspective on mining and international law.

In his chapter that follows, Professor Henseler focuses on the Strait of Hormuz. Perhaps no point on the world's oceans exemplifies "Strategic Maritime Crossroads" more directly than this vital chokepoint, the centerpiece of a region whose geography, politics, history, and resources influence world events and the global economy. Nations on every continent rely on the steady flow of energy and commerce from the Gulf to fuel their economic engines, while nations in the Gulf region rely on steady inflows through the Strait for a variety of their needs. Hormuz is a "two-way strait," and a busy one.

Defending freedom of navigation is unique to the global maritime commons. There is no global terrestrial commons, no international isthmus. Professor Henseler's article raises questions regarding the use of force to counter mining in this domain. Used thoughtfully, his article can promote discussion among commanders and policy makers. Rather than constrain the operating envelope for naval forces, the questions posed in Professor Henseler's article should prompt examination of rules of engagement (ROE) and policy to make sure operating forces have the right authorities to effectively deter, prevent, and respond to mining and help the lawyers "get to yes" for their operational bosses.

We are reminded of the historical cost of mines in world wars of the last century, in conflicts of the past generation, and in modern irregular warfare. We have had a century of tough lessons about recognizing the threat of mines too late—after mines are in the water—from Gallipoli in World War I to the US-led coalition in DESERT

STORM. Since the end of World War II, mines have damaged or sunk four times more US Navy ships than torpedoes and missiles and all other means of attack. Our challenge is to maintain the momentum we have gained in recognizing the relevance of countermine operations to develop policies and ROE that enable naval forces to deter and prevent enemy mining activity in defense of strategic access in vital maritime areas. Professor Henseler's legal questions are part of the conversation to maintain that momentum.

2   Could a Nation Maintain a Persistent MCM Presence in the SOH?

Yes. In order to effectively counter threats before mines are emplaced, or "left of splash," commanders must maintain a persistent ISR and fires presence. However, because the SOH is an international strait, ships and aircraft are somewhat restricted in their freedom of action. Units must proceed without delay, refrain from any threat or use of force against states bordering the strait, and refrain from any activities other than those incident to their normal modes of continuous and expeditious transit.[1] However, units may take steps to ensure self-defense, to include using off-board sensors (e.g., UUVs, UAVs, USVs) to collect indications and warning of hostile intent. Additionally, warships can launch and recover aircraft, and submarines can transit submerged. While merchant ships must respect properly designated sea lanes and the two traffic separation schemes in the SOH and its approaches, warships and government auxiliaries are not required to comply with them.[2] For military vessels and aircraft, the right of unimpeded transit passage exists "shoreline to shoreline."

Despite operational restrictions, commanders are privileged under international law to use a combination of transiting manned and unmanned air, surface, and subsurface assets to establish a desired level of presence. Additionally, a coastal nation bordering an international strait, such as Oman, could allow surface vessels to conduct operations in its TTS during peacetime and/or aircraft to loiter indefinitely in its airspace, to include above its territorial seas (TTS) in the SOH, provided they do not infringe on the transit passage rights of other vessels and aircraft. Finally, while military vessels possessing the capability to gather MW-related environmental information must transit continuously and expeditiously (vice loitering and conducting operations), they may do so from shoreline to shoreline.

---

[1]UNCLOS (1982), Art. 39.
[2]Commander's Handbook (2007), Para 2.5.3.1.

3   Could Iran Lawfully Mine Its TTS?

Yes, for national security purposes.[3] Pursuant to the United Nations Convention on the Law of the Sea (UNCLOS), a nation's TTS may extend 12 nautical miles (nm) from that nation's baseline, typically the low water line along the coast.[4] However, Iran has established a "straight baseline" system pursuant to its interpretation of UNCLOS, which several nations view as excessive.[5] Because Iran's straight baseline extends its internal waters and TTS, many nations would dispute how far out Iran could lawfully sow mines during peacetime.[6] Complicating matters, there are three islands claimed by both Iran and the United Arab Emirates in the vicinity of the Western Traffic Separation Scheme (WTSS). Iran has asserted that each island has a 12 nm TTS. The result is an excessive maritime claim where nearly the entire WTSS falls within Iranian-claimed TTS.

If Iran were to mine its claimed TTS with *armed* mines, it would be obligated to provide international notification because other nations possess the right of innocent passage through Iranian TTS.[7] Since the right of innocent passage can only be suspended temporarily, Iran would have to remove or render harmless its mines as soon as the security threat that prompted their emplacement was terminated.[8] However, if Iran were to use *controlled mines* (mines not yet armed), it would not be subject to either notification or removal requirements.[9] If Iran were to use floating mines, they must be directed against a military objective and become harmless within an hour of loss of control over them.[10]

4   Could Iran Lawfully Mine the SOH?

No. During peacetime, coastal nations may not "impede" the right of transit passage and thus may not emplace *armed* mines in an international strait.[11] While some have suggested that a nation could sow *controlled* mines in an international strait during peacetime, because the presence of controlled mines in the SOH would likely be discovered and impede shipping, the stronger position is that Iran could not sow controlled mines either.[12] Once an armed conflict begins, nations can lawfully mine

---

[3]Commander's Handbook (2007), Para. 9.2.2.

[4]UNCLOS (1982), Art. 5.

[5]*Ibid.* art. 7. *See also* Roach and Smith (2012), p. 89.

[6]On November 1, 2012 Iran fired warning shots at a U.S. MQ1 Predator Drone flying 16 nm from the Iranian coastline asserting that it had entered Iranian airspace over its claimed TTS, see New York Times (2012).

[7]Commander's Handbook (2007), Para. 9.2.2.

[8]*Ibid.*

[9]*Ibid.*

[10]See San Remo Manual, Art. 82.

[11]Commander's Handbook (2007), Para. 9.2.2.

[12]Heintschel von Heinegg (1994).

international straits but only if "safe and convenient alternative routes are provided."[13] However, assuming Iran's objective was to "close" the SOH, it would be impossible to meet this requirement because the SOH is the only way into and out of the Gulf.

5   Is Iranian Mining "An Act of War?"

Not always. Because a nation can lawfully mine its TTS during peacetime, assertions that any Iranian mining constitutes an "act of war" are legally inaccurate.[14] Given its excessive claims and the ambiguity of the law, Iran has several options to justify naval mining. As indicated earlier, the WTSS, which must be used by merchant ships, traverses Iranian-claimed TTS. Iran could mine the WTSS and suggest that ships have an alternate route to the south. Iran could also sow controlled mines in its TTS bordering the Eastern TSS asserting that vessels have a "safe and convenient route" on the Omani side or could mine its claimed TTS near the approaches to the SOH outside the Arabian Gulf. An Iranian justification for each scenario, that its national security trumps the mere impingement of maritime commerce, might be viewed by some as legitimate. As such, military commanders and policy makers must arrive at a mutual understanding of what would constitute *unlawful* Iranian mining before addressing if, when, where, and how force would be used to counter it.

6   Are There Any Rules Concerning Responses to Unlawful Mining?

Yes, but they are not "hard and fast." Nations can use force either in self-defense or in accordance with a United Nations Security Council Resolution (UNSCR). Per Article 51 of the UN Charter, nations possess an inherent right of individual and collective self-defense if an armed attack occurs.[15] Included is the right to act in anticipatory self-defense when an attack is imminent and no reasonable choice of peaceful means is available.[16]

---

[13]San Remo Manual (1995), Art. 89.

[14]Capaccio (2012): The U.S. Navy would move to stop any Iranian attempt to lay mines in the Strait of Hormuz or Persian Gulf as an "act of war" the international community wouldn't tolerate, the U.S. Navy's top Gulf commander said. "The laying of mines in international waters is an act of war," Admiral Fox said today. "We would, under the direction of the national leadership, prevent that from happening. We always have the right and obligation of self-defense and this falls in 'self-defense.' See also Fox News (2008): "U.S. Navy Commander Warns Iran: Don't Try Closing Gulf Oil Passageway".

[15]Charter of the United Nations (1945), Art. 51.

[16]Commander's Handbook (2007), Para. 4.4.3.1.

The International Court of Justice (ICJ) has, to some extent, addressed the issue of when mining might be considered an "attack" and what types of countermeasures would be lawful in response.[17] While ICJ decisions are not binding, a policy that would authorize the use of force "left of splash" would likely be influenced by them. Considerations related to naval mining gleaned from ICJ decisions include the following:

(1) A coastal State has no right to prohibit passage through an international strait in peacetime and the right of "freedom of maritime communication" ought to receive preference over any right that a nation might have to deny passage through an international strait.[18]

(2) If the right of access to ports is hindered by mines, freedom of maritime communications is infringed.[19]

(3) Elementary considerations of humanity are more exacting in peacetime than in war.[20]

(4) A mine strike that damages a single military or merchant vessel *might* be sufficient to trigger a nation's right of self-defense.[21]

(5) For a mine strike to be considered an armed attack a nation must specifically intend to harm another nation's vessel.[22] (Of note, many commentators disagree with this ICJ position).

(6) A nation must be able to attribute responsibility before it can act in self-defense.[23]

(7) Actions in self-defense must be necessary and proportionate and don't necessarily have to occur during the attack or in the minutes after the attack.[24]

(8) In determining what constitutes necessary and proportionate, the nature of the target upon which force is used must be considered (e.g., it must be a legitimate military target).[25]

(9) For a nation to exercise collective self-defense, a victim state must declare itself attacked and request assistance.[26]

(10) "Scale" and "effects" are critical elements in determining whether or not an action rises to the level of an armed attack.[27]

---

[17] See Corfu Channel Case (1949), Nicaragua Case (1986) and Oil Platforms case (2003).

[18] Stephens and Fitzpatrick (1999).

[19] Nicaragua Case (1986), Para. 253.

[20] Corfu Channel Case (1949), p. 22.

[21] Oil Platforms case (2003), paras. 64, 72. *See also* von Carlowitz (2005), p. 86.

[22] *Ibid.*, at Para. 64.

[23] *Ibid.*, at Paras. 51, 60–64.

[24] *Ibid.*, at Paras. 73–77.

[25] *Ibid.*, at Para. 73–77.

[26] Nicaragua Case (1986), Para. 199 and Oil Platforms case (2003), Para. 51.

[27] *Ibid.*, at Para. 195.

The ICJ specifically examined the U.S.'s use of force when it launched attacks in self-defense against Iranian oil platforms, naval vessels, and aircraft 4 days after the *USS Samuel B. Roberts* struck a mine in the Arabian Gulf in 1988.[28] The court found that the U.S.'s response was unnecessary because it was not convinced that Iran sowed the mine.[29] Since only one ship was hit and there was no loss of life, the court also found the U.S.'s reaction disproportionate.[30] However, the court did not suggest that the use of force in self-defense was unlawful because 4 days had elapsed between the mine strike and the reaction. Despite the court's ruling in 2003, world reaction in 1988 was favorable.

Another example regarding the use of force against a minelaying vessel also occurred during the Iran–Iraq "Tanker War." On September 21, 1987, the *Iran Ajr* was observed by U.S. helicopters laying mines at night in a channel used regularly by U.S. ships in the central Gulf. U.S. forces seized the Iranian vessel and subsequently destroyed it so it could no longer threaten U.S. and neutral vessels.[31] Nine armed Iranian-made mines were aboard, and charts found helped the Navy locate and disarm nine additional mines. In accordance with Article 51 of the Charter, on September 22, the U.S. notified the Security Council that it had acted in self-defense. The U.S. noted that it had previously informed the Iranian government on three occasions that it would take appropriate defensive measures against such provocative actions, which present an immediate risk to all ships, including those of the United States.[32] Iran did not seek a remedy for the sinking of the *Iran Ajar*, and the international response at the time was favorable.

The fact that the international community viewed both the U.S.'s reactions to Iranian minelaying in the Gulf as legitimate is important because if state practice attains a degree of regularity, and is accompanied by the general conviction among nations that behavior in conformity with that practice is obligatory, it then becomes customary international law binding on all nations.[33]

7   Could a Nation Use Force If Mines Are Emplaced Directly in the Path of a Vessel?

Yes. If a state or non-state actor was to sow a mine in the path of a military or merchant vessel, then it would be fair to characterize the act as an "armed attack" such that the victim nation would be justified acting in self-defense. The U.S. defines proportionate force as that amount of force that is limited in intensity, duration, and

---

[28]Oil Platforms case (2003).

[29]*Ibid.*, at Paras. 73–77.

[30]*Ibid.*

[31]Oil Platforms case (2003), Preliminary Objection Submitted by the United States of America, Dec. 16, 1993, p. 15.

[32]*Ibid.* at 16.

[33]Commander's Handbook (2007), Para. 5.5.1.

scope reasonably required to counter an attack or threat of attack and to ensure the continued safety of U.S. forces.[34] If a minelaying asset were to sow a mine directly in the path of another nation's military or merchant vessel and the other nation characterized the act as an armed attack, then it could request assistance in collective self-defense.

8   Could a Nation Use Force After a Mine Strike When the Mine Was Not Emplaced "Directly in the Path" of a Transiting Vessel?

Maybe. If the minelaying was attributable, then the nation whose vessel was damaged could assert that an armed attack occurred and might be justified in using necessary and proportionate measures in self-defense against a legitimate military target. Moreover, the victim nation could request assistance in collective self-defense.

9   During Peacetime, Could a Nation Use Force to Counter Mining in Sea Lanes Leading Toward the SOH and Its Approaches?

Not if a safe, alternative route exists. During peacetime, a nation can place controlled mines in international waters but only if required by "the most demanding requirements of individual or collective self-defense" and the mines "do not reasonably interfere with other lawful uses of the oceans."[35] While some dispute this U.S. position, it nonetheless opens the door to justifying mining international waters.[36] Because controlled mines do not constitute a hazard to navigation, international notice of their emplacement is not required.[37] As such, during peacetime, a nation could not use force to counter an Iranian minelayer about to, or in the act of emplacing, mines in a sea lane where a safe, alternative route exists. Commanders and policy makers would be wise to consider if there are any sea lanes in international waters, outside the SOH and its approaches, which, if mined, would fail to leave a safe, alternative route.

---

[34]*Ibid.*, at Para. 4.4.3.

[35]*Ibid.*, at Para. 9.2.2.

[36]Heintschel von Heinegg (1994), p. 76.

[37]Commander's Handbook (2007), Para. 9.2.2.

10   During Peacetime, Could Nations Use Force Against Minelaying Assets "Left of Splash" or "In the Act of" Mining the SOH or Its Approaches?

Yes, but not in self-defense. Given these circumstances, it would be difficult to justify using force in self-defense because the act of mining the SOH, while unlawful, would not constitute a direct attack on any state.

However, *nations should be able to use force left of splash or against assets in the act of unlawfully laying mines in the SOH or its approaches to ensure the freedom of maritime communications* for the following reasons:

(1) Nations cannot prohibit passage through an international strait in time of peace,

(2) The right of freedom of maritime communications must receive preference over any right of a coastal nation to deny passage through an international strait,

(3) Mining the SOH would deny warships and merchant ships access to ports in the Gulf, thus infringing on freedom of maritime communications,

(4) Mining a frequently trafficked international strait would likely cause significant damage and loss of innocent civilian life,

(5) There is no other safe or alternative route for shipping into or out of the Gulf, and

(6) The significant detrimental "effect" on the world economy that would result by waiting for the unlawful act to be committed *before* taking action would be too costly.

Using force *solely* to ensure the freedom of maritime communications would establish a novel precedent. Some would characterize such a use of force as either preemptive or preventive self-defense. Any use of force outside the traditional Article 51/UNSCR construct would be heavily scrutinized, and nations must be judicious when establishing precedent. Yet, in the wake of the 9/11 terrorist acts, the U.S. established precedent when it declared, in part based on the scale of the effects, that an armed attack occurred. The international response to the U.S. pronouncement was overwhelmingly favorable. Similarly, a proportionate use of force to keep the SOH open in order to prevent the devastating effect on the world economy would likely be well received by the international community, just as U.S. actions against Iranian minelayers were in the 1980s. Even Iran has been prepared to recognize that the uninterrupted flow of maritime commerce is a vital national security interest of the U.S. and presumably other similarly situated nations that rely on Gulf oil.[38]

This proposal is a very narrow exception to the traditional use of force construct. While there are other critical international strait "chokepoints" around the world,

---

[38]Oil Platforms case (2003), Para. 73.

there are safe, alternative (albeit more expensive) routes around nearly all of them. As such, it would be exceedingly difficult to meet all six proposed criteria to use force to ensure the freedom of maritime communications. Moreover, a nation could not use force unless there was an imminent threat of mining. Policy makers and commanders would need to carefully consider who in the chain of command should have the authority to make this determination.

11   Could Nations Use Force If Iran Did Mine the SOH or Its Approaches?

If forces were unable to act "left of splash" or "during the act" and Iran did mine the SOH, then any nation would be authorized to engage in minesweeping and hunting.[39] Nations could also maintain a persistent ISR and fires presence to ensure adequate self-defense of MCM assets for the following reasons. Firstly, the collective right to ensure the freedom of communications would trump the requirement that MCM assets proceed continuously and expeditiously. Secondly, minesweeping and hunting are the types of proportionate countermeasures envisioned by the ICJ to redress a knowing violation of international law that directly interferes with other nation's right to engage in maritime communications.[40] Lastly, if the right of inherent self-defense is to have any meaning in the narrow confines of the SOH, where MCM assets would be vulnerable to short or no-notice attacks, then nations ought to have the right to operate as required to provide adequate self-defense.

Commanders prefer to establish maritime and air superiority to protect relatively defenseless MCM assets. While the law allows forces to operate in the SOH as indicated above, it does not allow a nation to attack targets at sea and ashore *before* they represent an imminent threat. Determining what constitutes an imminent threat requires consideration of all relevant facts and circumstances at the time. For example, some might argue that coastal defense cruise missile sites that can fire without warning are by their very nature and location imminent threats. Commanders would be wise to discuss what might constitute an imminent threat, as well as who in the chain of command would be authorized to make such a determination.

References

Capaccio T (2012) U.S. would bock Iran from mining hormuz strait, Commander Says, Bloomberg, 12 February 2012. http://www.bloomberg.com/news/2012-02-12/u-s-would-block-iran-from-mining-hormuz-strait-commander-says.html. Accessed 5 Sept 2017
Charter of the United Nations (1945) http://www.un.org/en/charter-united-nations/. Accessed 5 Sept 2017

---

[39]Heintschel von Heinegg (1994), pp. 71–73.
[40]Stephens and Fitzpatrick (1999), p. 576.

Commander's Handbook (2007) The Commander's Handbook on the Law of Naval Operation, NWP 1-14M, 7.3; http://www.jag.navy.mil/documents/NWP_1-14M_Commanders_Hand book.pdf. Accessed 15 Jun 2017

Corfu Channel Case (1949) International Court of Justice (ICJ), United Kingdom of Great Britain and Northern Ireland v. Albania, Judgment, April 9, 1949 and December 15, 1949. http://www.icj-cij.org/docket/index.php?p1=3&p2=3&case=1&p3=4. Accessed 15 Jun 2017

Fox News (2008) U.S. Navy Commander warns Iran: don't try closing Gulf Oil passageway, 2 July 2008. http://www.foxnews.com/story/2008/07/02/us-navy-commander-warns-iran-dont-try-closing-gulf-oil-passageway.html. Accessed 5 Sep 2017

Heintschel von Heinegg W (1994) The international law of mine warfare at sea. Israel Yearb Hum Rights 23:75

Nicaragua Case (1986) International Court of Justice (ICJ) Military and Paramilitary Activities (1986) (Nicaragua. v. U.S.), June 27, 1986, 25 I.L.M. 1023. http://www.icj-cij.org/files/case-related/70/070-19860627-JUD-01-00-EN.pdf. Accessed 5 SepT 2017

Oil Platforms case (2003) International Court of Justice (ICJ) (Islamic Republic of Iran v. United States of America, Judgment, ICJ Reports 2003 [hereinafter Oil Platforms]. http://www.icj-cij.org/en/case/90. Accessed 5 Sept 2017

New York Times (2012) Defense Minister Confirms Iran Fired on US Drone, by Erdbrink T and Gladstone E, 9 November 2012. http://www.nytimes.com/2012/11/10/world/middleeast/iran-confirms-drone-shooting-episode.html?mcubz=0. Accessed 5 Sept 2017

Roach JA, Smith RW (2012) Excessive maritime claims, 3rd edn. Nijhoff, Leiden

San Remo Manual (1995) In: Doswald-Beck J (ed) San Remo manual on international law applicable to armed conflicts at sea. University Press, Cambridge

Stephens DG, Fitzpatrick MD (1999) Legal aspects of contemporary naval mine warfare. Loy L A Int Comp Law Rev 21:573

UNCLOS (1982) United Nations Convention on the Law of the Sea, 1833 U.N.T.S. 397

von Carlowitz L (2005) The World Court in the oil platforms case, in Sicherheit und Frieden, (23. Jg) 2/2005

Sean P. Henseler Commander, JAGC, USN (Ret.) is the Director of Operations for the College of Maritime Operational Warfare and Professor at the Naval War College in Newport, Rhode Island. While serving on active duty initially as a Naval Intelligence Officer, and later as a Judge Advocate General, Henseler made multiple combat deployments to include Operation Desert Shield, Operation Desert Storm, Operation Southern Watch, Operation Enduring Freedom, and Operation Iraqi Freedom. He retired in 2009 as the Howard S. Levie Military Chair of Operational Law at the Naval War College and since that time has been a professor at the college where he teaches operational level of war concepts and frequently consults at Navy Fleet Headquarters. He holds degrees from the Catholic University of America's Columbus School of Law (J.D), Georgetown University (M.A. National Security Studies), the Naval War College (M.A. National Security Studies, President's Honor Graduate), and Babson College (B.S. Business Management).

International Straits: Peacetime Rights and Obligations

Uwe Althaus

Abstract

The modern concept of transit passage came into play when coastal states agreed in 1982 to extend their territorial seas to a maximum of 12 nm, thereby removing most of the high seas passages through international straits. Before 1982, the legal situation was quite clear. Military ships and aircraft transiting through a strait enjoyed the operational freedoms of the high seas corridor while being reduced to innocent passage rights and obligations in the territorial waters (TTW) of the riparian states.

At first glance, it seems that Art. 39 of the United Nations Convention on the Law of the Sea (UNCLOS 1982) precisely defines the obligations and duties of ships and aircraft exercising the right of transit passage. However, digging deeper into the matter, it becomes clear that many questions at the interface of legal and operational issues remain open until today. The reason for this might be that the interest of most seafaring states to explicitly identify and write down rights and duties of their military aircraft or vessels in an international strait is limited. This approach clearly offers more operational leeway but is problematic for commanding officers of warships (COs) and legal advisors as they remain, to a certain extent, unaware of the precise legal demands while engaged in transit passage. This chapter not only focusses on legal problems but proposes possible operational and policy approaches as well.

U. Althaus (✉)
Germany Navy Headquarters, Rostock, Germany
e-mail: uwealthaus@bundeswehr.org

J. Schildknecht et al. (eds.), *Operational Law in International Straits and Current Maritime Security Challenges*, Operational Maritime Law 1,
https://doi.org/10.1007/978-3-319-72718-9_4

1   Introduction[1]

The concept of transit passage is relatively new in the law of the sea. It came into play when coastal states agreed in 1982 to extend their territorial seas to a maximum of 12 nm, thereby removing most high seas passages through international straits.[2] Before 1982, the legal situation was quite clear. Military ships and aircraft transiting through a strait enjoyed the operational freedoms of the high seas corridor while being reduced to innocent passage rights and obligations in the territorial waters (TTW) of the neighbouring states.

Although it seems that Art. 39 UNCLOS accurately defines the obligations and duties of ships and aircraft exercising the right of transit passage, many questions at the interface of legal and operational issues remain open. This is also true for most of the Operational Law (OpLaw) manuals.[3] The reason for this is somewhat unclear. It may either be that there is no recognizable consensus among the states or that the ability or interest of most seafaring states to explicitly identify and write down rights and duties of their military aircraft or vessels in an international strait is limited. The latter clearly offers more operational leeway but is problematic for commanding officers of warships (COs) as they remain, to a certain extent, unaware of the legal situation or status while engaged in transit passage. The same holds true for legal advisers, who should be able to give advice on all operational questions linked to transit passage rights.

The following findings will try to state what duties and obligations are undisputed while at the same time illustrating the gaps arising from various operational questions that COs may encounter while exercising the right of transit passage. Finally, these findings will propose solutions that represent a compromise between the necessary legal clarity and a sufficient degree of operational leeway that will allow COs to take all appropriate measures to ensure a safe, continuous and expeditious transit passage.

---

[1]This chapter exclusively deals with the rights and obligations of warships and military aircraft in an international strait during peacetime.

[2]The extension of the territorial to 12 nm has been codified with the adoption of *United Nations Convention on the law of the Sea* in 1982 UNCLOS (1982) making the rights and obligation within the territorial sea mandatory for all parties to the convention. The conference was convened in 1973. By then 66 had already claimed a 12 nm territorial sea limit, however without any right for recognition by the maritime major powers, *cf.* UN Division for Ocean Affairs and the Law of the Sea (1998).

[3]E.g. German Commander's Handbook (2002) and U.S. Commander's Handbook (2007).

2   The True Nature of the Right of Transit Passage

> In international straits, all military operations that are not in accordance with the right of innocent passage are prohibited unless they are necessary for a safe, continuous and expeditious transit.

As Art. 38 (2) UNCLOS[4] explicitly mentions the right of freedom of navigation and overflight. It may seem that the right of transit passage is derived from the regime of freedom of navigation on the high seas, only with due regard being paid to the sovereign rights of the adjacent states. However, the opposite is true: the right of transit passage must still be seen as an exceptional international right in sovereign foreign TTW, only with specific permissions that are strictly related to the needs of the conduct of the passage.[5] Article 39 UNCLOS states the duty of military aircraft and warships to refrain from activities other than those *incidental* to their normal mode of continuous and expeditious transit.

This suggests that it is not the normal mode of, e.g., a warship that is relevant—which is to carry out all kinds of military operations—but rather what a warship is required to do in order to ensure a safe, continuous and expeditious passage through the straits.

Though not mentioned in Art. 39 UNCLOS, the condition of a 'safe' passage[6] is the core of the concept of transit passage for military ships and aircraft.[7]

Similar to innocent passage, all warships are entitled to use force in self-defence. However, in innocent passage, most precautionary measures such as the training of artillery, the lowering of small boats for force protection, etc., are prohibited. Any threat stemming from inside the TTW can normally be avoided by simply not entering or leaving the TTW, thereby being able to have the entire spectrum of force protection measures available. The situation is completely different in an international strait that is overlapped by the TTW of neighbouring states. By nature, the TTW of the coastal states cannot be avoided, and the threat may be faced from

---

[4]The relevant part of Art. 38 (2) UNCLOS (1982) reads as follows: 'Transit passage means the exercise in accordance with this part of the freedom of navigation and overflight solely for the purpose of continuous and expeditious transit of the strait. . . .'.

[5]UNCLOS (1982) does not explain what activities could be incidental to their normal mode. Hence this part can be interpreted in various ways. George (2004), p. 27 considers 'an engagement in armed warfare' as one example of activities outside their normal mode.

[6]See Rule 30 of the San Remo Manual (1995): 'A Belligerents in transit passage . . . are permitted to take defensive measures *consistent with their security*, including launching and recovery of aircraft. . . .'

[7]*Cf.* German Commander's Handbook (2002), p. 85, highlights in its English version with regard to aircraft exercising the right of transit passage that 'Normal mode of transit means that all items of equipment which the aircraft is carrying and which are needed for the conduct of safe flight operations may be used'.

both sides of the strait. That is why the right to a safe journey is a highly important factor that accompanies the obligation to transit in a continuous and expeditious manner. Having said this, military operations that may be exercised on the high seas must not be carried out in transit passage if they do not meet the mentioned requirements.[8] Hence, the transit passage right is nothing more than an 'innocent passage right plus'.[9]

This is based on the following considerations: even though Art. 38(2) UNCLOS refers to the freedom of maritime navigation and the unimpeded right of overflight, Art. 39(1c) UNCLOS states that these rights may be exercised only within the context of a normal continuous and expeditious transit. If the authors of the UNCLOS had wanted to grant any ship passing through a strait the unlimited rights applying to the high seas, it would not have been necessary to refer to their normal mode of transit. Consequently, it would be more appropriate to call the right of transit passage an 'Innocent Passage plus' rather than a 'High Seas minus'. This argument is not negated by the fact that before territorial waters were widened to 12 nm, most straits also included a corridor where the rights of the high seas applied. It would be incorrect to conclude that the right of transit passage must be derived from the rights of the high seas as, prior to the widening, large parts of the straits were governed by the right of innocent passage only. Since the right of transit passage applies in the entire strait, this conclusion would basically mean that the right of the high seas—albeit with the known restrictions—would be in some form superimposed on the considerably more restrictive right of innocent passage. However, this would not constitute a balanced compromise between the claim to sovereignty of the relevant coastal states and the interests of the states operating ships in the strait.

Urgent operational requirements might force COs to depart from the principle stating that the rights of transit passage cease to exist where the strait is wider than 24 nautical miles. However, it must be stressed that such an exemption is not based on any explicit UNCLOS provision. There is no international treaty that provides a reliable definition of the geographical area of a strait in which the right of transit passage applies. A demarcation under customary law has not been established either. Likewise, it is evident for that very reason that appropriate borders or defined approaches or exit routes have not been marked on any nautical charts. Finally, it must be noted that the right of transit passage already represents an exception to the coastal states' claim to sovereignty and that extending this right to approaches and exit routes to/from the strait would even constitute a second exception. Against this backdrop, any further 'operational exemption' should be used extremely sparingly as there is always the risk that coastal states will not recognise the right of transit

---

[8]During the Third United Nations Conference on the Law of the Sea the head of the U.S. delegation John R. Stevenson stated with regard to an envisaged transit passage regime: 'The right is a narrow one—merely one of transiting the straits, not of conducting any other activities'; *see* Robertson (1979), p. 809.

[9]*Cf.* Treves (1991), pp. 945–950, who assesses the doctrine of transit passage as an exception to the principle of coastal state sovereignty over the territorial sea.

passage outside the area overlapped by the relevant coastal waters. This may drive states to feel compelled to stage diplomatic protests or even take military countermeasures.

3   Where to Pass through

> The right of transit passage applies throughout the strait. There is no obligation for warships including submarines or military aircraft to use designated transit corridors or Traffic Separation Schemes. Nor is there an obligation to complete the transit before conducting a turning maneuver.

The issue of transit passage lanes was discussed during the NATO Centre of Excellence for Operations in Confined and Shallow Waters (COE CSW) Istanbul Syndicate in 2013.[10] During the Syndicate, it was the general understanding among the members of the Syndicate (hereinafter Members) that these lanes were not necessarily the same as Traffic Separation Schemes (TSS) as the transit passage regime applies throughout the strait (requiring continuous and expeditious passage), while TSS often do not.

Furthermore, the obligation to use TSS may not apply to sovereign military ships; they may only be obliged to pay due regard to other traffic in the strait. However, warships and other sovereign vessels will normally comply with IMO-approved routing measures unless operational considerations warrant a deviation.[11] This point of view is especially beneficial for submerged transits of submarines that, in a TSS, would have difficulties to detect contacts overtaking from abaft abeam due to the sound and cavitation produced by their own propulsion systems. Likewise, these contacts change position much more slowly on the sonar screen than those coming from ahead, which makes it hard to plot them.

Are military ships and aircraft in transit passage authorised to come as close to the internal waters of the neighbouring states of a strait as the nautical circumstances (especially water depths) permit? Does this 'coast-to-coast approach' comply with the requirements of a continuous and expeditious transit?

---

[10] As a cooperative effort between the Combined Joint Operations from the Sea Centre of Excellence in Norfolk, U.S.A., the NATO Centre of Excellence for Operations in Confined and Shallow Waters (COE CSW) in Kiel, Germany, and the Maritime Security Centre of Excellence in Marmaris, Turkey, an international workshop on Maritime Situational Awareness was held in Istanbul, Turkey, from 9 to 11 October 2013. A legal syndicate (hereinafter Syndicate), consisting of legal advisors from Australia, France, Germany, New Zealand, Turkey and the United Kingdom, was an integral component of this workshop. The members of the legal syndicate focussed on the topic of international straits and examined legal issues that might be of operational relevance to the maritime nations in current and future maritime operations.

[11] U.S. Commander's Handbook (2007), pp. 2–6, 2.5.3.1.

It is a basic rule that the right of transit passage applies throughout the strait.[12] However, it is not sufficiently explicit to justify any type of manoeuvring during the passage through a strait.

It would certainly be too restrictive to order a CO to use a Traffic Separation Scheme at all times or at least to use or even stay near the equidistant line between the neighbouring states.

Any manoeuvring that results from the need for effective force protection to ensure a safe passage of the ship will in any case fulfil the criteria of a continuous and expeditious passage.[13]

Other well-founded operational reasons may be admissible, but the sovereign rights of the adjacent states must be taken into consideration.

However, due to potential political ramifications, COs should generally be advised to use a defined corridor that will prevent their actions from being perceived as a provocative act or even as a breach of sovereignty of a coastal state.

States should identify a corridor that will give COs sufficient operational leeway to carry out necessary FP measures and at the same time prevent them from being accused by neighbouring states of having violated transit passage rights (unless these states have excessive claims).

The right of transit passage must be exercised with the aim to travel from one part of the high seas or EEZ to another part of the high seas or EEZ. That, however, means neither that the strait cannot be passed multiple times nor that the transit has to be completed, i.e. that the entire strait has to be passed, before a turning manoeuvre may be performed. Turning manoeuvres may be conducted in the strait at all times. It is irrelevant at which point of the transit passage that the turning manoeuvre is performed. It is always possible that operational necessity (e.g., force protection) or an emergency may require a turning manoeuvre. However, it must be ensured that turning manoeuvres are not performed too often or in such a way that they constitute or appear to constitute patrol activities in the sea area concerned. This is because patrol activities cannot be reconciled with the obligation to conduct an expeditious and continuous passage through a strait and are thus prohibited without the coastal state's consent. Yet there are no established indicators or definitions stating from what point on a certain manoeuvre constitutes a patrol activity. Consequently, this presents another grey area under international law that provides some leeway for operators and constitutes in the same time a challenge for legal advisors.

---

[12] *Cf.* U.S. Commander's Handbook (2007), pp. 2–6, 2.5.3.1 ('shoreline-to-shoreline').

[13] *See supra* 1.2.

4   Territorial Scope of the Right of Transit Passage

> As long as no universally recognized demarcation of the beginning and end of an international strait exists, the right of transit passage should only be exercised in that portion of the sea that is overlapped by the TTW of the neighbouring states unless compelling operational consideration dictate the use of transit rights in the approach/exit routes to or from the international strait.

The most appropriate route to take into a strait was discussed at the Istanbul Syndicate,[14] with some of the Members arguing that any unit should remain in the high seas as long as possible before entering the overlapping part of the strait. Other Members said that it was already possible to transit through territorial waters at an earlier stage.

No universally valid definition exists as to where the right of transit passage through a strait commences or ends.[15] There is only legal certainty in the area where the territorial waters of the neighbouring states overlap.

During the Syndicate, there was a discussion of the term 'approaches', a term from the *U.S. Commander's Handbook*[16]: This manual introduces the concept of approaches to an international strait where transit passage rights apply as well. According to the manual, the right of transit passage starts in the approaches to the strait, i.e. in foreign TTW but still outside the overlapping part of the strait.[17] However, in this handbook, it remains unclear where the approaches exactly commence. In addition, the group discussed the term 'approaches' and debated if the concept was only espoused by the U.S.[18] or whether it represents customary international law.

No consensus was achieved among the Members, apart from the fact that the concept of approaches generally was not yet considered to represent customary international law.

It could be argued that the concept of approaches completely blurs the borders between innocent and transit passage. Transit passage is a very limited extension of the right of innocent passage. As an exception, it should be sufficiently defined; otherwise, it will become the rule rather than the exception. The unconditioned statement saying that transit passage may be applied in approaches[19] does not meet the requirement of an exceptional rule and in this way cannot have a basis in

---

[14]*See supra* at footnote 11.

[15]Langdon (2015), p. 209.

[16]*See supra* at footnote 12.

[17]See also Kraska (2013), p. 230 who states as one example the Strait of Hormuz.

[18]This concept is also reflected in the German Commander's Handbook (2002), p. 57.

[19]*See supra* at footnote 12; Kraska (2013), p. 229 and Roach and Smith (2012), p. 272.

international law. In general, this concept does not seem to be widely accepted by seafaring nations as there is not even a vague definition given by the U.S. as to where approaches commence or end.

International law is by nature always open to interpretations driven by various considerations. However, applying the concept of transit passage without any definition as to where the rights linked to it may be exercised poses an unacceptable legal risk to COs or, even worse, to military ships or aircraft that might be subject to military countermeasures.

As long as no recognised demarcation of an international strait is developed, transit passage rights should only be exercised in that portion of the sea that is overlapped by the TTW of the neighbouring states.[20]

Interpretations provided in relevant literature that extend the right of transit passage to the approaches and exits to/from the strait only do so based on operational considerations, especially on an effective protection of the transiting units.[21] However, this argument is exclusively based on operational considerations and is not properly reflected in international law as such. Only in cases where clear indications exist that the respective riparian state itself breaches international law; e.g., by allowing attacks carried out by armed groups from its shoreline on passing warships, the application of the concept of the 'approaches' may be legally justified as a proportionate countermeasure by the injured flag state.[22] If the riparian state does not commit wrongful acts, COs are advised to follow the rights and obligations of the regime of innocent passage until they reach the overlapping section of the strait.

However, there may exist compelling operational considerations (e.g., necessary force protection measures) outside the overlapped portion of the international strait that would from an operational standpoint require the use of transit passage rights. As a pure matter of policy and because no exact demarcation of an international strait exists, COs may exercise transit passage rights and should claim when challenged the use of this right in order to avoid the perception of an abuse of transit passage rights. The use of this grey area as a 'policy' right should be exceptional and used with extreme restraint as it bears the danger of an unwanted tension between the neighbouring state and the flag state of the passing vessel. Furthermore, such a behavior could undermine the function of international law that is to ensure or preserve peaceful relations among equal states.

In any case, the problem of an exact demarcation between the right of innocent and transit passage remains unsolved. This makes it difficult, if not impossible, for

---

[20]The line where the width of the strait exceeds 24 nautical miles.

[21]E.g. Langdon (2015), p. 209 argues that, if transit passage rights end as soon as the width of a strait exceeds 24 nautical miles, the transiting ship would be forced to adopt 'innocent passage mode' at that point or to plan its track through the exact point at which the median line splits into the 'V'. For him this requirement would be impractical or even dangerous because it would create a choke point through which many transiting vessels would have to pass in both directions.

[22]ILC (2001), Art.49; the injured state must in any case refrain from the threat or the use of force (Art. 50), Art. 39 b UNCLOS (1982) (Duties of ships and aircraft during transit passage).

neighbouring states to unequivocally identify whether a vessel may use transit passage or innocent passage rights.

5   Duty to Render Assistance

> Assistance in extremis during transit passage is permitted if the neighbouring states are not able to render assistance in time even if the requirement of a continuous and expeditious transit of a strait is not met.
>
> The duty to render assistance is not limited to the perils of the sea but also applies to evidently illegal attacks stemming from private ships.[23]

During the COE CSW Search and Rescue/Assistance at Sea Legal Workshop in Annapolis in 2015, there was a discussion[24] about the legality of a warship entering TTW and using force in *prima facie* contravening the restrictions imposed by the regime of innocent passage in extreme circumstances.

Article 98 UNCLOS imposes a general duty to render assistance at sea,[25] but some Members presented the legal academic argument[26] that this duty is limited to the high seas only.

The counterargument brought forward by the majority of the Members was that the duty to render assistance in TTW represents customary international law. Article

---

[23]The statement is restricted to private ships as warships or state vessels may be entitled to carry out law enforcement operations in their TTW. These vessels therefore enjoy the presumption of legality.

[24]The NATO COE CSW Search and Rescue/Assistance at Sea Legal Workshop held at the Naval Academy in Annapolis 6–10 April 2015 was attended by approximately 26 participants (hereinafter Members) from Germany, Denmark, Canada, the Netherlands, Nigeria, the United Kingdom, Austria, and the USA (of both the US Navy and the US Coast Guard). The workshop focussed on the right and the duty of warships or government vessels to conduct sea rescue and what is called 'assistance entry' missions, i.e. the rendering of assistance in territorial waters without the consent of the coastal state concerned. The workshop was rounded off by a discussion panel held at the U.S. DoD (Pentagon), Department of International Law. The workshop was unclassified; Chatham House Rule applied.

[25]Art. 98 (1) UNCLOS (1982) states that 'Each state shall require the master of a ship flying its flag to render assistance to any person found at sea in danger of being lost'.

[26]The reason given is that Art. 98 UNCLOS (1982) is contained in Part VII 'High Seas'. Yet its area of application remains disputed as all other articles of Part VII include an explicit reference to the high seas. Since this does not apply to Art. 98 UNCLOS (1982), which only states the general term 'at sea', Art. 98 UNCLOS (1982) may be interpreted as to be also applicable to territorial waters. Ultimately, this academic dispute may be left unsettled as the right of rendering assistance in territorial waters is recognised under customary law in those cases in which the relevant coastal state is unable to render assistance itself. For more information, *see* U.S. DoD (2010), p. 4 d.

18 (2) UNCLOS supports this argument, stating that innocent passage includes 'rendering assistance to persons, ships or aircraft in danger or distress'.[27]

Other Members expressed the view that the provisions of Art. 98 UNCLOS could only be applied for natural disasters or collisions ('to render assistance to any person found at sea in danger of being lost') and not for criminal acts. It was argued that the provisions of the basic Somalia Security Council resolution[28] supported this view as the UN felt the need to specifically legislate entry into TTW, which implies that they felt it was not covered by UNCLOS or any other legislation. However, this argument is not conclusive as the Somalia UNSCR regarding the fight against piracy does not deal with the duty to render assistance. The UNSCR instead authorises military operations against piracy (or, more accurately, armed robbery), which comprise the pursuit of fleeing perpetrators and their subsequent detention within the TTW of Somalia.

Another argument brought forward by the majority of the Members was that any counteraction taken in the wake of an attack constituted a law enforcement operation and was therefore only allowed to be carried out by the respective agencies of the coastal states or with their consent.

With regard to this argument, it should be stressed that the duty to render assistance ends immediately when the attacking private ship no longer poses a threat, whereas law enforcement from a general understanding goes far beyond that. A law enforcement action would include prosecution and subsequent arrest of a potential perpetrator.

While this may support the view that the duty to render assistance generally applies in innocent passage, there could be some doubt with regard to transit passage. Article 39(1c) UNCLOS, which covers the transit passage regime, was highlighted by some Members who may have a more restrictive interpretation than that provided under Art. 18(2) UNCLOS.

Article 39(1) UNCLOS states:

> Ships and aircraft, while exercising the right of transit passage, shall:
> c. refrain from any activities other than those incident to their normal modes of continuous and expeditious transit unless rendered necessary by force majeure or by distress.

Article 39 UNCLOS seems to be more restrictive, by removing the provision of 'in danger' contained in Art. 18(2) UNCLOS. Again, this argument is not convincing for the following reason: it was already pointed out that the concept of transit passage is an extension of the right of innocent passage, meaning that additional measures for a safe passage may be taken. Transit passage does not restrict the rights that warships enjoy while exercising the right of innocent passage. Article 39 UNCLOS reflects this finding by leaving out the obvious already contained in

---

[27]However, invoking Art. 18 (2) UNCLOS (1982) requires that the vessel is already exercising its right of innocent passage and does not provide the authority to enter the TTW as such.

[28]UNSCR 1816 (2008) states in OP 7 a that 'states. . . may enter the territorial waters of Somalia for the purpose of repressing acts of piracy and armed robbery at sea . . .'.

Art. 18 (2) UNCLOS. Thus, Art. 39 UNCLOS ('unless rendered necessary by force majeure or by distress') must be conceived as referring to not only the relevant ship's own distress but also that of another ship.[29] It is not necessary to repeat this right in the provision on transit passage as it is already part of innocent passage. Lastly, it should be undisputed that persons on board ships or aircraft that have come under attack by private ships are in imminent danger of life or limb. As a consequence, it must be stated that rendering assistance in an overlapped strait does not lead to a ship losing its right of transit passage.[30]

6   The Problematic Notion of 'Normal Mode': How to Pass Through

> The use of sonar, radar and depth sounders for the purpose of a safe navigation through the international strait is permitted as it is part of the normal mode of warships or submarines. The same holds true for the launching and recovering of aircraft, formation steaming, submerged transit of submarines and other adequate force protection measures.

Once again, *normal mode of transit* is key in this context. It means that, other than in foreign TTW, submarines may transit while submerged and that surface warships may carry out formation steaming and launch/recover aircraft during transit passage through such waters. Although this statement can be found in the *U.S. Commander's Handbook* and the *German Commander's Handbook*,[31] it seems to be incomplete as they remain silent as to the purpose of such measures.[32]

With reference to finding No. 1, all additional rights exercised must strictly be incidental to a safe, continuous and expeditious passage. Therefore, all the afore-mentioned rights must serve that purpose; otherwise, there would be literally no difference between high seas freedoms and transit passage rights. As a consequence, the launching and recovering of aircraft or small boats (RHIBs) is only permitted for Force Protection/safety reasons or to guarantee a safe passage in terms of navigation.[33] It is prohibited to launch aircraft in order to carry out offensive military

---

[29]*Cf.* Art. 18 (2) UNCLOS (1982) 'for the purpose of rendering assistance to persons, ships or aircraft in danger or distress'.

[30]Langdon (2015), *ibid.*, pp. 207–208.

[31]U.S. Commander's Handbook (2007), pp. 2–6, 2.5.3.1 and German Commander's Handbook (2002), p. 58.

[32]The term 'purpose' does in no way mean that the right to transit is determined by flag, cargo, destination or the military mission of the transiting vessel or aircraft but is rather linked to activities necessary to ensure a safe, continuous and expeditious passage.

[33]Cf. UK Handbook (2007), pp. 2–8 that states 'surface warships may transit in a manner consistent with sound navigational practices and the security of the force, including formation steaming and the launching and of aircraft'. Footnote 14 at *ibid.* adds: 'The freedom to launch and recover

operations whether inside or outside the strait (or to support such operations). Warships are also allowed to take all measures required for a safe passage through the strait and to employ the appropriate means, such as navigational radar, sonar or formation steaming. Medical evacuation flights are permitted in emergency situations only as the duty to render assistance even applies in sea areas that are governed by the right of innocence passage.[34] Replenishment at sea (RAS) may be carried out only if it still meets the requirement of a continuous and expeditious transit.[35] This is the case only in situations that could not be foreseen before entering the strait. In normal circumstances, RAS operations should not take place within international straits. Transiting of a submerged submarine through a strait not only is part of the normal mode but even constitutes the normal mode incidental to transit passage. A surfaced submarine is more vulnerable as most submarines are not able to counter asymmetric attacks due to a lack of suitable weaponry and manoeuvrability. Therefore, submarines may transit submerged as this is necessary for force protection.

As mentioned before, military aircraft are allowed to take off and land during a transit passage for the above-stated purpose only. This finding is not impacted by the undisputed fact that all military aircraft have the right to fly through or over a strait regardless of the military mission they may conduct outside the international strait.[36] That is because the right of transit passage can, by nature, only govern an aircraft's behaviour during transit or, in other words, in the area where the transit passage rights apply. This is illustrated by the following example: when a carrier strike group that has not yet entered the strait launches fighter aircraft whose mission is to provide close air support after having left the strait, then these aircraft—despite their combat mission—enjoy the right of unimpeded passage through the international strait. What is important in this context is if the operations are conducted in the area where the regime of the strait does apply. Both the purpose and the military mission associated with the passage of the fighter aircraft or the carrier strike group are irrelevant. This, in turn, means that the coastal states must not impede or deny the right of passage just because they might politically disagree with the military mission of the unit or strike group. However, aircraft are not allowed to take off and land in

---

helicopters can greatly improve situational awareness when transiting narrow international straits in an asymmetric threat environment. While it is legally permissible to launch and recover aircraft during transit, consideration for navigational safety often calls for an aircraft to be launched just prior to a warship's transit of an international strait, for it to overfly the strait ahead of the force, and then to be recovered on board once the warship has cleared the international strait.'

[34] *See supra* footnote 27.

[35] In general, replenishment during a transit passage reduces a vessel's speed of advance without any compelling reason and is thus not reconcilable with the requirement of an expeditious transit. An exception might be made if circumstances that have not been foreseeable require a replenishment operation as the vessel otherwise would not be able to continue at all or at a reduced speed of advance only.

[36] During the Search and Rescue/Assistance at Sea Legal Workshop (*see supra* footnote 23), it was brought forward that the right of aircraft to take off and land during transit passage regardless of the purpose of the activity is based on the right of overflight as such.

the area where the right of passage applies, unless this is necessary to ensure a continuous, expeditious and, above all, safe passage. In the above example, this would clearly not be the case as the fighter aircraft are explicitly dispatched not to ensure a safe transit passage but to conduct operations in an area where the right of transit passage does not apply. Military manuals often include a note stating that the take-off and landing of aircraft, especially those that form part of carrier strike groups, are incidental to the 'normal mode' of carrier strike groups.[37] However, this note tends to overlook the fact that in a strait, the 'normal mode' refers to the aforementioned purpose of safe passage and cannot be abstractly defined without taking into account this context. This restrictive interpretation of the term 'normal mode' can be bypassed in an operationally effective manner by deploying aircraft before entering or after leaving the strait. Given this option, there would be no imperative operational necessity to launch aircraft during the transit passage unless in extremely exceptional circumstances. Should the area of operations be that close to the strait that for security reasons it would not be possible to launch aircraft after having left the strait, this could also be done within the strait to ensure a safe passage of the carrier strike group. Again, what is important in this context are the arguments put forward to illustrate the operational necessity to the coastal state concerned.

7   The Right of Self-Defence During Transit Passage

Transit passage rights do not restrict the right of a transiting warship to use force in self-defence or collective self-defence[38] in case of an imminent attack or an actual attack.

During the Istanbul Syndicate session,[39] it was agreed that a warship conducting transit passage in peacetime could challenge suspicious contacts within a strait, with further action possible as long as it was conducted within the context of self-defence.

The question was raised as to whether there was any agreed common basis for the use of individual self-defence (as opposed to national self-defence) under international law. The consensus reached was that there did not seem to be such a common basis and that all countries operated under national law. All Members agreed that a certain level of 'imminence' of threat in the way of an imminent or actual attack was

---

[37] See supra footnote 30.

[38] The following reiterates what has been said during the Syndicate (see supra footnote 11) although it is not directly related to the transit passage regime.

[39] See supra footnote 11.

required before action could be taken in self-defence. This understanding may differ from the U.S. interpretation as their definition of self-defence is broader.[40]

The issue of the defence of property was also discussed, particularly with regard to 'mission-essential equipment'. The Members held different views concerning this issue, with some arguing that lethal force could not be used to protect equipment unless there was a direct link to an imminent loss of life if the equipment were stolen/destroyed. Others argued in favour of a more permissive interpretation, stating that lethal force could be used to defend items designated as 'mission-essential equipment', even if there was no imminent threat to life.

Although any rights that may be exercised in self-defence are subject to national regulations and interpretations, they are somehow limited by international law lest they constitute a breach of sovereignty. The Members agreed upon this being a general legal question not necessarily to be discussed under the topic of rights and obligations in straits. Still, it was stated that any proportional response to actual or imminent attacks on one's own or allied forces would not infringe on a state's sovereignty, no matter whether the response was taken to defend lives or property.

8   Conclusion

States should be careful not to exploit the legal borders of the right of transit passage to a maximum extent unless operational considerations provide no sound alternative. We have to keep in mind that in overlapped straits, military operations are conducted in the territorial waters of at least one neighbouring state. Excessive use or an unacceptably broad legal interpretation of the right of transit passage of the transiting nation might fuel the appetite of the coastal states to impose restrictions on fundamental navigational rights as a retaliatory measure. Using the right of transit passage in the proposed manner is one feasible way to prevent the neighbouring states from filing diplomatic protests or even taking military countermeasures to bring to an end what—from their standpoint—might constitute an abuse of transit passage rights. This holds true even if one can argue that the concept of the 'approaches' is a legally permissible interpretation of international law. However, even then, the political implications should not be neglected as it remains unclear how most of the riparian states interpret the respective UNCLOS provisions. Legal advisors, who should always be involved in the military planning process, must keep this aspect in mind at all times. They can contribute to an appropriate and balanced relationship between the claim to sovereignty made by the coastal states and any operational considerations that might have a decisive impact on how the right of transit passage

---

[40]According to the U.S. SROE, the use of force in self-defence is authorised in case of a hostile act or a hostile intent against the U.S. or U.S. forces, *cf.* U.S. DoD (2005), Enclosure A, 3 e and f. Both elements do not only include the use of force or the threat of an imminent use of force against the U.S. or U.S. forces but also force or the threat of force directly used to preclude or impede the mission and/or duties of U.S. forces. German forces can use force in self-defence in case of an attack or imminent attack against them or allied forces, cf. German Commander's Handbook (2002), p. 47.

is exercised. In accordance with the view presented in this contribution, exercising the right of transit passage in approaches to and exit routes from straits is only justified if otherwise a safe passage cannot be guaranteed, either for navigational reasons or for reasons related to appropriate self-protection. The legal advisor is responsible for encouraging the operators to consider this aspect during planning.

References

George M (2004) In: Oude Elfering AG, Rothwell D (eds) Oceans management in the 21st century. Brill/Nijhoff, Leiden

German Commander's Handbook (2002) Legal bases for the operations of Naval Forces (Un published)

ILC (2001) The International Law Commission, United Nations draft articles on responsibility of states for internationally wrongful acts with commentaries, http://legal.un.org/ilc/texts/instruments/english/commentaries/9_6_2001.pdf. Accessed 24 Oct 2017

Kraska J (2013) International maritime security law. Martinus Nijhoff

Langdon J (2015) In: Vincent P. Cogliati-Bantz (ed) The legal regime of straits: contemporary challenges and solutions, Hugo Caminos. Cambridge University Press, January 2015

Roach JA, Smith RW (2012) Excessive maritime claims, 3rd edn. Martinus Nijhoff, Leiden

Robertson HB Jr (1979) Passage through international straits: a right preserved in the third United Nations Conference on the Law of the Sea. Va J Int Law 20:801–857. http://scholarship.law.duke.edu/faculty_scholarship/104/. Accessed 24 Oct 2017

San Remo Manual (1995) In: Doswald-Beck J (ed) San Remo manual on international law applicable to Armed Conflicts at Sea. University Press, Cambridge

Treves T (1991) In: Depuy RJ, Vignes D (eds) A handbook on the new law of the sea, 2nd edn. Brill/Nijhoff, Leiden

UK Handbook (2007) UK operational law handbook – guide to maritime law (BR 3012), London, April 2005 (not published)

UN Division for Ocean Affairs and the Law of the Sea (1998) The United nations Convention on the Law of the Sea. A historical perspective, at http://www.un.org/Depts/los/convention_agreements/convention_historical_perspective.htm. Accessed 24 Oct 2017

United States Commander's Handbook on the Law of Naval Operations (2007) NWP 1-14M, 7.3. http://www.jag.navy.mil/documents/NWP_1- 14M_Commanders_Handbook.pdf. Accessed 10 July 2017

UNSCR 1816 (2008) http://www.un.org/en/sc/documents/resolutions/2008.shtml. Accessed 10 July 2017

U.S. DoD (2005) Chairman of the Joint Chiefs of Staff instruction, standing rules of engagement/standing rules on the use of force for US Forces, CJCSI 3121.01B, 12 June, 2005, http://www.jag.navy.mil/distrib/instructions/CJCSI%203121.01B13Jun05.pdf. Accessed 24 Oct 2017

U.S. DoD (2010) Chairman of the Joint Chiefs of Staff Instruction, CJCSI 2410.01D, August 31, 2010, Guidance for the exercise of right-of-assistance entry, https://hsdl.org/?abstract&did=723827. Accessed 24 Oct 2017

UNCLOS (1982) United Nations convention on the law of the Sea, 1833 U.N.T.S. 397

Uwe Althaus The author has been a Legal Adviser in the Armed Forces of Germany since 1990. He currently serves as the Head of the Operational Law Section at the German Navy Headquarters in Rostock. As a senior government official and Navy Captain (Res), he has completed assignments at the Army Command, Mürwik Naval Academy, the Fleet Command and the Strategy and Operations Directorate at the Federal Ministry of Defence in Germany. He has served as a legal adviser on missions abroad, both ashore and at sea. He has gained broad operational and legal expertise during four deployments in Kosovo. There he served as a legal adviser on the brigade level; two times he held the demanding position of the chief legal adviser of the Kosovo Force in the headquarters in Pristina. However, being a former submariner, his main focus is on legal questions concerning the law of the sea. He participated in the naval operations Enduring Freedom, UNIFIL and ATALANTA, where he served as the legal adviser of the German Force Commander on board German Frigates. The views expressed in this article are those of the author and do not necessarily reflect the position of the Federal German Government or the German Navy.

Belligerent Rights and Obligations in International Straits

Jörg Schildknecht

Abstract

As a cooperative effort between the Combined Joint Operations from the Sea Centre of Excellence in Norfolk, U.S.A.; the Centre of Excellence for Operations in Confined and Shallow Waters in Kiel, Germany; and the Maritime Security Centre of Excellence in Marmaris, Turkey, an international workshop on Maritime Situational Awareness was held in Istanbul, Turkey, from 9 to 11 October 2013. A legal syndicate, consisting of legal advisors from Australia, France, Germany, New Zealand, Turkey and the United Kingdom, was an integral component of this workshop. The participants of the legal syndicate focused on the topic of international straits and examined legal issues that might be of operational relevance to the maritime nations for planning current and future maritime operations. The findings of the syndicate were presented at the second Conference on Operational Maritime Law in Rome 2014 and following conferences in Lisbon 2015 and Turku 2016 (see Centre of Excellence for Operations in Confined and Shallow Waters http://www.coecsw.org, http://www.operationalmaritimelaw.org, accessed 06 Jan 2018). This chapter summarises the view of the majority of the participants who joined those events. In cases where opinions were divided, the author outlines the arguments brought forward and offers solutions. During both events, Chatham House Rule applied.

J. Schildknecht (✉)
Centre of Excellence of Operations in Confined and Shallow Waters, Kiel, Germany
e-mail: j.schildknecht@coecsw.org

This is a U.S. government work and its text is not subject to copyright protection in the United States; however, its text may be subject to foreign copyright protection 2018
J. Schildknecht et al. (eds.), *Operational Law in International Straits and Current Maritime Security Challenges*, Operational Maritime Law 1,
https://doi.org/10.1007/978-3-319-72718-9_5

1   Preliminary Remark

The San Remo Manual on International Law Applicable to Armed Conflicts at Sea (San Remo Manual), issued in 1995 by the International Institute of Humanitarian Law in San Remo, provided guidelines for determining what rights and obligations arise in an international armed conflict at sea. Along with its 'Explanations', the San Remo Manual contains essential statements on naval warfare in international straits in Part II Section II. The San Remo Manual is a useful reference for every legal advisor and operator who is associated with the law of naval warfare. Its findings are basically in line with international law. Where international law, mainly due to the lack of customary international law, cannot provide answers to legal questions, the San Remo Manual provides food for thought for a legal discourse. In particular, it offers considerations for new and unknown legal issues that have yet to occur.

With respect to belligerents' and neutrals' rights and obligations in international straits, it must be pointed out in advance that no or very little international practice exists when it comes to answering the question concerning the validity of the law of armed conflict (LOAC) on the one hand and general maritime law, in particular the 1982 peacetime provisions of the United Nations Convention on the Law of the Sea (UNCLOS),[1] on the other hand.

The San Remo Manual assumes that LOAC generally has priority over the rights granted under UNCLOS or respective customary international law when it comes to rights and obligations in international straits in an international armed conflict. This starting point was approved by the majority of the participants. The following basic premises are regarded as generally valid:

- A belligerent to an international armed conflict cannot arrogate peacetime rights in an international strait with regard to the other belligerent. For belligerents, only LOAC, including its legal regime of neutrality, is relevant.
- The peacetime right of transit passage in international straits applies to neutral-flagged ships.
- In an international armed conflict, the peacetime right of transit passage in international straits will become a supplementary doctrine of the law of neutrality in LOAC.

For international straits, the right of transit passage in accordance with Part III Section 2 of UNCLOS and corresponding customary international law applies to straits that are used for international navigation between one part of the high seas or an exclusive economic zone and another part of the high seas or an exclusive economic zone.[2]

With regard to the above-stated general premises, there was overall consensus about the following:

- Territorial waters of belligerent parties in an international strait are belligerent waters.

---

[1]UNCLOS (1982).
[2]See UNCLOS (1982), article 37.

- Belligerent forces in belligerent waters of an international strait do not have transit rights but are military targets.
- Territorial waters in an international strait that belong to neutral parties are neutral waters, where neutrals and belligerent forces enjoy transit rights.

As a critical point, it was examined in depth whether and how transit passages of neutral-flagged ships are to be granted in belligerent waters of an international strait.

2 Findings

2.1 The Right of Passage

> Belligerent warships, auxiliary vessels, and military and auxiliary aircraft may exercise the rights of passage through, under, or over neutral international straits provided by general international law.

The first part of the examination focused on the rights and obligations of belligerents in neutral waters comprising and forming an international strait or, as expressed in the San Remo Manual, 'in a strait comprised by neutral waters' or in 'a neutral international strait'. The majority agreed that the San Remo Manual's position laid down in number 23 fully reflects international customary law.[3]

Some participants expressly stressed the San Remo Manual's Explanations in number 23.2,[4] underlining that all legal positions shall only affect international straits that are not governed by existing multilateral treaties, such as the Turkish Straits under the 1936 Montreux Convention.[5]

> **Offensive Operations**
> Within and over neutral waters, including neutral waters comprising an international strait, belligerent acts by belligerent forces and the conduct of offensive operations are prohibited.[6]
>
> **Base for Naval Operations**
> Inter alia, the use of these neutral waters as a base for naval operations against adversaries is prohibited. In these waters belligerents may not use embedded command platforms for commanding belligerent acts or conduct

(continued)

---

[3]San Remo Manual (1995), Part II, Section II, No 23 with Explanations, pp. 102–103.
[4]*Ibid* at No 23.2, p. 103.
[5]Convention regarding the Regime of the Straits (1936).
[6]*See* San Remo Manual (1995), Part II, Section II, Explanations No 30, pp. 106–107.

offensive operations against enemy forces. The same applies to other platforms with the ability to essentially contribute to belligerent acts or offensive operations by means of coordinated command and control.[7]

No Sanctuary
Belligerent forces may not use neutral waters as a sanctuary.[8]

Self-Defence
The right of self-defence against unlawful actual and imminent attacks remains unaffected.[9]

The first sentence of number 15 of the San Remo Manual was examined as a starting point to answer the question of what belligerent acts in neutral straits are. The San Remo Manual states: 'Within and over neutral waters, including neutral waters comprising an international strait and waters in which the right of archipelagic sea lanes passage may be exercised, hostile actions by belligerent forces are forbidden.'[10] Further on, the San Remo Manual, referring to the Convention Concerning the Rights and Duties of Neutral Powers in Naval War of 1907 (Hague Convention XIII),[11] describes in number 16 what it understands is meant by hostile actions: 'Hostile actions within the meaning of paragraph 15 include, inter alia: (a) attack on or capture of persons or objects located in, on or over neutral waters or territory; (b) use as a base of operations, including attack on or capture of persons or objects located outside neutral waters, if the attack or seizure is conducted by belligerent forces located in, on or over neutral waters; (c) laying of mines; or (d) visit, search, diversion or capture.'[12]

Today, many warships are used as command platforms and have the possibility to command and control coordinated attacks on other units. Every warship contributes to a common recognised picture and gathers data and intelligence to send to its task force commander. Though often unrecognizable to third parties, warships in transit passage, in fact, have the ability to participate in an attack, by giving orders to another unit outside the international strait, or indirectly contribute to attacks, by information sharing.

Article 5 of the Hague Convention XIII[13] and respective customary international law prohibit belligerents from using neutral waters as a base of naval operations against their adversaries and, in particular, to erect wireless telegraphy stations or any apparatus for the purpose of communicating with the belligerent forces on land or at sea. In the past, the use of communication assets was seen as a major advantage of warfare. Now, we see that their importance has only increased. Superior

---

[7]*See* San Remo Manual (1995), Part II, Section I, No 15, 16 with Explanations, pp. 95–96.

[8]*See Ibid* at Explanations No 17, p. 97.

[9]*Cf.* San Remo Manual (1995), Part II, Section II, No 30, pp. 106–107.

[10]San Remo Manual (1995), Part II, Section I, Explanations in 15.1, p. 95.

[11]Hague XIII (1907).

[12]San Remo Manual (1995), Part II, Section I, No 16, p. 96.

[13]Hague XIII (1907).

situational awareness and the ability to create and use an undistorted maritime picture by data transmission for military decisions, combined with well-functioning command and control guaranteed by the ability of wireless communication with own troops, can be a decisive factor for victory in modern maritime warfare.

A warship in neutral waters or transiting in neutral waters of an international strait, acting as an operating command platform, can be seen as a violation of neutral rights. In this respect, the majority followed the San Remo Manual. Consequently, embedded force commands have to stop their offensive commanding of units, in general, when in neutral waters inside international straits. The same applies to any warship with the ability to essentially contribute to belligerent acts by means of coordinated command and control to other units.

The majority generally assumes that self-defence is legally permitted in neutral waters. However, in an international armed conflict, the question of distinguishing self-defence from belligerent acts arises, possibly resulting in the prohibition of some specific acts of self-defence if these constitute at the same time an unlawful belligerent act.

The San Remo Manual reflects the use of force for self-defence in number 22 by stating: 'Should a belligerent state be in violation of the regime of neutral waters, as set out in this document, the neutral State is under an obligation to take the measures necessary to terminate the violation. If the neutral state fails to terminate the violation of its neutral waters by a belligerent, the opposing belligerent must so notify the neutral state and give that neutral state a reasonable time to terminate the violation by the belligerent. If the violation of the neutrality of the state by the belligerent constitutes a serious and immediate threat to the security of the opposing belligerent and the violation is not terminated, then that belligerent may, in the absence of any feasible and timely alternative, use such force as is strictly necessary to respond to the threat posed by the violation.'[14]

The facts warranting a self-defence situation are not sufficiently described in the San Remo Manual. However, there was a common understanding among the participants that the definition of self-defence is up to the sovereign states and therefore a single and universal definition cannot exist. The limits of self-defence may vary, but there is a common accepted definition that describes a universally accepted core situation that any state would define as triggering a legal use of self-defence: whenever a unit is actually being attacked or threatened by an imminent attack, counteractions for the purpose of self-defence will be permissible according to international law.

Though accepting these fundamentals, there was no consensus among the participants on how to solve the issue that acting in self-defence may, in some cases, also be seen as an unlawful act under LOAC. Some stated that the right of self-defence supersedes the law of neutrality; some said the opposite. Scenarios that are laid down in the San Remo Manual extensively illustrate this problem and will be solved using the author's view:

To distinguish any acting in pure 'self-defence' from acting under *ius in bello*, the criteria of unlawfulness is recommended: self-defence (at least in neutral waters) may only be defined

---

[14]San Remo Manual (1995), Part II, Section I, No. 22 with Explanations, pp. 101–102.

as a situation where a unit is being actually *unlawfully* attacked, or threatened by an *unlawful* imminent attack. This unlawfulness will depend on LOAC rules, mainly with regard to neutrality.

This means that any response to a lawful attack from the adversary, meaning legally executed under LOAC, will not trigger a lawful response under the rules of self-defence. In other words, an attack by the enemy that is in accordance with LOAC in a situation of an armed conflict can never be seen as unlawful; therefore, it cannot lead to a reaction legally based on self-defence.

Not following this restrictive concept could lead to situations where reactions are justified by national rules of self-defence but are in violation of LOAC. Those states that have not yet properly synchronised the applicability of LOAC and national rules of self-defence for naval warfare in neutral territory may have difficulty to justify their self-defence policy under international law.

Further on, the San Remo Manual does not see a legal possibility for direct response unless there is an absence of any feasible and timely alternative; actions conducted otherwise would violate neutrality.[15]

The participants, in taking a more operational standpoint, did not see the San Remo Manual's approach conceivable. With regard to the need for immediate responses to threats in an armed conflict, it can be expected that belligerents will very easily assume that most threats to security would not be terminated by the neutral in a timely manner.

In a case of self-defence, meaning a unit is actually being attacked or threatened by an imminent attack, the neutral will likely always be simply unable to respond to the attack in a timely manner. As a result, it cannot be a question whether the neutral state is able or willing to prevent belligerent acts in its waters or not.[16]

When creating the San Remo Manual, one additional position in the Explanation states that taking armed defensive measures is only permissible in neutral waters if a belligerent was under an armed attack or immediate threat of attack (only) from that neutral state.[17] Another opinion was that measures taken in neutral waters were not a use of force against the territorial integrity of the neutral state but against the opposing belligerent and could be justified under a number of doctrines, including necessity and self-defence.[18]

The majority, clearly, did not follow the first position. This position definitely disregards international customary law on self-defence. It is a well-accepted practice that warships, while in territorial waters, have the right of self-defence against any (unlawful) attack whether in an armed conflict or not.

Acting in self-defence against unlawful attacks of the adversary in neutral waters reveals the failure of that neutral to prevent those incidents, what would be his key

---

[15]This approach has been further discussed in the San Remo Manual (1995), Part II, Section I, Explanation 22.3 and 22.4, p. 102.

[16]*Cf. ibid.* at Explanation to No 22.5; *see* also The Commander's Handbook (2017), 7.3.

[17]San Remo Manual (1995), Part II, Section I, Explanation 22.3, p. 102.

[18]*Ibid.*

international obligation. Acting in self-defence is a use of force against the attacker and not a violation of any neutral's rights.

Today, it is the United States' opinion, which a majority of the participants agreed on: 'Belligerents are also authorized to act in self-defence when attacked or threatened with attack while in neutral territory or when attacked or threatened from neutral territory.'[19] However, for neutral waters in international straits, the United States stated: 'Belligerent forces in transit may, however, take defensive measures consistent with their security, including the launching and recovery of aircraft and military devices, screen formation steaming, and acoustic and electronic surveillance, and may respond in self-defence to a hostile act or demonstrated hostile intent.'[20] The U.S. legal concept as a whole, unfortunately, remains imprecise due to the last half-sentence. It is doubtful whether, for transit passages in an international armed conflict, an attack will remain a *conditio sine qua non* to trigger self-defence or whether it will also be referred to the *aliud* of a hostile act or hostile intent under NATO understanding.[21] Moreover, the dilemma between acts of self-defence and belligerent acts in neutral waters as described here in Sect. 2.4 has not been raised by the U.S.

The Canadian Joint Doctrine Manual states: 'If the neutral state fails to terminate the violation of its neutral waters by a belligerent, the opposing belligerent must notify the neutral state and give it a reasonable time to terminate the violation',[22] and the 'belligerent may, in the absence of any feasible and timely alternative, use such force as is strictly necessary to respond to the threat posed by the violation'.[23] Although the Canadian Joint Doctrine Manual more generally refers to a threat instead of to an attack, and in this way leaves some room for preventive or pre-emptive measures, it does not promote more far-reaching rights to protect own forces as proposed in its earlier drafts.

The right of self-defence is not restricted to a single unit reacting to an attack related to it. Under the common agreed definition of collective self-defence, a unit will, in general, also have the right to defend other own or allied units against unlawful attacks. The creators of the San Remo Manual saw this challenge for transit passages but were not able to solve it, stating that it was not possible to draft a provision that would meet all contingencies.[24] The Explanation of the San Remo Manual describes hypothetical scenarios to underline this difficulty without giving a solution.[25] However, these situations must be solved to provide concrete guidance for commanders. They perfectly demonstrate the ambiguity between self-defence and belligerent acts in neutral waters.

---

[19]The Commander's Handbook (2017), No. 7.3.

[20]*Ibid* at No 7.3.6.

[21]MC 362/1, Appendix 1 to Annex A.

[22]Joint Doctrine Manual (2001), No 811 (1).

[23]*Ibid* at No 811 (2).

[24]San Remo Manual (1995), Part II, Section II, Explanation No 30.3, p. 107.

[25]*Ibid* at Explanation No 30.1, p. 106.

2.2   Passage Right Scenarios

▶   **First Scenario**
'Part of the task force is within neutral waters of a strait or an archipelago
and the part that is outside is brought under attack by the opposing
belligerent who is outside the neutral waters. Could the units within
neutral waters launch a counter-attack? Would this be a lawful defensive
measure?'[26]

▶   **Answer**
No. Any counter-attack would be a violation of neutrality. The case shows
allied units being actually attacked, but the attack by the other belligerent cannot be seen as unlawful: any belligerent has the right to attack
the adversary outside neutral waters under LOAC. Consequently, this is
not a situation of an unlawful attack as a premise for collective self-
defence, and as a result, a counter-attack would not be based on self-
defence; rather, it would be a belligerent act that is prohibited in neutral
waters.

▶   **Second Scenario**
'The unit or force within neutral waters is brought under attack by a unit
launching long-range missiles from outside neutral waters. Could the
units within neutral waters launch a counter-attack? Would this be a
lawful defensive measure?'[27]

▶   **Answer**
Yes. In the described situation, it is beyond doubt that the enemy unit is
actually attacking the unit or a second attack can be assumed as imminent. Any attack on belligerent units in neutral waters is a violation of
neutrality and is unlawful. A counter-attack is lawful because it is a case
of self-defence.

▶   **Third Scenario**
'A unit of the armed forces of the transiting force which is outside the
neutral waters and not a part of the transiting force is brought under
attack by an enemy unit outside neutral waters. Could the force within
neutral waters send aircraft to assist the unit under attack? Would this be
a lawful defensive measure?'[28]

---

[26]*Ibid.*

[27]San Remo Manual (1995), Part II, Section II, Explanation No 30.3, p. 107.

[28]*Ibid.*

▶ **Answer**

No. The attack by the enemy unit outside neutral waters would be lawful under LOAC. Own units outside neutral waters are lawful military targets for the adversary. Belligerent acts from inside neutral waters are prohibited. Aircraft from inside neutral waters are not allowed to start in order to engage the enemy. Delegating any aircraft, whether said aircraft is/are within or outside of neutral waters, from within neutral waters, during a transit passage, by effective means of command and control would be a use of neutral waters as a base for operations and would violate neutrality.

▶ **Fourth Scenario**

'A helicopter conducting anti-submarine surveillance ahead of the transiting force detects an enemy submarine lying in wait just outside neutral waters to attack the force upon its emergence. Could the helicopter attack the submarine? Would this be a lawful defensive measure?'[29]

▶ **Answer**

Yes. This case assumes that the enemy submarine will only attack when own forces leave neutral waters. It *prima facie* seems that there remains a possibility of no attack at all, and any later attacks by the submarine would be lawful belligerent acts. However, at the moment of threat assessment, the intention of the submarine would never be that clear to the commander. The question then always has to be if the mere positioning of the submarine can be understood as an imminent attack itself, at least under circumstantial evidence. In the reality of military warfare, it is very likely and has to be accepted that commanding officers will interpret this kind of positioning just outside neutral waters as a situation of an unlawful imminent attack by already reaching a sufficient level of threat to own forces in neutral waters. As a result, the enemy submarine may be targeted from inside neutral waters on the basis of self-defence.

2.3   Belligerent Waters

In an international armed conflict the territorial waters of a belligerent state comprising an international strait are belligerent waters. These belligerent waters are areas open to belligerent acts under the Law of Armed Conflict.

---

[29] *Ibid.*

For the majority, this ascertainment arises from the general precedence of the LOAC over the peacetime rights under UNCLOS and corresponding customary international law. It implies that the enemy's armed forces are military targets within these belligerent waters and that they cannot derive any special rights from the peacetime rights of transit passage in these waters in an international armed conflict.

2.4   Neutral Waters and Neutral States' Rights

> In international straits, neutral states enjoy the right of transit passage in neutral and belligerent waters.

The participants had a controversial discussion whether, and to what extent, neutral-flagged vessels should be granted transit rights in belligerent waters of an international strait.

The San Remo Manual states that neutral-flagged vessels should be granted transit rights in belligerent waters of an international strait[30] and at the same time incorporated an obligation of the neutral flag state 'as a precautionary measure, to give timely notice of its exercise of the rights of passage to the belligerent State'.[31]

The wording chosen in the San Remo Manual suggests that the right of passage does exist but that its use in the case of an international armed conflict is in the risk area of the neutral flag state and that, instead of the general right of conducting the transit passage, rather a legal exemption to peacetime rights is to be assumed. The majority did not want to follow this approach. The majority stipulated that in accordance with article 57 (4) of Protocol I to the 1949 Geneva Conventions,[32] it is rather the responsibility of a belligerent to plan his warfare in such a way that unrestricted rights of passage of neutrals are ensured and that inadvertent damage to neutrals is prevented. In this view, higher standards are to be applied while conducting collateral damage assessments and determining the enemy character of targets.

In the Explanations of the San Remo Manual with regard to straits, 'belligerent waters' and 'waters under the control of belligerent states' are considered synonymous.[33] It is the author's opinion that in adversary's waters of an international strait being *de facto* under effective control of the other belligerent, there will be a general

---

[30]San Remo Manual (1995), Part II, Section II, No 26, p. 104; Part II, Section II No 27, p. 105.

[31]*Ibid* at No 26, p. 104.

[32]AP I (1977).

[33]San Remo Manual (1995) Part II, Section II at Explanation No 26.2, p. 104.

obligation for the occupying belligerent to ensure undisturbed transit.[34] Here, especially the provision of piloting and escort services has to be considered.[35]

The majority was of the opinion that the rights of the neutrals in warfare are generally to be considered more robust than what was outlined in the San Remo Manual.

With respect to mining in international straits, the San Remo Manual states: 'Transit passage through international straits and passage through waters subject to the right of archipelagic sea lanes passage shall not be impeded unless safe and convenient alternative routes are provided.'[36] Correspondingly, the San Remo Manual states that mining of straits in an international armed conflict is not unlawful *per se*.[37] The San Remo Manual further outlines: 'belligerents may not exercise unlimited mining rights in those waters'.[38]

In the San Remo Manual's Explanations, it was subsequently discussed whether 'an alternative route should necessarily be situated within the strait or sea lane concerned' which led to the conclusion that 'alternatives for straits need not necessarily be within the same strait or provide identical facilities for shipping'.[39] And 'The alternative should in any event ensure the safety of shipping and accommodate the interests of shipping as much as possible'.[40] Furthermore, the San Remo Manual states that 'it was deemed necessary to rule out those cases in which either no alternative or only alternatives with unacceptable commercial consequences are offered by belligerents'.[41] And 'An extreme example of the latter situation could be that transit passage through Gibraltar straits would be impeded on the grounds that shipping could proceed through the Suez Canal and around the Cape of Good Hope'.[42]

The majority did not come to a common conclusion to restrict neutral rights as done in the San Remo Manual. However, there was a tendency among the participants in assuming that transit passage of neutrals through international straits in belligerent waters should not be impeded at all. It is therefore recommended not to adopt all notions of the San Remo Manual. First, they only refer to mining. As part of modern warfare, not only mining of belligerent waters but also other methods of

---

[34]To be seen as a general rule for naval warfare, *cf.* Institut de Droit International (1912), Section VI, Art. 96, p. 35.

[35]*Cf.* the legal concepts of the San Remo Manual (1995) in Part IV, Section I, Explanation No 88.3, p. 173.

[36]San Remo Manual (1995), Part IV, Section I, No 89, p. 174.

[37]*Ibid* at Explanation No 89.1, p. 174.

[38]*Ibid.*

[39]*Ibid* at Explanation No 89.2, p. 174.

[40]*Ibid.*

[41]*Ibid* at Explanation No 89.3, p. 174.

[42]*Ibid.*

naval warfare that have an impact on international straits, e.g. an enemy blockade or a temporary denial of the maritime area in order to carry out landing operations without disturbances, are conceivable.[43]

Disregarding cases where the access to passages could be denied by other military needs, the San Remo Manual, secondly, only refers to the Corfu Channel case[44] and the Hague Convention VIII[45] and XIII[46] of 1907. Neither in the Hague Conventions of 1907 nor in the court's decision in the Corfu Channel case nor in the corresponding memorials of the United Kingdom and Albania can a statement be found saying that mining of an international strait in an international armed conflict is prohibited or not. The only criterion has always been the necessity to notify other states if mines were laid by one of the belligerents off the coast of the adversary. Due to the subject the court had to decide in the Corfu Channel case, any statement with regard to the lawfulness of mining an international strait in an international armed conflict would have been an unnecessary *obiter dictum* because the mines that caused the death of 44 British sailors were assumed to be laid in late 1946.

Not taking this fact into account, the San Remo Manual only follows the precondition of the necessity of notification and adding only one further criterion for the lawfulness 'that the mines can only detonate against vessels that are military objectives'.[47] The San Remo Manual has thus not developed any further disqualifying hard criteria for the laying of mines in an international strait.

However, there have been attempts in history to prohibit the closure of straits in wartime. At the 1907 Hague Conference VII, the Netherlands proposed to prohibit minelaying in straits connecting two parts of the high seas in order to keep sea lanes of communication open for peaceful navigation.[48] This proposal met reservations from several states for their respective seas as some delegates stated that they had no instructions on the subject, and the Russian delegate doubted the conference's ability to deal with the question. As a result, the Committee suppressed all provisions relating to straits. Some delegates, however, indicated that they agreed with the Netherlands that those straits should not be mined. In the end, there was no clear indication what the existing law was considered to be.[49]

In a report to this Hague Conference, the Third Commission stated formally: 'the committee decided unanimously to suppress all provisions relating to straits, which should be left out of discussion by the present Conference. It was clearly understood

---

[43] *Cf.* San Remo Manual (1995), Part IV, Section VI, No 146, p. 212 and *ibid.* 146.6, p. 214: 'in the immediate area of naval operations, for example, in the vicinity of naval units, the belligerents' security interests outweigh the freedom of navigation of neutral merchant shipping. If neutral merchant vessel do not comply with such orders they may be presumed to have enemy character or hostile intent and may thus be treated as if they were enemy ships …'.

[44] ICJ Corfu Channel Case (1949).

[45] Hague VIII (1907), Art. 5.

[46] Hague XIII (1907).

[47] San Remo Manual (1995), Part IV, Section I, No 83, p. 172.

[48] *Cf.* Jia (1998), p. 92; Higgins (1909), p. 331 and Levie (1988), pp. 145–146.

[49] Levie (1988), pp. 145–146.

that under the stipulations of the Convention to be included nothing whatever has been changed as regards to the actual status of straits. But, so far as not inconsistent with the foregoing declarations, it has been considered as natural that the technical conditions established should be of general application.'[50]

It was not clear whether minelaying in international straits was permissible or not for the members of the 1907 Commission. However, during the Hague Convention XIII proceedings, when rights and duties of neutral powers were in debate, it was the general feeling that a neutral state could only suspend innocent passage in its territorial sea but not in straits uniting two open seas.[51] Thus, there were early indications of the nations' will not to hamper free trade of neutrals in international straits by the belligerents.

As a result, the Hague Conventions of 1907 must be regarded as agreements between states that generally only describe a minimum standard in naval warfare.[52] As international law has further developed with respect to the handling of the international straits, far-reaching restrictions of the LOAC in question can be assumed.

The San Remo Manual's style of legal argumentation already shows a beginning development but in total does not cover the area examined here in sufficient detail. The San Remo Manual's starting point is the fact that the LOAC takes precedence over passaging rights originating from peacetime law. The peacetime law of transit passage, which is now also reflected in the law of neutrality, is only considered to a limited extent. While basically accepting restrictions in international straits, the San Remo Manual builds up a simple principle of proportionality where only the neutrals' rights are considered and weighted without taking military requirements and purposes of the respective military action of the belligerent into account. In this respect, the San Remo Manual does not explicitly look on to what the purpose of minelaying and what the anticipated military advantage of it is. Apparently for the San Remo Manual, military requirements are considered as given *ab initio*. The San Remo Manual only states 'unacceptable commercial consequences'[53] as an isolated and very general argument against minelaying. Implicitly, the Corfu Channel case may support the San Remo Manual's argument as it was a case hardly of significance for the world economy in general and more theoretically could have affected neutral-flagged ships that may have used the waterway during the Second World War.

The San Remo Manual remained too focused on the Corfu Channel case and neglected the fact that some international straits became totally comprised of the territory of the adjacent states after the extension of the territorial waters from 3 to 12 nautical miles in 1982 and that, instead of the principle of innocent passage, the right of transit passage with its additional rights emerged. It would be contradictory

---

[50] *See at* Levie (1988), p. 145 with further references.

[51] Jia (1998), p. 92.

[52] *Cf.* Levie (1988), p. 146: 'minimum (and inadequate) regulation'.

[53] San Remo Manual (1995), Part IV, Section I, Explanation No 89.3, p. 174.

if a peacetime right agreement such as UNCLOS, on the one hand, widens states' rights by extending territorial waters and agrees to transit passage rights as compensation for the limitation of navigational rights and, on the other hand, would now be used for the interpretation of the law of armed conflict in a way to significantly reduce those peacetime rights. In contrary, it must generally be assumed that the new amended peacetime international law with UNCLOS was intended not to widen the LOAC but rather to restrict it. You cannot simply take away with one hand what was given with the other.

It is a fact that the law of neutrality as part of the *ius in bello* imposes restrictions on the belligerents and that its primary objective is to control the conduct of war between belligerents only. The law of neutrality protects neutrals from belligerent actions and is intended to limit the conflict to only the belligerents. Therefore, no state can generally claim rights that excessively strain the rights of neutrals or put them in danger of being involved in the armed conflict. The San Remo Manual's legal conception of 'unacceptable commercial consequences' with respect to the restriction of maritime traffic in international straits, and thus international world trade, expresses this correctly. It is a fact that some international straits have become major chokepoints of international maritime trade. The economy of every neutral state would often be directly or at least indirectly affected; therefore, it is mandatory not to restrict the rights of neutrals in international straits.

In this context, it must be kept in mind that the weighing of anticipated military advantages on the one hand and disadvantages for neutrals on the other hand would first and foremost be made by the belligerent. Decisions taken by the belligerent could have irreversible consequences for the economy of uninvolved third parties. A closure of an international strait would not be a mere question of legality following any theoretical discourses but would also be a question of presumed political acceptance by powerful neutrals. Presumably, those closures justified for whatever reason would most probably not be enforceable in the international community with regard to the major maritime trade routes and could at worst cause military reaction by neutrals.

Furthermore, the impact on the world economy may be minor in exceptional cases, but a single neutral state can be hit so hard by a closure that its shipping and economy would suffer unforeseeable impacts. Therefore, the volume of traffic passing through an international strait must generally play no role.[54] As a result, even significant military advantages that could be achieved by access denial of marine shipping should by no means justify a complete closure of an international strait for neutrals.

An autonomous attack and a distinction capability of mines as classification criteria for their legality of usage in international straits can be critical. There may

---

[54] *Cf.* legal notion of the United Kingdom, in Reply, July 30, 1949, ICJ Corfu Channel Case (1949), pp. 242–243; and *Ibid.* at merits of the court, p. 28.

well be mines that only recognise the signatures of enemy naval ships and do not attack neutral ships, or there is a possibility of controlled mines or unmanned underwater vehicles acting as movable mines. Nevertheless, the employment of any mine could bare the risk to bring neutral marine traffic to a halt since it must be taken into consideration that ship insurance companies could limit the insurance coverage for merchant vessels or increase their rates exorbitantly.

It should also be acknowledged that no matter what a mine is programed for, there cannot be a 100% guarantee that there will not be any malfunctions.

When possible impacts by belligerent parties on an international strait are assessed, this highway has to be considered as one entity.[55] The majority was of the opinion that if belligerent acts are to take place in belligerent waters of an international strait, the consequences on the possibility of transit passages in general have to be considered: if transit passages are generally possible due to the size of the international strait or the fact that the traffic separation schemes of the international strait are not within belligerent waters, but only in neutral waters, then there is no impact; the belligerent waters can be used for belligerent actions, e.g. for minelaying if the belligerent aspires a military advantage. An impediment could also be prevented by establishing other equally effective traffic schemes for neutrals in the same international strait.[56] This final conclusion already repeats an early statement of the Institut de Droit International in the year 1894: 'Straits which form a channel from one open sea to another can never be closed.'[57]

In the absence of practice, any argument relying on the function of the international law and its principles will eventually lead to an individual assessment mostly based on a prediction of a certain probability of states' future actions and reactions. In this respect, neither the San Remo Manual's proposals nor the proposals of this contribution are to be regarded as final interpretations of international law. Findings given here are therefore rather guidelines for *ordres de manoeuvre* that should become firmly established in *lex feranda*.

3   Recommendations

As a result of this examination of belligerent and neutral rights in international straits in an international armed conflict, it is recommended to states

---

[55]*Cf.* legal notion of the United Kingdom, in Reply, July 30, 1949, ICJ Corfu Channel Case (1949), p. 281; and *Ibid.* at Oral Pleadings, p. 585.

[56]*Cf.* Depuis (1911), p. 590: 'Il n'est pas nécessaires que le passage soit libre dans tous les détroits; il suffit qu'il le soit dans les détroits où il est indispensable, sous peine de supprimer une route commercial fréquentée; là où plusieurs détroits voisins permettent de passer, il suffirait qu'un seul demeurât ouvert à la navigation. ...'

[57]Higgins (1909), p. 467 with further references.

- to state their *opinio iuris* about the applicability of self-defence and its scope in neutral waters in times of an armed conflict, preferably in favour of adopting the condition of unlawfulness in their national self-defence definition;
- to expressively state their *opinio iuris* with regard to the closing and impediment of international straits by military operations, including minelaying, preferably in favour of restricting any closure of an international strait.

References

AP I (1977) Protocol Additional to the Geneva Conventions of 12 August 1949, and relating to the Protection of Victims of International Armed Conflicts [Protocol I], June 8, 1977, see https://www.icrc.org/ihl/INTRO/470. Accessed 06 Jan 2018

Convention regarding the Regime of the Straits (1936) League of nations treaty series, vol 173, pp 213 et seq

Depuis C (1911) Le Droit de la Guerre Maritime d'après les Conférences de la Haye et des Londres. Pedone, Paris. http://gallica.bnf.fr/ark:/12148/bpt6k61284745. Accessed 06 Jan 2018

Hague VIII (1907) Convention relative to the laying of automatic submarine contact mines, October 18, 1907. http://avalon.law.yale.edu/20th_century/hague08.asp. Accessed 06 Jan 2018

Hague XIII (1907) Convention concerning the rights and duties of neutral powers in Naval War, October 18, 1907. http://avalon.law.yale.edu/20th_century/hague13.asp. Accessed 06 Jan 2018

Higgins AP (1909) The Hague peace conferences and other international conferences concerning the laws and usages of war. University Press, Cambridge. https://archive.org/details/haguepeaceconfer00higguoft. Accessed 06 Jan 2018

ICJ Corfu Channel Case (1949) United Kingdom of Great Britain and Northern Ireland v. Albania, Judgment, April 9, 1949 and December 15, 1949, see at http://www.icj-cij.org/en/case/1. Accessed 06 Jan 2018

Institut de Droit International (1912) Session de Christiania, Réglementation des lois et coutumes de la guerre maritime dans les rapports entre belligérants (Manuel)

Jia BB (1998) The regime of straits in international law. Clarendon, Oxford

Joint Doctrine Manual (2001) Law of armed Conflict at the operational and tactical levels, Office of the Judge Advocate General, No 811 (1). https://www.fichl.org/fileadmin/_migrated/content_uploads/Canadian_LOAC_Manual_2001_English.pdf. Accessed 06 Jan 2018

Levie HS (1988) Commentary to 1907 Hague Convention VIII relative to the laying of automatic submarine contact. In: Ronzitti N (ed) The Law of Naval warfare: a collection of agreements and documents. Nijhoff, Dordrecht

MC 362/1. NATO Rules of Engagement, NATO Military Committee Document MC 362/1 (unclassified, undated)

San Remo Manual (1995) In: Doswald-Beck J (ed) San Remo Manual on International Law Applicable to Armed Conflicts at Sea. University Press, Cambridge

The Commander's Handbook (2017) The Commander's Handbook on the Law of Naval Operation, NWP 1-14M, Edition August 2017

UNCLOS (1982) United Nations Convention on the Law of the Sea, 1833 U.N.T.S. 397

Jörg Schildknecht is currently stationed as the Legal Advisor at the NATO Centre of Excellence for Operations in Confined and Shallow Waters (COE CSW) in Kiel, Germany. He is a civil servant and has held numerous positions throughout the German Navy. He taught law at the Luftwaffe Officers' School in Fürstenfeldbruck and at the German Naval Academy in Mürwik. He also served as Legal Advisor for the German Fleet Command and at the International Law Department of the German Ministry of Defense in Berlin. While deployed, Dr. Schildknecht served as Chief of a local headquarter in the Former Yugoslavian Republic of Macedonia, as Legal Advisor of Commander Maritime Task Force United Nations Interim forces in Lebanon and as Legal Advisor for European Naval Forces Atalanta in Northwood, and as Human Rights Advisor to the Commander of European Naval Forces Med in Rome. Mr. Schildknecht holds a Doctor Iuris of International Law from the University of Hamburg and is a Commander Senior Grade (Res.) in the German Navy. He expresses his own views and does not represent his government, NATO, the COE CSW or the participating states of the COE CSW.

The Legal Status of Greater and Lesser Tunbs Islands Including a Brief History of the Legal Dispute

Dorota Marianna Banaszewska

Abstract
Although not as well covered by the media as other disputes over island territories, the conflict between the Islamic Republic of Iran and the United Arab Emirates concerning the sovereignty over the Greater and Lesser Tunbs and Abu Musa is one of the most crucial current unresolved territorial questions.

The critical importance of the Greater and Lesser Tunbs due to their location in the Persian/Arabian Gulf and close to the Strait of Hormuz on the one hand and the historical ambiguities and uncertainties surrounding the islands on the other make the legal assessment of the ownership question over the islands particularly challenging.

The article focuses on the historical and legal dimension of the conflict: taking as starting point the rival historical claims by both States, the article shows that there is no conclusive evidence proving a valid historical title to the islands of any of the States. Subsequently, the article deals with the question of (mere) physical control over a territory and the consequences thereof, concluding that even if a State exercises effective control over a certain territory and hence has specific legal obligations towards other States that are inherent to that factual situation, this does not constitute a legal basis for its sovereignty claims over that territory. Finally, the article mentions briefly the possible modes of settling the dispute between the UAE and Iran.

D. M. Banaszewska (✉)
European-University Viadrina, Frankfurt (Oder), Germany
e-mail: dorota.banaszewska@gmail.com

J. Schildknecht et al. (eds.), *Operational Law in International Straits and Current Maritime Security Challenges*, Operational Maritime Law 1,
https://doi.org/10.1007/978-3-319-72718-9_6

1   Introduction

The echoes of a highly polarised discussion between the Islamic Republic of Iran
(hereinafter Iran) and the United Arab Emirates (hereinafter UAE) concerning the
ownership and sovereignty over the Greater and Lesser Tunbs and Abu Musa reach
the public opinion on a regular basis. In September 2013, the UAE Foreign Minister,
Sheikh Abdullah Bin Zayed Al Nahyan, renewed the UAE's demand concerning the
three islands in the following words:

> 'My Government expresses, once again, its regret regarding the continued Iranian occupa-
> tion of our three islands – Abu Musa and the Greater and Lesser Tunbs, and demands the
> restoration of the UAE's full sovereignty over these islands. (…).'[1] He also called upon the
> International Community to 'urge Iran to respond to the repeated peaceful, sincere calls of
> the United Arab Emirates for a just settlement of this issue, either through direct, serious
> negotiations or by referral to the International Court of Justice. (…)'.[2]

In response to that statement, Iran's representative rejected any UAE claims and
reiterated his State's full sovereignty over the islands.[3]

The territorial dispute between Iran and the UAE over the Greater and Lesser
Tunbs, as well as Abu Musa, is only one of the unresolved territorial questions in the
Persian/Arabian Gulf (hereinafter Gulf). The Gulf has a rich history of territorial and
boundary disagreements. However, the dispute over the ownership and sovereignty
of the three islands is a fundamental one as it constitutes a potential source of further
conflicts and not only affects the region itself but—due to the strategic importance of
the islands—may have far-reaching consequences for the economy and world peace.
The dispute concerning the Greater and Lesser Tunbs is as long as it is complicated,
in particular due to its multidimensionality. The economic and political aspects
impinge upon the legal arguments brought up by both States. Moreover, the ambig-
uous and often unclear or uncertain historical context, as well as the scarcity of
sources dealing independently with the topic, makes a legal assessment not a
particularly easy task. And yet the legal analysis of any territorial dispute depends
for the most part on the presented facts.

Irrespective of the political tensions around the topic and historical ambiguities,
this article intends, based upon independent sources, as well as Iranian and Arabic
sources, to provide a brief historical overview of the dispute and of the arguments
raised by both States, as well as a legal analysis of the situation. In literature, the
situation of the three islands is usually jointly discussed. However, since the actual
situation of Abu Musa, due to the 1971 Agreement,[4] is different than the case of the
Tunbs, the scope of this article is limited to the situation of the Greater and Lesser

---

[1] UN News Centre (2013).

[2] Ibidem.

[3] Ibidem.

[4] See infra point 3.

Tunbs which is in fact more unclear and precarious. The focal point of the article is a historical-legal dimension of the conflict.

2   Geographical Setting and Strategic Importance

Greater Tunb and Lesser Tunb are two relatively small islands that lie respectively at 26°15′N 55°16′E and 26°14′N 55°08′E in the eastern part of the Gulf, some 8 miles from each other, about 17 miles south-west from Iran's island Qeshm (or Qishm), about 46 miles from the Emirates of Ras al-Khaimah, about 30 miles from the Iranian port of Bandar Lengeh and close to the Strait of Hormuz.[5]

Greater Tunb is known in Farsi as Tunb-i-Bozorg and in Arabic as Tunb al-Kabir, both meaning Greater Tunb. Lesser Tunb is known in Farsi as Tunb-i-Kuchuk and in Arabic either as Tunb al-Saghir (both names meaning Lesser Tunb) or Nabiyu (Nabi) Tunb.[6]

Their geographical setting makes the islands important. The control over the islands is decisive for control over the export of oil from the Gulf, navigation and the sea lanes since most of the Gulf's oil exports are shipped by tankers through the Gulf and the Strait of Hormuz. Moreover, since they are located near the oil and gas fields, the islands are crucial for the security of the oil platforms as it would be very easy to seize, attack and sabotage the oil and gas fields from the islands. The sovereignty over the islands is also important with regard to the delimitation of the zones under the International Law of the Sea. Since the dispute over the islands can lead to further conflicts, it constitutes a destabilising factor in the region and a potential threat to international peace and security.

3   History of the Legal Dispute from the Perspective of Both States

The legal dispute of the sovereignty over the Lesser and Greater Tunbs is based on rival historical claims by both States. Many of the facts are still unclear or disputed by the States. The scarcity of independent sources makes it difficult to build a clear picture of the historical titles. Therefore, the historical roots of the dispute, after a brief general background, will be presented from the perspective of both sides and then assessed under public international law.

---

[5]See Hilal Al-Kaabi (1994), pp. 2–3 and Mojtahed-Zadeh (2015), pp. 26–27.
[6]Hilal Al-Kaabi (1994), pp. 2–3 and Mattair (2005), p. 7.

3.1   General Background

When, on 30 November 1971, Great Britain withdrew from the Gulf region, the
military forces of Iran took control over the Lesser and Greater Tunbs and Abu
Musa. Iran has held them, irrespective of the UAE regular protests, ever since.[7]

Great Britain began to exercise its influence in the Gulf region at the beginning of
the nineteenth century. The official reason given by Great Britain was the necessity
to grant protection against the pirate activities of the Qawasim (singular: al-Qasimi),
who according to the British East India Company launched attacks against British
and British-protected vessels in the waters of the Gulf, the Arabian Sea and the
Northern Indian Ocean. It has to be noted, however, that the label 'piracy' has been
recently opposed by some of the Arab historians, who maintain that the Qawasim
were only involved in the protection of the local trade.[8]

The Qawasim were Arab sheiks who operated in the eastern part of the Gulf but
mainly in Ras al-Khaimah and Bandar Lingeh. They were a major maritime power in
the region in the eighteenth century and developed extensive commercial relations
with other ports in the area and other countries, in particular India.[9]

The so-called *Pax Britannica*, literally peace imposed by British rule, was a
British system of truces, treaties as well as military means employed in order to
enforce the British interests and influence in different regions of the world in the
nineteenth century.[10]

The *Pax Britannica* began in point of fact for the Gulf region with the Treaty of
Perpetual Maritime Truce of 4 May 1853 between the East India Company and the
signatories of the General Treaty of 1820 (The General Treaty of Peace with the
Arab Tribes) prohibiting piracy against any vessel but permitting trade, that is the
Qawasim, their allies and Bahrain. The Treaty of Perpetual Maritime Truce gave the
East India Company the right to enforce maritime tranquillity in the Gulf region,
granting the British maritime hegemony in the Gulf. Whereas it required the local
Arab sheiks to refrain from retaliating against any external attacks and denied them
any right of self-defence, it provided at the same time that the British government
would watch over the maintenance of the peace that was concluded and ensure the
observance of the treaty provisions. A British squadron was stationed initially in Ras
al-Khaimah and thereafter for several years on the island Qeshm in order to ensure
the treaty observance and monitor the Qawasim.[11]

The end of the situation created by the *Pax Britannica* in 1971 was a turning point
for the Gulf region and its islands. After the British government decided on 4 January
1968 to withdraw its forces from the Gulf by 1971 and hence indicated the end of the
British control of the defence and foreign policy of the Trucial States, especially

---

[7]Gioia (2017), para. 16.

[8]Beeman (2009), p. 151; see also Ahmadi (2012), p. 8 and Mattair (2005), pp. 38–39.

[9]Beeman (2009), p. 151 and Mattair (2005), p. 34.

[10]Gough (2014), pp. 1–2.

[11]Ahmadi (2012), pp. 9–10; von Bismarck (2013), pp. 7–9 and Mattair (2005), p. 46.

throughout 1970 and 1971, Great Britain offered its good offices to lead discussions between Iran and Ras al-Khaimah (concerning the Lesser and Greater Tunbs) and Sharjah (concerning Abu Musa) with regard to the future fate of the three islands. The outcome of the discussions regarding Abu Masa was the Memorandum of Understanding of 29 November 1971 between Iran and the Ruler of Sharjah, in which neither Iran nor Sharjah relinquished their claims or recognised the territorial claims of the other party to Abu Masa. The control of the island was divided between Iran, which was allowed to exercise jurisdiction over the northern part of the island, and Sharjah, which was allowed to exercise jurisdiction over the southern part of the island. However, a compromise regarding the Tunbs between the Ras al-Khaimah sheikh Saqr and Iran was not reached.[12]

After Great Britain withdrew from the Gulf on 30 November 1971, Iran took control over the Lesser and Greater Tunbs.[13]

On 2 December 1971, the UAE proclaimed independence. At the time, the UAE consisted of six emirates, namely, Abu Dhabi, Dubai, Sharjah, Ajman, Umm al-Qawain and Fujairah. The Ras al-Khaimah joined the federation in February 1972. The UAE became a member of the United Nations (hereinafter UN) on 9 December 1971.[14]

On the same day, the UN Security Council considered the matter of the islands after a complaint filed earlier by Algeria, Iraq, the Libyan Arab Republic and the People's Democratic Republic of Yemen. Whereas Iran claimed that it always exercised sovereignty over the islands, the UAE did not recognise the Iranian claim and protested against the use of force by Iran to obtain control over the islands.[15] Eventually, the Security Council decided to

> defer consideration of the matter to a later date, allowing time for thorough third-party efforts to materialise.[16]

Until today, the matter has not been taken up by the Security Council and the political deadlock continues.

---

[12]Mattair (2005), pp. 114, 118, 120, 121 and Mojtahed-Zadeh (2015), pp. 115, 117 (reprinted text of the Memorandum of Understanding).

[13]Gioia (2017), para. 16.

[14]Mattair (2005), p. 125 and Mojtahed-Zadeh (2015), p. 43.

[15]UNSC Provisional Verbatim (1972).

[16]UNSC Decision (1971).

3.2   The Perspective of Iran

3.2.1   The Historical Supremacy of Iran in the Gulf Region and Its State Sovereignty Over the Islands

Iran claims that the Tunbs had for a lengthy period of time before the enforcement of *Pax Britannica* been in its possession. Iran maintains that, due to the geopolitical and historical factors, it has always had supremacy in the region. Iran's claim to possession of the islands dates back to mid sixth century BC, when Achaemenids consolidated their federative-like State and created a system of the Shahanshahi governance.[17]

According to a view presented by some Iranian scholars, the Arab raids on Iranian possessions in the Gulf region began in the times of the Sasanian Empire (224–685). However, after a period of disturbances, Nader Shah Afshar (1736–1747) restored stability in the region and sent a task force to take over the control over the southern coasts of the Gulf. Moreover, the researchers of Iranian origin claim that almost all Arab and Islamic historians and geographers of the early Islamic era confirmed that all the areas of the Gulf belonged to Iran.[18]

Hence, Iran claims to be the only State present in the region able to prove the exercise of sovereignty over the islands for centuries. In that vein, it denies the quality of 'statehood' with regard to the Arab territories in the Arab Peninsula before the second half of the twentieth century.[19]

Additionally, Iran backs its claim with linguistic considerations in that it contends that the word 'Tunb' is of Persian origin derived from a local Farsi dialect known as 'Tangistani Persian'.[20]

3.2.2   The Qawasim As Persian Subjects

Furthermore, the Iranian claim is based upon an assumption that the Qawasim that ruled and administered the Tunbs in the end of the nineteenth century became Persian subjects. The argument is that the Qawasim of Lingeh ruled the islands in their capacity as Persian officials and therefore the islands belonged to Iran.[21]

3.2.3   The Doctrine of Revocation

After the British left the Gulf region, Iran believed that it reclaimed its previous position in the region. Iran claimed that it resumed its earlier regional role in the wake of Britain. Iranian officials used many opportunities to communicate to the British their will to gain control over the islands; *inter alia*, the then Minister of Court, Assadollah Alam, during his talks with the British Foreign Secretary, Michael

---

[17]Ahmadi (2012), pp. 75–76 and Mojtahed-Zadeh (2015), p. 37.

[18]Mojtahed-Zadeh (2015), pp. 37–39.

[19]Ahmadi (2012), p. 61 and Mojtahed-Zadeh (2015), p. 37.

[20]Mojtahed-Zadeh (1995), p. 56.

[21]Said Zahlan (1978), p. 81.

Steward, mentioned that in Iran's opinion the British presence on the islands was illegal and hence Great Britain illegally wanted to hand them to the sheiks.[22]

3.2.4   A Package Deal with Great Britain

According to Iran, the question of the sovereignty over the islands was closely linked to the question of the sovereignty of Bahrain. Therefore, taking control over the islands was from the Iranian perspective an essential condition for the successful conclusion of the Bahrain dispute. Iran represents the view that it concluded a package deal with Great Britain and since it gave up Bahrain, it expected that Britain and the sheikdoms would compromise over the islands.[23]

3.3   The Perspective of the UAE

The UAE presents its own arguments concerning the dispute over the Greater and Lesser Tunbs. Partially, the arguments constitute the counterarguments to the rationale presented by Iran in the dispute over the islands.

3.3.1   A Priority in Occupation and Control

The first of the UAE arguments is that the early history of the islands is not clear and that the control over them changed many times through history. They argue that there was no supremacy of Iran in the region that would lead to a stabilised control over the territory over the islands. Iran has not provided evidence for a constant identity as a State throughout the millennia. According to the UAE, the Arab sheiks had priority in occupation over the islands since the sheiks hoisted their flag in the islands still not occupied by any of the governments. Therefore, their control of the Southern Gulf and the islands had been established long before the Persian coast was settled.[24]

Moreover, the UAE also relies upon linguistic arguments claiming that the name 'Tunb' is of Arab origin and actually means 'a long rope used to erect a tent'.[25]

3.3.2   The Qawasim Were Independent Rulers Exercising Their Sovereignty Over the Islands

From the UAE's perspective, contrary to the Iranian statement that the islands have stayed under the control of the Qawasim of Lingeh, who were Persian subjects, the islands have been controlled by the Qawasim sheiks of Ras-al-Khaima, who were independent rulers. According to the UAE, the two Qawasim factions separated, which was confirmed around 1870, when the sheiks of Ras al-Khaimah denied the Qawasim of Lingeh entry into the Tunbs and the ruler of Sharjah, Sheikh bin Sultan,

---

[22] Ahmadi (2012), pp. 75–76, 86.

[23] Ahmadi (2012), p. 84.

[24] Hilal Al-Kaabi (1994), pp. 11–12 and Mojtahed-Zadeh (2015), pp. 77–79.

[25] Al Roken (2001), p. 184.

sent off a group of armed men to Abu Masa to drive away ships belonging to the Qawasim of Lingeh. The UAE claim that after the receipt of a message of the Qawasim of the southern coast of the Gulf addressed to the Qawasim of Lingeh, in which the former protested against unauthorised visits of the latter to the islands, the Lingeh Qawasim accepted that the islands belonged to the Qawasim of the southern coast. Moreover, a map published by a German cartographer in 1864 indicates, according to the UAE, that the islands belonged to the Qawasim of the South.[26]

3.3.3 The Emirates As Protected States Were Subjects of Public International Law

The UAE maintains that the fact that it turned over the control of its foreign relations to Great Britain prior to 1971 does not influence the statehood of the emirates as the entities in question had a defined territory and permanent population under the control of their own government and only the control of the foreign relations was voluntarily turned over to the British. Therefore, it did not lack capacity to be a sovereign of the islands.[27]

3.3.4 Persian Occupation of the Islands was Temporary

The Persian occupation of the islands between 1880 and 1887, according to the UAE, lasted for a very short period of time and hence did not suffice to take over the control and sovereignty over the islands.[28]

4   Legal Assessment

4.1   The Factual Challenges Inherent to the Dispute Over the Islands

The biggest challenge concerning the legal status of the Tunbs lies in the lack of clarity and unanimity with regard to the historical facts. Both States present a contradictory course of events or interpretation thereof. Their arguments are more political than legal in their nature. Moreover, the lack of access to impartial historical sources limits the possibilities of legal assessment of the status of both islands. A thorough overview of Arabic and Farsi language historical sources would be indispensable in order to establish clear facts that could constitute a basis for the legal analysis. Notwithstanding these difficulties, the following legal assessment aims to present a complex analysis of the legal status of the islands, based on the aforementioned factual background and arguments of both States.

---

[26]Al Roken (2001), pp. 181, 189.

[27]Mattair (2005), p. 197.

[28]Hilal Al-Kaabi (1994), p. 25 and Al Roken (2001), p. 184.

4.2   The Assessment of the Arguments of the UAE and Iran

The linguistic arguments of both States, as well as the examples of administrative actions of the Iranian and UAE officials with regard to the islands, certainly may constitute an indication that a State has a historical link of some kind to a specific geographical region or exercises a certain level of control over a territory, but neither the linguistic derivation nor the administrative measures may *per se* constitute legally valid evidence for territorial title or sovereignty over a territory. Moreover, the arguments of both States concerning the priority in occupation or the location of the islands, although politically fetching, are also not convincing from the standpoint of public international law since a title by discovery is only an inchoate one, if not supported by evidence of effective occupation, and a title based on contiguity has no standing in international law.[29] The question of whether Great Britain was entitled to exercise some of the sovereign rights over the islands on behalf of the emirates depends directly on the question of whether the emirates might and could be considered as States within the meaning of public international law. Although there are some good indications that the emirates had a defined territory and permanent population under governmental control, here again there is a lack of sufficient clarity, based upon historical facts, with regard to the permanency of the population and the criterion of an established government. Therefore, in the case at stake, the evidence concerning a valid historical title to the islands proving the sovereignty is inconclusive. What ought to be done in such situation from the legal point of view is discussed in detail below.

4.3   The Actions of Iran and the Prohibition of Threat or Use of Force in International Relations

Article 2 (4) of the Charter of the United Nations (hereinafter UN Charter)[30] prohibits the threat or use of force and calls on all Members to respect the sovereignty, territorial integrity and political independence of other States. A comprehensive prohibition also constitutes a part of customary international law.[31] Taking control over a territory with military force constitutes a breach of the prohibition to use force unless this territory is derelict or unclaimed or a State has a valid legal title to this territory.[32] Regarding the taking of control over the Lesser and Greater Tunbs by Iran after Great Britain withdrew from the Gulf on 30 November 1971, an original acquisition of the islands was not possible since the territory was neither derelict or unclaimed. If the Tunbs were a *terra nullius* at the time, as a general principle, Iran could acquire their territory by means of occupation. However, the Tunbs were not

---

[29]PCA (1928), pp. 846, 855.

[30]UN Charter (1945).

[31]Compare *inter alia* Dinstein (2011), p. 89f. and Randelzhofer (2002), Article 51 para. 3.

[32]Epping (2014), p. 65.

and are not a *terra nullius*. One of the States has sovereign rights over the islands. Otherwise, it would be necessary to come to a conclusion that Great Britain exercised sovereignty over the islands. However, Great Britain has not claimed that it exercised—if any—originary or derivative sovereign rights over the territory of the islands. If this was the case, it could effectively give these rights over to the UAE. Nevertheless, the understanding of the situation between Great Britain and the UAE is rather that the rights were exercised on behalf of the sheikdoms. This brings us back to the question already asked. Moreover, although the islands do not actually have a population, thereby eliminating the possibility for the principles on the self-determination of peoples as codified in Article 1 (2) of the UN Charter at first glance, it may still be possible to apply these principles *mutatis mutandis* to a territory that does not constitute 'nobody's' land but has a disputed and inconclusive history in order to exclude any possible 'colonial' title over the disputed territory. There remains, hence, still the question of whether Iran or the UAE has a valid legal title to that territory that could not be disputed by another State.

Therefore, it has to be analysed whether Iran had a valid legal title to the islands or acquired the territory of the islands in a derivative way. If it is not the case, the actions of Iran constitute a breach of the prohibition on the use force by States in international relations both under Article 2 (4) of the UN Charter and under the rules of customary international law.

4.4 The Situation of the Tunbs Under the Rules Concerning the Determination of Borders in Public International Law

In the light of the aforementioned factual uncertainties, it is already doubtful whether Iran could have had a valid undisputed legal title to the islands in 1971. Nevertheless, a closer look shall be given to the rules on the determination of borders in international law and their application in the present case.

State borders are established either in international treaties, including mainly peace treaties, or according to the principle of undisputed possession, that is a situation in which one State has accepted, over a long period of time without any objections, a demarcation made unilaterally by another State.[33] With regard to the demarcation, maps are of particular importance. However, it has to be distinguished between the official maps, some of which constitute annexes to international treaties and hence either primary or supplementary means of treaty interpretation,[34] and private maps. The private maps, although being an indication with regard to the demarcation, do not have the legal force of evidence.

In the dispute concerning the Tunbs, there is no international treaty regarding directly the legal status of both islands concluded between the UAE and Iran, such as the Memorandum of Understanding of 29 November 1971 between Iran and the

---

[33]See *inter alia* ICJ (1962) and Epping in: Ipsen, supra note 33, p. 55.
[34]Compare ICJ (1962), p. 33f. and ICJ (1959), pp. 220, 225f.

Ruler of Sharjah concerning Abu Masa. Irrespective of the question of whether the alleged package deal with Great Britain, as claimed by Iran, shall be considered valid and legal in the light of public international law, there is no sufficient evidence that such a package deal was concluded between Iran and Great Britain. In the case at stake also, the principle of undisputed possession is not applicable since each of the Sates has been continuously claiming their exclusive title to the territory of the Tunbs. Both States also claim the existence of various maps in favour of their alleged legal title to the islands; however, none of the maps has a quality of an official map. Therefore, Iran, although exercising control over the Tunbs, does not have a legal title to those territories deriving from an international treaty, based on an official map or grounded on the principle of undisputed possession.

4.5   A Derivative Acquisition of the Islands: Annexation and Article 2 (4) of the UN Charter

Annexation, understood as taking over fully and definitely control over a territory of a foreign State by another State by force or at least against the will of the territory owner, used to be an accepted mode of acquiring title to territory under traditional international law,[35] but it is no longer legal in the light of the aforementioned prohibition to use force in international relations. Although some of the UN Members are ready to tacitly accept in some cases the *status quo* after the effective control over a territory had been taken over by force and against the will of the territory owner, which was, for instance, the case of Tibet taken over by the People's Republic of China in 1951 or the occupation of the Chadian oasis Aouzou by Libya in 1994, annexation as a way to obtain a foreign territory is without doubt contrary to the prohibition to use force in international relations. The acceptance of an illegal state on the one hand and the comprehensive prohibition to use force on the other would lead to an unsolvable contradiction. Even if it is disputed to what extent the principle *ex inuira lex non oritur*, according to which a violation of law cannot constitute a precedent for it or lead to the legality of such action itself, applies in the public international law, in that case the principle of legality overrides the principle of effectiveness due to the significance and extensiveness of the prohibition to use force in international relations. Therefore, no State is entitled to unilaterally and by force establish its borders with the neighbouring States.[36] Moreover, States are under a legal obligation not to recognise as lawful territorial changes effected by means of annexation.[37]

If the Tunbs were a *terra nullius* at the time, as a general principle Iran could acquire their territory in a legal way by means of occupation. The relevant question in this context would be whether the Iranian effective military occupation would be

---

[35] See Epping (2014), p. 65f and Hofmann (2017), para. 1.

[36] Compare Epping (2014), p. 68.

[37] Hofmann (2017), para. 15.

contrary to Article 2 (4) of the UN Charter since the prohibition to use force in international relations stops the acquisition of State's territory.[38] It was generally accepted by States that an effective occupation of a nobody's land could lead to its legal acquisition.[39] However, it is not clear whether this would still hold accurate today in the light of Article 2 (4) of the UN Charter as the conflict between Iran and the UAE has led to an emergence of a threat to international peace and security. Nevertheless, as already stated above, since the Tunbs are not a *terra nullius*, this is rather a theoretical question with regard to the situation of the islands.

Since Iran does not have an undisputed legal title to the Tunbs and took over the control over both islands by using military force in 1971, there is no possibility that Iran obtained the territory of the islands in a derivative way through annexation that would be compatible with the prohibition to use force in international relations. Hence, Iran also does not have a derivative legal title to the islands.

Certainly, the State exercising effective control over a certain territory has specific legal obligations towards other States that are inherent to that factual situation. However, the international responsibility or liability following from the effective control over a territory does not entail any sovereignty or legitimacy of title over the territory. As stated by the ICJ in its Advisory Opinion concerning Namibia:

> The fact that South Africa no longer has any title to administer the Territory does not release it from its obligations and responsibilities under international law towards other States in respect of the exercise of its powers in relation to this Territory. Physical control of a territory, and not sovereignty or legitimacy of title, is the basis of State liability for acts affecting other States.[40]

Nevertheless, a reverse conclusion, that is, that a physical control over a territory alone could entail a legal title to that territory, is—as stated above—not tenable in the light of current public international law.

4.6   Possible Modes of Settling the Dispute Between the UAE and Iran

In the case at stake, in which the factual background and the existence of a valid legal title to the islands is highly disputed by both States, the most effective solution would be an action from the UN Security Council. Instead of deciding to 'defer consideration of the matter to a later date, allowing time for thorough third-party efforts to materialise',[41] the Security Council should play a more active role in finding the solution to the unclear legal status of the islands. Due to the political and economic significance of the islands, as well as their location, it is not far-fetched to say that any further escalation of the dispute between the UAE and Iran may lead to

---

[38]Epping (2014), p. 65ff.

[39]Compare Epping (2014), p. 69ff.

[40]ICJ (1971), p. 54.

[41]See supra point 3.1.

the emergence of a threat to international peace and security. Whether the UN Security Council is able and willing to play such role in the resolution of the dispute over the Tunbs is not a question of law but a question of current politics.

The procedures to bring both States to the negotiating table may include good offices or dispute resolution by means of mediation or conciliation and might be initiated by international institutions such as the UN. A ruling of the ICJ or an impartial arbitral tribunal would be certainly an option granting a stable solution to the dispute between the UAE and Iran. Also, bilateral negotiations may lead to a successful outcome. However, in the present case, it seems that the major problem is the lack of will of the States involved to resolve the issue. Nevertheless, it has to be stressed that both the UAE and Iran are obliged to resolve the territorial dispute over the Lesser and Greater Tunbs in a peaceful way.

5   Conclusion

The transfer of power from Great Britain to the Arab sheikdoms in the Gulf was complicated and led to the emergence of numerous boundary disputes. Some of them have already been resolved. The particular difficulty with the legal assessment of the status of the Greater and Lesser Tunbs lies in the lack of a clear factual background. Since lawyers shall ideally work with clearly established facts, a background work of impartial historians consisting of the gathering or verification of the historical data from various Arabic, Farsi and other sources would be of utmost importance in order to establish the facts that are at present disputed by both States. Nevertheless, in the current situation, the only solution not contradictory to public international law is a peaceful settlement of the dispute between both States. The actions of Iran that took unilateral control over the islands by means of military force are contrary to one of the basic principles of *ius ad bellum*, which is the prohibition to use force in international relations. If one asks the question of whether a peaceful solution of the dispute over the Tunbs is still possible, one has to be reminded that both disputes over Bahrain and a part of Kuwait ended peacefully. Therefore, the possibility of a peaceful solution of the dispute over the Tunbs, as politically difficult as it may be, is not completely unrealistic.

References

Ahmadi K (2012) Islands and international politics in the Persian Gulf, Abu Musa and the Tunbs in strategic perspective. Routledge, New York

Al Roken MA (2001) Dimensions of the UAE–Iran dispute over Three Islands. In: Al Abed I, Hellyer P (eds) United Arab Emirates: a new perspective. Trident Press Ltd, London

Beeman WO (2009) Gulf society. In: Potter LG (ed) The Persian Gulf in history. Palgrave Macmillan, New York, pp 147–163

Dinstein Y (2011) War, aggression and self-defence, 5th edn. Cambridge University Press, Cambridge

Epping V (2014) Völkerrechtssubjekte. In: Ipsen (ed) Völkerrecht, 6th edn. C.H. Beck Verlag, Munich, p 65

Gioia A (2017) Persian Gulf, Max Planck Encyclopedia of Public International Law Online. http://
opil.ouplaw.com/home/EPIL. Accessed 25 Oct 2017

Gough B (2014) Pax Britannica, ruling the waves and keeping the peace before Armageddon.
Palgrave Macmillan, London

Hilal Al-Kaabi M (1994) The question of Iranian occupation of the Islands, Greater Tunb, Lesser
Tunb, and Abu Musa Belonging to the United Arab Emirates,17 May 1994, US Army War
College, www.dtic.mil/cgi-bin/GetTRDoc?AD=ADA280066. Accessed 25 Oct 2015

Hofmann R (2017) Annexation. Max Planck encyclopedia of public international law online, http://
opil.ouplaw.com/home/EPIL. Accessed 25 Oct 2015

ICJ (1959) Case concerning sovereignty over frontier land case (Belgium v. Netherlands), ICJ Rep.
p 209

ICJ (1962) International Court of Justice (hereinafter ICJ), case concerning the Temple of Preah
Vihear (Cambodia v. Thailand), ICJ Rep. p 6

ICJ (1971) Legal consequences for States of the continued presence of South Africa in Namibia
(South West Africa) notwithstanding Security Council Resolution 276 (1970), Advisory Opinion, 21 June 1971, ICJ Rep. p 16

Mattair TR (2005) The three occupied UAE Islands, The Tunbs and Abu Musa. The Emirates
Center for Strategic Studies and Research, Abu Dhabi

Mojtahed-Zadeh P (1995) The Islands of Tunb and Abu Musa: an Iranian argument in search of
peace and cooperation in the Persian Gulf. SOAS, University of London, London

Mojtahed-Zadeh P (2015) Maritime political geography, The Persian Gulf Islands of Tunbs and
Abu Musa. Universal Publishers, Boca Raton

PCA (1928) Permanent Court of Arbitration, Island of Las Palmas (or Miangas) Case (Netherlands
v. United States of America), Arbitral Award of 4 April 1928. RIAA II:829–871

Randelzhofer A (2002) Article 51. In: Simma B (ed) The charter of the United Nations. A
commentary, 2nd edn. Oxford University Press, Oxford

Said Zahlan R (1978) The origins of the United Arab Emirates. Palgrave Macmillan, London

UN Charter (1945) Charter of the United Nations of 26 June 1945 UN Conference on International
Organization Doc., vol. XV (1945), 335

UN News Centre (2013) http://www.un.org/apps/news/story.asp?NewsID=46124#.Vjalk7cvdD8.
Accessed 25 Oct 2017

UNSC Provisional Verbatim (1972) Record of the sixteen hundred and tenth meeting of the UN
security council, 9 December 1971, S/10436

UNSC Decision (1971) decision of 9 December 1971, Official Records, 26th yr., Resolutions and
Decisions of the Security Council, p 11

von Bismarck H (2013) British policy in the Persian Gulf 1961–1968, conceptions of informal
Empire. Palgrave Macmillan, London

Dorota Marianna Banaszewska The author is former a research assistant and a doctoral candi-
date in Public International Law at the Chair of Public Law, especially Public International Law,
European Law and Foreign Constitutional Law, European-University Viadrina in Frankfurt (Oder),
Germany, as well as a Polish attorney at law (*adwokat*) and German *assessor iuris*.

After havening successfully completed the studies of German and Polish laws at the European-
University Viadrina (Germany) and Adam-Mickiewicz University (Poland), Ms. Banaszewska
completed a three-year-long training for Polish attorneys at law in order to practice law in Poland
and passed two German Legal State Exams in order to become a fully qualified lawyer in Germany
(*assessor iuris*). Her legal education also includes studies in Institut d'études politiques de Paris
(France).

Part II

Maritime Safety and Maritime Security

International Law and Search and Rescue

Rick Button

Abstract

This article provides a broad overview of several international law and policy issues that search and rescue (SAR) authorities worldwide should consider. First, the article will discuss the global SAR system's international framework and organization implemented by coastal states. While not perfect, the global SAR system provides an important basis on which coastal states can build cooperative relationships to enable them to conduct this important lifesaving mission more effectively. Second, this article will review the SAR responsibilities and international legal requirements placed on shipmasters and coastal states as they work together in coordinating and conducting maritime SAR operations. In addition, this section also will briefly discuss the tragic issue of mixed migration by sea from a SAR perspective. Third, this article will address two additional SAR-specific issues that legal advisers and policy makers need to consider: the responsibilities and requirements of a ship or aircraft when conducting a rescue operation within another coastal state's territorial sea and the issue of forcibly evacuating a person from a vessel when doing so is, in the judgment of the SAR responders on scene, the only way to save the person's life. May SAR responders use force to compel a person to abandon his vessel? What type of force should be considered? The discussion of each of these unique operational issues will provide points to consider from both policy and international law perspectives.

This article was originally published in Naval War College Review, Winter 2017, Vol. 70, No. 1.

R. Button (✉)
United States Coast Guard, Washington, DC, USA
e-mail: Richard.A.Button@uscg.mil

J. Schildknecht et al. (eds.), *Operational Law in International Straits and Current Maritime Security Challenges*, Operational Maritime Law 1,
https://doi.org/10.1007/978-3-319-72718-9_7

1   Introduction

Treasury Department
Office of the Secretary
Washington, D.C.
November 15, 1897

*Sir: The best information obtainable gives the assurance of truth to the reports that a
    fleet of eight whaling vessels are icebound in the Arctic Ocean, somewhere in the
    vicinity of Point Barrow, and that the 265 persons who were, at last accounts, on
    board these vessels are in all probability in dire distress. These conditions call for
    prompt and energetic action, looking to the relief of the imprisoned whalemen. It
    therefore has been determined to send an expedition to the rescue.*

*Believing that your long experience in arctic work, your familiarity with the region
    of Arctic Alaska from Point Barrow, south, and the coast line washed by the
    Bering Sea, from which you but recently returned, your known ability and
    reputation as an able and competent officer, all especially fit you for the trust,
    you have been selected to command the relief expedition. Your ship, the Bear, will
    be officered by a competent body of men and manned by a crew of your own
    selection. The ship will be fully equipped, fitted, and provisioned for the perilous
    work in view, for such it must be under the most favorable conditions. . ..*

*You are hereby given full authority and the largest possible latitude to act in every
    emergency that may arise, and while impossibilities are not expected, it is
    expected that you, with your gallant officers and crew, will leave no avenue of
    possible success untried to render successful the expedition which you
    command. . ..*

*Mindful of the arduous and perilous expedition upon which you are about to enter, I
    bid you, your officers and men, Godspeed upon your errand of mercy, and wish
    you a successful voyage and safe return.*[1]

The search for and rescue of persons in distress is a centuries-old, time-honored
tradition. The above instructions provided to Captain Francis Tuttle of the
U.S. Revenue Cutter Service over a century ago, as he prepared his crew to rescue
whalers trapped in ice in the Arctic Ocean, epitomize the dedicated efforts of
mariners and coastal states in saving lives at sea.

This lifesaving tradition continues unabated today, albeit with new challenges.
The long-standing challenges provided by harsh weather and sea conditions, long
distances, and limited available search-and-rescue (SAR) resources remain the same.
However, since Captain Tuttle's successful rescue, international and national SAR
organizations, practices, procedures, capabilities, and technologies have continued
to improve. There is now a greater commitment and resolve by the international
community to work together to save lives at sea.

---

[1]Gage (1897), pp. 5–10.

Owing to the unique hazards encountered by ships as they ply the world's oceans and by aircraft on transoceanic flights, as well as the challenges to coordinating and conducting maritime lifesaving operations, coastal states implemented national SAR systems and SAR organizations to search for and rescue those in distress at sea. However, prior to the 1970s, there was no standardized system globally for organization, coordination, and conduct of SAR operations. Seeking to harmonize these organizations and procedures, the international community, through the International Maritime Organization (IMO), established in 1979 the International Convention on Maritime Search and Rescue (SAR Convention). The SAR Convention provides an internationally standardized foundation and framework for coastal states to work together in implementing a global maritime SAR system.[2] The IMO describes how the SAR Convention was developed to provide a plan for and implementation of a system to save the lives of persons in distress at sea more effectively:

> The 1979 Convention... was aimed at developing an international SAR plan, so that, no matter where an accident occurs, the rescue of persons in distress at sea will be co-ordinated by a SAR organization and, when necessary, by co-operation between neighbouring SAR organizations.

Although the obligation of ships to go to the assistance of vessels in distress was enshrined both in tradition and in international treaties... there was, until the adoption of the SAR Convention, no international system covering search and rescue operations. In some areas, there was a well-established organization able to provide assistance promptly and efficiently; in others, there was nothing at all.[3]

Under the internationally recognized foundation provided through the SAR Convention, each coastal state organizes its maritime SAR authorities and organization on the basis of its available SAR resources, unique geographic challenges, political considerations, cultural influences, available funding, and domestic SAR legal framework. Each country's national and agency-specific SAR organizations then develop policies, procedures, tactics, and training to implement their respective national SAR system, which then becomes an integral component of the global SAR system. Through this internationally standardized and organized framework, coastal states work together in responding to and rescuing those imperiled at sea.

This article pursues several objectives. First, it seeks to provide a broad overview of the global SAR system's international framework and organization as set forth in the annex to the SAR Convention and implemented by coastal states. Despite that implementation over the past 45 years, many people remain unaware of the existence of a standardized, global, maritime SAR system. While not perfect, the global SAR system provides an important basis on which coastal states can build cooperative relationships to enable them to conduct this important lifesaving mission more effectively.

---

[2]SAR Convention (1979); number of contracting states 2017: 106.
[3]Ibid.

Second, the article focuses on the specific SAR responsibilities and international legal requirements placed on shipmasters and coastal states as they work together in coordinating and conducting maritime SAR operations; both are important lifesaving partners. Passenger ships, cargo ships, and warships of all types transit across the world's oceans every day. In many instances, one of these ships may be the only available SAR resource in the vicinity of a person in distress and could make the difference between life and death. The coastal state is responsible for coordinating the SAR operation and supporting the responding shipmaster. The article discusses several international conventions that form the legal basis for this important lifesaving relationship. The responsibilities of a warship in rendering assistance to persons in distress also are considered.

This section also will discuss the tragic issue of mixed migration by sea from a SAR perspective. The question that needs to be considered is whether these mixed-migration incidents—in which thousands of persons are taking to the sea, in many instances fleeing for their lives—and the ensuing response actions should even be considered SAR operations conducted under the SAR Convention or instead law-enforcement/national border security incidents.

Third, this article will address two additional situations that SAR legal advisers and policy makers should consider and for which they should develop policy and prepare SAR responders.

First, under international law, the responsibilities and requirements of a ship or aircraft when conducting a rescue operation within another coastal state's territorial sea will be considered. The shipmaster's duty to render assistance to persons in distress does not stop at a coastal state's territorial sea boundary. When such a situation occurs, can a ship at sea, on being notified of persons in distress, enter a coastal state's territorial sea to render assistance? Can an aircraft enter into a coastal state's airspace over its territorial sea to assist in a rescue operation? Seven different scenarios will be presented to highlight the distinctions and limitations of rescue operations within a coastal state's territorial sea.

Second, this article will address the issue of forcibly evacuating a person from a vessel when doing so is, in the judgment of the SAR responders on scene, the only way to save the person's life. May the SAR responder use force to compel a person to abandon his vessel? What type of force should be considered? SAR authorities should develop policies and procedures in preparation for the day when a person in distress does not want to leave his vessel even in a life-threatening situation.

This article does not provide exhaustive legal analyses of these various issues. Its purposes are to provide a synopsis of the international law addressing these subjects and to address questions that SAR authorities and responders should consider in developing future SAR policies and procedures. It is my hope that this article will provide the reader with a better understanding of the legal framework for the global SAR system and serve as an impetus for further discussion of these important topics.

2   Overview: Global Search-and-Rescue System

The thing I constantly think about—we were so, so very lucky. The difference between our ship and the Titanic is we weren't caught in the middle of the ocean... If we had been caught in the middle of the ocean, most of these people wouldn't have survived.—Mike Kajian, passenger on board Costa Concordia[4]

The world's oceans constitute a dangerous environment that covers approximately 70% of the earth's surface. The centuries-old duty of the mariner transiting the world's oceans to render assistance to those in distress at sea was implemented formally through several international conventions.[5] However, large-scale disasters at sea in the early twentieth century, many involving significant loss of life, continued to plague the shipping community. The continued loss of life made it apparent that, alone, this duty to render assistance was insufficient; an international SAR system for organizing, coordinating, and conducting rescues at sea was required.

Before the adoption of the SAR Convention, there was no overarching international plan for coordinating the conduct of maritime lifesaving operations. Some maritime regions did have coastal states that implemented robust, effective, national SAR systems, while others had very limited or no SAR resources or coordinating structures to render assistance to persons in distress. There was no internationally recognized system to coordinate and conduct SAR operations because there was no governing international regime to standardize SAR processes and procedures.

The adoption of the SAR Convention filled this gap by instituting a framework under which coastal states could implement their respective national SAR systems,[6] including the establishment of rescue coordination centers (RCCs) and rescue subcenters (RSCs) to coordinate operations within a coastal state's SAR region.[7]

Soon after the IMO's SAR Convention came into force in 1985, it became apparent that additional guidance was required. To assist states in meeting their SAR obligations under the SAR Convention, as well as the comparable requirements

---

[4]Jones (2013).

[5]These international conventions will be discussed in greater detail later in this chapter.

[6]The annex to the SAR Convention (1979) mandates (paragraph 2.1.2) that "Parties shall either individually or, if appropriate, in co-operation with other States, establish the following basic elements of a search and rescue service: (1) legal framework; (2) assignment of a responsible authority; (3) organization of available resources; (4) communication facilities; (5) co-ordination and operational functions; and (6) processes to improve the service including planning, domestic and international co-operative relationships and training. Parties shall, as far as practicable, follow relevant minimum standards and guidelines developed by the Organization."

[7]The annex to the SAR Convention (1979) provides (paragraphs 1.3.4, 1.3.5, and 1.3.6, respectively) the following definitions: "Search and Rescue Region: An area of defined dimensions associated with a rescue co-ordination centre within which search and rescue services are provided"; "Rescue co-ordination centre: A unit responsible for promoting efficient organization of search and rescue services and for co-ordinating the conduct of search and rescue operations within a search and rescue region"; "Rescue sub-center: A unit subordinate to a rescue co-ordination center established to complement the latter according to particular provisions of the responsible authorities."

that the International Civil Aviation Organization (ICAO) mandated in the Convention on International Civil Aviation ("Chicago Convention"),[8] both organizations jointly developed the three-volume *International Aeronautical and Maritime Search and Rescue Manual* (IAMSAR manual).[9] This reference provides guidelines and procedures to assist states in developing and harmonizing their respective aeronautical and maritime SAR organizations, planning, and operations, as well as providing the basis for coordinating and conducting SAR operations among states.

Developed for the SAR manager, the IAMSAR manual, volume 1 *(Organization and Management)*, "attempts to ensure that managers understand the basic concepts and principles involved in SAR, and to provide practical information and guidance to help managers establish and support SAR services."[10] Volume 2 *(Mission Co-ordination)* provides guidance and information to personnel who plan and coordinate SAR operations.[11] Volume 3 *(Mobile Facilities)* was developed for carriage on board vessels and aircraft that may be called on to assist in a SAR operation.

Volume 1 explains the IMO and ICAO's purpose for developing the IAMSAR manual:

> ICAO and IMO jointly developed this Manual to foster co-operation between themselves, between neighbouring States, and between aeronautical and maritime authorities. The goal of the Manual is to assist State authorities to economically establish effective SAR services, to promote harmonization of aeronautical and maritime SAR services, and to ensure that persons in distress will be assisted without regard to their locations, nationality, or circumstances. State authorities are encouraged to promote, where possible[,] harmonization of aeronautical and maritime SAR services.[12]

Within the global SAR system, roles and responsibilities also have been developed to provide for the efficient organization and implementation of a coastal state's national SAR system. There are three primary levels of coordination: (1) the SAR coordinator (SC) is that person or agency with the responsibility for the management and oversight of a coastal state's SAR organization[13]; (2) the SAR mission

---

[8]Convention on International Civil Aviation (1944).

[9]IAMSAR manual (2013).

[10]The annex to the SAR Convention (1979) defines (paragraph 1.3.3) *search and rescue service* as "[t]he performance of distress monitoring, communication, co-ordination and search and rescue functions, including provision of medical advice, initial medical assistance, or medical evacuation, through the use of public and private resources including co-operating aircraft, vessels and other craft and installations."

[11]IAMSAR manual (2013), vol. 1, p. v.

[12]Ibid., pp. 1–1 (paragraph 1.1.3). It should also be noted (paragraph 1.3.1) that SAR services can be established by individual states or regionally: "These services can be provided by States individually establishing effective national SAR organizations, or by establishing a SAR organization jointly with one or more other States."

[13]Ibid., p. xiii. The SC is defined as "[o]ne or more persons or agencies within an Administration with overall responsibility for establishing and providing SAR services and ensuring that planning for those services is properly co-ordinated." Volume 2 goes on to state (paragraph 1.2.2) that "SCs have the overall responsibility for establishing, staffing, equipping, and managing the SAR system, including providing appropriate legal and funding support, establishing RCCs and rescue

coordinator (SMC) is the official temporarily assigned to coordinate, direct, and supervise a SAR operation[14]; and (3) an on-scene coordinator (OSC) may be assigned by the SMC to coordinate SAR operations on scene when multiple resources are working together within a specified area.[15] Additionally, an aircraft coordinator (ACO) can be assigned by the SMC or OSC in a SAR operation if the response involves multiple aircraft. The ACO would be responsible for flight safety and for ensuring effective use of the aircraft in the conduct of the operation.[16]

2.1   Search-and-Rescue Regions

Implementation of the international SAR framework mandated by the SAR Convention necessitated the division of the world's oceans into a patchwork quilt of maritime SAR regions in which each coastal state assumed responsibility for coordinating and conducting SAR operations.[17] It is commonly assumed that coastal states establish their SAR regions unilaterally. However, SAR region lines of delimitation are only provisional; the SAR Convention mandates that coastal states with adjacent SAR regions enter into cooperative agreements to establish their respective SAR regions formally.[18] These SAR agreements not only delimit the SAR regions but ideally serve as the basis for cooperation and coordination between coastal states in the conduct of SAR operations.[19]

---

sub-centres (RSCs), providing or arranging for SAR facilities, co-ordinating SAR training, and developing SAR policies. SCs are the top level SAR managers; each State normally will have one or more persons or agencies for whom this designation may be appropriate."

[14]Ibid., vol. 1, p. xiii. The SMC is defined (paragraph 1.2.3) as "[t]he official temporarily assigned to co-ordinate response to an actual or apparent distress situation." See also ibid., vol. 2, pp. 1–2.

[15]Ibid., vol. 1, p. xii. The OSC is defined (paragraph 1.2.4) as "[a] person designated to co-ordinate search and rescue operations within a specified area." See also ibid., vol. 2, pp. 1–3.

[16]Ibid., vol. 1, p. xi. The ACO is defined (paragraph 1.2.5) as "[a] person or team who co-ordinates the involvement of multiple aircraft in SAR operations in support of the SAR mission co-ordinator and on-scene co-ordinator." See also ibid., vol. 2, pp. 1–3.

[17]Comparable to the annex to the SAR Convention (1979), the annex 12 of the Chicago Convention (1944) (Search and Rescue) provides the framework for contracting states to implement an aeronautical global SAR system. The SAR system under the Chicago Convention (1944) also has aeronautical SAR regions worldwide, in which contracting states are responsible for coordinating SAR operations. This global aeronautical SAR system complements, or stands in parallel to, the maritime system.

[18]The annex to the SAR Convention (1979) states (paragraph 2.1.4): "Each search and rescue region shall be established by agreement among Parties concerned. The Secretary-General shall be notified of such agreements."

[19]SAR agreements can be bilateral or multilateral. For example, in 2011, the eight Arctic nations (Canada, Denmark, Finland, Iceland, Norway, Russia, Sweden, and the United States) concluded an agreement that delimited the entire Arctic region into aeronautical (Chicago Convention (1944)) and maritime (SAR Convention (1979)) SAR regions between the parties. It also formalized SAR cooperation and coordination among the eight states. Agreement on Cooperation on Aeronautical and Maritime Search and Rescue in the Arctic (2011).

One practical benefit in developing a global SAR system is that with the world-wide assignment of maritime SAR regions, states are not required to provide SAR services for their own citizens wherever they travel. Coastal states provide SAR services to anyone in distress within a SAR region, without regard to the person's nationality, status, or circumstances.[20]

Two other important factors need to be understood regarding coastal states' implementation of SAR services within their maritime SAR regions.[21] First, a maritime SAR region is not an extension of a coastal state's national "boundaries" but rather a geographic area in which the coastal state accepts responsibility to coordinate SAR operations.[22] This is an especially important concept to understand since a coastal state may extend a large portion of its maritime SAR region into the high seas.[23] Second, the SAR Convention does not mandate that a coastal state must have all the SAR resources necessary to respond to a distress within its entire maritime SAR region. As previously stated, SAR regions only define a geographic area in which a coastal state is responsible for "coordinating" SAR operations.[24] The requirements of the SAR Convention build on the time-honored tradition of shared responsibility for coordinating and conducting lifesaving operations at sea. All available resources should be used to save lives: local, regional, national, and international; volunteer; commercial and shipping; aircraft; etc.[25] The circumstances

---

[20]IAMSAR manual (2013), vol. 1, pp. 1–5 (paragraph 1.6.3).

[21]See note 11 for a definition of *search and rescue service*. The coastal state is responsible for the coordination and conduct of SAR operations within its SAR region.

[22]The annex to the SAR Convention (1979) (paragraph 2.1.7) is very clear on this point: "The delimitation of search and rescue regions is not related to and shall not prejudice the delimitation of any boundary between States." The IAMSAR manual (2013), vol. 1, pp. 2–8 (paragraph 2.3.15 [e]) goes on to state that "[a]n SRR [SAR region] is established solely to ensure that primary responsibility for co-ordinating SAR services for that geographic area is assumed by some State. SRR limits should not be viewed as barriers to assisting persons in distress.... In this respect co-operation between States, their RCCs and their SAR services should be as close as possible."

[23]The High Seas Convention (1958), article 1, defines *high seas* as "all parts of the sea that are not included in the territorial sea or in the internal waters of a State."; number of parties 2017: 77. UNCLOS (1982), which replaced the High Seas Convention (1958), states in article 86: "The provisions of this Part apply to all parts of the sea that are not included in the exclusive economic zone, in the territorial sea or in the internal waters of a State, or in the archipelagic waters of an archipelagic State." UNCLOS (1982) entered into force: 16 November 1994; number of parties 2017: 167.

[24]The annex to the SAR Convention (1979) (paragraph 2.1.9) states: "Parties having accepted responsibility to provide search and rescue services for a specified area shall use search and rescue units and other available facilities for providing assistance to a person who is, or appears to be, in distress at sea." (See note 59 for the definition of *SAR facilities* and *SAR units*.) The annex to the SAR Convention (1979) allows for the use of any resources to save lives at sea. The national administration must be able to coordinate the response to persons in distress though the RCC/RSC.

[25]The IAMSAR manual (2013), vol. 1, paragraph 2.1.1, provides an excellent overview when describing SAR as an international *system:* "The SAR system, like any other system, has individual components but must work together to provide the overall service. Development of a SAR system typically involves establishment of one or more SRRs, along with capabilities to receive alerts and to co-ordinate and provide SAR services within each SRR. Each SRR is associated with an RCC.

of a particular distress incident should dictate what available resources can and should be used most effectively.

2.2   Rescue Coordination Center (RCC)/Rescue Subcenter (RSC)

The coastal state's RCCs and RSCs are the backbone of the global SAR system. They are responsible for the organization of SAR services and the coordination and conduct of SAR operations within maritime SAR regions.[26] The annex to the SAR Convention requires assignment of one RCC or RSC to each maritime SAR region.[27] The RCC should be located where it can perform its coordination function most effectively, have 24-h availability, be staffed with trained personnel, have the ability to receive distress alerts, and maintain plans of operation for different types of distress scenarios.[28]

In situations in which an RCC may not be able to coordinate SAR services effectively over a specific geographic area within its SAR region, a coastal state's SAR authority can establish an RSC to exercise responsibility for coordinating SAR operations within a designated search-and-rescue subregion (SRS).[29] The RSC, which can be just as capable as an RCC, may be a delegated authority to coordinate

---

For aeronautical purposes, SRRs often coincide with flight information regions (FIRs). The goal of ICAO and IMO conventions relating to SAR is to establish a global SAR system. Operationally, the global SAR system relies upon States to establish their national SAR systems and then integrate provision of their services with other States for world-wide coverage."

[26]Ibid., pp. 2–3, paragraph 2.3.1.

[27]The annex to the SAR Convention (1979) (paragraph 2.3.1) states: "Parties shall individually or in co-operation with other States establish rescue co-ordination centres for their search and rescue services and such rescue sub-centres as they consider appropriate." It should be noted that under the Chicago Convention (1944)'s annex 12, the global aeronautical SAR system also requires contracting states to make provision for an aeronautical RCC (ARCC); one ARCC is assigned for each aeronautical SAR region. By comparison, under the global maritime SAR system, a maritime RCC (MRCC) coordinates maritime SAR operations in a designated maritime SAR region. When nations implement a national SAR system in which a particular RCC coordinates both aeronautical and maritime SAR, it is known as a joint RCC. Where a coastal state has instituted both ARCCs and MRCCs, aeronautical and maritime SAR authorities must work closely together to ensure the various types of SAR operations with overlapping aeronautical and maritime SAR regions are effectively coordinated. When considering the coordination between aeronautical and maritime SAR services, the annex to the SAR Convention (1979) (paragraph 2.4.1) states: "Parties shall ensure the closest practicable co-ordination between maritime and aeronautical services so as to provide for the most effective and efficient search and rescue services in and over their search and rescue regions." This same imperative is established as a recommendation in the Chicago Convention (1944)'s annex 12, paragraph 3.2.2.

[28]IAMSAR manual (2013), vol. 1, pp. 2-4–2-5.

[29]Ibid., p. xiv. *Search-and-rescue subregion* is defined as "[a] specified area within a search and rescue region associated with a rescue sub-centre." For example, the U.S. Coast Guard maintains two RSCs (RSC San Juan, Puerto Rico, and RSC Guam) that coordinate SAR operations with their respective SRSs.

SAR operations independently within its SRS. However, an RSC generally has fewer responsibilities than its associated RCC.[30]

The global SAR system, while not perfect, continues to improve every year as nations work together to save lives at sea. SAR authorities worldwide understand their responsibilities under the SAR Convention. Lessons learned from SAR cases are developed and shared among international SAR authorities and organizations. Coastal states in many regions of the world are realizing that effective SAR services cannot be provided independently. In these regions, coastal states are working together to develop regional SAR plans and cooperative arrangements to implement regional SAR systems based on the framework mandated in the SAR Convention. There is still plenty of work to be accomplished, but through the IMO and ICAO positive improvements to the global SAR system continue to be made.

2.3   Obligations of the Shipmaster and the Coastal State: Persons Rescued at Sea

In May 2014, a U.S. rescue coordination center was notified that a passenger ship, transiting on the high seas, had come across what appeared to be a dilapidated vessel with a large number of persons on board in the vicinity of a coastal state. On the basis of the size and condition of the vessel and the presence of thirty-nine persons on board, the passenger ship embarked the persons, consistent with its international obligation to render assistance to those in distress at sea.

Even though the passenger ship was in the vicinity of this coastal state, the rescue of the thirty-nine survivors occurred in the maritime SAR region of a second coastal state. After the thirty-nine survivors were safely on board, the passenger ship resumed its transit to the second coastal state, its next port of call. During its transit, the shipmaster notified the authorities of the rescue and that his ship had embarked the thirty-nine survivors. However, upon arrival, the authorities made no effort to coordinate the disembarkation of the survivors in their country or to another place of safety, as required by the SAR Convention. As a result, the passenger ship was forced to retain the thirty-nine survivors on board when it departed for its next port of call, in the United States.

Because of the coastal state's failure to meet its obligation to coordinate the disembarkation of the survivors to a place of safety as required by the SAR Convention, the passenger ship was forced to continue to bear the burden of caring for the thirty-nine survivors upon departure. Subsequently, the U.S. Coast Guard was notified of the situation, contacted the passenger ship, and arranged for a rendezvous at sea between the passenger ship and a Coast Guard cutter. As planned, the passenger ship met with the cutter, which facilitated the at-sea transfer of the thirty-nine survivors without incident.

---

[30]Ibid., pp. 2–9.

In effect, the United States, in particular the U.S. Coast Guard, was forced to assume the responsibility to coordinate the disembarkation and disposition of the survivors rescued by the passenger ship on behalf of the coastal state. Once the transfer was complete, the passenger ship was released from its obligations and continued its transit to the United States.[31]

This actual incident illustrates what is required of ships transiting the world's oceans and of coastal states implementing the global SAR system. In this incident, the shipmaster fulfilled his duty to render assistance to persons rescued at sea. However, the coastal state refused to assist in coordinating the disembarkation of the survivors or to relieve the shipmaster of his obligation to care for the survivors. As a result, in this instance, the global SAR system failed. It cannot be stressed enough that both the shipmaster *and* the coastal state must be active participants in the global SAR system—both must be committed to saving lives at sea.

What follows is a description of the duties and obligations of shipmasters and coastal states in ensuring the success of maritime lifesaving operations. It is important for both to be cognizant of their responsibilities, as well as for each to develop processes and procedures to implement the global SAR system.

2.3.1 Shipmaster

Ships at sea are the eyes and ears of the global SAR system. In many instances, it is ships that receive notification of persons in distress, and they can be the first SAR resources available to render assistance. Ships conduct lifesaving operations every day in the world's oceans and generally welcome the opportunity to save lives.

Three international conventions formally enshrine in international law the important duty of the shipmaster to render assistance to persons in distress at sea.[32] Compliance with this duty is essential to preserving the integrity of the global SAR system.

---

[31]The facts portrayed in this vignette are known by the author, who attests to their accuracy. The vignette is presented for consideration of the legal and policy issues involved.

[32]Oxford Dictionary, s.v. "international law," www.oxforddictionaries.com/: "A body of rules established by custom or treaty and recognized by nations as binding in their relations with one another." Commander's Handbook (2007), p. 20 further describes international law as "that body of rules that nations consider binding in their relations with one another. International law derives from the practice of nations in the international arena and from international agreements. International law provides stability in international relations and an expectation that certain acts or omissions will effect predictable consequences. If one nation violates the law, it may expect that others will reciprocate. Consequently, failure to comply with international law ordinarily involves greater political and economic costs than does observance. In short, nations comply with international law because it is in their interest to do so. Like most rules of conduct, international law is in a continual state of development and change."

First, the Safety of Life at Sea (SOLAS) Convention of 1974 is one of the most important treaties concerning merchant ship safety.[33] Chapter V, regulation 33, states:

> The master of a ship at sea which is in a position to be able to provide assistance, on receiving information from any source that persons are in distress at sea, is bound to proceed with all speed to their assistance, if possible informing them or the search and rescue service that the ship is doing so. This obligation to provide assistance applies regardless of the nationality or status of such persons or the circumstances in which they are found. If the ship receiving the distress alert is unable or, in the special circumstances of the case, considers it unreasonable or unnecessary to proceed to their assistance, the master must enter in the log-book the reason for failing to proceed to the assistance of the persons in distress, taking into account the recommendation of the Organization to inform the appropriate search and rescue service accordingly.[34]

Second, the United Nations Convention on the Law of the Sea (UNCLOS), in article 98, provides that shipmasters have a duty to render assistance to persons in distress:

> 1. *Every State shall require the master of a ship flying its flag, in so far as he can do so without serious danger to the ship, the crew or the passengers:*
>   (a) *to render assistance to any person found at sea in danger of being lost;*
>   (b) *to proceed with all possible speed to the rescue of persons in distress, if informed of their need of assistance, in so far as such action may reasonably be expected of him;*
>   (c) *after a collision, to render assistance to the other ship, its crew and its passengers and, where possible, to inform the other ship of the name of his own ship, its port of registry and the nearest port at which it will call.*[35]

Note that article 98 is addressed to the flag state; it is the flag state that must ensure that any ship flying its flag renders assistance to persons in distress at sea. The shipmaster has the duty to render assistance "so far as he can do so without serious danger to the ship, the crew or the passengers."[36]

---

[33]The IMO website explains that the SOLAS Convention in its successive forms is generally regarded as the most important of all international treaties concerning the safety of merchant ships. The first version was adopted in 1914, in response to the *Titanic* disaster, the second in 1929, the third in 1948, and the fourth in 1960. The 1974 version includes the tacit acceptance procedure—which provides that an amendment shall enter into force on a specified date unless, before that date, objections to the amendment are received from an agreed number of Parties. As a result the 1974 Convention has been updated and amended on numerous occasions. The Convention in force today [SOLAS (1974)] is sometimes referred to as amended.

[34]SOLAS (1974), p. 268. SOLAS (1974) applies to vessels on international voyages, commercial vessels in particular. SOLAS (1974) allows exceptions for warships (and others) but encourages these ships to act in a manner consistent with its provisions. Entered into force: 25 May 1980; number of contracting states 2017: 162.

[35]UNCLOS (1982), article 98.

[36]Commander's Handbook (2007), pp. 1–1, states: "Although the United States is not a party to the 1982 LOS Convention, it considers the navigation and overflight provisions therein reflective of customary international law and thus acts in accordance with the 1982 LOS Convention, except for

Third, the Salvage Convention in article 10 states:

1. *Every master is bound, so far as he can do so without serious danger to his vessel and persons thereon, to render assistance to any person in danger of being lost at sea.*
2. *The States Parties shall adopt the measures necessary to enforce the duty set out in paragraph 1.*
3. *The owner of the vessel shall incur no liability for a breach of the duty of the master under paragraph 1.*[37]

Notably, there are circumstances in which a shipmaster would *not* be duty bound to aid persons in distress. For example, a shipmaster is not required to place his ship and crew in undue peril in order to attempt to render assistance.[38] In addition, there is no duty to attempt to render assistance in instances where doing so would be impracticable or futile.[39]

All three conventions affirm the shipmaster's duty to render assistance to persons in distress at sea and to treat any rescued survivors humanely while on board the ship.[40] Most shipmasters realize that, if the situation were reversed and they

---

the deep seabed mining provisions." Additionally, the duty for U.S. shipmasters to render assistance is stipulated in the United States Code (USC); 46 USC § 2304(a)(1) states: "A master or individual in charge of a vessel shall render assistance to any individual found at sea in danger of being lost, so far as the master or individual in charge can do so without serious danger to the master's or individual's vessel or individuals on board." Additionally, "A master or individual violating this section shall be fined not more than $1,000, imprisoned for not more than 2 years, or both." However, as further stated in 46 USC § 2304, this obligation does not apply to U.S. warships.

[37] Salvage Convention (1989); entered into force: 14 July 1996; number of contracting states 2017: 67.

[38] E.g., the Salvage Convention (1989), article 10, requires a shipmaster to render assistance "so far as he can without serious danger to his vessel, her crew and her passengers." This is also stipulated in SOLAS (1974), chapter V, regulation 33, paragraph 1, quoted in the text above, where the shipmaster must make a determination about whether he can render assistance to a person in distress.

[39] E.g., the annex to the SAR Convention (1979) (paragraph 4.8.1) states: "Search and rescue operations shall continue, **when practicable**, until all reasonable hope of rescuing survivors has passed" (emphasis added). According to paragraph 4.8.4, "If a search and rescue operation on-scene becomes **impracticable** and the rescue co-ordination centre or rescue sub-centre concludes that survivors might still be alive, the centre may temporarily suspend the on-scene activities pending further developments, and shall promptly so inform any authority, facility or service which has been activated or notified" (emphasis added).

[40] SOLAS (1974), chapter V, regulation 33, paragraph 6, states: "Masters of ships who have embarked persons in distress shall treat them with humanity, within the capabilities and limitations of the ship."

themselves were in distress, they would want another ship to provide the same assistance.[41]

Does the same treaty law concerning the shipmaster's duty to render assistance to persons in distress apply to warships?[42] The complex nature of military operations at sea means that diverting a warship to assist in a SAR operation and embark survivors can pose a challenge, especially when attempting to coordinate survivor disembarkation with a coastal state's SMC. And while conducting a maritime SAR operation can be difficult for a warship during peacetime, it can be even more complicated during armed conflict.

Interestingly, the SOLAS (chapter V, regulation 33) and Salvage (article 10) Conventions do not apply to warships and other noncommercial, state-owned vessels; the conventions do not mandate that these classes of vessels render assistance to persons in distress.[43] However, it remains customary international law[44] for

---

[41]Guidelines on the Treatment of Persons Rescued at Sea (2004) provide general guidance (paragraph 5.1) for shipmasters. "SAR services throughout the world depend on ships at sea to assist persons in distress. It is impossible to arrange SAR services that depend totally upon dedicated shore-based rescue units to provide timely assistance to all persons in distress at sea. Shipmasters have certain duties that must be carried out in order to provide for safety of life at sea, preserve the integrity of global SAR services **of which they are part**, and to comply with humanitarian and legal obligations" (emphasis added).

[42]UNCLOS (1982), article 29, defines *warship* as "a ship belonging to the armed forces of a State bearing the external marks distinguishing such ships of its nationality, under the command of an officer duly commissioned by the government of the State and whose name appears in the appropriate service list or its equivalent, and manned by a crew which is under regular armed forces discipline." See also Commander's Handbook (2007), p. 2-1.

[43]SOLAS (1974), chapter I, regulation 3, lists the following classes of ships that are exempted from complying with the regulations unless specifically stated in a particular regulation: (1) ships of war and troopships; (2) cargo ships of less than 500 gross tons; (3) ships not propelled by mechanical means; (4) wooden ships of primitive build; (5) pleasure yachts not engaged in trade; and (6) fishing vessels. Additionally, the Salvage Convention (1989), article 4, details the nonapplicability of the convention to "State-owned vessels": "1. Without prejudice to article 5, this Convention shall not apply to warships or other non-commercial vessels owned or operated by a State and entitled, at the time of salvage operations, to sovereign immunity under generally recognized principles of international law unless that State decides otherwise. 2. Where a State Party decides to apply the Convention to its warships or other vessels described in paragraph 1, it shall notify the Secretary-General thereof specifying the terms and conditions of such application."

[44]In Case Hasan v. United States of America (2010), the U.S. District Court for the Eastern District of Virginia, in its opinion and order, provided an overview of customary international law: "[the] body of rules that nations in the international community universally abide by, or accede to, out of a sense of legal obligation and mutual concern." In addition, the Statute of the International Court of Justice (1945), article 38(1)(b), describes customary international law as "a general practice accepted as law.". This understanding of customary international law is further affirmed in the Commander's Handbook, which states (p. 20): "The general and consistent practice among nations with respect to a particular subject, which over time is accepted by them generally as a legal obligation, is known as customary international law. Customary international law is the principal source of international law and is binding upon all nations."

states to ensure that their warships act in a manner consistent with this requirement.[45] By comparison, UNCLOS does impose this obligation on the flag state to require masters to comply with article 98. The SAR Convention, as previously stated, provides the framework for coastal states to implement the global SAR system; however, it does *not* "carve out" an exemption for certain classes of vessels from complying with its requirements. A party to the SAR Convention is obligated to ensure that *all* ships under its flag render assistance to persons in distress.[46]

Under the SAR Convention, a coastal state may receive notification of a person in distress, assume the role of SMC, and have its RCC contact a warship in the vicinity of a distress incident to divert and render assistance. If the warship is in a position and is able to render the assistance, the commanding officer (CO) should do so when the SMC so requests. If it is the CO who becomes aware of persons in distress, he should contact the coastal state whose SAR region the ship is transiting and relay any information concerning the distress incident. The coastal state would assume SMC and coordinate the response with the CO, including the disposition of any survivors once embarked on the warship.

Can the CO of a warship at sea decide *not* to render assistance to persons in distress, even if the warship is in a position to do so and could provide timely assistance but—owing to other "operational commitments"—is considered "not available"? Who would decide, in a particular instance, whether the CO of a warship can be relieved of his duty to render assistance to persons in distress? While this may be considered a difficult situation, the overall answer is *no*. For example, under U.S. Navy and Coast Guard policy, the CO always retains the duty to render assistance to persons in distress at sea if able to do so.[47] It also can be argued that,

---

[45] For example, in the United States, the requirement for COs of warships to render assistance to persons in distress at sea is mandated in U.S. Navy Regulations (1990), article 0925 (Assistance to Persons, Ships and Aircraft in Distress): "1. Insofar as can be done without serious danger to the ship or crew, the commanding officer or the senior officer present as appropriate shall: a) proceed with all possible speed to the rescue of persons in distress if informed of their need for assistance, insofar as such action may reasonably be expected of him or her; b) render assistance to any person found at sea in danger of being lost; c) afford all reasonable assistance to distressed ships and aircraft; and d) render assistance to the other ship, after a collision, to her crew and passengers and, where possible, inform the other ship of his or her identity." U.S. Coast Guard Regulations (1992), article 4.2-5 (Assistance), provides a similar mandate for the COs of U.S. Coast Guard ships to render assistance to persons in distress. These respective regulations make no distinction between peacetime and wartime operational requirements. (Note: rendering assistance to persons in distress under the law of armed conflict is not considered within the scope of this article.)

[46] The annex to the SAR Convention (1979) applies to its contracting states. It is the contracting state that is obligated to ensure its ships comply with their obligation to render assistance at sea. See also paragraph 2.1.10.

[47] The disembarkation of survivors can be conducted in several ways: (1) by the warship transferring survivors at sea to another craft to ensure it can resume normal operations; (2) by the SMC coordinating disembarkation with the coastal state that would be the warship's next port of call; or (3) in any other way that would relieve the warship of its burden to care for the survivors. As stated previously, the SMC should strive to minimize the impact on the warship (SAR Convention (1979), paragraph 3.1.9).

with this historical and universal principle enshrined in the SOLAS Convention, the Salvage Convention, and UNCLOS, the CO's duty to render assistance to persons in distress constitutes customary international law as well. This is especially relevant during peacetime when, considering the circumstances of the distress incident, a warship may be the only available resource capable of conducting a lifesaving operation. The circumstances on scene and the CO's coordination with the SMC and his operational chain of command should dictate the best course of action to ensure that persons in distress are rescued.

2.3.2 Coastal State

Under the SAR Convention, a state has the responsibility to implement the global SAR system.[48] To fulfill this mandate, the coastal state establishes a national SAR system that effectively coordinates SAR operations to render assistance when notified of persons in distress.[49] If the most effective SAR resource available for a particular SAR operation is a merchant ship (or any other vessel best suited to render the assistance), the SMC should divert the ship to save lives.

As the shipmaster fulfills this duty to render assistance to persons in distress, he has an expectation that the coastal state will fulfill its own obligation to assist in coordinating the disembarkation of survivors rescued at sea to a place of safety and to minimize the impact on his ship. For example, the SMC should do everything possible to limit the deviation of a ship from its intended course to assist persons in distress. Granted, there are times when a particular ship is the only SAR resource available. However, diversion of a merchant ship in particular should be limited, if at all possible. Additionally, the SMC should reconsider ever diverting a merchant ship from its intended port of call to a different port to disembark rescued survivors. Such a diversion can cause significant logistical and liability challenges for the ship, shipping company, and shipping agent and should be avoided.[50] While these types of SAR cases may be challenging for the SMC, who very well may be required to coordinate survivor disembarkation and disposition with another coastal state, the global SAR system will benefit when the shipmaster knows that the SMC will

---

[48] The annex to the SAR Convention (1979) (paragraph 2.1.1) states: "Parties shall, as they are able to do so individually or in co-operation with other States and, as appropriate, with the Organization, participate in the development of search and rescue services to ensure that assistance is rendered to any person in distress at sea."

[49] Additionally, the coastal state must coordinate the SAR response regardless of who the persons in distress are. The annex to the SAR Convention (1979) (paragraph 2.1.10) makes this requirement very clear: "Parties shall ensure that assistance be provided to any person in distress at sea. They shall do so regardless of the nationality or status of such a person or the circumstances in which that person is found."

[50] A more appropriate course of action than diverting a ship from its next port of call would be to have the ship rendezvous with and transfer SAR survivors to a SAR unit for further transport to a place of safety.

minimize the impact on his ship's intended voyage when he renders assistance to persons in distress.[51]

This relationship between the shipmaster and the coastal state is crucial to the effectiveness of the global SAR system. While the shipmaster has the duty to render assistance to persons in distress, the coastal state is obligated to coordinate the SAR operation effectively and efficiently in support of the responding shipmaster. Without a cooperative relationship, a ship has limited incentive to render aid to a distressed vessel, as opposed to passing by so as to meet its arrival time at its next port of call. Coastal-state support of ships saving lives at sea is a critical component of the global SAR system and is enshrined in the SAR Convention[52]:

> Parties shall co-ordinate and co-operate to ensure that masters of ships providing assistance by embarking persons in distress at sea are released from their obligations with minimum further deviation from the ships' intended voyage, provided that releasing the master of the ship from these obligations does not further endanger the safety of life at sea. The Party responsible for the search and rescue region in which such assistance is rendered shall exercise primary responsibility for ensuring such co-ordination and co-operation occurs, so that survivors assisted are disembarked from the assisting ship and delivered to a place of safety.... In these cases, the relevant Parties shall arrange for such disembarkation to be effected as soon as reasonably practicable.[53]

As mentioned above, a "place of safety" is an important concept in the global SAR system for both the coastal state and the shipmaster. The IAMSAR manual, volume 1, describes a "place of safety" as

> [a] location where rescue operations are considered to terminate; where the survivors' safety of life is no longer threatened and where their basic human needs (such as food, shelter and medical needs) can be met; and, a place from which transportation arrangements can be made for the survivors' next or final destination. A place of safety may be on land, or it may be on board a rescue unit or other suitable vessel or facility at sea that can serve as a place of safety until the survivors are disembarked at their final destination.[54]

---

[51] Guidelines on the Treatment of Persons Rescued at Sea (2004) provide the priorities for rendering assistance to persons rescued at sea. Paragraph 3.1 states in part: "When ships assist persons in distress at sea, co-ordination will be needed among all concerned to ensure that all of the following priorities are met in a manner that takes due account of border control, sovereignty and security concerns consistent with international law: 1) **Lifesaving**: All persons in distress at sea should be assisted without delay; 2) **Preservation of the integrity and effectiveness of SAR services**: Prompt assistance provided by ships at sea is an essential element of global SAR services; therefore it must remain a top priority for shipmasters, shipping companies and flag States; and 3) **Relieving masters of obligations after assisting persons**: Flag and coastal States should have effective arrangements in place for timely assistance to shipmasters in relieving them of persons recovered by ships at sea" (emphasis added).

[52] The SAR Convention (1979) is the means by which parties have agreed to fulfill their duty to render assistance in most circumstances. However, the duty to render assistance continues to exist for every mariner. If it appears that the process agreed to in the SAR Convention (1979) will not result in timely and effective assistance in a particular situation, a shipmaster is still under obligation to come to the aid of the person in distress.

[53] Annex to the SAR Convention (1979), paragraph 3.1.9.

[54] IAMSAR manual (2013), vol. 1, p. xiii.

Identifying a place of safety should be coordinated between the shipmaster and the coastal-state SMC responsible for coordinating the SAR operation. The priority always should be to minimize the impact on the ship that conducted the rescue and has survivors on board.[55] A place of safety may not be necessarily a location that is most advantageous to the survivors. However, it should be a location where all the criteria defining a place of safety can be achieved. It cannot be overemphasized that the SMC has the primary responsibility for determining the place of safety, in coordination with the ship that rendered the assistance.[56]

Additionally, the coastal state's SMC, in coordinating a SAR operation, must remember that under the SAR Convention a ship diverted to render assistance[57] is considered a *SAR facility*, not a *SAR unit*, and should not be considered necessarily a place of safety simply because the survivors are no longer in distress.[58] Unlike a SAR unit, which has the equipment and trained personnel to conduct SAR operations, a ship diverted to render assistance to persons in distress may not have the resources on board to care for what may be large numbers of survivors properly or to meet the criteria for a place of safety.[59] When a ship is diverted to render assistance, the coastal state, in coordinating disembarkation, should take into

---

[55]A place of safety very well may be the ship's next port of call. The goal of the SAR Convention (1979) is to minimize the impact on the ship. However, a life raft, even with ample rations, is *not* considered a place of safety. According to the SOLAS (1974), a life raft is considered a lifesaving appliance and does not meet the requirements for or the definition of a place of safety. The SOLAS (1974), chapter III, regulation 3, explains that a lifeboat or life raft is a *survival craft*, "capable of sustaining lives of persons in distress from the time of abandoning the ship." Persons afloat in a life raft must still be considered "in distress" until appropriate assistance is rendered and the persons are delivered to a place of safety.

[56]The Convention on Facilitation of International Maritime Traffic (1965) mandates that states that must coordinate the disembarkation of persons rescued at sea. Section 7.C (Emergency Assistance) affirms this important requirement, stating in part, "7.8 Standard. Public authorities shall facilitate the arrival and departure of ships engaged in: ... the rescue of persons in distress at sea in order to provide a place of safety for such persons." In addition, standard 7.9 states, "Public authorities shall, to the greatest extent possible, facilitate the entry and clearance of persons, cargo, material and equipment required to deal with situations described in Standard 7.8.";entered into force: 5 March 1967; number of contracting states 2017: 115.

[57]Or any other vessel that diverts to render assistance to persons in distress.

[58]The annex to the SAR Convention (1979) (paragraph 1.3.7) defines *search and rescue facility* as "[a]ny mobile resource, including designated search and rescue units, used to conduct search and rescue operations." By comparison, *search and rescue unit* is defined (paragraph 1.3.8) as "[a] unit composed of trained personnel and provided with equipment suitable for the expeditious conduct of search and rescue operations." The IAMSAR manual (2013), vol. 1, goes on to state (pp. 2–10, paragraph 2.5.3) that SAR units "may be under the direct jurisdiction of the SAR service or other State authorities or may belong to non-Governmental or voluntary organizations."

[59]Guidelines on the Treatment of Persons Rescued at Sea (2004) stipulate (paragraph 6.13) that "[a] n assisting ship should not be considered a place of safety based solely on the fact that the survivors are no longer in immediate danger once aboard the ship. An assisting ship may not have appropriate facilities and equipment to sustain additional persons on board without endangering its own safety or to properly care for the survivors. Even if the ship is capable of safely accommodating the survivors and may serve as a temporary place of safety, it should be relieved of this responsibility as soon as alternative arrangements can be made."

consideration the number of survivors rescued, the ship's estimated time of arrival at its next port of call, the survivors' condition, and other critical factors.[60] Normally, the SMC would coordinate survivor disembarkation at the ship's next port of call or with another coastal state[61] to limit complications and minimize the impact on the ship that conducted the rescue.[62]

If either the coastal state or the shipmaster fails to fulfill the obligations under international law, the global SAR system becomes ineffective. If a shipmaster ignores persons in distress because of the potential time delay and logistical challenges associated with rescuing the survivors or if the coastal state does not fulfill its obligation to coordinate SAR operations within its maritime SAR region, as well as to disembark rescued survivors, the system is threatened—and lives imperiled on the world's oceans can be lost. Both the shipmaster and the coastal state are responsible for saving lives at sea.

2.4 Mixed Migration by Sea

Mixed migration by sea is a difficult problem that afflicts many regions of the world.[63] Tragically, lives are lost every year when overloaded boats are overturned

---

[60]Guidelines on the Treatment of Persons Rescued at Sea (2004) further explain (paragraph 6.15) this important aspect of coordinating the disembarkation of any persons rescued at sea: "The Conventions, as amended, indicate that delivery to a place of safety should take into account the particular circumstances of the case. These circumstances may include factors such as the situation on board the assisting ship, on scene conditions, medical needs, and availability of transportation or other rescue units. Each case is unique, and selection of a place of safety may need to account for a variety of important factors."

[61]On 10–11 December 2014, the U.S. Coast Guard participated in the annual Dialogue on Protection Challenges, in Geneva, Switzerland, on the theme "Protection at Sea." The meeting, sponsored by the UNHCR, focused on mixed migration at sea. During the meeting, an International Chamber of Shipping (ICS) representative made an excellent point: It is the shipmaster who must determine whether to deviate from his intended voyage and transit to the "nearest port of call" or to continue to the ship's "next port of call." Coastal states need to understand and support the shipmaster's decision, which will take into account important on-scene conditions as well as other logistical and risk factors. The "nearest port" may not be a viable option for the shipmaster. The coastal state needs to respect the shipmaster's decision and coordinate disembarkation of survivors accordingly. "Shipping Industry Calls on Governments to Address Migrants at Sea Crisis," *International Chamber of Shipping,* www.ics-shipping.org/.

[62]In 2015 IMO/UNHCR/ICS jointly published an excellent resource, the Rescue at Sea Guide (2015). In discussing the action required by governments and RCCs in coordinating a merchant ship rendering assistance to persons in distress, it states: "Governments have to coordinate and cooperate to ensure that Masters of ships providing assistance by embarking persons in distress at sea are released from their obligations with minimum further deviation from the ship's intended voyage, and have to arrange disembarkation as soon as reasonably practicable." It goes on to state (p. 12) that "the Government responsible for the SAR region in which the rescued persons were recovered is primarily responsible for providing a place of safety or ensuring that such a place of safety is provided."

[63]Kumin (2014) provides a good overview of what is considered *mixed migration by sea:* "Contemporary irregular migration is mostly 'mixed,' meaning that it consists of flows of people who are

and hundreds, if not thousands, of people perish; others perish in extremely poor and hazardous conditions in overloaded boats unfit to make an ocean voyage. People engage in at-sea migrations for many reasons; these include desperate pursuit of a better life, if not survival. Regional problems and challenges have resulted in these mass migrations; proposing solutions goes well beyond the scope of this article. However, the sheer number of "persons in distress" has stretched the limits of the global SAR system. Merchant ships, other vessels, and coastal-state resources are tasked to render assistance. Many are not equipped or manned to support dozens, if not hundreds, of persons who may remain on board an assistance-rendering vessel for several days.

In March 2015, a meeting to address unsafe mixed migration at sea took place at IMO headquarters on Albert Embankment, London, United Kingdom.[64] Participants at the meeting included representatives of the IMO member states, intergovernmental organizations, and nongovernmental organizations, as well as senior representatives from the IMO, the UN High Commissioner for Refugees (UNHCR), the International Organization for Migration (IOM), and several other UN agencies. Challenges concerning mixed migration at sea were discussed. In his opening address, Koji Sekimizu, IMO secretary-general, succinctly stated the problem: "The issue of mixed migration by sea, including irregular migration, has been a serious concern for decades—if not longer. But, in recent years, it has reached epidemic proportions, to the extent where the whole system for coping with such migrants is being stretched up to, and sometimes beyond, its breaking point."[65]

Several statistics presented at the meeting highlight the critical nature of this problem:

• "The conflict in Syria, which enters its fifth year in March 2015, has caused the largest displacement crisis of our time. There are now more than 3.2 million Syrian refugees, a number that is growing by 100,000 every month."[66]
• In 2014, over 200,000 people were rescued and over 3000 deaths were reported in the Mediterranean Sea alone as a result of unsafe, irregular, and illegal sea passages.[67]

---

on the move for different reasons but who share the same routes, modes of travel and vessels. They cross land and sea borders without authorization, frequently with the help of people smugglers. IMO and UNHCR point out that mixed flows can include refugees, asylum seekers and others with specific needs, such as trafficked persons, stateless persons and unaccompanied or separated children, as well as other irregular migrants. The groups are not mutually exclusive, however, as people often have more than one reason for leaving home. Also, the term 'other irregular migrants' fails to capture the extent to which mixed flows include people who have left home because they were directly affected or threatened by a humanitarian crisis—including one resulting from climate change—and need some type of protection, even if they do not qualify as refugees."

[64]IMO Secretariat (2015), pp. 1–2.

[65]Sekimizu (2015), p. 1.

[66]Boyer (2015), p. 10: "The scale and protracted nature of the crisis is challenging the ability of the international community to meet the continuing need for essential, life-saving humanitarian aid."

[67]Sekimizu (2015), p. 1.

- In the first 6 months of 2015, 137,000 refugees and migrants crossed the Mediterranean Sea.[68] This compares with 75,000 in the same period in 2014, marking an 83% increase over 2014.[69]
- More than 1800 migrants have perished in at-sea migration attempts so far in the first 6 months of 2015.[70]
- In mid-April 2015, 800 people died in the largest maritime refugee disaster on record, highlighting the significant increase in migrants dying or missing at sea.[71]
- There are reports of dozens of migrants dying from hypothermia after being recovered by SAR resources, demonstrating the dangerous nature of these unsafe maritime transits in dilapidated vessels.[72]
- In the first 3 months of 2015, over 700 merchant vessels were diverted from their routes to recover and rescue migrants making unsafe passages just in the Mediterranean Sea alone.[73]

The interplay between mixed migration by sea and SAR presents an extremely difficult challenge because of the complex humanitarian nature of these operations. Many coastal states consider each mass migrant incident a SAR case that should be conducted under the SAR Convention and coordinated by a coastal-state SMC, through the RCC. However, this is not the case.[74] Some incidents may include persons in distress; however, many more appropriately could be considered law-enforcement or border security events.[75] In addition, care must be taken to

---

[68]United Nations High Commissioner for Refugees UNHCR (2015), p. 2.

[69]IMO Secretariat (2015).

[70]Ibid.

[71]United Nations High Commissioner for Refugees UNHCR (2015), p. 2.

[72]IMO Secretariat (2015), p. 2.

[73]Ibid.

[74]The summary conclusions from an 8–10 November 2011 UNHCR experts meeting in Djibouti, see United Nations High Commissioner for Refugees UNHCR (2011), state (paragraph B.7): "The specific legal framework governing rescue at sea does not apply to interception operations that have no search and rescue component."

[75]Considering the level of concern for the safety of persons or craft that may be in danger, the SMC will determine in which emergency phase (uncertainty, alert, or distress) to classify the SAR incident. (IAMSAR manual (2013), vol. 2, paragraph 3.3.1.) In particular, the annex to the SAR Convention (1979) (paragraph 1.3.13) defines *distress phase* as "[a] situation wherein there is a reasonable certainty that a person, a vessel or other craft is threatened by grave and imminent danger and requires immediate assistance." In many mixed-migration operations the SAR Convention (1979) would not apply necessarily because the circumstances of the incident may not meet the criteria for any of the three emergency phases.

ensure that migrants are not refugees.[76] Refugees should be afforded the protections required under the Convention Relating to the Status of Refugees, 1951.[77]

The condition of the vessel, the weather on scene, and the persons on board, as well as the judgment of the SAR unit or facility on scene and the SMC should dictate whether a migrant incident triggers the rendering of assistance to persons in distress under the SAR Convention or its treatment as a national border/law-enforcement action. Determining whether large numbers of persons in a mass-migration scenario are in distress can be particularly challenging for the SMC. The global SAR system is activated when a person declares he is in distress or when SAR authorities are notified of a person in distress. However, in many recent mixed-migration-at-sea operations, migrant vessels have been declaring that they are "in distress" so that their "survivors" will be transferred to a merchant ship or other SAR unit and transported to a place of safety. This continues to be an ongoing, difficult problem in the Mediterranean Sea, in particular.

Another difficulty is that, while the shipmaster is required to embark persons assisted, the coastal state has no specific international mandate to receive the survivors from the ship.[78] The RCC is required to coordinate the disembarkation of rescued survivors; however, some coastal states refuse to assist the ship and receive the migrants. Unfortunately, the SAR Convention does not impose a duty for a coastal state to accept migrants from a merchant ship, even if the incident occurred within the coastal state's SAR region.[79] Kathleen Newland provides a good summary of this problem:

---

[76]It is important to understand the differences among *refugees, asylum seekers,* and *economic migrants*. (1) The Rescue at Sea Guide (2015) provides a good description of the difference between a refugee and an asylum seeker. An asylum seeker is a person who "is seeking international protection and whose claim has not yet been finally decided. Not every asylum-seeker will ultimately be recognized as a refugee. Refugee status is 'declaratory'—that is, determining refugee status does not make a person a refugee, but rather recognizes that a person is a refugee." The guide goes on to state that "[r]escued persons who do not meet the criteria of the Refugee Convention (1951) definition of a 'refugee,' but who fear torture or other serious human rights abuses or who are fleeing armed conflict may also be protected from return to a particular place ('refoulement') by other international or regional human rights or refugee law instruments." (2) There is also a difference between refugees and economic migrants. In its 50th-anniversary issue, "The Wall behind Which Refugees Can Shelter," of its *Refugees* publication the UNHCR states: "An economic migrant normally leaves a country voluntarily to seek a better life. Should he or she elect to return home they would continue to receive the protection of their government. Refugees flee because of the threat of persecution and cannot return safely to their homes in the circumstances then prevailing.", see: Most Frequently Asked Questions about the Refugee Convention (2001).

[77]The Refugee Convention (1951), article 1A(2), defines *refugee* as a person who, "owing to a well-founded fear of being persecuted for reasons of race, religion, nationality, membership of a particular social group, or political opinion, is outside the country of his nationality, and is unable to or, owing to such fear, is unwilling to avail himself of the protection of that country." The Convention entered into force: 22 April 1954; number of parties 2017: 145.

[78]Annex to the SAR Convention (1979), paragraph 3.1.9.

[79]"the SAR Convention (1979) only lays down an obligation of coordination and cooperation and does not necessarily entail an explicit duty to allow disembarkation in a particular port.", see Mallia (2014).

The intersection of maritime law and refugee law thus leaves ship owners, masters, and crews in a quandary. They must pick up refugees and asylum seekers whose lives are in danger, but no state is required to take them in.

The ship itself cannot be considered a "place of safety"—indeed, carrying a large number of unscheduled passengers may endanger the crew and passengers themselves, owing to overcrowding, inadequate provisioning, and the tensions of life in close quarters. The inability to disembark rescued passengers in a timely fashion and return to scheduled ports of call creates a profound disincentive for the maritime industry to engage actively in search and rescue missions.[80]

The IMO may want to consider developing an international convention to provide the international community with a basis for coordinating and conducting these challenging mixed-migration-at-sea operations.[81]

3   Assistance Entry

The United States Coast Guard received notification that a vessel was hard aground on rocks in a coastal state's territorial sea, with three persons on board. The Coast Guard diverted a Coast Guard cutter that was available to render assistance. The Coast Guard notified the coastal state's authorities of the incident. The Coast Guard cutter arrived, remained outside the territorial sea, and established communications with the vessel aground. Those on the vessel communicated their concern regarding the deteriorating condition of the vessel

---

[80]Newland (2013). This was also affirmed in the report (paragraph C.10) of United Nations High Commissioner for Refugees UNHCR (2011), "Fundamentally, a core challenge in any particular rescue at sea operation involving asylum-seekers and refugees is often the timely identification of a place of safety for disembarkation, as well as necessary follow-up, including reception arrangements, access to appropriate processes and procedures, and outcomes. If a shipmaster is likely to face delay in disembarking rescued people, he/she may be less ready to come to the assistance of those in distress at sea. Addressing these challenges and developing predictable responses requires strengthened cooperation and coordination among all States and other stakeholders implicated in rescue at sea operations".

[81]The IAMSAR manual (2013), vol. 2, p. xviii, defines *mass rescue operation* (MRO) as "[s]earch and rescue services characterized by the need for immediate response to large numbers of persons in distress, such that the capabilities normally available to search and rescue authorities are inadequate." The question is whether a mixed-migration-at-sea incident would actually include "persons in distress"; and, if there are large numbers of persons involved, would the incident be classified as an MRO? In many instances, these incidents could be considered illegal trafficking in persons; it would seem that the United Nations Convention on Transnational Organized Crime (TOC Convention (2004))—in particular annex II, Protocol to Prevent, Suppress and Punish Trafficking in Persons, Especially Women and Children—would be more applicable than the SAR Convention (1979). The TOC Convention (2004) entered into force: 29 September 2003; number of parties 2017: 185. If mixed-migration-by-sea incidents do not primarily constitute the rescue of persons in distress, and are not adequately addressed in the TOC Convention (2004), the international community may want to consider developing an international instrument that would serve as the basis for the coordination and conduct of these maritime operations.

and adverse weather conditions. The vessel stated that the coastal state's authorities were on scene but were not providing any assistance. The coastal state's authorities notified the Coast Guard that the on-scene Coast Guard cutter was not authorized to enter the state's territorial sea to conduct a rescue operation, and indicated that the vessel in distress should arrange for local commercial salvage.

Because of the deteriorating on-scene conditions, in which the vessel was listing sixty degrees and taking on water; the adverse weather; the lack of support from the coastal state's authorities on scene in assisting the vessel; and the presence on board of a sixty-five-year-old crewmember who began to experience symptoms of a heart attack, the Coast Guard cutter made the decision to enter the territorial sea to conduct a rescue operation. The Coast Guard cutter rescued the three persons on board and their personal property.[82]

The incident described above highlights the complex challenges, from an international law and policy perspective, facing any shipmaster or aircraft commander attempting to fulfill his duty to render assistance to persons in distress, particularly in another coastal state's territorial sea.[83] Does the shipmaster have a duty to rescue persons in distress even in another coastal state's territorial sea? Are aircraft also obliged to conduct these types of rescue operations? What are the implications for a warship or military aircraft conducting a rescue operation in a coastal state's territorial sea?[84] The problem is that these rescue operations can cause unintended concern for the coastal state if the ship's or aircraft's purpose for entering its territorial sea is misconstrued.

While not specifically defined, the principle of assistance entry (AE) is established through international conventions[85] and customary international law.[86]

---

[82]The facts portrayed in this vignette are known by the author, who attests to their accuracy. The vignette is presented for consideration of the legal and policy issues involved.

[83]In defining *territorial sea,* UNCLOS (1982), article 2, states: "1. The sovereignty of a coastal State extends, beyond its land territory and internal waters and, in the case of an archipelagic State, its archipelagic waters, to an adjacent belt of sea, described as the territorial sea. 2. This sovereignty extends to the air space over the territorial sea as well as to its bed and subsoil." Article 3 continues, "Every State has the right to establish the breadth of its territorial sea up to a limit not exceeding 12 nautical miles, measured from baselines determined in accordance with this Convention."

[84]The Commander's Handbook (2007) (paragraph 2.4.1) defines *military aircraft* as "all aircraft operated by commissioned units of the armed forces of a nation bearing the military markings of that nation, commanded by a member of the armed forces, and manned by a crew subject to regular armed forces discipline."

[85]For example, AE is envisioned in UNCLOS (1982). In describing innocent passage, article 18 provides for the assistance of persons in distress: "2. Passage shall be continuous and expeditious. However, passage includes stopping and anchoring, but only in so far as the same are incidental to ordinary navigation or are rendered necessary by *force majeure* **or distress or for the purpose of rendering assistance to persons, ships or aircraft in danger or distress**" (emphasis in bold added).

[86]At the 1991 convening of IMO's Sub-Committee on Lifesaving, Search and Rescue, the United States submitted to the subcommittee a note which argued (paragraph 3) the U.S. position that "[t]he obligation to rescue persons in distress regardless of nationality is based on the principle and time-

In support of this mandate to rescue persons in distress anywhere on the seas, the U.S. Coast Guard developed policy for the conduct of AE rescue operations within a coastal state's territorial sea by Coast Guard ships and aircraft.[87] To ensure compliance with international conventions, AE rescue operations policy should respect three principles: (1) the sovereign right of a state to control and regulate entry into its territorial sea, (2) the humanitarian need to assist persons in distress quickly and effectively without regard to nationality or circumstances, and (3) that entry into a coastal state's territorial sea does not require seeking or receiving permission from the coastal state to conduct the rescue operation in its territorial sea.[88]

What follows are seven different AE scenarios that SAR authorities and legal advisers should consider in developing national and agency-specific AE policies, accompanied in each case by an overview of the applicable international legal and policy concerns. It is important to work through the issues and prepare positions that can be provided to the shipmaster and the aircraft commander for guidance. When persons are in distress and a government ship or aircraft is in a position to render assistance, valuable time should not be wasted seeking guidance and legal advice before rendering the necessary assistance.[89] These discussions should occur; however, legal positions and policies should be developed *before* any of these scenarios are encountered.

---

honored tradition that those at sea will, wherever they can without undue risk, assist others in danger or distress. . ... Thus, coastal state's right to control activities in its territorial seas is balanced with the requirement to rescue those in distress from perils of the sea", see Note USA to IMO (1991). This U.S. paper was also discussed at the 65th session of IMO's Legal Committee, duly recorded in Report of the IMO Legal Committee (1991). While several delegations shared the U.S. position, the committee agreed "that there existed no right of assistance entry in public international law **at present;** this principle is neither embodied in any convention, nor established by customary law. Many delegations emphasized in this connection that it was important not to upset the delicate balance between the duty to render assistance, on the one hand, and the sovereign right of coastal States to control entry into or operation in their waters on the other" (emphasis added). Over the two decades since the Legal Committee reached this conclusion, the concept of AE has continued to become established as a standard principle enshrined through international conventions and customary international law.

[87]This article uses the term "AE rescue operation," not "SAR operation." When a ship or aircraft enters a coastal state's territorial sea to render assistance to persons in distress, the purpose is to *rescue,* not *search* for, survivors. Scenario D addresses this distinction further.

[88]United States Coast Guard Addendum to the United States Search and Rescue Supplement to the International Aeronautical and Maritime Search and Rescue Manual (2013), pp. 1–45, paragraphs 1.8.1.4 and 1.8.1.5. See also Chairman of the Joint Chiefs of Staff instruction (2013), p. 2. Note: the U.S. Coast Guard uses the term "assistance entry" (AE), while the U.S. Department of Defense (DoD) uses the term "right of assistance entry" (RAE) when discussing the conduct of rescue operations in a coastal state's territorial sea.

[89]SOLAS (1974) does not apply to warships. UNCLOS (1982) and the Salvage Convention (1989) do not limit what types of vessels can conduct an AE rescue operation in a coastal state's territorial sea. However, the emphasis of this article is on AE rescue operations conducted by government ships (including warships).

3.1   Scenario A

A government ship transiting on the high seas receives a distress broadcast and diverts to render assistance to a person in distress in a coastal state's territorial sea. Does the ship need to obtain the coastal state's consent to enter its territorial sea to render assistance to the person in distress?

In this scenario, the government ship would not be required to obtain consent from the coastal state before rendering assistance to persons in distress in the coastal state's territorial sea. However, the shipmaster should notify the coastal state of his intention to render the assistance, the approximate distress location, and the ship's intention to transit into the state's territorial sea to conduct the rescue operation. UNCLOS and the SOLAS and Salvage Conventions mandate that the shipmaster has the duty to render assistance to persons in distress throughout the oceans.[90]

While the coastal state exercises sovereignty over its territorial sea, that sovereignty is not unlimited. In the case of AE, the coastal state has limited ability to interfere with the entry of a ship conducting a rescue operation.[91] Likewise, the assisting ship is also limited in its operations within a coastal state's territorial sea. For example, (1) there must be persons in distress before a government ship may enter into a coastal state's territorial sea to render assistance, and (2) there is a limitation on what activities the ship may conduct during an AE rescue operation. Specifically, the government ship is limited to *rescuing* persons in distress only.

There are conditions that should be met for a ship to conduct AE. For example, U.S. Coast Guard policy affirms that a Coast Guard SAR unit may conduct AE into a coastal state's territorial sea to render assistance to a person in distress if, in the judgment of the CO, the on-scene situation meets the following three criteria: (1) there is reasonable certainty (on the basis of the best available information, regardless of source) that a person is in distress, (2) the distress location is reasonably well known, and (3) the SAR unit (or SAR facility) is in position to render timely and effective assistance.[92]

---

[90]UNCLOS (1982), article 98(1)(a), specifically states that the shipmaster has a duty to "render assistance to any person found **at sea** in danger of being lost" (emphasis added). SOLAS (1974), chapter V, regulation 33, requires "[t]he master of a ship at sea, which is in a position to be able to provide assistance, on receiving information from any source that persons are in distress **at sea**, ... to proceed with all speed to their assistance" (emphasis added). Similarly, the Salvage Convention (1989), article 10, paragraph 1, requires "[e]very master ..., so far as he can do so without serious danger to his vessel and persons thereon, to render assistance to any person in danger of being lost **at sea**" (emphasis added). All three conventions make no geographical distinction concerning the obligation of the shipmaster to render assistance to persons in distress. The duty to render assistance should be considered to apply on the high seas and territorial sea of any coastal state.

[91]For example, UNCLOS (1982), article 2, states: "The sovereignty over the territorial sea is exercised **subject to this Convention and other rules of international law**" (emphasis added).

[92]United States Coast Guard Addendum to the United States Search and Rescue Supplement to the International Aeronautical and Maritime Search and Rescue Manual (2013), pp. 1–46, paragraph 1.8.2.4. As will be discussed later in this section, U.S. Coast Guard and DoD SAR policy allows for both aircraft and surface units to conduct AE rescue operations.

Additionally, because of the urgency to take immediate action to rescue persons in distress, AE should not be delayed while the coastal state is notified of the government ship's intention to render assistance in its territorial sea. Even if the assistance to a person in distress already is being coordinated by the coastal state's RCC, as envisioned in the SAR Convention, the government ship's duty to render timely assistance remains.[93]

3.2   Scenario B

A government ship transiting on the high seas receives a distress broadcast and diverts to render assistance to a person in distress in a coastal state's territorial sea. Can the ship use its embarked helicopter and small boat to assist in the rescue operation? Can a military aircraft transiting in oceanic airspace also divert and enter a coastal state's airspace to assist in the rescue operation, or must the aircraft first obtain permission from the coastal state? Can a military aircraft enter a coastal state's territorial sea even if no surface unit is participating in the rescue operation?

There is no international instrument that expressly prevents a government ship from using its embarked aircraft or small boat in rendering assistance to a person in distress. Embarked aircraft and small boats should be considered an extension of the ship[94]; all available resources necessary to the lifesaving operation should be used, even if the location of the distress incident is in a coastal state's territorial sea.[95]

In addition to a ship using an embarked aircraft for an AE rescue operation, any other available aircraft made aware of a distress can and should divert to render assistance in a coastal state's territorial sea.[96] The use of an aircraft for an AE rescue

---

[93]The SAR Convention (1979) was never intended to limit or restrict any available warship or other ship in the conduct of immediate lifesaving assistance to persons in distress, even in a coastal state's territorial sea. The annex to the SAR Convention (1979) (paragraph 4.3) states: "Any search and rescue unit receiving information of a distress incident shall initially take immediate action if in the position to assist and shall, in any case without delay, notify the rescue co-ordination centre or rescue sub-centre in whose area the incident has occurred."

[94]Chairman of the Joint Chiefs of Staff instruction (2013), paragraph 4.d.

[95]It should be emphasized that UNCLOS (1982) and SOLAS (1974) and Salvage Convention (1989) were never intended to restrict or hamper a ship's use of its available SAR resources (e.g., embarked aircraft or small boat) that could be used in a lifesaving operation.

[96]The use of U.S. military aircraft in the conduct of RAE operations is also contemplated. Chairman of the Joint Chiefs of Staff instruction (2013), paragraph 6.c(2), states, "An operational commander may render immediate rescue assistance by deploying a U.S. military aircraft (including aircraft embarked aboard military ships conducting RAE operations) into the national airspace within U.S.-recognized foreign territorial seas or archipelagic waters when all four of the following conditions are met: (a) A person, ship, or aircraft within the foreign territorial sea or archipelagic waters is in danger or distress from perils of the sea and requires immediate rescue assistance; (b) The location is reasonably well known; (c) The U.S. military aircraft is able to render timely and effective assistance; and (d) Any delay in rendering assistance could be life-threatening."

operation would be governed by the same criteria placed on use of a surface rescue unit.[97]

The legal justification for the use of an aircraft in the conduct of an AE rescue operation cannot rest solely on UNCLOS; both articles 18 and 98 are silent on whether aircraft can assist persons in distress in a coastal state's territorial sea.[98] However, the SAR Convention *does* consider the use of aircraft in the conduct of SAR operations.[99] This makes sense since the purpose of the SAR Convention is to implement the global SAR system, which provides the international framework for organizing and standardizing SAR processes and procedures in the coordination and conduct of lifesaving operations. To carry out this purpose, the SAR Convention supports the use of any and all rescue capabilities that can be used during a SAR operation, including rescue operations within any coastal state's territorial sea.[100]

---

[97]For example, the United States Coast Guard Addendum to the United States Search and Rescue Supplement to the International Aeronautical and Maritime Search and Rescue Manual (2013), paragraph 1.8.2.5, states that "Coast Guard rescue aircraft may conduct an AE rescue operation in a coastal State's territorial sea, when in the judgment of the aircraft commander: (a) There is reasonable certainty (based on the best available information regardless of source) that a person is in distress; (b) The distress location is reasonably well known; and (c) The SAR unit (or SAR facility) is in position to render timely and effective assistance."

[98]Article 18(2) of UNCLOS (1982) concerns *ships* in the conduct of innocent passage in a coastal state's territorial sea. See also note 84.

[99]The annex to the SAR Convention (1979) promotes using all available means for rendering assistance to persons in distress. For example, in the conduct of search operations, paragraph 3.1.3 states: "Unless otherwise agreed between the States concerned, the authorities of a Party which wishes its rescue units to enter into **or over** the territorial sea or territory of another Party solely for the purpose of searching for the position of maritime casualties and rescuing the survivors of such casualties, shall transmit a request, giving full details of the projected mission and the need for it, to the rescue co-ordination centre of that other Party, or to such other authority as has been designated by that Party" (emphasis added). While paragraph 3.1.3 describes the requirement for aircraft entering into a coastal state's territorial sea for the purpose of *searching,* the aircraft would not be required to seek permission for the conduct of an AE rescue operation. The criteria for the conduct of an AE rescue operation by an aircraft should be met prior to rendering any assistance in a coastal state's territorial sea (see notes 97 and 98).

[100]The United States Coast Guard Addendum to the United States Search and Rescue Supplement to the International Aeronautical and Maritime Search and Rescue Manual (2013) does provide a note of caution on the use of aircraft and ships in the conduct of an AE rescue operation. Paragraph 1.8.1.6 states: "Customary practice for aircraft conducting AE rescue operations in a coastal State's territorial sea is not as fully developed as for vessels (e.g., nations may recognize the right to conduct AE rescue operations more readily for vessels than for aircraft). In addition, the conduct of AE rescue operations by nonmilitary vessels is apt to cause less coastal State concern than entry by military vessels. Therefore, safety of the rescue unit must be considered in light of the views of the coastal State whose territorial sea or overlying airspace is being entered."

3.3   Scenario C

Can a government ship "rescue" property while rendering assistance to a vessel in distress (e.g., personal property on board the vessel, floating in the water, etc.) in a coastal state's territorial sea, in addition to rendering assistance to persons in distress? To render the necessary assistance, can the ship tow the imperiled vessel into safe waters? After the ship brings any survivors on board, can it "rescue" the vessel and property, if they are still salvageable?[101]

The international conventions mandating a shipmaster's duty to render assistance to persons in distress do not contemplate the "rescue" or "recovery" of property in an AE rescue operation in a coastal state's territorial sea.[102] It is a person in distress who is assisted, not property. Therefore, the requirements for the conduct of an AE rescue operation should not be applied to the recovery of property. However, it can be argued that the recovery of property incidental to the conduct of an AE rescue operation is appropriate. This may include, for example, the recovery of critical medicine a survivor may require, towing a vessel that would facilitate the rescue of the persons in distress, and towing a disabled vessel.

Unless other arrangements are made between the shipmaster and the coastal state, the government ship contemplating the recovery of property *not* incidental to the AE rescue operation and within the coastal state's territorial sea should (1) complete the AE rescue operation, (2) depart the coastal state's territorial sea, and (3) seek permission to reenter the territorial sea to recover or salvage the property. This also would include the recovery of illegal contraband that could be used for any prosecution of the survivors if they were conducting a smuggling operation (e.g., narcotics).

---

[101]The Salvage Convention (1989), article 1(a), defines *salvage* as "any act or activity undertaken to assist a vessel or any other property in danger in navigable waters or in any other waters whatsoever."

[102]It is at this point where U.S. Coast Guard and DoD AE policy set forth in Chairman of the Joint Chiefs of Staff instruction (2013), differ. The United States Coast Guard Addendum to the United States Search and Rescue Supplement to the International Aeronautical and Maritime Search and Rescue Manual (2013) states (paragraph 1.8.2.6[b]) that Coast Guard rescue assets shall not conduct an AE rescue operation "[t]o rescue (or salvage) property (other than in limited cases, such as for the retrieval of medical supplies, or other property that may assist in the conduct of the lifesaving operation)." In contrast, Chairman of the Joint Chiefs of Staff instruction (2013), allows for the rescue of property: "RAE applies only to rescues in which the location of the persons **or property** in danger or distress is reasonably well known" (emphasis added). As mentioned previously (note 89), another difference is that the Coast Guard uses the term "assistance entry," while DoD uses "right of assistance entry." The Coast Guard prefers *AE,* believing the term advances the service's objectives in international engagements. Many nations view AE solely as a duty, not a right, even a limited one. While the distinction between a "duty" and "right" has legal significance, the practical distinctions are minimal, since international support exists for entry into a coastal state's territorial sea to render assistance to those in distress.

3.4   Scenario D

A government ship transiting on the high seas receives a distress broadcast and enters a coastal state's territorial sea to render assistance to a person in distress. After a reasonable amount of time, it cannot locate the distress incident location. Can the ship conduct a search in an attempt to locate the person in distress?

While no international instrument permits a coastal state to refuse entry of a government ship into its territorial sea to conduct an AE rescue operation, the SAR Convention does require authorization from the coastal state to conduct a search for persons in distress. If the ship conducting the AE rescue operation is unable to locate the persons in distress in a reasonable amount of time, then the proper course of action would be (1) to depart the coastal state's territorial sea and (2) to seek permission to conduct a search coordinated by the coastal state's SMC through the RCC responsible for the SAR region in which the person in distress is (presumably) located.[103]

3.5   Scenario E

A government ship transiting on the high seas receives a distress broadcast from a vessel taking on water in a coastal state's territorial sea. The shipmaster notifies his command authority that he is diverting to render assistance. The command authority coordinates notifying the coastal state that the ship is entering its territorial sea to render assistance to the vessel. The coastal state notifies the command authority that its SAR facility is en route to provide assistance and advises the ship that its assistance is not required. What should the shipmaster do? What should the ship's command authority do?

A government ship's duty to conduct an AE rescue operation is not nullified because the coastal state reports it has dispatched SAR facilities or units to rescue a person in distress. If, in the judgment of the shipmaster, the coastal state's assistance

---

[103]The annex to the SAR Convention (1979) (paragraph 3.1.2) states: "Unless otherwise agreed between the States concerned, a Party should authorize. . . immediate entry into or over its territorial sea or territory of rescue units of other Parties solely for the purpose of **searching** for the position of maritime casualties and rescuing the survivors of such casualties" (emphasis added). As previously noted (note 100), the annex continues (paragraph 3.1.3): "Unless otherwise agreed between the States concerned, the authorities of a Party which wishes its rescue units to enter into or over the territorial sea or territory of another Party solely for the purpose of **searching** for the position of maritime casualties and rescuing survivors of such casualties, shall transmit a request, giving full details of the projected mission and the need for it, to the rescue co-ordination centre of that other Party, or to such authority as has been designated by that Party" (emphasis added). In addition to Coast Guard policy not authorizing the conduct of an AE rescue operation to recover property or to search for persons in distress, the United States Coast Guard Addendum to the United States Search and Rescue Supplement to the International Aeronautical and Maritime Search and Rescue Manual (2013) also states (paragraph 1.8.2.6) that an AE rescue operation cannot be conducted (1) to assist persons not in distress, or (2) within a coastal state's internal waters or over its landmass.

is inadequate or not timely, then the distress still may be ongoing, and his duty would continue regardless of the coastal state's assertions or intent. This decision must rest with the shipmaster on scene, who has the duty to render the assistance.[104] However, if the coastal state's SAR unit is able to arrive on scene and conduct the rescue, the shipmaster's duty to render assistance is fulfilled.

3.6   Scenario F

Do the same requirements for a government ship to render assistance in a coastal state's territorial sea apply in international straits while transiting?[105]

The shipmaster's duty to render assistance to persons in distress applies throughout the ocean, whether in the territorial sea, in straits used for international navigation, in archipelagic waters, in the exclusive economic zone, or on the high seas.[106]

3.7   Scenario G

A government ship transiting on the high seas receives a distress broadcast from a vessel under attack by armed robbers while transiting through a coastal state's territorial sea. The government ship diverts to render assistance. Would this incident be considered an AE rescue operation?

This scenario should not be considered AE; UNCLOS (article 98), as well as the SOLAS (chapter V, regulation 33) and Salvage (article 10) Conventions, would not apply. Additionally, if the incident is not considered a rescue operation, then the SAR Convention also would not apply.[107] The issue is whether a vessel under attack

---

[104]SOLAS (1974), chapter V, regulation 33, requires the master of a ship at sea that is in a position to render assistance to persons in distress to provide that assistance. Stating that the *master* is required to render assistance demonstrates that it is the master who determines whether a person is in distress.

[105]The Commander's Handbook (2007), paragraph 2.5.3.1, describes *international straits* as follows: "Straits that are used for international navigation between one part of the high seas or an exclusive economic zone and another part of the high seas or an exclusive economic zone are subject to the legal regime of transit passage. Transit passage exists throughout the entire strait (shoreline-to-shoreline) and not just the area overlapped by the territorial sea of the coastal nation (s). Under international law, the ships and aircraft of all nations, including warships, auxiliary vessels, and military aircraft, enjoy the right of unimpeded transit passage through such straits and their approaches." *Transit passage* is defined as "the exercise of the freedoms of navigation and overflight solely for the purpose of continuous and expeditious transit in the normal modes of operation utilized by ships and aircraft for such passage." See also UNCLOS (1982), part III (Straits Used for International Navigation).

[106]Nordquist (2012), vol. 3, *Articles 86 to 132*, p. 177.

[107]While the annex to the SAR Convention (1979) does not explicitly state that law-enforcement actions are not coordinated and conducted within the framework of the global SAR system, the IAMSAR manual (2013), vol. 2, does provide guidance for assistance in "other than SAR operations" (see note 113). Another excellent guide for determining what generally would be

should be considered to be "in distress" (from a SAR perspective), with any response to be coordinated under the requirements of the SAR Convention. Interestingly and appropriately, there is no formal definition of *distress* in the SAR Convention or any other international convention.[108] This gives a person in extremis wide latitude in determining whether to declare distress and seek assistance. However, a vessel under attack should not be considered in distress, with any response to be coordinated under the SAR Convention; it would be more appropriate to consider this type of incident a law-enforcement or military operation.[109]

This does not mean, however, that a coastal state's RCC cannot coordinate a response in support of law-enforcement authorities or military resources that may be used to assist the ship under attack. The coordination and conduct of this type of operation would be implemented through a coastal state's national policies and procedures. In addition, if persons are injured during the response, the operation could include the medical transport of injured persons, which would be considered a SAR operation.

This position—that a vessel under attack is not considered "in distress"—was affirmed in a 2015 legal ruling in the U.S. Court of Appeals for the Fourth Circuit. The case highlighted the important distinction among antipiracy, law-enforcement, and military actions and SAR operations. The court's ruling provides an important distinction that warrants consideration by law-enforcement, military, and SAR authorities; in some coastal states, the coordination, policies, processes, procedures,

---

considered a "SAR case" is paragraph 4.c of Chairman of the Joint Chiefs of Staff instruction (2013), which states that RAE is conducted by U.S. military ships in support of "the time-honored mariners' duty under customary international law of rendering rapid and effective assistance to persons, ships, or aircraft in imminent **peril at sea** without regard to nationality or location" (emphasis added). The Chairman of the Joint Chiefs of Staff instruction (2013) goes on (paragraph 5.c) to define *perils of the sea* as "accidents and dangers peculiar to maritime activities including storms, waves, and wind; grounding; fire, smoke, and noxious fumes; flooding, sinking, and capsizing; loss of propulsion or steering; and other hazards of the sea." This definition provides not only a good understanding of when U.S. military ships should conduct AE rescue operations, but also a broad characterization for when the SAR Convention (1979) would apply and when activation of the global SAR system is warranted.

[108]The annex to the SAR Convention (1979) does provide (paragraph 1.3.13) a definition of *distress phase* (see note 76). The coastal-state SMC makes the determination of whether this definition applies considering the circumstance of a particular SAR operation. If a person declares that he is in distress, the SMC normally would activate the coastal state's distress phase processes and procedures to provide the necessary assistance.

[109]Walker (1995), p. 169, provides a good overview of what should be considered a distress: "'Distress,' as used in UNCLOS (1982) Articles 18, 39, 98 and 109, and as incorporated by reference in UNCLOS (1982) Articles 45 and 54, means an event of grave necessity, such as severe weather or mechanical failure in a ship or aircraft; or a human-caused event, such as a collision with another ship or aircraft. The necessity must be urgent and proceed from such a state of things as may be supposed to produce in the mind of a skillful mariner or aircraft commander a well-grounded apprehension of the loss of the vessel or aircraft and its cargo, or for the safety or lives of its crew or its passengers."

and resources used to conduct these types of actions very well may not be the same as those used to conduct SAR operations.[110]

In 2011, during NATO-conducted antipiracy operations in the Gulf of Aden and the Indian Ocean, a U.S. warship engaged *Jin Chun Tsai 68 (JCT 68)*, a fishing vessel from Taiwan that pirates had hijacked more than a year earlier and were using as a mother ship for pirate operations. On board *JCT 68* were pirates and three hostages; the latter consisted of the original shipmaster, Wu Lai-Yu, and two Chinese crew members. During the engagement, the warship used disabling fire to stop the vessel. After the pirates surrendered, the warship's boarding team went on board *JCT 68*. Three of the pirates and Wu had been killed during the warship's use of disabling fire. Subsequently, the pirates and the two remaining Chinese crew members were removed from the vessel. The following day, *JCT 68* was sunk intentionally—with Wu's body still on board, as the NATO task force commander directed.

Wu's widow subsequently initiated legal action against the United States in the District Court for the District of Maryland, seeking damages for her husband's death and the loss of *JCT 68*. The court granted the government's motion to dismiss the legal action, reasoning that the complaint was not a legal issue to be decided in a court of law. Wu's widow appealed the ruling in the Court of Appeals for the Fourth Circuit; the court of appeals affirmed the district court's decision to grant the government's motion. In determining whether a vessel under attack is considered "in distress," any response to which would fall under the requirements of the SAR Convention, the court of appeals affirmed an important distinction concerning the action the warship in question conducted:

> Plaintiff is likewise mistaken in categorizing the USS Groves's engagement with the Jin Chun Tsai 68 as a "Good Samaritan" action, or a "rescue operation" analogous to the rescue by the U.S. Coast Guard of distressed mariners. . ... The focus of the USS Groves's operation was to stop the depredations of the pirates, in part by depriving the pirates of their stolen mother ship. Sinking the Jin Chun Tsai 68 was part of the course of action worked out by the military commanders to further maritime security. The district court correctly recognized that because the Jin Chun Tsai 68 was sunk under direct NATO orders, the court could not adjudicate plaintiff's claim that the decision to sink the vessel was negligent or unlawful.[111]

This distinction is important when considering the conduct of SAR operations under the SAR Convention. Some coastal states may train and equip SAR units that would be responsible for conducting SAR operations only, not law-enforcement or military actions. Additionally, SAR authorities may rely on volunteer SAR organizations or seek the assistance of Good Samaritans in the vicinity of a vessel or persons in distress to assist in a particular SAR operation. The global SAR system was never envisioned to support other types of actions.[112]

---

[110]Case Wu Tien Li-Shou v. United States of America (2015).

[111]Ibid., p. 38.

[112]The IAMSAR manual (2013), vol. 2, also recognizes this important distinction. In paragraph 7.4.2 it states: "In situations such as piracy or armed robbery against ships where the ship or crew is in grave and imminent danger, the master may authorize the broadcasting of a distress message,

In summary, any ship or aircraft conducting an AE rescue operation must notify the coastal state of the intended course of action. Because of the perceived imminence of the distress and the urgency to take immediate action, the shipmaster or aircraft commander is not required to seek permission from the coastal state to fulfill his duty to render assistance and save lives. Even if the coastal state notifies the ship or aircraft rendering assistance that it has dispatched a SAR unit, if the shipmaster or aircraft commander believes the coastal-state SAR unit will not arrive in a timely manner, the duty to render assistance remains, and the shipmaster or aircraft commander must continue the rescue operation. The SAR Convention was never intended to limit or restrict a ship or aircraft that is available to render assistance to persons in distress. However, it would be appropriate for the shipmaster to coordinate the AE rescue operation with the coastal state's RCC, which should assume SMC of the SAR case. The shipmaster or aircraft commander, in communicating his actions to the coastal state, must ensure there is no misunderstanding about the craft's intent to conduct an AE rescue operation. Saving lives is the priority, even in a coastal state's territorial sea.

4   Forcible Evacuation for SAR

In 2011, the U.S. Coast Guard was notified that a twenty-four-foot sailboat registered in the United States and with one person on board was possibly in distress. The reporting source had received a voice mail from the person's satellite phone late in the evening stating, "Emergency, emergency," and nothing more. The last report received placed the sailboat seventy miles south of the United States and thirty miles offshore. The Coast Guard assumed SMC for the SAR operation and launched a Coast Guard aircraft and diverted a Coast Guard cutter to render assistance.

The aircraft located the sailboat, was able to see the person moving on deck, but was unable to hail him on the radio. It did appear to the aircraft that the sailboat's boom was damaged. The Coast Guard cutter arrived on scene and sent a boarding team to the sailboat to assess the situation. The boarding team

---

preceded by the appropriate distress alerts (MAYDAY, DSC, etc.), using all available radiocommunications systems. Also, ships subject to the SOLAS (1974) are required to carry equipment called the Ship Security Alert System (SSAS) for sending covert alerts to shore for vessel security incidents involving acts of violence against ships (i.e., piracy, armed robbery against ships or any other security incident directed against a ship). ... National procedures can vary but the role of the RCC, if involved, is usually to receive the SSAS alert and inform the security forces authority that will be in charge of the response. Actions taken by the RCC upon receiving a covert SSAS alert include: ... **place SAR resources on standby, if appropriate, since it may become a SAR case**" (emphasis added). This section in vol. 2 is placed in chapter 7, which is titled "Emergency Assistance Other than Search and Rescue," emphasizing that a law-enforcement action should not initially be considered a SAR operation as envisioned in the SAR Convention (1979); however, a SAR case may arise out of a law-enforcement action.

*confirmed the boom was destroyed and the sailboat's only outboard engine had
fallen off the vessel.*

*The boarding team advised the person that he should evacuate the vessel for his own
safety, but he refused. However, the Coast Guard cutter and its boarding team on
the sailboat realized that due to the condition of the sailboat the person's life was
in jeopardy. In consultation with the Coast Guard SAR chain of command, the
Coast Guard cutter compelled the person to depart the sailboat with the cutter's
boarding team. The cutter determined that the sailboat was in such a dilapidated
state that it was unsalvageable; the sailboat was marked and abandoned at sea.
The survivor was transferred to the Coast Guard cutter and returned to the
United States.*[113]

Finally, this article considers the challenge of compelling a person to abandon his
vessel to save his life. Thankfully, SAR authorities encounter such situations only
infrequently; a person in distress who requests assistance normally wants to leave his
vessel if the SAR responders on scene believe it necessary for his safety.[114]

The international conventions do not address specifically the use of force to
compel a person to abandon his vessel in a life-threatening situation. The intent
here is to provide a very brief overview and discussion of this issue, in order for
coastal states and SAR authorities to consider whether national and agency-specific
SAR policies are adequate and well understood by all levels in the SAR chain of
command. As can be seen in the scenario related above and in the fishing vessel
Northern Voyager SAR case described below (which resulted in a lawsuit against the
U.S. Coast Guard), these incidents can and do occur.

SAR authorities should consider several questions:

- What if an SMC is notified that a vessel is in distress and dispatches a SAR unit to
  render assistance but the vessel's captain refuses to disembark, even though in the
  judgment of the SAR unit on scene he will perish if he does not abandon the
  vessel?
- What if a merchant ship is diverted to render assistance but the vessel's captain
  refuses to abandon the vessel? The ship's crewmen most likely would not be
  trained in the use of force; they are merely fulfilling their duty to assist in the
  lifesaving operation. What advice should the SMC give to the shipmaster?
- What if the crew or passengers wish to evacuate a vessel in distress but the
  vessel's captain refuses to allow them to depart? What should the SAR unit or

---

[113]The facts portrayed in this vignette are known by the author, who attests to their accuracy. The
vignette is presented for consideration of the legal and policy issues involved.

[114]This discussion is based on SAR cases that would be coordinated and conducted under the SAR
Convention (1979) and would not normally apply to a mixed-migration-at-sea incident, which
might or might not constitute a SAR case. The unique nature of mixed-migration-at-sea operations
would require development of unique processes and procedures to meet the requirements of those
types of operations.

SAR facility on scene do? Should the use of force be contemplated to allow passengers and crew members to disembark the vessel in distress?

- If necessary, should force be used to compel the person in distress to leave his vessel? Does it matter whether the SAR unit is trained in the use of force? What type of force and extent of use should be contemplated?
- What are the legal implications of compelling a person against his will to abandon his vessel in what is perceived to be a life-threatening situation?
- What if the forcible evacuation of a person is being contemplated on a vessel of a different flag state?[115] How does that complicate the proposed use of force?

These are difficult questions applied to challenging, life-threatening situations—and SAR authorities should address them before this type of incident occurs. Forcibly compelling a person to abandon his vessel presents the SAR responder on scene who is attempting to provide the lifesaving assistance with a difficult situation and may result in controversy, property loss, and litigation.

In the United States, there is only one lawsuit that primarily discusses a SAR unit compelling a person in distress to abandon his vessel to save his life. In *Thames Shipyard and Repair Company v. United States*, the owner and insurer of the U.S.-documented fishing vessel *Northern Voyager* sued the United States, alleging that the disabled vessel sank, in part, because the U.S. Coast Guard compelled the vessel's captain to leave against his will.[116]

In November 1997, after losing its starboard rudder off the northeastern coast of the United States, the 144-foot *Northern Voyager* experienced significant flooding in the steering compartment, which was threatening to flood the vessel's engineering compartment as well. *Northern Voyager*'s captain notified the Coast Guard of the situation, which assumed SMC and dispatched two SAR units to provide additional pumps and render any other assistance that *Northern Voyager* might require. Despite the crew's attempts to curtail the progressive flooding, the fishing vessel developed a port list, settled further in the water, and was threatening to capsize and sink without warning with the crew members and Coast Guard personnel on board. The SAR units on scene, in contact with the SMC at the RCC coordinating the response, decided the only course of action left was to evacuate the remaining crew members before the vessel sank. When the Coast Guard personnel on *Northern Voyager*

---

[115]United Nation Convention on Conditions for Registration of Ships (1986), article 2, defines *flag State* as "a State whose flag a ship flies and is entitled to fly." Article 1 indicates that a flag state must "exercise effectively its jurisdiction and control over such ships with regard to identification and accountability of shipowners and operators as well as with regard to administrative, technical, economic and social matters." Additionally, UNCLOS (1982) article 91 states: "1. Every State shall fix the conditions for the grant of its nationality to ships, for the registration of ships in its territory, and for the right to fly its flag. Ships have the nationality of the State whose flag they are entitled to fly. There must exist a genuine link between the State and the ship. 2. Every State shall issue to ships to which it has granted the right to fly its flag documents to that effect." Walker (1995), pp. 193–195, provides a detailed explanation of the term *flag State* as used in UNCLOS (1982).

[116]Case Thames Shipyard and Repair Company v. United States (2003).

informed the captain that it was time to abandon ship, he refused to leave. The Coast Guard personnel informed him that if he did not cooperate, he would be compelled to depart, using force if necessary. As a result, the remaining members of *Northern Voyager*'s crew, the captain, and the assisting Coast Guard personnel evacuated the vessel. The fishing vessel sank a short while later.

Both the district court and the court of appeals held that U.S. law protected the Coast Guard's decision to evacuate the captain forcibly from the life-threatening situation that occurred on *Northern Voyager*.[117] The Supreme Court of the United States declined to review the case.[118]

In contemplation of both the operational and legal difficulties involved in forcibly evacuating a person from his vessel, even in a life-threatening situation, the Coast Guard does provide guidance to SAR units and the Coast Guard SAR chain of command. Coast Guard policy provides that, if time permits, the SAR unit on scene should consult with the SMC but that the SAR unit can evacuate a person forcibly from his vessel if it judges that (1) a true life-threatening situation exists and (2) the vessel to be abandoned in fact does require immediate assistance.[119] If time further

---

[117]In particular, both the district court and the court of appeals held that the discretionary function exception to liability under 46 USC § 742 (the Suits in Admiralty Act, which allows for a limited waiver of the U.S. federal government's sovereign immunity from civil lawsuits) and 46 USC § 781 (the Public Vessels Act, which allows for legal action against the United States for damages caused by a public vessel) protected from further judicial review the Coast Guard's decision to evacuate the master forcibly from *Northern Voyager*.

[118]The court of appeals brief included the following comment: "The facts of this case lead us to conclude that the Coast Guard reacted rationally, and that human life could reasonably have been deemed to be at serious risk had Captain Haggerty and his crew not been removed. The *Northern Voyager*, without steering, was rolling in 6–8 foot ocean seas. Water was pouring in. She was developing an increasing port-side list. The fishing boat's only access port was on the starboard side. The Coast Guardsmen on the vessel reported progressive flooding, raising the possibility that the ship would capsize, trapping all on board. While arguments can perhaps be made in light of 20-20 hindsight tending to minimize the potential dangers had the master and his fellows been allowed to remain, we see no basis to doubt the objective reasonableness of the Coast Guard's on the scene decision to remove them." However, Judge Torruella on the Court of Appeals concurred in part in and dissented in part from the majority's recognition of the Coast Guard's authority to compel the master forcibly to abandon his ship, thus preventing him from continuing efforts to save it. He wrote: "With due respect, there is no authority in law, practice, or maritime tradition that validates such action by the Coast Guard, nor am I aware of the government's having claimed such extraordinary powers before the inception of the case." He concluded that the discretionary function exception did not shield the United States from liability, because a decision cannot be shielded from liability if the decision maker is acting without actual authority. In the judge's view, "Such a momentous shift in policy and such an extraordinary grant of authority should not be undertaken absent a clear legislative mandate expressed both in the text of the statute and in its legislative history." For those interested in this issue, this case is well worth reading.

[119]Coast Guard SAR policy states that a voluntary evacuation of a person should be considered the preferred alternative to removing the person forcibly from his vessel. The United States Coast Guard Addendum to the United States Search and Rescue Supplement to the International Aeronautical and Maritime Search and Rescue Manual (2013) (paragraph 4.2.2) states: "Although the Coast Guard does have the authority to compel a mariner to abandon their vessel in a life threatening situation, it is always preferable that a mariner voluntarily evacuate when necessary. Coast Guard

permits, the decision to evacuate a person forcibly from his vessel should be made at the most competent operational and legal level in the SAR chain of command.[120]

In summary, SAR authorities should consider whether their current SAR policies and procedures provide adequate guidance for this challenging "forcible evacuation" scenario; if not, they should give further thought to developing new or improved policies and procedures for their SAR chain of command.

5   Summary

The global SAR system, while not perfect and in need of continuous improvement, does provide a means of notification about and response to persons in distress at sea. As long as people continue to sail the world's oceans, there will be a need to provide effective lifesaving services to those who need assistance.

International conventions provide the legal foundation for each coastal state to implement a national SAR organization. Coastal states must develop the SAR processes and procedures and provide the ships, boats, aircraft, and dedicated personnel that conduct lifesaving operations at sea. Ships plying the world's oceans are important contributors to the global SAR system and normally are willing to come to the aid of those in distress. When ships render assistance in a SAR operation, the SMC must work with the shipmaster to coordinate the response and delivery of the survivors to a place of safety, thereby limiting the impact on the shipmaster.

This article considered the conduct of AE rescue operations in a coastal state's territorial sea and some different AE scenarios that may be encountered. While AE rescue operations occur infrequently, SAR authorities nonetheless should develop national and agency-specific policies for ships and aircraft that may be required to conduct these operations and ensure that their commanders understand them.

Finally, this article discussed the difficult situation of a person who refuses to abandon his vessel even when the SAR unit on scene believes that evacuation is the only option left to save lives. While SAR authorities encounter such situations very

---

personnel should endeavor to use all means, including powers of persuasion, to encourage a mariner to evacuate, when appropriate. Forcible and/or compelled evacuations should only be conducted when a life-threatening emergency exists, and there is an immediate need for assistance or aid." Additionally, the decision to evacuate a person forcibly from his vessel to save his life should, if possible, be made in consultation with the SMC. The SMC, if time permits, should consult legal counsel. However, if time is of the essence and the situation is life threatening, then SAR policy should allow the SAR unit on scene to make the decision to remove a person forcibly from his vessel to save his life. Policies, procedures, and training must be developed and implemented to ensure that SAR units, SMCs, legal counsel, and the SAR organization chain of command can effectively manage this type of scenario.

[120]It should also be noted that from a U.S. legal perspective, a person who refuses to abandon his vessel at the request of the U.S. Coast Guard to save his own life has committed no crime, which makes the contemplated use of force even more difficult.

infrequently, national and agency-specific policies and guidelines should be developed to address this type of incident.

References

Agreement on Cooperation on Aeronautical and Maritime Search and Rescue in the Arctic (2011) 12 May 2011. oaarchive.arctic-council.org/. Accessed 05 Sept 2017

Boyer G (2015) Development dimensions of mixed migration (presentation, high-level meeting to address unsafe mixed migration by Sea, London, March 2015. http://www.imo.org/en/About/Events/Documents/migrantspresentations/y%20undp%205%20march%20Development%20Dimensions%20of%20Mixed%20Migration%20Flows%20March%202015.pdf. Accessed 05 Sept 2017

Case Hasan v. United States of America (2010) https://www.courtlistener.com/opinion/2476901/united-states-v-hasan/. Accessed 05 Sept 2017

Case Wu Tien Li-Shou v. United States of America (2015) U.S. District Court for the District of Maryland, 4th Cir., 23 January 2015. http://caselaw.findlaw.com/us-4th-circuit/1690428.html and https://content.next.westlaw.com/Document/I8824f413e70211e3a795ac035416da91/View/FullText.html?contextData=(sc.Default)&transitionType=Default&firstPage=true&bhcp=1. Accessed 10 Oct 2017

Case Thames Shipyard and Repair Company v. United States (2003) Northern Voyager Limited Partnership; OneBeacon America Insurance Company f/k/a/ Commercial Union Insurance Company, Plaintiffs, Appellants, v. United States, Defendant, Appellee. Nos. 02-1619, 02-1620. Decided: November 26, 2003. http://caselaw.findlaw.com/us-1st-circuit/1173624.html. Accessed 10 Oct 2017

Chairman of the Joint Chiefs of Staff instruction (2013) Guidance for the exercise of right-of-assistance entry, CJCSI 2410.01D (3 September 2013). http://www.jcs.mil/Portals/36/Documents/Library/Instructions/2410_01.pdf?ver=2016-02-05-175013-783. Accessed 05 Sept 2017

Chicago Convention (1944) Convention on international civil aviation, 7 December 1944, 9th ed. 2006, ICAO doc. 7300

Commander's Handbook (2007) The commander's handbook on the law of naval operations, U.S. Navy/Marine Corps/Coast Guard. www.jag.navy.mil/documents/NWP_1-14M_Commanders_Handbook.pdf. Accessed 10 Oct 2017

Gage LJ (1897) U.S. secretary of the treasury, to captain francis tuttle, revenue cutter service, "Letter of Instructions," 15 November 1897, in Report of the Cruise of the U.S. Revenue Cutter Bear and the Overland Expedition for the Relief of the Whalers in the Arctic Ocean, from November 27, 1897, to September 13, 1898 (Washington, DC: Government Printing Office, 1899). www.uscg.mil/

Guidelines on the Treatment of Persons Rescued at Sea (2004) adopted 20 May 2004, IMO Resolution MSC.167(78). http://www.imo.org/en/OurWork/Facilitation/personsrescued/Documents/MSC.167(78).pdf. Accessed 05 Sept 2017

High Seas Convention (1958) Convention on the High Seas, 29 April 1958, U.N.T.S. 450, p. 11, into force 30 September 1962. https://treaties.un.org/doc/Publication/UNTS/Volume%20450/v450.pdf. Accessed 05 Sept 2017

IAMSAR (2013) International Aeronautical and Maritime Search and Rescue Manual (2013), IAMSAR, IMO/International Civil Aviation Organization. CPI Group, Croydon

IMO Secretariat (2015) Outcome of the inter-agency high-level meeting to address unsafe mixed migration by sea: note by the secretariat (LEG 102/INF.3), Legal Committee 102nd Session (9 March 2015). http://iidmaritimo.org/instituto/wp-content/uploads/2016/04/LEG-102-INF.3-Outcome-of-the-inter-agency-High-level-meeting-to-address-unsafe-mixed-migration-by-sea-Secretariat.pdf. Accessed 17 Sept 2017

Jones M (2013) A year later, Oshkosh survivor of cruise ship crash still cruising. Milwaukee-Wisconsin Journal Sentinel, 14 January 2013. www.jsonline.com/

Kumin J (2014) The challenge of mixed migration by sea. Forced Migration Review, no. 45 (February 2014). www.fmreview.org/. Accessed 05 Sept 2017

Mallia P (2014) The MV salamis and the state of disembarkation at international law: the undefinable goal. Am Soc Int Law Insights 18(11). (15 May 2014). https://www.asil.org/insights/volume/18/issue/11/mv-salamis-and-state-disembarkation-international-law-undefinable-goal. Accessed 05 Sept 2017

Most Frequently Asked Questions about the Refugee Convention (2001) United Nations High Commissioner for Refugees (UNHCR), 01 June 2001. http://www.unhcr.org/news/stories/2001/6/3b4c06578/frequently-asked-questions-1951-refugee-convention.html.   Accessed 06 Oct 2017

Newland K (2013) Troubled waters: rescue of Asylum seekers and refugees at sea, migration information source (1 January 2003). http://www.migrationpolicy.org/article/troubled-waters-rescue-asylum-seekers-and-refugees-sea. Accessed 05 Sept 2017

Nordquist MH (2012). In: Nandan SN, Rosenne S (eds) United Nations convention on the law of the sea: a commentary. Brill

Note USA to IMO (1991) Note "SAR on or over Foreign Territorial Seas" of the United States of America to IMO's sub-committee on lifesaving, search and rescue, submitted 19 January 1991 (LSR 22/8/4)

Oxford Dictionaries., www.oxforddictionaries.com. Accessed 05 Sept 2017

Refugee Convention (1951) Convention relating to the status of refugees, UNHCR, 25 July 1951. http://www.unhcr.org/3b66c2aa10. Accessed 6 Oct 2017

Report of the IMO Legal Committee (1991) Report of the legal committee on the work of Its Sixty-Fifth Session, 11 October 1991, LEG 65/8

Rescue at Sea Guide (2015) A guide to principles and practice as applied to refugees and migrants (2015).   http://www.ics-shipping.org/docs/default-source/resources/safety-security-and-operations/imo-unhcr-ics-rescue-at-sea-guide-to-principles-and-practice-as-applied-to-refugees-and-migrants.pdf?sfvrsn=25. Accessed 05 Sept 2017

Salvage Convention (1989) International convention on salvage, 28 April 1989. http://www.dutchcivillaw.com/legislation/consalvage.htm. Accessed 6 Oct 2017

SAR Convention (1979) International convention on maritime search and rescue, into force 22 June 1985.   http://www.imo.org/en/About/conventions/listofconventions/pages/internationalconvention-on-maritime-search-and-rescue-(sar).aspx. Accessed 5 Sept 2017

Sekimizu K (2015) IMO Secretary-General, speech at High-Level Meeting to Address Unsafe Mixed Migration by Sea. IMO Headquarters, London, p 1. http://www.imo.org/en/About/Events/Documents/migrants4march/Z%20IMO%20High-Level%20meeting%20to%20address%20Unsafe%20Mixed%20Migration%20by%20Sea.pdf. Accessed 05 Sept 2017

SOLAS Convention (1974) International convention for the safety of life at sea, into force 25 May 1980. http://www.imo.org/en/About/conventions/listofconventions/pages/internationalconvention-for-the-safety-of-life-at-sea-(solas),-1974.aspx. Accessed 5 Sept 2017; Consolidated Edition, 2009 (London: IMO, 2009)

Statute of the International Court of Justice (1945) http://legal.un.org/avl/pdf/ha/sicj/icj_statute_e.pdf. Accessed 05 Sept 2017

The Convention on Facilitation of International Maritime Traffic (1965) 9 April 1965. http://www.ifrc.org/Docs/idrl/I258EN.pdf. Accessed 05 Sept 2017

TOC Convention (2004) United Nations convention against transnational organized crime and the protocols thereto, New York 2004. https://www.unodc.org/documents/middleeastand northafrica/organised-crime/UNITED_NATIONS_CONVENTION_AGAINST_TRANSNA TIONAL_ORGANIZED_CRIME_AND_THE_PROTOCOLS_THERETO.pdf.   Accessed 06 Oct 2017

United Nations Convention on the Law of the Sea (1982) (UNCLOS) 1833 U.N.T.S. 397

United Nation Convention on Conditions for Registration of Ships (1986) Not in force. http://unctad.org/en/PublicationsLibrary/tdrsconf23_en.pdf. Accessed 05 Sept 2017

United Nations High Commissioner for Refugees UNHCR (2015) The sea route to Europe: the Mediterranean passage in the age of refugees (1 July 2015). http://www.unhcr.org/5592bd059.pdf. Accessed 05 Sept 2017

United Nations High Commissioner for Refugees UNHCR (2011) Refugees and Asylum-Seekers in Distress at Sea – how best to respond?, Expert Meeting in Djibouti, 8 to 10 November 2011, Summary Conclusions at http://www.refworld.org/pdfid/4ede0d392.pdf. Accessed 06 Oct 2017; overwiev at http://unhcr.org/cgi-bin/texis/vtx/search?page=search&skip=117&docid=&cid=49aea93aa7&scid=49aea93a57&comid=4ef33aa76. Accessed 06 Oct 2017

United States Coast Guard Addendum to the United States Search and Rescue Supplement to the International Aeronautical and Maritime Search and Rescue Manual (2013) COMDTINST M16130.2F (January 2013). http://ppgroup.uscgaux.info/manuals/USCG_SAR_Addendum.pdf. Accessed 05 Sept 2017

U.S. Navy Regulations (1990) https://doni.documentservices.dla.mil/navyregs.aspx. Accessed 05 Sept 2017

U.S. Coast Guard Regulations (1992) http://govdocs.rutgers.edu/mil/cg/CIM_5000_3B.pdf. Accessed 05 Sept 2017

Walker GK (1995) Definitions for the law of the Sea: terms not defined by the 1982 convention. Martinus Nijhoff

Rick Button is the Chief, Coordination Division, Office of Search and Rescue, United States Coast Guard Headquarters, Washington, D.C., and serves as the Secretary to the United States National Search and Rescue Committee. Mr. Button conducts outreach and education, coordinates Coast Guard and United States, national and international search and rescue policy and management issues, is the program manager for the Amver search and rescue ship reporting system and Coast Guard support for the Search and Rescue Satellite Aided Tracking (SARSAT) program. Mr. Button retired from the Coast Guard in 2006 after serving 22 years on active duty and has served 11 years in his current position. During his Coast Guard career, Mr. Button served on several Coast Guard cutters and twice served as commanding officer. Mr. Button is a 1984 graduate of the United States Coast Guard Academy and is a licensed Master Mariner.

A Review of Selected Measures for Reducing Potential Conflict Among Naval Vessels in the South China Sea

David Letts

Abstract
The South China Sea is an area that is subject to numerous competing sovereignty claims over the many maritime features that exist in the region. None of these claims appear capable of easy resolution, and a number of the States directly involved, as well as States that have an interest in the preservation of passage and overflight rights through and over the South China Sea, have used their military forces as the means by which they have sought to exert influence in this region. Fears that the increased presence of military vessels and aircraft might lead to unintended outbreak of armed conflict have been constantly raised by academic and political commentators with the contention from some that armed conflict is an inevitable outcome of this increased military presence. However, this article undertakes a review of these concerns and reaches the conclusion that the likelihood of conflict inadvertently occurring is low. In particular, the requirement to ensure the continued flow of maritime trade throughout the South China Sea is likely to drive State behaviour away from any desire for armed conflict as a means of resolving the various tensions and claims that exist in the region.

This contribution is a refined and revised version of a presentation given by the author at the 23rd Annual ANZSIL Conference in Wellington, New Zealand, on 4 July 2015. Comments on the presentation from those present at the Conference were of considerable assistance in finalising this contribution.

D. Letts (✉)
Centre for Military and Security Law, Australian National University College of Law, Canberra, ACT, Australia
e-mail: david.letts@anu.edu.au

143

J. Schildknecht et al. (eds.), *Operational Law in International Straits and Current Maritime Security Challenges*, Operational Maritime Law 1,
https://doi.org/10.1007/978-3-319-72718-9_8

1   Introduction

As ongoing tensions affect relations between States that have an interest[1] in the
South China Sea,[2] there may be an aura of inevitability regarding the likelihood of
conflict at sea occurring among naval vessels of some of the States that have made
claims of sovereignty over the maritime features that exist in the region.[3] However,
tensions in the South China Sea have existed for many decades, and notwithstanding
that incidents have occurred at sea, for the most part these incidents have not resulted
in the outbreak of any significant level of conflict.

A number of reasons can be posited for this situation. One key reason is that
mariners are notoriously cautious about deliberately putting their vessels in
situations where danger of collision or sinking is likely, especially as the potential
consequences arising from a vessel being sunk are obviously grave. Accordingly,
there is a reduced likelihood that 'accidental' conflict will arise. Also, the maritime
domain is actually quite well regulated in terms of both hard (black letter) law as well
as a growing number of soft law[4] instruments (although the latter is not the focus of
this chapter). Another reason is that the maritime domain has some unique
characteristics that mitigate against conflict arising. The consequence is that
measures that have been put in place by States to lessen the potential for conflict
occurring at sea have, in the main, had the desired dampening effect.

By way of a preliminary consideration, one may question why particular attention
should be paid to this topic when serious conflicts at sea are such an infrequent
aspect of the modern age—at least when compared to the use of air power and land
forces as instruments of national power. The answer is really quite simple when the
amount of world trade that travels by sea, and especially through the South China
Sea, is considered. According to the International Maritime Organization, 'international shipping transports about 90% of global trade to peoples and communities all
over the world'.[5] The immediate and obvious consequence of any disruption in that

---

[1]The main claimant states are China (both the People's Republic of China and the Republic of
China), Vietnam, the Philippines, Malaysia; Brunei and Indonesia have smaller claims in the region.

[2]It is noted that the term 'South China Sea' is not universally accepted as being the correct name for
the sea areas in South East Asia that are the subject of competing sovereignty claims. Other names
used include: the South Sea, the East Sea, the West Philippine Sea and the South East Asian Sea.

[3]Sovereignty claims and disputes involve China (and Taiwan), the Philippines, Vietnam, Malaysia,
Brunei and Japan: Council on Foreign Relations (2017).

[4]Finding a widely accepted definition of 'soft law' is problematic. One approach could be to adopt
the definition used in the Australian Law Dictionary 2nd ed (2013) which defines soft law as
'Norms not satisfying the Positivist Sources Thesis or the criteria for international law in the Statute
of the International Court of Justice Article 38'. Difficulties associated with identifying a definition
of soft law have also been recently identified by Weeks (2014), pp. 181–216 esp. pp. 181–186. In
this contribution the term 'soft law' will be used to describe instruments that have been agreed
between States and/or their navies but which do not meet the criteria described in Article 38 (1)(a) of
the Statute of the International Court of Justice.

[5]See International Maritime Organization (n.d.).

percentage of trade in terms of the impact on the world's economy necessitates periodic analysis of this topic.

As a means of setting the context for the discussion in this chapter, it is interesting to reflect upon some of the remarks that were made at the 14th Asia Security Summit (widely known as the Shangri-la Dialogue), in Singapore on 29–31 May 2015. For example, the United States Secretary of Defense, Dr. Ashton Carter, stated that 'The United States is deeply concerned about the pace and scope of land reclamation in the South China Sea, the prospect of further militarisation, as well as the potential for these activities to increase the risk of miscalculation or conflict among claimant states'.[6] Australia's (then) Defence Minister stated that 'Australia has a legitimate interest in the maintenance of peace and security in this part of the world (i.e. South East Asia), including the preservation of respect for international law, unimpeded trade and freedom of navigation'.[7] Similar expressions of concern were made by other high-ranking delegates at the Shangri-la Dialogue.[8]

These comments reflect a consistent line of thought among politicians and commentators that some level of threat to the current order of maritime freedoms and rights in the Asian region does exist and not only in relation to tensions arising in the South China Sea. Therefore, examination of the measures that have been adopted to reduce tension at sea (and the potential for conflict) provides a salutary balance to counter some of the more pessimistic reporting that occurs on the topic.

The focus of the analysis being undertaken in this chapter will be on the South China Sea through examining a selection of legal issues that might impact upon any conflict at sea that might arise in that region. To achieve this task, initial comment will outline the meaning of 'armed conflict' and 'armed attack' in order to understand threshold issues that have been set by international law and consider their applicability to hostile conduct at sea. This will be followed by a brief overview of how naval operations at sea are regulated before examining certain elements of the 1982 UN Convention on the Law of the Sea.[9] Next, the key features of the maritime operating environment will be addressed, and an outline of the impact of those features on the likelihood of conflict at sea arising will take place.[10] Finally, consideration of the implications for naval operations in the South China Sea will occur prior to the provision of some concluding remarks.

---

[6]Carter (2015).

[7]Andrews (2015), Speech at 14th IISS Asia Security Summit. Mr. Andrews was replaced as Australian Minister for Defence in September 2015 by Senator The Hon Marise Payne.

[8]Transcripts of speeches from the Opening Session and Plenary Sessions of the 2015 Shangri-la Dialogue can be found at: https://www.iiss.org/en/events/shangri%20la%20dialogue/archive/shangri-la-dialogue-2015-862b; these sentiments were echoed at the 2016 Shangri-la Dialogue and 2017 Shangri-la Dialogue.

[9]LOSC (1982).

[10]It is recognised that vessels from government agencies other than navies are regularly deployed in maritime regions where tensions are fragile, including the South China Sea, and there is potential for conflict to arise among and between these vessels. For example, see Kraska and Monti (2015). Nevertheless, the focus of this contribution is primarily limited to issues which involve naval forces.

2   The Meaning of Conflict

It is not the major purpose of this contribution to canvass a complete history of conflict in order to reach a satisfactory description that can be used to comprehensively cover the range of military activity that might eventuate in the South China Sea. Instead, a convenient starting point has been chosen, perhaps arbitrarily, by travelling back 70 years and considering that despite the prohibition contained in the UN Charter[11] on States resorting to the threat or use of force in settling their international differences, the reality is that since 1945 there have been numerous occasions throughout the world in which armed conflict has occurred.

At the time of writing, the International Institute of Strategic Studies Armed Conflict Database reports that there are 42 active conflicts underway throughout the world[12] yet none of these conflicts has any significant maritime dimension. It is also noted that post-1945 conflicts have not been restricted to any particular geographical area, and conflicts that have occurred have varied greatly in terms of the characterisation of the conflict as international armed conflict (IAC) or non-international armed conflict (NIAC), the length of conflict and the intensity of the fighting.[13] However, by far the vast majority of post-1945 armed conflicts have involved battles between land forces, with relatively few examples of conflict occurring in the maritime environment.

But there should be no misapprehension. There is undoubtedly the potential for conflict to emerge between vessels at sea, and in some post-1945 cases this potential has been realised with consequent loss of life and destruction of vessels.[14] Thus, one of the questions raised by this contribution is to ask why, even when tensions have escalated between States since 1945, and even when these tensions have resulted in armed conflict occurring between land (and air) forces, has there not been, in most cases, corresponding major battles among naval forces. Prior to 1945, this was certainly not the case, as the examples of World War II, World War I and the Russo–Japanese War of 1904–1905 demonstrate.

2.1   'Armed Conflict' and 'Armed Attack'

It is apparent that not every hostile or heated interaction between vessels will result in characterisation of the incident as being an 'armed conflict' or even comprising an 'armed attack' in the sense that the consequence of the interaction would result in the

---

[11]UN Charter (1949), Article 2(4).

[12]IISS (2015).

[13]See AP II (1949) Article 1.

[14]The most notable instance was, perhaps, the war between Argentina and the United Kingdom over the Falkland Islands (or Islas Malvinas) in 1982 when vessels from both belligerents were attacked and sunk. Some other relatively recent armed conflicts (both IAC and NIAC) involving naval vessels include the Korean War, the Vietnam War, Israel/Egypt, Sri Lanka and Iraq (1990–1991 and 2003).

immediate applicability of the laws of armed conflict and/or invoke the right of self-defence (as a matter of law). While the preceding statement points to a requirement for precision in determining the character or nature of any given incident, even a cursory examination of judicial decisions and academic literature will disclose that such precision is lacking once factual circumstances are taken into account.

For example, in the often quoted Tadic decision, the Appeals Chamber of the International Criminal Tribunal for the Former Yugoslavia used the following criteria as the basis for determining whether an international armed conflict exists: 'an armed conflict exists whenever there is a resort to armed force between States'.[15] Although this is a seemingly straightforward proposition, the reality when factual circumstances are taken into account is not so clear as there are interpretative issues to be addressed in order to determine if the facts support the conclusion that 'resort to armed force between States' has actually occurred. The situation in relation to NIAC is even more obscure with many instances of States taking considerable effort to avoid recognition that activities taking place within their territory might reach the threshold where the law of armed conflict would apply.[16]

In trying to determine whether a maritime incident would amount to a 'resort to armed force between States', some guidance can be taken from the Oil Platforms[17] decision in 2003. In that judgment, the International Court of Justice could 'not exclude the possibly that the mining of a single military vessel might be sufficient to bring into play the "inherent right of self-defence"'[18] (which arises following an armed attack) with the consequential outcome that an IAC might arise between two States. However, based on the facts that were relevant in the case that was considered by the ICJ, the Court was unable to conclude that action taken by the United States against Iranian oil platforms was justified.[19]

The issue of use of force in the maritime context was also considered in the Guyana/Suriname Arbitration.[20] Following a ruling by the Arbitral Tribunal that it possessed jurisdiction to deal with the issue, arguments were raised by Guyana and Suriname in relation to the nature of the activity that took place at sea on 3 June 2000. In essence, the key point was whether the action of the Suriname officials amounted to a threat or use of force in contravention of the prohibition in Article 2 (4) of the UN Charter[21] or constituted legitimate law enforcement activities.[22] After

---

[15]ICTY (1996), para 70; see also Greenwood (1996).

[16]Perhaps the most famous example being the refusal of the British government to ever recognise that an armed conflict existed in Northern Ireland during the period 1968–1998. The period is commonly referred to as 'The Troubles'.

[17]ICJ (2003).

[18]Ibid at para 72.

[19]There is a large volume of material which has analysed the Oil Platforms decision, ICJ (2003). See for example, Garwood-Gowers (2004).

[20]Guyana and Suriname Award (2007), pp. 1–144.

[21]UN Charter Article 2(4).

[22]Guyana and Suriname Award (2007), para 425–447.

considering the facts and relevant authorities,[23] the Tribunal found that while '...
force may [legitimately] be used in law enforcement activities provided that such
force is unavoidable, reasonable and necessary',[24] the actions of Suriname did
constitute '... a threat of the use of force in contravention of the Convention, the
UN Charter and general international law'.[25]

Extrapolating the approach taken by the International Court of Justice to the
situation that exists in the South China Sea, there would clearly need to be a high
level of certainty that a conflict between vessels was of sufficient gravity to constitute an 'armed attack' and therefore a situation that warranted at least the consideration of a response using force in self-defence, let alone the actual use of force.
Further distinction in this area can be made on the basis that some attacks may be
minor (the infamous 'mere frontier incident' described by the International Court of
Justice in the Nicaragua case[26]), but this approach also provides challenges in
determining precisely which attacks would fall on the appropriate side of the line.[27]

Although the preceding discussion is extremely brief, the main point is that when
considering the characterisation of activities taking place among vessels in the South
China Sea, there are threshold considerations that must be addressed before any
determination of the nature of the activity can occur. In simple terms, not every
hostile action will be one that will automatically result in an armed conflict existing
as a matter of law, nor will every action necessarily invoke a legal right of armed
response in self-defence.

3   Regulation of Activities at Sea

There is a wide body of law regulating the activities of vessels at sea that has
applicability in both times of armed conflict and times of peace. Many aspects of
this law have been codified and agreed among States to deal with issues as diverse as
vessel traffic management/collision avoidance[28] and vessel passage regimes in
various maritime zones,[29] while other laws deal with issues like the prevention of
the pollution of the ocean by vessels[30] and measures to deal with terrorism threats at

---

[23]In particular, those cited below in this article at footnote 49.

[24]Ibid and Guyana and Suriname Award (2007), para 445.

[25]Ibid.

[26]ICJ (1986).

[27]See the discussion of this aspect of the ICJ's Nicaragua decision in Dinstein (2011), pp. 208–212;
see also Klabbers (2015), in Weller (ed) (2015) pp. 501–502 for analysis of the differing reasoning
provided by the ICTY in the Tadic decision and the ICJ in Nicaragua and Oil Platforms.

[28]For example, the 1972 Convention on the International Regulations for Preventing Collisions at
Sea (COLREGs).

[29]For example LOSC (1982) Articles 17–20, Articles 38–39, Articles 52–54, Article 87 and Article
90.

[30]The 1973 International Convention for the Prevention of Pollution from Ships had not entered
into force when the 1978 Protocol Relating to the International Convention for the Prevention of

sea.[31] Some, but not all, of the codified laws are also reflective of customary international law in the maritime domain.[32] Additionally, only some, but not all of the codified laws, are applicable to naval vessels.[33]

Notwithstanding the mixed applicability of laws to naval vessels, it is entirely plausible that the increase in regulation of maritime activity that has occurred in recent years has had a consequential influence on the behaviour of vessels generally and naval vessels in particular. One result of this influence is that there have been relatively few instances in the past 50 years where interaction between naval vessels from States that could be considered as being 'politically opposed' has resulted in a heightened risk of conflict between those vessels. Those instances where conflict has erupted have invariably been as a result of wider geopolitical and strategic factors involving the flag States of the vessels concerned and have involved clear and deliberate action.[34]

It is true that tensions at sea have, on occasion, risen. There have been instances where diplomatic relations between states have become very fragile (e.g., the Black Sea 'bumping' incident of 1988,[35] the 'cod wars'[36] that occurred between Iceland and the UK in the 1970s, the 'Whiskey on the rocks'[37] incident in 1981 and protests

---

Pollution from Ships was finalised and so the 1973 Convention was subsumed by the 1978 Protocol and the two instruments are used together and commonly referred to as MARPOL (73/78). The International Maritime Organisation website notes that MARPOL (73/78): is the main international convention covering prevention of pollution of the marine environment by ships from operational or accidental causes. The MARPOL Convention was adopted on 2 November 1973 at IMO. The Protocol of 1978 was adopted in response to a spate of tanker accidents in 1976–1977. As the 1973 MARPOL Convention had not yet entered into force, the 1978 MARPOL Protocol absorbed the parent Convention. The combined instrument entered into force on 2 October 1983. In 1997, a Protocol was adopted to amend the Convention and a new Annex VI was added which entered into force on 19 May 2005. MARPOL (73/78) has been updated by amendments through the years.

[31] SUA Convention (1988).

[32] The navigation and passage regimes in the LOSC (1982) are the main examples.

[33] For example, notwithstanding disagreement which exists regarding the precise scope of application, it is clear that as a general proposition the provisions of LOSC (1982) apply to warships: see LOSC (1982) Articles 29–32 and 95–96; this situation is contrasted with MARPOL (73/78) Article 3(3) which clearly excludes the application of MARPOL (73/78) from warships, naval auxiliaries and other ships owned/operated by a State and being used on government non-commercial service.

[34] The most obvious example is the 1982 Falklands/Malvinas conflict which had a heavy involvement of naval forces and witnessed significant loss of vessel and life on both the UK and Argentine sides.

[35] In February 1988 two Soviet warships 'bumped' into USS Yorktown and USS Caron after the two United States Navy vessels entered Soviet territorial waters while claiming to be undertaking innocent passage: see Kraska and Pedrozo (2013), pp. 255–257 for further details of this incident.

[36] The 'cod wars' were a series of clashes between the UK and Iceland which primarily occurred in the 1960s and 1970s and included a large number of incidents when vessels from both sides rammed into each other. Both the Icelandic and UK governments were attempting to preserve/enforce fishing rights: see Ingimundarson (2003); see also Hart (1976).

[37] A Soviet 'Whiskey' class submarine became stranded on rocks in Swedish internal waters on 28 October 1981 and remained there until 5 November 1981; see Jacobsson (1997), pp. 516–518.

at French nuclear testing in the Pacific[38] during the 1970s), but none of these instances have resulted in an armed conflict ensuing. In terms of incidents that have occurred in the South China Sea, there have been numerous occasions upon which tensions have been heightened during recent decades, and these incidents have involved many of the claimant States in the region.[39]

However, and perhaps somewhat paradoxically in terms of the proposition being advanced in this chapter, in the South China Sea there have been instances where armed conflict has occurred, but these instances have been limited in scale and scope and did not extend beyond the immediate environs of each dispute.[40] In this sense, the relatively small scale of naval confrontation is in contrast to the seemingly constant state of IAC and NIAC that has been a blight on the world during the past 70 years.[41]

4   The Impact of the 1982 Law of the Sea Convention

A variety of legal instruments have been used by various actors in the international community to try and reduce the likelihood of armed conflict erupting at sea. Descriptions of these measures vary as do the nature of the activities undertaken by naval forces to reduce tensions outside of formal legal processes.

In terms of 'hard' international law, the starting point must be the 1982 UN Convention on the Law of the Sea[42] (LOSC), which contains provisions that specifically deal with the rights and obligations of States, and their warships, in the maritime zones that are established (or recognised) under the LOSC. For example, in the territorial sea, where coastal State sovereignty and jurisdiction is

---

[38]Both Australia and New Zealand protested against French nuclear testing in the South Pacific during the 1970s and both States initiated proceedings (unsuccessfully) against France. See Nuclear Tests (Australia v. France) (1974), p. 253; Nuclear Tests (New Zealand v. France), Judgment, (1974), p. 457. In addition, in June 1973 New Zealand sent two frigates to the Muroroa test zone (see NZ History (2015)) after France had refused to abide by the ICJ's Interim Protection Order. See Nuclear Tests (New Zealand v. France), Interim Protection, Order of 22 June (1973), p. 135.

[39]Examples include: the seizing of USS Pueblo by North Korea in January 1968; numerous and ongoing challenges to warship passage in the region involving a wide variety of States and in a range of maritime zones; the interception and mid-air collision between a Chinese PLA-N J-8 aircraft and a United States Navy EP-3 aircraft on 1 April 2001; challenges to a task force of Royal Australian Navy warships in April 2001; the interception and challenge to USNS Impeccable and USNS Victorious in 2009; and the incident involving USS Cowpens and PLA-N's aircraft carrier/training ship Liaoning in December 2013.

[40]The most noticeable incident occurred in the 1974 'Battle of the Paracel Islands' between China and the Republic of Vietnam when the PLA-N inflicted heavy losses on the Vietnamese forces; more than 70 military personnel were killed; see Tri and Collin (2014).

[41]As noted above at n12 there are at least 42 conflicts currently underway throughout the world.
[42]LOSC (1982).

strongest, a warship has the same passage rights[43] as any other vessel—subject to certain key restrictions.

In the territorial sea, all vessels are required to refrain from any activity that is prejudicial to the coastal State's peace and security.[44] This seems a straightforward requirement, but of course there is an element of detail missing. For example, who decides what activity constitutes 'prejudicial'? Is this a test that is left solely to the discretion (and vagaries) of coastal State interpretation? Must there be consistency among States so that activity that is regarded as 'prejudicial' by one coastal State must necessarily be considered prejudicial by another? Can, in some instances, the mere presence of a warship in a coastal State's territorial sea amount to being 'prejudicial'? The answers to all of these issues are not universally agreed, and variance that does exist could, potentially, be the cause of tension and eventually lead to armed conflict arising at sea.

Another restriction in the territorial sea directly affecting naval vessels is that air capable warships are not, absent coastal State consent, permitted to conduct flying operations in the territorial sea as LOSC Article 19(2)(e) denotes that '... the launching, landing or taking on board of any aircraft' is one of the activities that will be considered prejudicial to the peace, good order or security of the coastal State if it takes place in the territorial sea. Again, this seems like a fairly straightforward issue,[45] and for those who wonder about unmanned aerial vehicles, LOSC Article 19 (2)(f) seems to have that issue covered too—providing that the UAV can be characterised as a 'military device'.

A further restriction is found in LOSC Article 20, which requires that submarines and other underwater vessels navigate on the surface and show their flag in the territorial sea. The reason behind this requirement could be described as self-evident in the sense that one of the obvious tasks that a submarine might be given is to operate in an area close to another State's coastline and obtain information regarding that State in a manner that is not readily detected. Of course, from the coastal State's point of view, this covert activity would likely be regarded as extremely prejudicial to the security interests of the coastal State.

Perhaps the most famous (or infamous) example of a foreign submarine being detected in close proximity to the coastline of another State occurred on 28 October 1981, admittedly before the 1982 LOSC had been concluded, when a Soviet submarine struck a 'rocky islet in Gasefjarden' in a military protection zone within Swedish internal waters.[46] The submarine remained stuck until 5 November 1981 before being towed into international waters by Swedish vessels whereupon it was greeted by a waiting flotilla of Soviet naval vessels that had been deployed in the area in order to assist the submarine after it had run aground. Interestingly, despite

---

[43]LOSC (1982) Articles 17 and 18.

[44]LOSC (1982) Article 19(1).

[45]The vexed question of sovereignty, especially in the South China Sea, is certainly not straightforward.

[46]Jacobsson (1997), above n37 p. 516.

tensions being very high between the Soviet Union and Sweden as a result of the submarine's presence, there were no shots fired at the Soviet submarine or the Soviet warships that moved to the immediate environs (but outside of the Swedish territorial sea).[47] The presence of unidentified underwater contacts in Swedish waters is not only a matter of Cold War history, as evidenced by an incident that Sweden dealt with in October 2014 when responding to evidence of unauthorised submarine activity in its waters.[48]

The preceding discussion has shown that even with the hard law areas of LOSC, there remain plenty of uncertainties and ambiguities that rely on other mechanisms for interpretation and fidelity. For example, LOSC Article 25 permits a coastal State to '... take the necessary steps in its territorial sea to prevent passage which is not innocent', but there is no further elaboration contained in LOSC to determine what action might legitimately constitute 'necessary steps'. Instead, the law looks to State practice, and in particular a number of seminal cases/incidents[49] that have occurred in the maritime domain, in order to determine whether the steps taken by a coastal State in furtherance of its sovereign rights have exceeded those that can be considered 'necessary'. Unsurprisingly, during peacetime operations, these cases/incidents have heavily criticised any use of force that results in serious injury or death to persons as a result of using levels of force that are considered excessive. These cases/ incidents serve as a clear indicator that restraint among, and between, naval forces should be the initial focus that underpins maritime interaction at sea. It is this understanding, which arises from both legal requirements[50] and maritime custom, that limits the potential for armed conflict to occur.

While differing State interpretation of a number of LOSC articles might be thought to provide some impetus for real conflict to arise at sea, the reality is that States are reportedly bellicose but direct action is not likely to follow. A further example illustrates this point as it was reported in 2015 that Indonesia was considering invoking the provisions of Article 52(2) of the Law of the Sea Convention[51] to suspend temporarily the right of innocent passage in its archipelagic waters. This reported action was supposedly aimed primarily at Australia as a response to some of the measures that have been taken by Australia in dealing with a variety of maritime border security threats in its northern approaches.[52] However, the report was not

---

[47]Ibid.

[48]Pollard and Scrutton (2014).

[49]The I'm Alone (1929), 3 UNRIAA p. 1609, the Red Crusader (1961) and the MV Saiga No. 2 (1999).

[50]See for example LOSC (1982) Article 94 which imposes duties upon the flag state in relation to vessels that fly its flag; these duties include measures that are necessary for ensuring safety at sea.

[51]LOSC (1982).

[52]IHS Maritime Fairplay, 25 June 2015, p. 9. LOSC (1982) Article 52(2) stipulates that 'The archipelagic State may, without discrimination in form or in fact among foreign ships, suspend temporarily in specified areas of its archipelagic waters the innocent passage of foreign ships if such suspension is essential for the protection of its security'. Accordingly, if such action was taken by Indonesia and it purported to apply only to Australian vessels, or vessels on passage to/from

followed by any attempt to realise the purported threat, and it therefore represents another speculative dip in the ocean of uncertainty regarding maritime activity that has been growing in scale and frequency during recent years.

As noted earlier, a similar approach has been adopted in the LOSC too, in relation to the rights and duties of vessels and coastal States in the territorial sea.[53] However, the use of subjective measures does raise potential issues regarding consistency of approach between and among maritime user States and coastal States, which, if not adequately understood, could be a factor in causing tensions to rise at sea.

5   The Maritime Environment

Perhaps, then, there is another dimension that is relevant in this area? The uniqueness of the maritime environment, and commonalities among those who work and serve at sea, could provide part of the explanation for the present relatively low level of conflict that exists at sea and also provide an explanation why the potential for conflict at sea is currently assessed as being relatively low. Stretching the concept a little further, a look at some of the characteristics that mould activities that occur in and around the maritime domain can prove illuminating.

The very nature of the maritime environment, especially in the relatively confined spaces of the South China Sea, when compared with terrestrial regions, is clearly a distinguishing feature. The existence of a wide range of maritime features, which may encompass disputed claims of sovereignty (as is the case in the South China Sea), as well as qualifications that arise over the type of sovereignty that is exercised, is indeed unique. For example, although the sovereignty of a coastal state exists over the territorial sea,[54] it is qualified in the sense that the right of innocent passage exists contemporaneously for 'ships of all States'.[55] This situation simply does not exist in relation to land territory where the sovereignty exercised by a State is absolute. Accordingly, the maritime environment has an inherent uniqueness that arises because of the geographical characteristics that are part of its uniqueness and that are also clearly distinguishable from activity that takes place on land.

Australia, legitimate questions could be raised regarding the validity of a suspension which is applied in this manner. It is also noted that archipelagic sea lanes passage (including overflight) is non-suspendable: see LOSC (1982) Article 54 which applies LOSC Article 44 *mutatis mutandis* to archipelagic sea lanes passage.

[53] For example, see LOSC (1982) Article 19(2) in relation to those activities of a foreign ship in the territorial sea which are considered to be prejudicial and Article 25 which specifies that a coastal State may take the 'necessary steps' in its territorial sea to prevent passage which is not innocent.

[54] LOSC (1982) Article 2.

[55] Ibid, Article 17.

Next, consideration of the impact arising from the professional (or perhaps epistemic)[56] community of maritime professionals (and naval officers as a subset of that community) is a factor that warrants some attention. The maritime environment is one in which those who serve at sea develop an element of comraderie, understanding and appreciation for the role(s) undertaken by others who serve in that same environ. This concept is one that is steeped in maritime history rather than being the subject of any detailed academic consideration, but nevertheless it contains a real and meaningful element in terms of creating a universal common bond among seafarers. It has been suggested that this bond arises from '... their professional pride and their wider view of the world which their land based colleagues often do not understand',[57] which certainly may be a significant factor in determining the effect and influence of the maritime environment on the conduct and practice of mariners. It is assessed that the concept is not an isolated or vague notion either, as is evidenced from reports that were published after some recent interaction between United States Navy and PLA-N vessels in the South China Sea.[58] The issue was also illustrated in the fictional scenario portrayed in the movie *The Hunt For Red October*,[59] where a key part of the plot lay in the ability of Soviet and American naval officers to know intuitively what each of them was likely to do as the submarine chase unfolded.

The final issue that will be briefly considered in this context is the preponderance of 'maritime confidence building measures' (MCBMs)[60] that exist (especially when compared with the terrestrial arena) and the role that MCBMs are purported to play in shaping the maritime environment. MCBMs may be aimed solely at commercial activities or solely at naval or military activities or in some cases could contain elements of both. MCBMs serve two primary purposes: '... helping to build maritime regimes that provide good order at sea ... and ... they serve as "building blocks" for habits of cooperation and dialogue that reduce tensions and promote peace and stability'.[61] MCBMs can include measures such as arrangements for port visits by naval forces, agreements to hold naval exercises, procedures for the conduct

---

[56]An 'epistemic' community is one in which there is shared knowledge based on a set of commonalities among the community. In the case of mariners there is commonality in language (jargon), training in basic concepts of seamanship and navigation as well as more specific commonalities which exist among naval experts in terms of warfare and tactical operations. See the discussion in Davis Cross (2014).

[57]See Shashikumar (1996), p. 101.

[58]In the report Philippines, Japan, US hold talks to enhance defense cooperation (Laude 2016) the Commanding Officer of the USS Chung-Hoon commented that interaction with the PLA-N disclosed a navy that '... prides itself with professional communications and interactions'.

[59]A film released in 1990 in which the captain of a Soviet submarine defects, with his submarine, to the USA.

[60]The existence of MCBMs has been the subject of considerable academic comment, and effort on the part of those governments which have adopted MCBMs, for many years. The utility of MCBMs has periodically been questioned: see generally Bateman and McCaffrie (1995) in Cox (ed) (1995), pp. 83–96.

[61]Ibid pp. 9–10.

of passage exercises between ships when encountering each other (either planned or on an 'ad-hoc' basis) and meetings between senior naval officials where they get to know each other personally and understand the operational environment in which their navies operate.[62] MCBMs can also include activities that take place in the shadows of commercial Defence exhibitions whereby naval personnel interact and exchange views as part of their attendance at such exhibitions.[63]

One other MCBM that has been used in a different region is the NATO/UE/CMF Shared Awareness and De-confliction (SHADE) meetings among navies operating in the East African region and the Middle East Area of Operations. The 37th SHADE meeting in December 2015 was attended by 80 representatives from 30 States,[64] and this meeting provides a unique opportunity for all interested parties to assemble together in an environment where potential conflict issues can be discussed openly and frankly.

The continued reliance on, the development of, and the use of MCBMs are an indication that States see utility and value in their ongoing existence. At the very least, the existence of a wide range of MCBMs provides a non-confrontational mechanism whereby relationships can be fostered, concepts discussed and perspectives understood. In this manner, MCBMs have an ongoing utility in the maritime environment, and accordingly they play a supporting role in the reduction of tension at sea.

6   Implications for Naval Operations in the South China Sea

Instances of naval confrontation in the South China Sea are not new, but as noted earlier in this chapter there have been relatively few occurrences in recent times.[65] Nevertheless, the impact of naval conflict in the region on the development of international law, and in particular the law of naval warfare, has been noteworthy. Indeed, the means and methods of warfare employed during the Russo–Japanese War in 1904–1905 was one of the factors that influenced the inclusion of naval warfare issues in the Hague Peace Conference of 1907.[66] Significantly, although the Conventions that emerged from the 1907 Conference are more than 100 years old, they still represent the most comprehensive suite of 'black letter' laws of naval warfare and would therefore have direct applicability in the event that a conflict at sea did occur.

When considering the potential impact of naval confrontation in the South China Sea, there are two aspects of the laws of armed conflict that arise: the *jus ad bellum*[67]

---

[62] ASPI (2013), pp. 10–11.

[63] See for example Minnick (2015).

[64] Combined Maritime Forces (2015).

[65] See White (2015).

[66] See Letts and McLaughlin (2016), pp. 269–271; see also Haines (2014), pp. 418–420.

[67] *Jus ad Bellum* refers to the legality of a war.

and the *jus in bello*.[68] Each of these components of the law of armed conflict has different characteristics as the former is concerned with the legality of a state resorting to the use of armed force while the latter is concerned with the legality of how that armed force is used once a conflict is underway.

The applicable legal framework for the *jus ad bellum* is now influenced by the prohibitions placed upon the use of force by States that is contained in the UN Charter,[69] especially Articles 2(4) and 2(7), as moderated by the recognition that States retain the right to use force when exercising their right of self-defence—enshrined in Article 51 of the Charter. Although there have been instances in the South China Sea of aggressive behaviour by States, recent rhetoric from States involved (or interested) in the region is that they wish to see disputes settled without the use of force. For example, then Australian Defence Minister Andrews stated that 'Australia has made clear its opposition to any coercive or unilateral actions to change the status quo in the South and East China Sea'.[70]

This assessment should, however, be tempered with acknowledgement that there have been clashes and aggressive action in the region. The sinking of the Republic of Korea vessel Chenoan in March 2010, with the loss of the vessel and the lives of 46 Republic of Korea sailors, is a salient reminder that the threat of aggressive action in the region is very real.[71] Similarly, China's positioning of an oil platform in waters in the vicinity of Vietnam in April/May 2014, and again in January 2016, provides a notable recent example of provocative action that could have resulted in conflict arising.[72]

In terms of the *jus in bello*, the actions of States in the South China Sea over the past few years seem to include tactics that are deliberately designed to keep incidents below the threshold at which it could be considered that an armed conflict exists. The use of fishing vessels, coast guard vessels and other craft that do not have the capability to participate fully in armed conflict at sea could be viewed as evidence of States wishing to use methods and means of harassing or disrupting that do not fall within the ambit of the *jus in bello*.[73] Nevertheless, tactics adopted from naval warfare, such as Anti-Access Area Denial (A2AD), are becoming an increasing feature of the operations in the area, and threats against vessels (and aircraft) have

---

[68]*Jus in Bello* refers to the laws governing the conduct of hostilities once an armed conflict has commenced. See Dinstein (2011), pp. 5–19 for a detailed discussion of the complexities and considerations which arise when dealing with the interplay between the two concepts.

[69]UN Charter (1949) Article 2(4).

[70]Andrews (2015) Speech at 14th IISS Asia Security Summit.

[71]The Chenoan was subsequently salvaged and the cause of the sinking was investigated by a Joint Civilian-Military Investigation Group led by the Republic of Korea, with participants from five other nations. The Group concluded that the Democratic People's Republic of Korea had been responsible for the sinking, but this finding was denied by the DPRK. See UNSC Presidential Statement S/PRST/2010/13.

[72]See Hunt (2016).

[73]See for example, Kraska and Monti (2015), pp. 450–467.

occurred.[74] However, progress has also occurred, as is evidenced by the adoption of maritime confidence building measures such as the involvement of the Chinese Navy (PLA-N) in Exercises RIMPAC 2014 and RIMPAC 2016.[75]

Accordingly, the potential for hostile confrontation to occur in the South China Sea is blurred by the somewhat confusing and inconsistent behaviour of States in the region. The interests of States are difficult to reconcile, and there are significant numbers of naval and other maritime assets, from a large number of States, in the region. The legal framework to deal with incidents, from both *jus ad bellum* and *jus in bello* perspectives, already exists, although it is hoped that circumstances will not deteriorate to the level where these laws become directly relevant.

7   Conclusion

The analysis undertaken in this short contribution does not purport to be either comprehensive or conclusive. In many ways, this chapter represents the start of a journey that might never end as the underlying structural issues that directly affect the likelihood of conflict at sea occurring in the South China Sea are unresolved and likely to remain so for the foreseeable future. Accordingly, a series of conundrums and contradictions might be the only plausible outcome.

Nevertheless, the opening premise of this chapter—that despite the existence of tensions among States in the region, likelihood of conflict at sea occurring is actually quite low—remains valid. There will inevitably be continued inflammatory rhetoric emanating on the issue of how to avoid conflict in the South China Sea, with the character of this discourse depending on the differing perspectives of those who are commenting. For example, reports from international relations practitioners and theorists are likely to reflect their assessment of the geopolitics at play. Legal commentators, especially those who are legal positivists, are likely to focus on perceived divergences from the key legal principles that exist in the LOSC and question any lack of adherence to those principles. Finally, serving (and perhaps former) members of naval forces are likely to be influenced by a mix of the two, but with an ongoing dialogue concentrated on getting a practical outcome in any given circumstance.

In any case, it is considered that the practicalities and necessity of maritime trade through the region will limit the scope for conflict at sea to occur as it is undoubtedly in the national interest of all states that are involved in the South China Sea to preserve the ability for unhindered freedom of navigation to remain in place.

---

[74]See Townshend and Medcalf (2016) p. 7.

[75]However, note there were calls to exclude China from RIMPAC 2016 but these calls were not heeded; see Kan (2016); but contrast with Secretary of Defense Carter's statement that China is still invited to RIMPAC 2016: Eckstein (2016).

References

Andrews K (2015) Speech presented at the 14th IISS Asia security summit, Singapore, 29–31 May 2015

ASPI (2013) Maritime confidence building measures in the South China Sea conference. In: Special Report. Available via DIALOG. https://www.aspi.org.au/publications/special-report-maritime-confidence-building-measures-in-the-south-china-sea-conference/SR55_MCBM.pdf. Accessed 29 Apr 2016

Bateman S, McCaffrie J (1995) Maritime confidence and security building measures (MSCBMs) in Asia Pacific: challenges, prospects and policy implications. In: Cox GA (ed) Issues in maritime strategy. Defence Publishing Centre, Australia

BBC. More information about: the troubles. http://www.bbc.co.uk/history/troubles. Accessed 29 Apr 2016

Carter A (2015) The United States and challenges of Asia-Pacific security. Speech presented at the 14th IISS Asia security summit, Singapore, 29–31 May 2015

Combined Maritime Forces (2015) Maritime industry and international naval forces reaffirm commitment to counter-piracy efforts at the 37th SHADE conference in Bahrain. https://combinedmaritimeforces.com/2015/12/16/maritime-industry-and-international-naval-forces-reaffirm-commitment-to-counter-piracy-efforts-at-the-37th-shade-conference-in-bahrain/. Accessed 5 May 2016

Council on Foreign Relations (2017) China's maritime disputes. https://www.cfr.org/asia-and-pacific/chinas-maritime-disputes/p31345#!/p31345. Accessed 8 Apr 2016

Davis Cross MK (2014) European integration and security epistemic communities. http://www.e-ir.info/2014/01/09/european-integration-and-security-epistemic-communities/. Accessed 28 Apr 2016

Dinstein Y (2011) War aggression and self-defence, 5th edn. Cambridge University Press, Cambridge

Eckstein M (2016) SECDEF Carter: China still invited to RIMPAC 2016 despite South China Sea tension. In: USNI News. Available via DIALOG. https://news.usni.org/2016/04/18/secdef-carter-china-still-invited-to-rimpac-2016-despite-south-china-sea-tension

Garwood-Gowers A (2004) Case note – oil platforms: did the ICJ miss the boat on the law on the use of force? Melb J Intl Law 45:241–256

Greenwood C (1996) International law and the tadic case. Eur J Int Law 7:265–283

Haines S (2014) 1907 Hague Convention VIII relative to the laying of automatic submarine contact mines. Int Law Stud 90:412–445

Hart JA (1976) The Anglo-Icelandic Cod War of 1972–1973: a case study of a fishery dispute. University of California, Berkeley

Hunt K (2016) South China Sea: Vietnam says China moved oil rig into contested waters. http://edition.cnn.com/2016/01/20/asia/vietnam-china-south-china-sea-oil-rig/. Accessed 6 May 2016

IHS Maritime Fairplay, 25 June 2015. https://magazines.IHS.com/Maritime/Fairplay

IISS (2015) Armed conflict database. https://acd.iiss.org/en. Accessed 13 Apr 2016

IISS (2016) The IISS Shangri-La dialogue 2016. https://www.iiss.org/en/events/events/archive/2016-a3c2/june-4a2d/sld2016-70d7. Accessed 6 June 2017

IISS (2017) The IISS Shangri-La dialogue. https://www.iiss.org/en/events/shangri-la-dialogue. Accessed 6 June 2017

Ingimundarson V (2003) Fighting the Cod Wars in the Cold War: Iceland's challenge to the western alliance in the 1970s. RUSI J 148(3):88–94

International Maritime Organization. Introduction to the IMO. http://www.imo.org/en/About/Pages/Default.aspx. Accessed 15 July 2015

Jacobsson M (1997) Sweden and the law of the sea. In: Treves T, Pineschi L (eds) The law of the sea: the European Union and its member states. Martinus Nijhoff, The Hague

Kan S (2016) Rescind China's invitation to join RIMPAC. In: Pacific Forum CSIS. Available via DIALOG. http://us8.campaign-archive2.com/?u=fdfd9b07c6818bebcd9951d95&id=a400569ea1&e=61fac75afc. Accessed 15 Apr 2016

Klabbers J (2015) Intervention, armed intervention, armed attack, threat to peace, act of aggression, and threat or use of force: what's the difference? In: Weller M (ed) The Oxford handbook of the use of force in international law. Oxford University Press, Oxford

Kraska J, Monti M (2015) The law of naval warfare and China's maritime militia. Int Law Stud 91:450–467

Kraska J, Pedrozo R (2013) International maritime security law. Brill, Leiden

Laude J (2016) Philippines, Japan, US hold talks to enhance defense cooperation. http://www.philstar.com/headlines/2016/03/09/1561042/philippines-japan-us-hold-talks-enhance-defense-cooperation. Accessed 11 Mar 2016

Letts D, McLaughlin R (2016) Naval warfare. In: Liivoja R, McCormack T (eds) Routledge handbook of the law of armed conflict. Routledge, New York

Mann T (ed) (2013) Australian law dictionary, 2nd edn. Melbourne, Oxford University Press

Minnick W (2015) IMDEX: China on charm offensive at show. http://www.defensenews.com/story/defense/international/asia-pacific/2015/05/20/imdex-singapore-china-charm-offensive/27642535/. Accessed 25 May 2015

NZ History (2015) HMNZS Otago sails for Mururoa test zone. http://www.nzhistory.net.nz/hmnzs-em-otago-em-departs-for-mururoa-to-oppose-french-nuclear-tests. Accessed 14 Apr 2016

Pollard N, Scrutton A (2014) Sweden says credible reports of foreign submarine in its waters. http://www.reuters.com/article/us-sweden-deployment-idUSKCN0I80T320141019.   Accessed 15 Apr 2016

Shashikumar N (1996) World shipping competition. In: Lovett WA (ed) United States shipping policies and the world market. Quorum Books, Westport

Townshend A, Medcalf R (2016) Shifting waters: China's new passive assertiveness in Asian maritime security. In: Lowy Institute Report. Available via DIALOG. https://www.lowyinstitute.org/publications/shifting-waters-china-s-new-passive-assertiveness-asian-maritime-security

Tri NM, Collin KSN (2014) Lessons from the battle of the Paracel Islands. http://thediplomat.com/2014/01/lessons-from-the-battle-of-the-paracel-islands/. Accessed 15 Apr 2016

UNSC (2010) Statement by the president of the security council. In: United Nations Security Council. Available via DIALOG. http://www.un.org/press/en/2010/sc9975.doc.htm. Accessed 6 May 2016

Weeks G (2014) The use and enforcement of soft law by Australian public authorities. Fed Law Rev 42(1):181–216

White H (2015) South China Sea not the place to get all bolshie. In: The Canberra Times. Available via DIALOG. http://www.canberratimes.com.au/comment/south-china-sea-not-the-place-to-get-all-bolshie-20150607-ghipzt. Accessed 10 June 2015

International Instruments and Court Rulings

1972 Convention on the International Regulations for Preventing Collisions at Sea (COLREGs) 1050 UNTS 16

AP II (1949), Protocol Additional to the Geneva Conventions of August 12, 1949, and Relating to the Protection of Victims of Non-International Armed Conflicts, https://ihl-databases.icrc.org/ihl/INTRO/475?OpenDocument. Accessed 27 October 2017

Guyana and Suriname Award (2007), Arbitral Tribunal Constituted Pursuant to Article 287, and in accordance with Annex VII, of the United Nations Convention on the Law of the Sea in the Matter of an Arbitration between Guyana and Suriname, Award of 17 September 2007, RIAA Volume XXX

ICJ (1986), Military and paramilitary activities in and against Nicaragua (Nicaragua v United States of America) (Merits), 1986 ICJ Reps 14 (27 June 1986)

ICJ (2003), Case Concerning Oil Platforms (Islamic Republic of Iran v United States of America), 2003 ICJ Reps 161 (6 November 2003)

ICTY (1995), The Prosecutor v Dusko Tadic, Case No. IT-94-1-1, Decision on the Defence Motion for Interlocutory Appeal on Jurisdiction, 27 October 1995

LOSC (1982), UN Convention on the Law of the Sea (10 December 1982) 1833 UNTS 397

MARPOL (73/78)., International Maritime Organization. International convention for the prevention of pollution from ships, http://www.imo.org/en/About/Conventions/ListOfConventions/Pages/International-Convention-for-the-Prevention-of-Pollution-from-Ships-%28MARPOL%29.aspx. Accessed 14 Apr 2016

MV Saiga No. 2 (1999), Case (Saint Vincent and The Grenadines v Guinea), ITLOS Case No. 2 1999

Nuclear Tests (Australia v France), Judgment, ICJ Reps 1974

Nuclear Tests (New Zealand v France), Interim Protection, Order of 22 June 1973, I.C.J. Reports 1973

Nuclear Tests (New Zealand v. France), Judgment, ICJ Reps 1974

Protocol Additional to the Geneva Conventions of August 12 1949

Relating to the Protection of Victims of Non-International Armed Conflicts Article 1, June 8 1977. 1125 UNTS 609

SUA Convention (1988), Convention for the Suppression of Unlawful Acts Against the Safety of Maritime Navigation, 1678 UNTS 222, http://www.un.org/en/sc/ctc/docs/conventions/Conv8.pdf. Accessed 27 October 2017

The I'm Alone (1929), 3 UNRIAA

The Red Crusader (1961), 35 ILR, http://legal.un.org/riaa/cases/vol_XXIX/521-539.pdf. Accessed 27 October 2017

UN Charter (1945), Charter of the United Nations, adopted June 26th 1945, UN Conference on International Organization Doc., vol. XV (1945), p. 335

David Letts is a Commodore (ret.) of the Royal Australian Navy, where he served for more than 30 years both at sea and ashore as a supply (logistics) officer and as a legal officer. He is now an Associate Professor at the Australian National University College of Law in Canberra, Australia, and he is also one of the Co-Directors of the Centre for Military and Security Law at the ANU College of Law. He is an elected member of the International Institute of Humanitarian Law in San Remo, Italy, and is a frequent public commentator on legal issues that affect maritime operations. David's assistance as a maritime law expert is regularly sought by national and international bodies, including the International Committee of the Red Cross.

What Went Wrong When Regulating Private Maritime Security Companies

Ian M. Ralby

Abstract

When regulating private maritime security companies arose as a pressing issue in 2012, a number of key actors made a conceptual choice that turned out to be a mistake. The discussion centered on whether private maritime security companies (PMSCs) were primarily a subset of the security industry or the maritime industry. At the time, PMSCs' principal activity was to provide armed guards on ships transiting the High Risk Area off Somalia. Since they were then considered necessary supernumeraries to the crews of commercial vessels, representatives of the shipowners won the argument that PMSCs should be treated as part of the broader maritime industry. The main regulatory initiatives, therefore, were divorced from existing private security accountability initiatives and were developed in such a way as to suit the needs of commercial vessels in transit. This approach, however, has proved shortsighted. Even after the first successful attacks in 5 years, armed transits off Somalia are a fraction of what they used to be in terms of both frequency and financial value. But the PMSCs that have survived this bust period have sought and found work performing other services in the maritime space. Unfortunately, however, those activities are generally not covered by the regulatory initiatives that were produced under the erroneous notion that private maritime security companies are more maritime service providers than security service providers. The consequence, therefore, is that the private maritime security industry, as it currently operates, is largely unregulated.

To understand the nature of this accountability gap, it is necessary to review (1) the private security regulatory initiatives that were rejected when addressing PMSCs, (2) what has been done to regulate PMSCs specifically, and (3) what

I. M. Ralby (✉)
I.R. Consilium, LLC, Baltimore, MD, USA
e-mail: imralby@irconsilium.com

This is a U.S. government work and its text is not subject to copyright protection in the United States; however, its text may be subject to foreign copyright protection 2018
J. Schildknecht et al. (eds.), *Operational Law in International Straits and Current Maritime Security Challenges*, Operational Maritime Law 1,
https://doi.org/10.1007/978-3-319-72718-9_9

PMSCs are now doing. Only then can this analysis really delve into why current measures do not adequately cover the private maritime security industry.

1   Introduction

Private security companies have a troubled history of high-profile incidents, frequently involving civilian casualties and other human rights violations. While some of the concerns that accompany the private security industry on land seemed inapplicable to the private maritime security industry's provision of armed guards on ships transiting the High Risk Area off Somalia, some of the newer activities in which PMSCs are now involved raise a broad spectrum of legal, policy and human-rights-related issues. When discussing private security, the name Blackwater is frequently invoked as a reminder of what an unregulated industry looks like.[1] In the most infamous incident, guards from that American firm, while protecting a US State Department convoy, opened fire in Nisor Square, Iraq, killing 17 civilians in September 2007.[2] Not until April 2015, however, were the guards from that incident convicted and sentenced for their criminal conduct in a US court.[3] Consequently, that case has been held up for the last decade as the icon of unaccountability in the private security sector. No direct corollary exists with regard to the private maritime security sector, however.

Ironically, the nearest maritime parallel, initially called the "maritime Nisor Square," did not even involve private security guards.[4] An Italian vessel protection detail—made up of serving Italian Navy personnel on active duty—became embroiled in an international incident for allegedly killing Indian fisherman within Indian waters.[5] Nearly all the facts of the case remain in dispute, and relations between the states remain strained in the ongoing effort to resolve the matter, but it is not a PMSC case.[6] Another Indian case, in which the *M/V Seaman Guard Ohio* was arrested, along with her crew, on its way into Indian waters for having allegedly been a floating armory, also misses the mark.[7] The ten members of the crew and 25 guards who were aboard spent four years in a hotly contested legal battle in India and were only acquitted in November of 2017.[8] And while this is a PMSC case relevant to the present analysis, the guards did not fire their weapons and are not alleged to have killed anyone or violated anyone's human rights, making it quite different from a Nisor Square analogy.

---

[1] Thurnher (2008) and Scahill (2007).

[2] Apuzzo (2014a).

[3] Apuzzo (2014b).

[4] Wiese Bockmann and Katz (2012).

[5] BBC News (2012).

[6] Mitra (2016).

[7] BBC News (2013).

[8] Maritime Executive (2017).

In the absence of public concern and scrutiny, therefore, little attention has been paid to the adequacy of regulatory initiatives for private maritime security companies. Furthermore, extensive fanfare has accompanied the PMSC-related instruments that do exist, creating the impression that the question of accountability has been effectively resolved.[9] This analysis, however, finds that existing measures are inadequate. Not only does that inadequacy leave the industry and its clients exposed to potential liability; it also creates concern that potential victims of improper activity would not have any recourse. Furthermore, a maritime incident truly akin to Nisor Square would potentially damage the credibility of all regulatory initiatives pertaining to private security—maritime and land alike. While the architects of the current system felt that PMSCs were more "maritime" than "security" in their character, it is unlikely that the general public would agree. Therefore, the claim that the private maritime security industry is regulated would, if exposed to be inaccurate in a high-profile case, call into question all the efforts to regulate private security writ large. This article concludes, therefore, that steps must be taken to fill this accountability gap.

2   The Private Security Regulatory Initiatives That Were Rejected

2.1   The Montreux Document

A decade ago, the letters "PMSC" had nothing to do with maritime security. They formed an acronym for "private military and security company"—a term used to describe the corporate entities that were offering armed services for hire in Iraq and Afghanistan.[10] While initially met with a degree of uncertainty, private military and security companies were being viewed with concern and trepidation, given the perception of a legal vacuum surrounding them.[11] That year, the International Committee for the Red Cross (ICRC) teamed up with the International Law Division of the Swiss Foreign Ministry to initiate a process to identify existing international laws that constrained the behavior of these companies and the states that interacted with them.[12] They formed a group of 18 states[13] that worked to develop a document that would both restate those international legal obligations and articulate a series of "good practices" to guide future interaction between states and the industry.[14]

---

[9]Seatrade Maritime News (2013).

[10]Percy (2007).

[11]Mlinarcik (2006).

[12]Chesterman (2011).

[13]Participating States of the Montreux Document (2017): inter alia Afghanistan, Angola, Australia, Austria, Canada, China, France, Germany, Iraq, Poland, Russia, Sierra Leone, South Africa, Sweden, Switzerland, Ukraine, the United Kingdom and the United States (see:, International Committee of the Red Cross).

[14]Ralby (2016).

For 2 years, those states, together with the ICRC, held a series of expert discussions and industry engagements to develop a collective position on private military and security companies.[15]

On September 17, 2008, 17 of the states—Russia dropped out the day before— signed the Montreux Document on Pertinent International Legal Obligations and Good Practices for States Related to Operations of Private Military and Security Companies during Armed Conflict.[16] The Document "recalls existing legal obligations of States and PMSCs and their personnel... and provides States with good practices to promote compliance with international humanitarian law and human rights law during armed conflict."[17] Despite this focus on armed conflict settings, however, the Document specifically notes that its principles are applicable to all settings in which private military and security companies operate.[18] Having said that, there is no mention of maritime security in the Document, and armed transits on commercial vessels were not part of the discussion at that time.

2.2   The International Code of Conduct

Following adoption of the Montreux Document, which now has 54 states and three international organizations "participating" as signatories,[19] the Human Rights division of the Swiss Foreign Ministry, this time without the partnership of the ICRC, launched a second initiative in 2009 to develop a code of conduct for the private military and security companies themselves.[20] The United States and United Kingdom, together with the industry, and a select group of civil society organizations, academic institutions, and independent experts collaborated with the Swiss Government on developing what was ultimately named the International Code of Conduct for Private Security Service Providers (ICoC).[21] Unlike the Montreux Document, the ICoC does not use the term PMSC and is not limited in its application to armed conflict settings.

The ICoC, which references the "Respect, Protect, Remedy" framework that was later set forth in the United Nations Guiding Principles on Business and Human Rights,[22] establishes a set of principles to which all signatories agree to adhere. In essence, the ICoC says that the private security providers that sign it will abide, at all times, by international human rights standards, as well as applicable laws and the industry-specific guidance set forth in both the Montreux Document and the Code of

---

[15]Overview of the Montreux Document (2017).

[16]Overview of the Montreux Document (2017).

[17]Montreux Document (2008).

[18]Montreux Document (2008), Preface ¶ 5.

[19]Participating States of the Montreux Document (2017).

[20]Wilton Park (2009).

[21]ICoC (2010).

[22]United Nations Guiding Principles on Business and Human Rights (2011).

Conduct itself. From an international legal standpoint, this is a significant commitment. In other words, even in the absence of legal obligations regarding human rights, the companies will voluntarily hold themselves responsible to abide by the principles articulated in international human rights law. Technically, that body of law only applies to states. States, in turn must develop national legislation to hold individuals accountable to the international principles. Thus, the ICoC ensures that private security providers will abide by all international human rights law principles, even when operating in inadequate or nonexistent national legal jurisdictions.

The ICoC was developed by a multistakeholder process.[23] In the final months of the negotiations, the issue of maritime security was raised. As the author pointed out at the time, the applicable legal regimes and the relevant stakeholders for maritime security had not adequately been incorporated into the process to extend the Code, as it was drafted, to private maritime security operations. While the then nascent maritime security industry did have some representation in the discussions, the ICoC, on its terms, does not apply to maritime security. Paragraph 13 of the Code states that it is "applicable to the actions of Signatory Companies while performing Security Services in Complex Environments."[24] Complex environments are defined as "any areas experiencing or recovering from unrest or instability, whether due to natural disasters or armed conflicts, where the rule of law has been substantially undermined, and in which the capacity of the state authority to handle the situation is diminished or non-existent."[25] While an argument could be made that this definition could include both territorial waters and flag state responsibilities on the high seas, it is unmistakably written with a land-based mindset.[26] More on point, however, paragraph 7 explicitly clarifies that once auditable, measurable standards are drafted on the basis of the Code and once external, independent governance and oversight mechanisms are established, the stakeholders agree "thereafter to consider the development of additional principles and standards for related services, such as training of external forces, the provision of maritime security services and the participation in operations related to detainees and other protected persons."[27] No such "additional principles" have yet been developed. In other words, the ICoC does not currently apply to maritime security on its face.

At the time the Code was completed and signed on November 9, 2010, there was considerable discussion of needing to develop a "maritime annex" as soon as possible in order to extend its principles to operations on the water. Based on those discussions, the now defunct Security Association for the Maritime Industry (SAMI) encouraged its prospective members to sign the Code as a display of commitment to regulatory initiatives. As a result, several hundred private maritime

---

[23]IPOA, BAPSC, PASA (2009).

[24]ICoC (2010), ¶ 13.

[25]ICoC (2010), Definitions.

[26]The author was involved in the drafting and can speak to the mindset of the drafters at the time; this is not speculation or inference.

[27]ICoC (2010), ¶ 7.

security providers signed the ICoC, swelling the number of signatories in favor of those that provided maritime services. Unfortunately, however, the slow pace of progress on developing governance and oversight mechanisms meant that, even at the time of writing this present analysis, more than 7 years later, no maritime annex yet exists. Conceptually, however, the Respect, Protect, Remedy framework and the commitment to abide by international human rights law principles, regardless of any legal requirement to do so, are equally applicable in maritime operations as they are on land. Therefore, in practice, many have decided to consider the spirit of the ICoC applicable to maritime security, even if the terms of it are not.[28]

2.3   The ICoC Association

An entire volume could be produced on the machinations that led to the eventual establishment of the International Code of Conduct Association (ICoCA),[29] along with its first 4 years of operation. The Code set ambitious timelines and a rigid procedure for how a select portion of stakeholders should proceed to develop what became the ICoCA. The ICoC was signed by an initial 58 companies on November 9, 2010, and the ICoCA was due to be operational by November 2011. Unfortunately, however, it was not stood up until September 19, 2013. Since the focus of the present analysis is on maritime security, there is not much to be said about the ICoCA, except that in February 2016, it recognized the ISO 28007-1 (2015) Standard, which will be discussed below as part of its certification process.[30] Effectively, this means that companies certified to the ISO Standard may now also seek "certification" within the ICoCA.

2.4   ANSI/ASIS PSC.4 Standard

In October 2010, after the ICoC was finished, but not yet formally signed, ASIS International, one of the top security-related standards drafting organizations, as well as the world's largest security-related trade association, initiated the development of a formal American National Standard based on the Code of Conduct. This initiative, while funded by the US Department of Defense, was insulated from US control and involved representatives from 26 countries—far more than the ICoC negotiations themselves—and spread across those who are providers of security, those who are customers of security, and those who take a general interest in it.

The logic of developing an American National Standards Institute (ANSI) Standard was that it would be the most credible and fastest way, following the rigorous international procedures that govern business standards, to produce an international

[28]Ralby (2011).

[29]Articles of Association of the International Code of Conduct Association (2013).

[30]International Code of Conduct Association, Certification Procedures (2016).

standard with the International Organization on Standardization (ISO). Standards have two key components—requirements and implementation guides.[31] Requirements are broadly drafted statements of the general aims of the Standard. Implementation guides, on the other hand, goes into greater detail on how to meet those requirements within a particular context. Those implementation guides can be further enhanced by annexes explaining anything that needs to be addressed in even greater depth. So the first ANSI/ASIS PSC Standard, known as PSC.1, provides the requirements and implementation guide, as well as detailed annexes for business operations to be conducted in conformance with the ICoC on land. It is the first business Standard to incorporate human rights obligations, making it noteworthy in its own right as a groundbreaking development.[32]

The Standards Series continued, with PSC.2, a conformity assessment standard for the auditors; PSC.3, a maturity model to help guide phased implementation of the standard; and finally, PSC.4, a maritime security implementation guide to the requirements of PSC.1. In other words, PSC.4 operationalized the human rights principles of the ICoC, combined them with general private security requirements, and tailored them to the specific context of private maritime security. The principal advantage of this approach, as well, was to give a company that provides both land and maritime security the opportunity to pursue a single audit, grounded in the same requirements, for the entirety of its operations. Furthermore, from an accountability perspective, it meant that the human rights principals of the ICoC were made an auditable requirement of all private maritime security operations—whether providing armed guards on ships, protecting offshore oil platforms, advising a seismic survey vessel on security or anything else that the company might do on, in, above or near the water.

2.5   None of the Above

All of these initiatives—the Montreux Document, the ICoC, the ICoCA, and the ANSI/ASIS PSC Standards Series—were rejected when it came to regulating private maritime security. In doing so, several arguments were made:

1. Private maritime security is more a subset of the maritime industry than the security industry and thus should be regulated accordingly.
2. Private maritime security is purely commercial—there are no government clients—so governments should only have a say through the International Maritime Organization (IMO) and flag or home state requirements.
3. Maritime security is inherently international, and most of the companies are in Britain anyway, so it would be inappropriate to use an ANSI Standard.

---

[31] Siegel (2011).
[32] Ralby (2015a).

4. Human rights are not a principal concern in the maritime security context, except insofar as the protection of seafarers is concerned.
5. The IMO is the central focal point for all regulatory requirements.

These arguments, widely articulated and repeated in the discussions of how to proceed with regulating private maritime security during the boom of the industry in 2011, led to the rejection of the above initiatives. They further helped shape the regulatory developments discussed in the next section. And they ultimately helped to create the gaps in accountability that the private maritime security industry faces today—particularly the conceptual notion that maritime security is more maritime than security.

3   What Has Been Done to Regulate PMSCs

3.1   IMO Circulars

The International Maritime Organization "is the United Nations specialized agency with responsibility for the safety and security of shipping and the prevention of marine pollution by ships."[33] Throughout the rise of private maritime security companies, it has remained resolute in insisting that it neither supports nor condemns shipowners for choosing to employ armed guards.[34] In providing guidance to shipowners on avoiding pirate attacks, the IMO developed several iterations of Best Management Practices (BMP), the last of which was BMP 4. As that guidance states, "The use, or not, of armed Private Maritime Security Contractors on board merchant vessels is a matter for individual ship operators to decide following their own voyage risk assessment and approval of respective Flag States. This advice does not constitute a recommendation or an endorsement of the general use of armed Private Maritime Security Contractors."[35]

In the event that armed guards are hired, the IMO has issued guidance on their use.[36] The Maritime Safety Committee (MSC) has produced a number of relevant circulars including the following:

- MSC.1/Circ.1405—Interim Guidance to Shipowners, Ship Operators and Ship Masters on the use of Privately Contracted Armed Security Personnel (PCASP) on Board Ships in the High Risk Area;
- MSC.1/Circ.1406—Interim Recommendations for Flag States regarding the use of PCASP on Board Ships in the High Risk Area;

---

[33]Website of the International Maritime Organization, *About IMO*, July (2014). http://www.imo.org/About/Pages/Default.aspx. Accessed 7 Jul 2017.
[34]IMO Private Armed Security (2017).
[35]Best Management Practices (2011), 8.15.
[36]IMO Private Armed Security (2017).

- MSC.1/Circ.1408—Interim Recommendations for Port and Coastal States regarding the use of PCASP on Board Ships in the High Risk Area;
- MSC.1/Circ.1443—Interim Guidance to Private Maritime Security Companies providing PCASP on Board Ships in the High Risk Area;
- MSC.1/Circ.1444—Interim Guidance for Flag States on Measures to Prevent and Mitigate Somalia-Based Piracy.

Despite not having a position on the matter, therefore, the IMO has nevertheless produced considerable guidance regarding armed guards on ships transiting the High Risk Area off Somalia.

Furthermore, the IMO has taken a position with regard to the Montreux Document and the ICoC. In MSC Circular 1443, the IMO explains its stance:

> The Montreux Document on Pertinent International Legal Obligations and Good Practices for States related to Operations of Private Military and Security Companies during Armed Conflict and the International Code of Conduct for Private Security Service Providers (ICoC) are useful reference points for PMSC, but are not directly relevant to the situation of piracy and armed robbery in the maritime domain and do not provide sufficient guidance for PMSC. The Montreux Document, which addresses States, restates rules of international law and provides a set of good practices for States, although it should be noted that international humanitarian law is applicable only during armed conflict. The ICoC, which addresses the private security industry, identifies a set of principles and processes for private security service providers related to support for the rule of law and respect for human rights, but is written in the context of self-regulation and only for land-based security companies, and is therefore not directly applicable to the peculiarities of deploying armed guards on board merchant ships to protect against acts of piracy and armed robbery at sea.[37]

Consequently, IMO does not adopt the loose construction described in the last section whereby the spirit of the ICoC is deemed to apply to PMSCs even if the terms of the Code are not directly applicable. From a strict legal standpoint, the IMO is correct in its analysis, though, given the multistakeholder nature of the processes that created the ICoC, perhaps overreaching in its comment on "self-regulation."

The IMO position, however, must be viewed in light of its mission. As the specialized UN agency responsible for safety and security of shipping, its primary concern is the ability of commercial vessels to engage in maritime commerce. The "spirit" of a voluntary instrument created by an ad hoc process that did not include the key maritime stakeholders was not sufficient for it to feel comfortable about the accountability and responsibility of armed guards on ships. Consequently, and at the behest of some of the shipowner associations—Baltic and International Maritime Council (BIMCO) foremost among them—the IMO determined in 2012 that an international standard would be the most suitable approach to addressing its concerns surrounding PMSCs.[38]

---

[37]IMO Interim Guidance to Private Maritime Security Companies (2012).
[38]IMO Private Armed Security (2017).

3.2   ISO 28007

This is where a crucial decision regarding private maritime security was made. Essentially, there were two options for how regulation of PMSCs could proceed. In the first instance, the maritime stakeholders could join the line of activity, starting with the Montreux Document, that focused on human rights and broad-spectrum responsibility for the private security industry. The opportunity presented was to start with the requirements section of the ANSI/ASIS PSC.1 Standard and, taking those general security and human rights obligations, craft a maritime-specific implementation guide that would cover the private maritime security industry in all its activities (the PSC.4 Standard discussed above, Sect. 2.4). The other option, however, was to divorce PMSCs from private security and marry them to the maritime industry. In this approach, a new line of activity would need to be initiated, deriving from IMO guidance and shipowner interests and rejecting the private security initiatives. Believing that it was in their best interests since their clients at the time were primarily commercial shippers, the private maritime security companies, through SAMI and the UK's Security in Complex Environments Group (SCEG), selected this latter option.

Key portions of the maritime industry—particularly the shipowner associations, led by BIMCO—together with PMSC trade associations—led by SAMI and SCEG—and individuals within the International Organization for Standardization (ISO) proposed that the IMO reject the private security industry initiatives and mandate the development of a separate international standard. The IMO, in line with its own responsibilities and mandate, accepted that approach. Those same actors then proceeded, in a matter of months, to develop a Publicly Available Specification (PAS) focused on armed security on ships. Based on ISO 28000, a Standard concerning security in the supply chain, and drafted concurrent to ANSI/ASIS PSC.4, ISO PAS 28007 was titled "Guidelines for Private Maritime Security Companies (PMSC) providing privately contracted armed security personnel (PCASP) on board ships." The limitation of the scope, even in the title, indicates how much the Standard was focused on exclusively addressing the private maritime security activities that were important to the shipping industry and the needs of the IMO.

Given the IMO position articulated in MSC.1Circ.1443, efforts were made to distance the new Standard, ISO PAS 28007, from the ICoC. The author was privy to discussions during the Standard development whereby key actors made it clear that there was no interest, among at least some of those stakeholders, in addressing human rights issues directly in this new maritime security standard. It was argued that the concerns that had led to the ICoC were simply not applicable in the maritime context. The main concern was, understandably, the protection of seafarers, so it was determined that there was not a need to address the rights of local communities. The absence of any meaningful human rights provisions, however, led to extensive criticism of the PAS.[39]

As a PAS, ISO 28007 had to be reviewed within 3 years and either rescinded or turned into a formal standard. In 2015, therefore, it was revised and formally turned into ISO 28007-1. Some human rights considerations were added, and were recognized by commentators, but considerable room for improvement still remains.[40] In particular, there is no requirement of human rights training, no mention of human rights violations as a metric for vetting, no incorporation of human rights into due diligence processes, insufficient guidance for assessment and prioritization of human rights risks, and no requirement to remediate negative human rights impacts.[41]

The biggest concern raised over ISO 28007-1, however, has been the limited nature of its scope. It is, in many respects, a misnomer to consider it a standard for private maritime security. Rather, it is a standard for armed guards on ships offering protection to commercial vessels in transit. But that is what the IMO and the shipping community wanted and needed, so it should come as no surprise. The problem, however, is that, as it has turned out, the private maritime security industry is actually more closely related to the security industry than the maritime industry. The IMO, BIMCO, and other maritime industry representatives looked after the needs and interests of their constituencies and produced a standard consistent with their mandates. But the private maritime security industry has left itself greatly exposed, as armed transits only constitute a fraction of its work at this stage. The analysis below reviews some of the activities in which PMSCs are now engaged that are not covered by the standard.

3.3   Nongovernmental Initiatives

Before moving on, however, it is worth mentioning that there are other initiatives relevant but not central to this analysis. BIMCO produced a standard contract for private security called GUARDCON, which itself greatly enhanced the accountability of PMSCs to shipowners by creating consistent contractual obligations. As

---

[39]DeWinter-Schmitt (2014). ("Two key issues neglected in the ISO/PAS 28007 are the responsibility of maritime security companies to respect human rights and to carry out human rights due diligence processes. There is also no mention of conducting human rights risk analyses or engaging with affected communities and stakeholders during that process. In fact, there is no mention that maritime security operations can potentially impact on human rights. Furthermore, there are no stipulations for human rights trainings for personnel, and the requirements for grievance mechanisms are inadequate. While there is a provision that no one under 18 should be employed to carry weapons, there is no reference to avoiding the worst forms of child labor or other gross human rights violations. The ISO/PAS 28007 is simply not a human rights standard.").

[40]DeWinter-Schmitt (2015). ("While these [human rights] additions warrant recognition, there is still room for strengthening the human rights provisions of the ISO 28007-1 if it is to truly reflect the [UN Guiding Principles on Business and Human Rights].").

[41]DeWinter-Schmitt (2015).

GUARDCON also applies to raising the standard for guards on ships, however, it is similar to ISO 28007-1 in that it meets the maritime industry's needs but does not cover the nontransit activities of the private security industry.

A number of the same individuals involved in the development of ISO PAS 28007 subsequently teamed up with a London barrister to develop a uniform set of rules for the use of force (RUF) in the maritime context. These RUF 100 Series Rules at one point were considered for potentially becoming annex to the ISO PAS 28007 and were ultimately used as an optional annex to GUARDCON. From a legal standpoint, the rules are vague, inconsistent, and expressly based on inapplicable legal sources. Given their lack of deference for the nuances of flag state laws, the rules are more likely to create potential liability for both the PMSCs and the shipowners who use them than they are to resolve any practical issues. Using them could lead to seriously problematic consequences for the private maritime security industry and potentially the maritime industry as well—particularly if required as a matter of contract. This purely private initiative effectively seeks to supplant governmental guidance on rules for the use of force and, in the process of doing so, creates confusing conflict between applicable laws and these "universal" rules.

The normative basis for the RUF 100 Series includes a limited smattering of human rights conventions and a number of instruments and cases that address the prohibition on the use of force by states—a fundamentally different legal concept than the use of force by individuals.[42] While the principles stated at the outset of the Rules are largely fine, the Rules themselves not only create confusion with regard to states' laws on the use of force but also are internally confusing when put into practice. Fundamentally, though, the RUF 100 Series ignores the legal diversity among sovereign states with regard to the use of force and the concept of self-defense. Even within the Anglo-American system, there are considerable divides between the American concept of use of force and that of the UK. Given the number of different flag states under whose laws PMSCs may operate, it simply does not make sense why one would create legally inconsistent "rules" rather than guidance on how to develop use of force protocols in line with the applicable law. Unlike ISO 28007-1, which leaves gaps in accountability, RUF 100 Series, if followed, could actually lead to legal liability.

While not a private initiative, a "Handbook on the Use of Force of Private Security Companies," both land and maritime, has also recently been published by the nongovernmental organization Oceans Beyond Piracy (OBP).[43] Unlike the RUF 100 Series, this was not a privately driven undertaking but a collaborative effort initiated by the UN Office of Drugs and Crime (UNODC) that included input from a wide range of governmental, industry, and expert stakeholders. Consistent with and deferential to both international and domestic laws, the handbook provides guidance for how private security companies should approach use of force, what must be considered, and what should be done to ensure legal compliance. If embraced and

---

[42]Ralby (2015b).

[43]Drew and McLoghlin (2016).

used responsibly, this handbook could greatly help reduce the problem of uncertainty surrounding private security companies' authority to use force in carrying out their responsibilities.

4   Private Maritime Security Beyond Transits

4.1   The Current State of Transits and Decline in the Industry

Many of the private maritime security companies that were established in response to piracy off the coast of Somalia have gone out of business.[44] As piracy against commercial vessels had virtually disappeared and has only minimally reemerged in that region, shipowners have lost the appetite for purchasing elite security services, or even any security at all. While a security team used to be comprised of four former western military professionals, teams are frequently now comprised of two individuals from developing states with various degrees of experience. With this decline in the use of armed personnel, the use of ISO 28007 has also declined. As one commentator wrote in 2015:

> ISO 28007 has not worked. Some have it; some do not. There are many buyers who do not require it. There are many sellers who do not bother. BIMCO's recent endorsement of ISO 28007 may help. It may be too late. Buying patterns are entrenched. Too many stand outside Anglo-centric regulatory initiatives. It is easy to do so, legally and practically. As former Royal Marines increasingly price themselves out of the market for guards, a once Anglo-centric market along with its regulatory attire becomes increasingly irrelevant.[45]

The decline in the threat picture has led to a decline in the tolerance of high costs for security. That drop in the market has therefore corresponded to a drop in the quality of services being offered. So even in the specific context for which ISO 28007-1 was developed, market forces have undermined its utility.

The collapse in the armed transit market has had other knock-on consequences as well. SAMI went into voluntary liquidation on account of the dramatic contraction in the number of PMSCs.[46] The industry, therefore, has no maritime-specific association of international reputation now to speak on its behalf. And many of the companies are either engaging more in littoral and land-based work or selling themselves to land-based security providers, further blurring the line between private security and private maritime security—the problematic conceptual division on which the regulatory thrust toward ISO 28007 was initiated.

---

[44]Quartz (2016).

[45]Bennett (2015).

[46]Splash 24/7 (2016).

4.2   Other Private Maritime Security

The private maritime security companies that continue to exist have had to diversify their offering in order to survive the downturn in the demand for armed transits. This process of exploring new forms of operation is likely to continue throughout the coming years as new maritime challenges—like mass migration or even potential naval conflict—arise and other activities, like counterpiracy, become cyclical.

One of the fastest-growing areas of private security work is in the training of foreign personnel. As states in the developing world are overcoming "sea blindness" and beginning to enhance their maritime law enforcement capacity, they are increasingly turning to private companies to provide both training and operational support. As there is no oversight for the training that is offered, and no standards for private maritime security trainers, however, the quality of these undertakings varies dramatically. In one instance, for example,[47] a private maritime security company was found to be training the local maritime police in a West African state on BMP 4 (the guidance for shipowners on how to avoid Somali piracy), RUF 100 Series (the private initiative addressed above, Sect. 3.3, that is inconsistent with international and national laws), and ISO 9001 (the main business management system standard of dubious utility for a law enforcement organization). These three items were advertised as the key pillars of the training program, but they are completely inappropriate for a state law enforcement agency, except as perhaps something about which to be aware.

Historically, as well, training has been a source of maritime security problems as much as it has been an approach to addressing them. Building coastal capacity with regard to armed security, in the absence of corresponding work to develop the local economy and enhance the rule of law, can actually lead to the development of a well-trained criminal element. In Somalia, a PMSC entered into contracts in 2000 with the breakaway province of Puntland to provide antipiracy and other coastal guarding services.[48] That contract has since been heavily criticized. News stories also suggest that other PMSCs may have more recently entered into similar arrangements with the Puntland authorities.[49] Indeed, some fault these security companies with having trained the pirates who caused so much havoc in the region.[50] The ISO 28007 Standard does not address this issue at all.

Other activities in which PMSCs now engage include the protection of offshore platforms, the guarding of waterside facilities with maritime jurisdictional components, the protection of seismic survey vessels, the provision of fishery enforcement activities, and other similar services, either armed or unarmed. While some of this work, if on ships, could be covered by the ISO 28007 Standard, most of it is not. Indeed, one of the most legally problematic offerings of private maritime

---

[47]Information gleaned from interviews in country, plus company's promotional material.

[48]Kinsey et al. (2009).

[49]Houreld (2011) and Mazzetti and Schmitt (2011).

[50]The Hidden Paw (2009).

security on ships that has not been covered by the Standard is the provision of unarmed security on ships for which the forces of coastal states provided armed security. This model, prevalent in West Africa, is used to address the legal prohibition on the transport of weapons into the territorial seas of the states. In other words, since PMSCs cannot provide armed security in the territorial waters of West African states, shipowners hire them and they, in turn, hire the local navy, coast guard, or maritime police. This mix of private unarmed guards and local armed forces constitutes the security for the vessel throughout its time in territorial seas. The concern, however, is the legal obligations incurred by a private actor if they are found to be in "effective control" over the state forces. There are a number of unexplored legal concerns surrounding this dynamic of PMSCs leading a security operation involving state forces. In one instance, for example, a company hired the personnel of the local navy, not realizing that they were, at the time, operating outside the chain of command. With those moonlighting naval personnel aboard, they then accidentally sailed into a neighboring state's waters where they were boarded by the local armed forces.[51] This highly contentious international incident, if litigated, could have yielded some unfavorable results for the PMSC, whose negligence in hiring armed, uniformed navy sailors rather than hiring the navy itself may have been blamed for the incident. ISO 28007 does not offer any guidance for how to avoid such liability or how to treat the unclear legal relationship when a PMSC directs the security operation involving local forces on a ship. Significant legal consideration on this matter is warranted, and no published analysis exists on the matter.

At the more extreme end of the spectrum of PMSC activities, there have been a few ventures into armed escort work that has begun to move toward quasi-naval activities. In 2008, the infamous American firm Blackwater purchased a vessel and sought to provide armed maritime security services.[52] For a variety of reasons, that initiative failed. More recently, however, a similar initiative has been launched in West Africa and is seeking contracts. This work is not addressed by the ISO 28007 Standard.

Finally, the issue of floating armories created significant concern at the height of armed transits as they were established to support counterpiracy operations in the Indian Ocean. At the peak, roughly 25 were in operation, varying in size and location. The cost, however, indicates how successful the business was for the companies that ran them. A floating armory off Sri Lanka (established once the Sri Lankan Government stopped allowing its territory to be used) costs $4000 USD per transfer—meaning the embarkation or disembarkation of kit, personnel, and weapons. One private maritime security company might have paid for 40 transfers per month, amounting to $160,000 USD per month.[53] And with dozens of companies

---

[51] Information gleaned from interviews in the region.

[52] Sengupta (2008).

[53] Data taken from interviews with private maritime security companies regarding their interaction with floating armories.

operating, floating armories were highly lucrative businesses. Not covered by ISO 28007, however, the floating armories have not been regulated internationally. Only a few state-based initiatives sought to regulate the use of the armories by their own nationals, but no regulation of the armories themselves has even been attempted.

The *M/V Seaman Guard Ohio*, a patrol vessel owned and operated by AdvanFort, an American private maritime security company, and flagged in Sierra Leone, is probably the most well-known floating armory. On October 12, 2013, the *Seaman Guard Ohio* was intercepted by the Indian Coast Guard outside the High Risk Area within Indian waters and was arrested for being an illegal floating armory. A fisherman had allegedly alerted the Coast Guard that there were armed personnel aboard and that it had been improperly refueling with subsidized diesel. While the owners claimed that the ship was in Indian waters to avoid a storm, in the charges, Indian officials claimed that it was not authorized to enter Indian waters. Thirty-five weapons were impounded, along with 5700 rounds of ammunition, and the 25 members of the crew were arrested. There were no Indian licenses or permits for the weapons and ammunition.

The legal case was considered to have significant implications for Indian maritime sovereignty, especially after the *Enrica Lexie* incident discussed earlier.[54] As there was a factual dispute as to whether the vessel was in territorial waters or the contiguous zone when it was arrested, as well as a legal issue as to whether it was allowed in the waters in the first place, the case became a diplomatic incident as much as a legal one. Despite all the lobbying by other states and parties, the Indian courts found jurisdiction over the case regarding the purchase of the fuel in its customs zone.[55] Initially, the Madras High Court ruled that the ship had entered the waters for safe harbor from a storm but that the purchase of subsidized fuel did still constitute a potential violation.[56] The Court wrote: "I hold that the anchoring of MV Seaman Guard Ohio within our territorial sea was out of necessity and their action is saved by the principle of 'innocent passage' contemplated by Section 4(1) of the Territorial Waters, Continental Shelf, Exclusive Economic Zone and Other Maritime Zone Act, 1976 and Article 18 and 19 of UNCLOS. Therefore, the crew and the security guards cannot be prosecuted for an offence under the Arms Act."[57] Subsequently, however, the court changed its position, and on January 11, 2016, all ten crew members and 25 guards were sentenced to 5 years in prison and a fine of 3000 rupees each.[58] In November 2017, an appeals court reversed the decision, acquitted all 35 individuals and returned the fines they had paid (footnote to Maritime Executive).

The case is likely to continue to draw controversy, but it highlights the legal uncertainty surrounding floating armories. The division line between PMSC activities in different contexts—providing armed guards on ships, unarmed

---

[54]Black (2013).

[55]Anandan (2013).

[56]Subramani (2014).

[57]*Quoted in Id.*

[58]Selvaraj (2016).

oversight of local naval personnel, training of local law enforcement, protection of offshore or shore-side infrastructure, services that amount to floating armories, and any number of other activities—is, however, too blurry to say that some belong to the security industry while others belong to the maritime industry. From a regulatory standpoint, therefore, the approach taken to address armed guards on ships using ISO 28007 met the immediate needs of the shipowners and the IMO but left the private maritime security industry, especially as it stands today, largely unregulated.

5   Conclusion

Though many PMSCs signed the ICoC, its principles remain voluntary. And while ISO 28007-1, in conjunction with other substantive human-rights-related activities, may be adequate for certification to the ICoCA, there does not seem to be any market driver to push the remaining portions of the industry to undergo such a certification process. Thus, PMSCs now have a few options. PMSCs can choose not to offer armed transits and just operate in the unregulated space, joining the ICoCA or getting certified to ISO 28007-1 as a matter of preference rather than necessity. But even offering armed transits does not require companies to pursue ISO 28007-1 certification as shipowners can elect to hire a cheaper, uncertified company against the suggestion of the IMO. Consequently, in real terms, there is no real regulation of the PMSC industry. A standard of limited scope exists, and a voluntary and technically inapplicable code of principles exists, but neither are absolutely required.

From a short-term standpoint, the effort to develop ISO 28007 did address the immediate best interests of its main backers—shipowners and the IMO. Unfortunately, however, the PMSCs themselves did not stand up to push for a more comprehensive set of regulations that would have covered the spectrum of their activities—present and future. If they had, they would not be as exposed as they are now. While it made sense that their principal clients—commercial shippers—and UN's specialist agency for regulating shipping had substantial voices in how things would proceed, the irony is that it would have ultimately been better for everyone to have taken a more comprehensive approach. The ANSI/ASIS PSC.4 Standard did take that approach, but, even though it would have become a proper ISO Standard around the same time ISO 28007 PAS was converted into ISO 28007-1, the national affiliation of the American Standards body was further cause for rejecting the security-industry-based approach. The waters are now muddied by unregulated PMSC activities, further complicating the global threat picture for shippers. So the key decisions that were made—that PMSCs are more maritime than security, that PMSCs will only ever work for commercial clients, that an ANSI standard would have been too limiting for the international nature of the industry, that human rights were not a serious concern for PMSCs, and that the IMO needed to be the focal point for all regulatory activities—have all proved to have been shortsighted.

The PMSC industry is struggling at the moment, but it is not dead. And tough times mean corners are perhaps cut in trying to make ends meet. Consequently, serious consideration should be applied to devising effective means of regulating and overseeing the full spectrum of activities performed by private maritime security companies before an undesirable event occurs. PMSCs, while sometimes said to be regulated by ISO 28007-1 and even by the ICoC, are actually operating with little to no international or national accountability. The dangers of an unregulated private security industry are now well known. It is time, therefore, to recognize that private maritime security companies are part of the private security industry and take proactive steps to address its current lack of regulation, governance, and oversight.

References

Anandan S (2013) 'Floating Armoury' poses a legal conundrum, The Hindu, 16 October 2013. http://www.thehindu.com/news/national/floating-armoury-poses-a-legal-conundrum/arti cle5237673.ece. Accessed 13 Jan 2018

Apuzzo M (2014a) Blackwater guards found guilty in 2007 Iraq Killings, New York Times, 22 October 2014. http://www.nytimes.com/2014/10/23/us/blackwater-verdict.html?_r=0. Accessed 13 Jan 2018

Apuzzo M (2014b) Ex-Blackwater guards given long terms for killing Iraqi Civilians, New York Times, 13 April 2014. http://www.nytimes.com/2015/04/14/us/ex-blackwater-guards-sen tenced-to-prison-in-2007-killings-of-iraqi-civilians.html?_r=0. Accessed 13 Jan 2018

Articles of Association of the International Code of Conduct Association (2013) http://www.icoca. ch/en/articles_of_association. Accessed 13 Jan 2018

BBC News (20 February 2012) Indian Police detain Italian Navy Security Guards. http://www.bbc. com/news/world-asia-india-17093224. Accessed 13 Jan 2018

BBC News (18 October 2013) MV Seaman Guard Ohio: India police arrest crew of US Ship. http:// www.bbc.com/news/world-asiaindia-24577190. Accessed 13 Jan 2018

Bennett T (2015) Maritime security at a crossroads, The Maritime Executive, 26 April 2015. http:// www.maritimeexecutive.com/features/maritime-security-at-a-crossroads. Accessed 13 Jan 2018

Best Management Practices (2011) IMO MSC.1/Circ.1339 (2011), BMP4: best management practices for protection against Somalia based piracy

Black N (2013) Criminal jurisdiction over maritime security in the Indian Ocean. Cornell Int Law J Online 1:77

Chesterman S (2011) Lawyers, guns and money: the governance of business activities in conflict zones. Chicago J Int Law 11:321, 334

DeWinter-Schmitt R (2014) Why the ISO Standard for maritime security – ISO/PAS 28007 – is not a security and human rights standard, human analytics, 23 October 2014. http://human-analytics.net/iso-standard-maritime-security-isopas-28007-security-human-rights-standard/. Accessed 13 Jan 2018

DeWinter-Schmitt R (2015) New ISO standard on private maritime security companies reflects some progress on human rights, 20 May 2015. http://human-analytics.net/new-iso-standard-private-maritime-security-companies-reflects-progress-human-rights/. Accessed 13 Jan 2018

Drew P, Robert McLoughlin R (2016) Handbook on the use of force by private security companies, oceans beyond piracy. http://oceansbeyondpiracy.org/publications/use-force-handbook-private-security-companies. Accessed 13 Jan 2018

Houreld K (2011) Puntland (Somali Region) defies Federal Government over Saracen Deal. Associated Press, (28 January 2011). http://laaska.wordpress.com/2011/01/28/puntland-somali-region-defies-fed-govt-over-saracen-deal/. Accessed 13 Jan 2018

ICoC (2010) The International Code of Conduct for Private Security Service Providers (2010). http://icoc-psp.org/. Accessed 13 Jan 2018

IMO Interim Guidance to Private Maritime Security Companies (2012) MSC.1/Circ.1443 – Interim guidance to private maritime security companies providing PCASP on board ships in the high risk area. http://www.imo.org/en/OurWork/security/secdocs/documents/piracy/msc.1-circ.1443.pdf. Accessed 13 Jan 2018

IMO Private Armed Security (2017) http://www.imo.org/en/OurWork/Security/ PiracyArmedRobbery/Pages/Private-Armed-Security.aspx. Accessed 13 Jan 2018

International Code of Conduct Association, Certification Procedures (2016) http://www.icoca.ch/ en/certification. Accessed 13 Jan 2018

IPOA, BAPSC & PASA (6 June 2009) Industry statement. http://www.humanrights.ch/home/ upload/pdf/090617_Nyon_Declaration.pdf. Accessed 13 Jan 2018

Kinsey C, Hansen S, Franklin G (2009) The impact of private security companies on Somalia's governance network. Camb Rev Int Aff 22(1):152–154

Maritime Executive (27 November 2017) Seaman Guard Ohio Crew Acquitted. https://maritime-executive.com/editorials/seamanguard-ohio-crew-acquitted. Accessed 13 Jan 2018

Mazzetti M, Schmitt E (20 January 2011) Blackwater founder said to Back Mercenaries, Washington Post. http://www.nytimes.com/2011/01/21/world/africa/21intel.html?_r=1& pagewanted=all. Accessed 13 Jan 2018

Mitra D (2016) India, Italy Spar over Marines issue again as Ad-hoc tribunal reviews Enrica Lexie case, The Wire, 30 March 2016. http://thewire.in/26752/india-italy-spar-over-marines-issue-again-as-ad-hoc-tribunal-reviews-enrica-lexie-case/. Accessed 13 Jan 2018

Mlinarcik JT (2006) Private military contractors & justice: a look at the industry, blackwater & the Fallujah incident. Regent J Int Law 4:129

Montreux Document (2008) The Montreux Document on pertinent international legal obligations and good practices for states related to operations of private military and security companies during armed conflict, U.N. doc. A/63/467-S/2008/636, at Preface 2 (2008). http://www.eda. admin.ch/psc. Accessed 13 Jan 2018

Overview of the Montreux Document (2017) The Montreux Document, Swiss Federal Department of Foreign Affairs. https://www.eda.admin.ch/eda/en/home/foreign-policy/interna tional-law/international-humanitarian-law/private-military-securitycompanies/montreux-docu ment.html. Accessed 13 Jan 2018

Participating States of the Montreux Document (2017) International Committee of the Red Cross. http://www.eda.admin.ch/eda/en/home/topics/intla/humlaw/pse/parsta.html. Accessed 13 Jan 2018

Percy S (2007) Morality and regulation. In: Chesterman S, Lehnardt C (eds) From mercenaries to market: the rise and regulation of private military companies

Quartz (18 April 2016) Piracy on the high seas is in decline, and so is the anti-piracy industry. http:// qz.com/664036/piracy-on-thehigh-seas-is-on-the-decline-and-so-is-the-anti-piracy-industry/. Accessed 13 Jan 2018

Ralby I (2011) Maritime security and the ICoC. J Int Peace Oper 7(3), https://issuu.com/ipoa/docs/ journal_v7_n3/14. Accessed 13 Jan 2018

Ralby I (2015a) Accountability for armed contractors, Fletcher Secur Rev, 12 January 2015. https:// docs.wixstatic.com/ugd/c28a64_8622580aa7754ec4adbb1bc9d9541d2a.pdf. Accessed 13 Jan 2018

Ralby I (2015b) Private military companies and the Ius ad Bellum. In: The Oxford handbook of the use of force in international law. Oxford University Press. Chapter 53

Ralby I (2016) The Montreux Document: the legal significance of non-legal instrument (Chapter 10). In: Private military and security contractors: controlling the corporate warrior. Rowman & Littlefield

Scahill J (2007) Blackwater: the rise of the world's most powerful mercenary army. Nation Books, New York

Seatrade Maritime News (2013) At last, An accepted international standard for maritime security. http://www.seatrademaritime.com/news/europe/at-last-an-accepted-global-standard-for-maritime-security.html. Accessed 13 Jan 2018

Selvaraj A (2016) US anti-piracy vessel seaman guard ohio crew members sentenced to jail in Tamil Nadu, Times of India, 11 January 2016. http://timesofindia.indiatimes.com/india/US-anti-piracy-vessel-MV-Seaman-Guard-Ohio-crew-members-sentenced-to-jail-in-TamilNadu/articleshow/50530239.cms. Accessed 13 Jan 2018

Sengupta K (2008) Blackwater gun boats will protect ships, The Independent, 19 November 2008. http://www.independent.co.uk/news/world/africa/blackwater-gunboats-will-protect-ships-1024582.html. Accessed 13 Jan 2018

Siegel M (2011) ASIS webinar, 15 April 2011

Splash 24/7 (19 April 2016) SAMI goes into liquidation after membership halves. http://splash247.com/sami-goes-into-liquidationafter-membership-halves/. Accessed 13 Jan 2018

Subramani A (2014) Madras High Court quashes criminal case against Crew of US Ship, Times of India, 10 July 2014. http://timesofindia.indiatimes.com/india/Madras-high-court-quashes-criminal-case-against-crew-of-US-ship/articleshow/38147206.cms. Accessed 13 Jan 2018

The Hidden Paw (11 May 2009) Somali pirates directed by British consultants. http://szamko.wordpress.com/2009/05/11/somalipirates-directed-by-british-consultants/. Accessed 13 Jan 2018

Thurnher JS (2008) Drowning in blackwater: how weak accountability over private security contractors significantly undermines counterinsurgency efforts. 2008-JUL Army Law 64

United Nations Guiding Principles on Business and Human Rights (2011) http://www.ohchr.org/Documents/Publications/GuidingPrinciplesBusinessHR_EN.pdf. Accessed 13 Jan 2018

Website of the International Maritime Organization, About IMO July 2014. http://www.imo.org/About/Pages/Default.aspx. Accessed 13 Jan 2018

Wiese Bockmann M, Katz A (2012) Shooting to kill pirates risks blackwater moment. Bloomberg, 8 May 2012. http://www.bloomberg.com/news/articles/2012-05-08/shooting-to-kill-pirates-risks-blackwater-moment. Accessed 13 Jan 2018

Wilton Park (6 June 2009) Private military and security companies: working toward an international code of conduct. Business & Human Rights Resource Centre. http://www.business-humanrights.org/Links/Repository/818115/link_page_view. Accessed 13 Jan 2018

Dr. Ian Ralby is a recognized expert in maritime law and security and the interdiction of transnational crime. He is a leading authority on the regulation, governance, and oversight of private security companies, having been involved in national and international efforts to develop accountability and standards for the private security industry. Much of his work focuses on the intersection of law and security, particularly in the maritime space. Dr. Ralby is an Adjunct Professor of Maritime Law and Security at the US Department of Defense's Africa Center for Strategic Studies, a nonresident Senior Fellow at the Atlantic Council, a "Key Opinion Former" on Maritime Security at NATO, and the CEO of his own consultancy, I.R. Consilium. He speaks and publishes widely on matters of international relations, law, and security. He holds a JD from William and Mary Law School and a PhD in Politics and International Studies from the University of Cambridge.

'. . .in These Exceptional and Specific Circumstances. . .': The EU Military Operation Against Human Smuggling and Trafficking in the Southern Central Mediterranean

Jouko Lehti

Abstract

The year 2015 was marked by a dramatic increase in the irregular migration to Europe, one of the primary routes being from Libya across the Southern Central Mediterranean to Southern Italy. Following the drowning of hundreds of persons in April 2015, the European Union (EU) adopted a ten-point action plan of the immediate actions to be taken in response to the crisis situation in the Mediterranean. One of those actions is a systematic effort to capture and destroy vessels used by the human smugglers, which was put into practice by establishing in May 2015 the EU military operation, EUNAVFOR MED operation SOPHIA. Under the EU Mandate, the operation will contribute to the disruption of the business model of human smuggling and trafficking networks in the Southern Central Mediterranean. Following the increase of migration at sea, the United Nations Security Council authorised UN Member States and regional organisations to conduct certain essential military activities in the fight against migrant smuggling and human trafficking.

This contribution discusses the military activities of the European Union from a legal point of view. Focus of the study is on the mandate of the European Union and the UN Security Council resolution 2240 (2015) while operating on the high seas. Special attention will be paid to five specific questions faced by the operation: flag state consent; rescue of persons at sea; disembarkation of rescued and apprehended persons; collection, storing and transition of personal data; and use

The author is a Military Legal Advisor in the Defence Command Finland, who served in the Operation Headquarters of the EUNAVFOR MED operation SOPHIA from its establishment in May 2015 until February 2016. All the views expressed are those of the author and do not reflect the official policy or position of the EUNAVFOR MED operation SOPHIA or the Finnish Defence Forces.

J. Lehti (✉)
Defence Command Finland, Helsinki, Finland
e-mail: jouko.lehti@mil.fi

J. Schildknecht et al. (eds.), *Operational Law in International Straits and Current Maritime Security Challenges*, Operational Maritime Law 1,
https://doi.org/10.1007/978-3-319-72718-9_10

of force. It may be concluded that the EU has opened a new page in the application and development of public international law with the EUNAVFOR MED operation SOPHIA by introducing mechanisms of a regional organisation within a legal framework designed for state activities. The operation has not encountered such legal obstacles that would endanger the carrying out of the EU mandate. However, a continuous study of the legal framework of the Common Security and Defence Policy in the fight against human smuggling and trafficking is required.

1   Introduction

In April 2015, the European Union faced one of the most disastrous events on its borders when several hundreds of migrants drowned outside Lampedusa, an Italian island between Sicily and Tunisia. These events sparked an unprecedented political reaction, during which the Member States decided to use military means to tackle human smuggling and trafficking for the first time in the history of the Common Security and Defence Policy of the EU. This was not done in isolation but as part of a ten-point action plan on migration devised by the Council. To name a few, the other activities of non-military nature adopted by the Union have included so far several measures tightening the control on its external borders, political initiatives aiming at the decrease of the migrant flow to Europe and the revision of the asylum procedures.[1] The international community did not stand idle in the development of the events. The United Nations Security Council adopted, after a period of intense consultations, a resolution authorising the employment of essentially military measures against the criminal business model of human smuggling and trafficking.[2]

The main flow of irregular migrants to Europe on the so-called Central Mediterranean route is from the western coastal Tripolitania region of Libya, which serves as the main stronghold of the human smugglers and traffickers in the region.[3] Therefore, it is hardly surprising that alongside EUNAVFOR MED operation SOPHIA, also other European, national and international activities are taking place in the Southern Central Mediterranean. Such activities include FRONTEX operation TRITON,[4] EUBAM Libya,[5] bilateral training programmes, UNSMIL[6] and several NGO activities, to name just a few.

---

[1]Council Meeting (2015), Joint Foreign and Home Affairs Council (2015) and Special Meeting of the European Council (2015).

[2]UNSCR 2240 (2015).

[3]IOM (2015).

[4]The border security operation under Italian control of the European Agency for the Management of Operational Cooperation at the External Borders of the Member States of the European Union (FRONTEX) established by Council Regulation (EC) 2007/2004.

[5]EU Border Assistance Mission (EUBAM) in Libya established on 22 May 2013 to support the Libyan authorities in improving and developing the security of the country's borders.

[6]United Nations Support Mission to Libya, a civilian mission of the United Nations established on 16 September 2011 by United Nations Security Council Resolution 2009 (2011).

2   EU Mandate of EUNAVFOR MED Operation SOPHIA

The Council gave, on 18 May, the EU Mandate for the operation with a decision establishing a European Union military operation in the Southern Central Mediterranean (EUNAVFOR MED) with Operation Headquarters (OHQ) in Rome, Italy.[7] The preparations at the OHQ began with the development of an Operation Plan for the conduct of the operations and the Rules of Engagement guiding the use of force. The operational activities began with the approval of these two fundamental military documents within EU Council decision to launch the operation on 22 June 2015.[8]

The operation will be conducted in three phases according to the EU Mandate. As specified in articles 2 and 6, the transition between the phases is based on the assessment of the EU Council and the decision of the Political and Security Committee (PSC). The first phase of the operation concentrated on the collection of information and intelligence in the area of operations (AOO), which was specifically limited to the high seas. The next step in the efforts of disrupting the criminal business model was established on 3 October 2015, when the Council decided to move on 7 October 2015 to the first sub-phase of the second phase of the operation under point (b) (i) of article 2(2) of the EU Mandate. This sub-phase authorises the EU Naval Force to 'conduct boarding, search, seizure and diversion on the high seas of vessels suspected of being used for human smuggling or trafficking' in accordance with applicable international law. The sub-phase is specifically limited to only the high seas.[9]

The EU Mandate entails a second sub-phase, which foresees the aforementioned activities in accordance with any applicable UN Security Council resolution or consent by the coastal state concerned, on the high seas or in the territorial and internal waters of that state. In the third phase, the operation would be authorised to, in accordance with 'any applicable UN Security Council resolution or consent by the coastal state concerned, take all necessary measures against a vessel and related assets, including through disposing of them or rendering them inoperable, which are suspected of being used for human smuggling or trafficking, in the territory of that state, under the conditions set out in that Resolution or consent'. As mentioned above, the main route for human smuggling and trafficking in the Central Mediterranean is the area of Tripolitania. Therefore, Libya is the most relevant coastal state in terms of consent for operations in the waters and land territory of the coastal states in the region.[10]

---

[7]EU Mandate (2015). The name of the operation was later changed to 'EUNAVFOR MED operation SOPHIA' after the name of a baby born on a German vessel which rescued her mother on 22 August 2015 off the coast of Libya as part of the operation. See also: Council Decision 1926 (2015) amending Council Decision 778 (2015) on a European Union military operation in the Southern Central Mediterranean (EUNAVFOR MED).

[8]Council Decision 972 (2015) launching the European Union military operation in the southern Central Mediterranean (EUNAVFOR MED).

[9]EU Mandate (2015), article 2(2)(b)(i).

[10]EU Mandate (2015), article 2(2)(b)(ii) and 2(3).

The legal basis for military activities under the EU Mandate is based on the public international law. There is no specific legal framework in the Union that would apply within the Common Security and Defence Policy (CSDP) operations for military assets deployed countering cross-border criminality, such as the one applicable to the European border control mechanisms under FRONTEX. In fact, the EU Mandate relies heavily on applicable international agreements within the framework of the United Nations rather than on any specific EU legislation. Special reference is made to the United Nations Convention on the Law of the Sea (UNCLOS) and the Protocols Against the Smuggling of Migrants by Land, Sea and Air (Smuggling Protocol) and to Prevent, Suppress and Punish Trafficking in Persons, Especially Women and Children, supplementing the United Nations Convention Against Transnational Organized Crime.[11]

The operation cannot enter into the territory of a third state without an applicable legal framework considering the third state's consent and any applicable UN Security Council resolution. Therefore, the future of the EU mandate is based on the assumption that there will be readiness from the Libyan side, as well as from the international community, to enable the conduct of the military activities in the Libyan waters and the land territory. The progress in the UN-backed peace negotiations, including the Libyan Political Agreement, which foresees the establishment of a Government of National Unity, is a step forward for a legal framework of the next phases as it commits the participants also to activities of countering irregular migration. At the time of this article's publication, the EU Council had not yet made a decision on the transition to the future phases due to the lack of applicable Libyan consent and UN Security Council resolution.

3   UN Security Council Resolution 2240(2015)

The United Nations Security Council adopted resolution 2240(2015) as a response to the 'recent proliferation of, and endangerment of lives by, the smuggling of migrants and trafficking of persons in the Mediterranean Sea off the coast of Libya'.[12] The adoption of UNSCR 2240(2015) must be seen in the wider context of international efforts of restoration of law and order in the region and especially in Libya. The resolution is not only authorising EUNAVFOR MED operation SOPHIA specifically, although it does recognise the central role of the European Union in the fight against human smuggling and trafficking. The authorisations adopted under Chapter VII of the UN Charter are given to UN Member States and regional organisations. This is a well-founded solution given that there are several state actors involved in the Southern Central Mediterranean contributing to the disruption of human smuggling and trafficking activities.

---

[11]EU Mandate (2015), preamble (6) and article 2(2)(b)(i).
[12]UNSCR 2240 (2015), preamble.

The resolution underlines in several paragraphs the principles of international law related to the safety of life at sea and the respect of human rights. The authority to conduct inspection and seizure of suspected vessels under paragraphs 7 and 8 of UNSCR 2240(2015) are limited to the high seas off the coast of Libya. Even though the Security Council recognised that the crisis situation is not limited only to the southern central part of the Mediterranean, it acted only in one geographical area exploited by human smugglers and traffickers. The resolution underlines the severe situation in Libya, where human smuggling and trafficking is not the only form of severe cross-border criminality. It does not provide authorisation for similar activities in other parts of the Mediterranean or generally on the high seas.[13]

Hence, UNSCR 2240(2015) is neither an operational mandate for EUNAVFOR MED operation SOPHIA nor a specific endorsement of the efforts of the Union in the control of migration flows on its external borders. Instead, it is a specific extension to the international legal framework applicable to the fight against cross-border crime of human smuggling and trafficking. It should be seen in the wider context of UN Security Council resolutions concerning Libya. The following act of the Security Council was the adoption of resolution 2259(2015), which recognised the Libyan Political Agreement and urged the international community to support Libya, although it did not provide specific authorities under Chapter VII.[14]

---

4 Flag State Consent and UNSCR 2240(2015)

Under international law, the operation is required to obtain consent of a flag state for vessels with nationality. UNCLOS recognises the right of visit under article 110 for a warship in a limited number of cases. Related to irregular migration, there are two operational cases that may be thought to apply to the right of visit. The first one is to verify the nationality of a vessel that is not flying a flag. This is also the most realistic option as most of the vessels suspected of human smuggling and trafficking in the Southern Central Mediterranean are not flying a national flag. Instead, they are mostly overcrowded unseaworthy rubber dinghies and fishing vessels. The second one is for vessels that are conducting slave trade. The problem with the terminology of UNCLOS is that it does not specify slavery, and it remains subject to debate whether the slavery under UNCLOS could be partly synonymous to the crime of human trafficking. In the end, only criminal investigation and other law enforcement activities may verify the nature of the possible crime.

The obligation of obtaining flag state consent is underlined also by UNSCR 2240 (2015). However, the resolution does recognise that an inspection of a suspected vessel may be conducted even without consent provided that good faith efforts have been exhausted to obtain the consent. The resolution does not provide specific guidance on what constitutes good faith efforts. It is also the first time that the

---

[13]UNSCR 2240 (2015), preamble, paragraphs 7 and 8.
[14]UNSCR 2259 (2015).

concept has been used related to a European Union military operation. A similar mechanism was established in UNSCR 2182(2014) on Somalia for the arms and coal embargo regime. Their comparison is, however, difficult as the phenomenon it addresses is fundamentally different. Human smuggling and trafficking are crimes that are not direct material and financial support fuelling an ongoing armed conflict as is the case under UNSCR 2182(2014), even though it does contribute to the funding of the armed groups. The legal framework surrounding these crimes relates to the specific questions of protection of human rights and victims of the crimes in the maritime environment, not an embargo regime.[15]

5   Rescue of Persons at Sea

The obligation to rescue persons in distress is central to the law of the sea on the high seas. The principles are laid down in article 98 of UNCLOS and in chapter 5 of the 1974 International Convention for the Safety of Life at Sea (SOLAS), as well as the 1979 International Convention on Maritime Search and Rescue (SAR). The rescue efforts are coordinated by responsible rescue coordination centres, requesting assistance and facilitating the disembarkation of the rescued persons. Especially from the military perspective, an essential question is how far the right actually extends from the high seas to the territorial waters of a nation as it presents fundamental questions in relation to the fight against the crime of human smuggling and trafficking, as well a state's sovereignty. The question is not so much related to the existence of the actual duty to render assistance to those in danger but instead to the coordination and the extension of the rescue efforts and the disembarkation of the persons who have been rescued: the latter question will be discussed in the following section.

The Rescue Coordination Centre (RCC) in Rome has, in practice, assumed the responsibilities of the coordination of SOLAS events off the coast of Libya as there is no functioning RCC in that area. The vessels involved in the rescue operations are often not only vessels of the EUNAVFOR MED operation SOPHIA and other military and Coast Guard Units vessels, also merchant vessels and NGO-based rescue vessels. Even though the Libyan internal situation is very volatile, it must be noted that the Libyan Coast Guard authorities also conduct search and rescue activities from time to time.

Extending the rescue activities to the Libyan territorial waters might seem obvious from a purely humanitarian point of view. The international legal basis for conducting rescue operations in the territory of another country, with the need to establish contact with the coastal state, would seem to be embedded in UNCLOS and SOLAS. Both conventions consider the safety at sea to be the paramount consideration in any rescue activities. Although article 98 of UNCLOS concerning the duty to render assistance applies to the high seas, also in the territorial sea the passage

---

[15]For a detailed study on questions related to the right of visit and related UN Security Council resolutions, see for example: Kraska (2010) and Wilson (2015).

under article 18 includes also the rendering assistance to persons, ships or aircraft in danger or distress. Under article 19, the passage is innocent so long as it is not prejudicial to the peace, good order or security of the coastal state. The rights of the coastal state related to an innocent passage are designed to support the safety of navigation, not to hamper it. Thus, it seems to support the right to render assistance even in the absence of coastal state consent for the entry into territorial waters for that purpose also by warships.

Especially in the case of Libya, there are two important factors to be considered. Firstly, the duty to inform the national authorities is greatly dependent on the availability of a governmental, legally responsible interlocutor. The Government of National Accord was established with the Libyan Political Agreement, but the basic governmental structures are still largely not capable of carrying out their functions due to the volatile situation. Secondly, there is a disagreement of the geographical area of the territorial waters as Libya holds a widely contested view that the Gulf of Sirte is, as a historic bay, part of its internal waters. The law of the sea does not support the Libyan view, *inter alia*, as it has not been recognised as a historic bay by other nations. Thus, there seems to be no legal basis forbidding the entry for the sole purpose of the rescue operations in the Libyan territorial waters, including the Gulf of Sirte, under the coordination of the responsible RCC.

6   Disembarkation of Rescued and Apprehended Persons

During the rescue operations, EUNAVFOR MED operation SOPHIA is also authorised to apprehend persons suspected of human smuggling and/or trafficking. Under the coordination of the responsible RCC, a port of safety will be designated for the rescued persons. The humanitarian situation dictates this approach. The closest possible port of disembarkation in Libya is not an option due to the security and human rights situation in the country. This issue is of special concern to the European Union Member States, which also are all members of the Council of Europe, under which the European Court of Human Rights (ECHR) issues legally binding decision on the application of the European Convention on Human Rights.

In a recent case, *Hirsi Jamaa and Others v. Italy*, the ECHR concluded that a violation of the *non-refoulement* principle had taken place when migrants were returned to their original point of departure in Libya by the Italian authorities even if they did not exercise physical control over the persons.[16] Hence, unless the human rights record in the country improves, there is no other legally sound option than to disembark the rescued persons in the European Union. This policy is, however, not without criticism as it has been seen as supportive to the criminal business model as new tactical and technical procedures of the smugglers appear in which less and less fuel and water is given to the smuggling vessels expecting that the rescue will take place well before the European Union borders.

---

[16]ECHR (2012).

Due to security and human rights considerations, the rescued and apprehended persons are being disembarked to the European Union territory, mostly to a port of safety in Southern Italy designated by the Italian Ministry of Interior under the RCC coordination. In practical terms, the Italian RCC has assumed the role of coordinating the rescue events in lack of a functioning Libyan RCC. There is currently no specific legal framework for the disembarkation of apprehended and rescued persons in Italy by the operation. As such, the practice is based on the Italian national rules and regulations, as well as taking advantage of the local authorities. The persons who have been apprehended because of their suspected involvement in the human smuggling/trafficking criminal activities fall under the Italian jurisdiction. The Italian Ministry of Interior, more specifically the Direzione Nazionale Antimafia (DNA, National Anti-Mafia Directorate), is responsible for the organisation of the investigation and prosecution of persons apprehended by the operation.

In the disembarkation, the operation takes advantage of the already existing procedures of FRONTEX. The operation and FRONTEX have established a detailed framework for the cooperation, including an upper level agreement on the forms of cooperation, of more detailed common standard operating procedures. Under this framework, FRONTEX has deployed liaison officers to the OHQ and the vessels deployed to the operation. Deployment of FRONTEX liaison officers on board the military vessels of the troop-contributing nations quite naturally requires the consent of both FRONTEX and the flag state of the vessel. An important factor is that on board EUNAVFOR MED operation SOPHIA vessels, FRONTEX liaison officers do not conduct law enforcement activities, such as arrests of suspected human smugglers and traffickers.[17] Currently, there is no general European legal framework in the Common Security and Defence Policy that would be directly applicable to the transfer of suspected criminals between EU Member States participating in EU military operations. National legislation of a Member State may prohibit the disembarkation of apprehended persons to another without a specific applicable legal framework. In such a case, it would be subject to the nation in question to establish other legal mechanisms than those of the operation to fulfil its national legal requirements, such as acting on national basis and possibly relying on international agreements concerning the disembarkation.

7   Collection and Transition of Personal Data

Collection and transition of personal data are included in the EU mandate. The operation has a supportive task towards relevant EU bodies and the respective law enforcement authorities of the EU Member States by transmitting personal data to them. Collection of the personal data is limited only to the characteristics likely to assist in the identification of persons taken on board ships participating in the operation, including fingerprints, as well as certain particulars, with the exclusion

---

[17]European Union Exchange of Letters (2015).

of other personal data.[18] The data may be transmitted to relevant law enforcement authorities of the EU Member States, as well as to respective Union bodies. This obviously excludes a number of actors from the distribution of the personal data, such as other international organisations involved in the fighting against human smuggling and trafficking networks.

The data collection of the operation is therefore limited in the form of which it may be collected. This is fully in line with the limits of the operation; the operation is not pure law enforcement aimed in the traditional sense of conducting identification and investigation in view of prosecution of crimes of human smuggling and trafficking. The operation was established in order to identify the business model of the criminal networks and to contribute to their disruption.

The possibility of collecting personal data, however, demonstrates how close the operation still is to the traditional law enforcement activities. It is also a demonstration of the comprehensive approach of the Union towards emerging crisis that cannot be solved only by civilian or military means. Currently, there is no common European framework for the law enforcement activities resulting from the operation, and thus the national law of the Member States applies. More specifically, the law of a Member State, particularly Italy, in which the disembarkation of the suspected human smugglers/traffickers takes place, would apply to such personal data.

8   Use of Force and the Rules of Engagement

The use of force in any EU military operation is limited by the applicable international law, especially international humanitarian law (IHL) and human rights law (HR), as well as national legislation of the troop-contributing nations (TCNs), including the national interpretation of the self-defence and the more specific operational guiding documents, most importantly the Operation Plan (OPLAN) and the Rules of Engagement (ROE).[19] In the case of the EUNAVFOR MED operation SOPHIA, IHL is, at least for the time being, not applicable; the current non-international armed conflict in Libya has not affected the units of the operation, and the operation has not engaged with any of the armed groups participating in the conflict. Hence, the international legal background for the use of force in the operation derives from international human rights norms, especially those deriving from the European Convention on Human Rights and related jurisprudence of the ECHR.

---

[18]EU Mandate (2015), article 2(4). Characteristics referred to in the article are limited to those that are likely to assist in the identification of persons taken on board ships participating in the operation, including '*fingerprints, as well as the following particulars, with the exclusion of other personal data: surname, maiden name, given names and any alias or assumed name; date and place of birth, nationality, sex; place of residence, profession and whereabouts; driving licenses, identification documents and passport data*'.

[19]EU Mandate (2015), preamble and articles 2, 5 and 6.

The ROEs are based on the minimum level of force necessary to achieve the set political and military goals in specific cases. The development of the operational documents concerning the use of force is based on the mandate in each of the phases and applicable international legal framework, including the applicable UN Security Council resolutions. The OPLAN and the ROE were authorised on the political level at the launch of the operation for the first phase of the operation in view of information gathering, and ROEs have been authorised also for the second phase on the high seas.[20] In the current phase, it is designated especially to support all aspects of stopping, boarding, searching, seizing and diverting the suspected human smuggler/trafficker vessels in international waters. Special consideration in this case is placed on the requirements and limitations of UNSCR 2240(2015), which authorises in these exceptional and specific circumstances the inspection and seizure of vessels suspected on reasonable grounds to be used for migrant smuggling or human trafficking from Libya.

Under no circumstance may the ROE expand the authorisation for the use of force beyond the applicable law, nor does it limit the inherent right of self-defence under national legislation. The use of force is always subject to the application of the basic principles of necessity and proportionality. This derives directly from the human rights obligations applicable to the operation. Certain specific legal regimes may have to be considered, including the law of the sea, especially the general requirement of flag state consent for operations on vessels flying a national flag,[21] the identification of appropriate measures against the smuggling of migrants by sea as understood by the Protocol against the Smuggling of Migrants,[22] as well as the regime applicable to the rescue of persons at sea.[23]

ROE and its interpretation are always guided by the more specific OPLAN, drafted based on the political level guidance in the EU, most importantly the EU Mandate. Especially, the protection of third persons is a key factor in balancing the use of force. The importance of the consideration of the human rights obligations and detailing their practical implementation in the operational context has been highlighted both by the political decision-makers and legal experts.[24]

In the context of the operation, the use of force is restricted by several legal and political factors. Apart from the domestic self-defence regulations, the possible use of force is conducted on a field that is very different from traditional crisis management operations. The nature of the operation as a naval operation aimed at the disruption of criminal business models of human smuggling and trafficking, which—unlike piracy—are not considered as universal crimes, makes it unique. The use of force is more limited and closer to the traditional law enforcement use of force than that available for crisis management. Therefore, it may be concluded that

---

[20]Council Decision 972 (2015).

[21]UNCLOS (1982), articles 92, 94 and 110.

[22]Protocol against the Smuggling of Migrants (2000), especially article 8.

[23]UNCLOS (1982), article 98, SOLAS (1974) and the SAR Convention (1979).

[24]See for example Capaldo (2015).

individual right of self-defence of a person and others and the requirement to protect and secure the safety of third persons are in fact the primary legal considerations dictating the use of force in the operation, surpassing others.

9   Conclusion

EUNAVRFOR MED operation SOPHIA is historical from many perspectives. The use of not only civilian but also military assets of the EU Member States to counter organised crime of human smuggling and trafficking is without precedence. Also, the speed in which the operation was established and began to operate as part of coordinated comprehensive efforts is worth noting on both the political and military levels in the EU, demonstrating the ability of the Member States to respond to humanitarian crisis on its borders with also military means. The United Nations Security Council also has shown its willingness to apply the authorities of Chapter VII of the UN Charter to situations where organised criminal groups based in a country in a non-international armed conflict endanger the lives of thousands.

A continuous study of the legal framework of the Common Security and Defence Policy in the fight against human smuggling and trafficking is required. Especially, the relation between the CSDP and other EU policies in such a complex environment—should similar activities be needed in the future—needs to be studied. The cooperation between an EU military force and the law enforcement authorities is a key to success in such operations to guarantee an effective legal finish. The collection, storing and transfer of personal data for law enforcement purposes require a review as it is notably a new area of cooperation. The use of force in an essentially law-enforcement-related operation is an area where the delicate balance between the human rights obligations, especially avoiding at all costs any damage to third persons on the one hand and on the other hand the measures needed in the countering of the most serious forms of organised crime, must continuously be evaluated.

The ways in which the European Union conducts the operation can be defined as a combination of traditional naval peacetime operations and law enforcement activities in which the military is used as a tool to facilitate crime fighting efforts of its Member States. The military side of it includes the possibility to gather information of the criminal activities and personal data of persons encountered during the operation. It is further guaranteed by the authority to use necessary and proportional force should the situation so require. The disembarkation of the persons on board the assets as a result of their apprehension or rescue to the European Union territory is adding to the conclusion of the operation in a legally sound fashion. The establishment of the EUNAVFOR MED operation SOPHIA demonstrates that it is possible to apply the already existing international, European and national legal frameworks swiftly to counter in a coordinated fashion unprecedented situations if the necessary political will and determination exist. Similar multinational operations may be conducted not only within the legal context of the EU Common Security and

Defence Policy but also within the international community at large, as demonstrated by the wording of UNSCR 2240(2015).

References

Capaldo GZ (2015) The EUNAVFOR MED operation and the use of force. Am Soc Int Law 19 (27). Meijers Committee, CM1513, Military action against human smugglers: legal questions concerning the EUNAVFOR Med operation, 23 September 2015. https://www.asil.org/insights/volume/19/issue/27/eunavfor-med-operation-and-use-force. Accessed 5 July 2017

Council Decision 972 (2015) (CFSP) 2015/972 of 22 June 2015 launching the European Union military operation in the southern Central Mediterranean (EUNAVFOR MED). http://eur-lex.europa.eu/legal-content/EN/TXT/?uri=CELEX%3A32015D0972. Accessed 5 July 2017

Council Decision 1926 (2015) (CFSP) 2015/1926 of 26 October 2015 amending decision (CFSP) 2015/778 on a European Union military operation in the Southern Central Mediterranean (EUNAVFOR MED). http://eur-lex.europa.eu/legal-content/EN/TXT/PDF/?uri=CELEX:32015D1926&from=EN. Accessed 26 Oct 2017

Council Meeting (2015) Outcome of the council meeting, 3385th Council meeting, Foreign Affairs and Home Affairs, Luxembourg, 20 April 2015 (8146/15, (OR. en), PRESSE 28, PR CO 20), European Commission - Press release

ECHR (2012) European court of human rights: CASE OF HIRSI JAMAA AND OTHERS v. ITALY (Application no. 27765/09) JUDGMENT Strasbourg, 23 February 2012. http://hudoc.echr.coe.int/eng#{%22appno%22:[%2227765/09%22]}. Accessed 5 July 2017

EU Mandate (2015) Council decision (CFSP) 2015/778 of 18 May 2015 on a European Union military operation in the Southern Central Mediterranean (EUNAVFOR MED)

European Union Exchange of Letters (2015) On the operational cooperation between the European Agency for the Management of the Operational Cooperation at the External Borders of the Member States of the European Union (Frontex) and EUNAVFOR MED, concluded on 14 July 2015. http://www.consilium.europa.eu/en/press/press-releases/2015/04/23-special-euco-statement/. Accessed 5 July 2017

IOM (2015) International Organization for migration: migration trends across the Mediterranean: connecting the dots, prepared by Altai Consulting for IOM MENA Regional Office, June 2015. https://publications.iom.int/books/migration-trends-across-mediterranean-connecting-dots. Accessed 5 July 2017

Joint Foreign and Home Affairs Council (2015) Ten point action plan on migration, Luxembourg, 20 April 2015. http://www.consilium.europa.eu/en/meetings/jha/2015/04/20/. Accessed 5 July 2017

Kraska J (2010) JAGC, USN - Broken Taillight at Sea: the peacetime international law of visit, board, search, and seizure. Ocean Coast Law J 16:1

Protocol against the Smuggling of Migrants (2000) The protocol against the smuggling of migrants by land, sea and air supplementing the United Nations Convention against Transnational Organized Crime, https://www.unodc.org/documents/southeastasiaandpacific/2011/04/som-indonesia/convention_smug_eng.pdf. Accessed 26 Oct 2017

SAR Convention (1979) International convention on maritime search and rescue (1979), into force 22 June 1985, http://www.imo.org/en/About/conventions/listofconventions/pages/international-convention-on-maritime-search-and-rescue-(sar).aspx. Accessed 05 Sept 2017

SOLAS (1974) International convention for the safety of Life at Sea, into force 25 May 1980, http://www.imo.org/en/About/conventions/listofconventions/pages/international-convention-for-the-safety-of-life-at-sea-(solas),-1974.aspx. Accessed 05 Sept 2017; Consolidated Edition, 2009 (IMO, London, 2009)

Special meeting of the European Council (2015) 23 April 2015 – statement, 23/04/2015, 22:15, Statements and remarks, 204/15, Home Affairs, Foreign affairs & international relations

UNCLOS (1982) United Nations Convention on the Law of the Sea (1982), 1833 U.N.T.S. 397

UNSCR 2240 (2015) United Nations: Security Council, S/RES/2240 (2015), Security Council Distr.: General 9 October 2015, Resolution 2240 (2015). http://www.un.org/en/sc/documents/resolutions/2015.shtml. Accessed 5 July 2017

UNSCR 2259 (2015) United Nations: Security Council, S/RES/2259 (2015), Security Council Distr.: General 23 December 2015, Resolution 2259 (2015). http://www.un.org/en/sc/documents/resolutions/2015.shtml. Accessed 5 July 2017

Wilson B (2015) The Mediterranean migrant crisis: key considerations for the UN Security Council. Harvard NSJ, Online Article. http://harvardnsj.org/2015/10/mediterranean-migrant-crisis/. Accessed 5 July 2017

Jouko Lehti is a Military Legal Advisor in the Legal Division of the Defence Command Finland specialised in international and operational issues. He graduated as a lawyer in 2005 and has served in the Finnish Defence Forces as a legal advisor since 2008. He served as a legal advisor in the Operation Headquarters of the EUNAVFOR MED operation SOPHIA in Rome, Italy, from its establishment in May 2015 until February 2016. He has also served as a legal advisor in the Operation Headquarters of the operation 'EUFOR RCA' in Larissa, Greece, and in the Finnish Contingent of the operation 'ISAF' in Mazar-i-Sharif, Afghanistan.

From Piracy to Palermo: The Changing Challenges of Maritime Crime

Oliver Clark

Abstract

To the untrained eye, the only way to counter criminality in international waters is via the use of navies operating in a constabulary role across the oceans of the world. They certainly have a role to play, but it would be a mistake to say that just because warships provide a solution in one scenario the same 'business model' would continue to deliver success in another.

In this article, the author seeks to demonstrate why the successes displayed by maritime forces off the coast of Somalia in countering piracy cannot have the same effect when redeployed in the Mediterranean, where smuggling and human trafficking are now stealing the headlines as the biggest maritime blight on Europe. He does so by first explaining why navies were free to operate effectively around the Horn of Africa through the legal framework, both internationally and domestically, that enabled that operation. He then contrasts that with the lack of a similar legal framework in the Mediterranean that has rendered impotent any international efforts to deter criminal gangs from operating freely around the coast of Libya.

The author concludes that, unless more is done to combat the root causes of transnational crime ashore, navies will continue to focus on delivering a short-term means to address the symptoms rather than seeking a permanent cure.

Lt Cdr Oliver Clark RN is a UK lawyer; however, the views and opinions expressed in this article are his own and are not intended to reflect national or Royal Navy policy.

O. Clark (✉)
Joint Helicopter Command, Hampshire, UK
e-mail: oli.clark210@mod.gov.uk

J. Schildknecht et al. (eds.), *Operational Law in International Straits and Current Maritime Security Challenges*, Operational Maritime Law 1,
https://doi.org/10.1007/978-3-319-72718-9_11

195

1   Introduction

Transnational organised crime, specifically migrant smuggling at sea and human trafficking, as described by the Palermo Convention,[1] has become a key political, economic and strategic concern in recent years. The burgeoning number of migrants and refugees flooding into Europe has started to push the Schengen Agreement to breaking point and has been a source of significant tension between the European powers. At the same time, the former blight on the Indian Ocean that was piracy has seen substantial decline, and as such there has been a shift in political focus away from the threat of global piracy towards the human tragedy that is unfolding on our doorstep.

Recent academic articles have tried to draw parallels between these crimes, extrapolating from this the need for parallel solutions. Although some similarities exist, they are fundamentally different. Whilst both are crimes, the political motivation that drives the global response distinguishes between the economic impact of pirated ships and their subsequent ransoms, and the human impact of children being washed up on a beach. The solution to both takes the form of maritime law enforcement operations, but recognition of the differences is vital for success.

Criminality, be it piracy, smuggling or trafficking, depends on opportunity and the lack of regional stability to deal with it. Whilst the business model for each criminal enterprise differs widely, failure of regional States to take appropriate action is a significant factor. As such, whilst the world's navies will have a role in suppression, it is on land that the ultimate solutions must lie.

This article therefore seeks to examine the way in which the threat of piracy has been met and, through a number of measures, repressed. It then goes on to consider the UN's response to the challenges in the Mediterranean and the entirely different way that the problems need to be addressed. Finally it offers a note of caution: first in drawing comparisons between the two areas of transnational crime and second in the level of ambition that ought to be exercised in response to the crisis.

---

2   The Wave of Piracy

Combatting piracy is a politically comfortable operation for nations to engage in. Piracy has the potential to exist across the globe wherever international maritime commerce is concentrated into choke points, such as the waters off the coast of Somalia. Testament to the global interest in countering piracy is the fact that maritime forces engaged in operations off the coast of Somalia include NATO, the EU, CMF and ships from China, India, Japan, and Russia, amongst others.

Piracy is a crime, codified by UNCLOS,[2] over which all nations have universal jurisdiction. On the high seas, if piracy takes place, any State may seize a pirate ship

---

[1]United Nations Convention against Transnational Organised Crime (2000).
[2]UNCLOS (1982), Arts.100–105.

and arrest the persons on board. This is a rare exception to the general rule on the high seas that jurisdiction lies with the flag State[3] of the suspect ship.

It may be an obvious point to make, but since piracy is a crime, combatting piracy takes the form of a law enforcement, peacetime, operation. This means that 'counter-piracy operations' place restrictions on warships that would not otherwise exist if pirates were the 'enemy'. Although force, including lethal force, may be used in self-defence, one cannot plan to kill pirates—they cannot be targeted as if they were combatants. That is not to say that pirates have not been killed during the course of counter-piracy operations, but that is never the aim of any interdiction.

To expand upon this point a little further, during constabulary operations, self-defence is the only situation in which a pirate can be intentionally killed and it not amount to murder. One does not accidentally kill or seriously injure a pirate in self-defence; one intends to do so; it is just that the intention did not arise until such a time as the pirate posed an imminent threat to life. Thus, a boarding party may conduct a boarding and be prepared to kill, but it should never be the case that they intend to do so.

Even if the ROE were to allow the use of minimum force, which by definition includes deadly force, the situation in which that level of force would be used would be when the pirates pose an imminent threat to the life of either the hostages or the boarding party. So whilst there is clear intent to kill; the justification for doing so is to prevent loss of innocent life. Pirates remain, at the end of the day, suspected criminals – not combatants – and should be treated as such.

This is in line with the judgement on the use of force in peacetime operations, in *MV Saiga (No 2)*,[4] according to which, in cases of 'boarding, stopping and arresting' a vessel, international law

> Requires that the use of force must be avoided as far as possible and, where. . .unavoidable, it must not go beyond that which is reasonable and necessary in the circumstances. Considerations of humanity must apply. . .
>
> The normal practice. . .is first to give an auditory or visual signal to stop,. . . [then to take other action], including the firing of shots across the bows of the ship. It is only after the appropriate actions fail that the pursuing vessel may, as a last resort, use force. Even then, the appropriate warning must be issued. . .and all efforts should be made to ensure that life is not endangered.

It may be the case that a pirate is killed unintentionally (e.g., when using disabling fire, a bullet might ricochet and hit a pirate). In such a case, under UK law, it could be considered an unlawful killing on the ground of gross negligence or involuntary manslaughter. Either way, there is no intention to kill. In such a case, one would expect there to be an investigation into whether the person firing the weapon did so negligently or in an unreasonably dangerous, and therefore unlawful, way.

If no negligence is found, and the death is pure accident, then it is not manslaughter because there is no gross breach of the duty of care. Likewise, if the disabling fire

---

[3]The State to which the ship is registered and whose flag it flies.

[4]ITLOS M/V 'Saiga' (No.2) (1999), 1355.

was a lawful act, then one of the ingredients of involuntary manslaughter (that an unlawful act took place) is absent. In both cases, although death of a pirate has occurred outside of self-defence, the killing would not amount to murder on account of the lack of intent.

There is always the risk of someone being wounded or killed on either side during a counter-piracy operation, as there is in any constabulary operation, where weapons and criminals are involved. However, it is the intent that is crucial and distinguishes the use of lethal force in self-defence, which is lawful, from that of deliberate targeting, which is not.

When pirates withdraw from the high seas, under UNCLOS, unless they retreat into your territorial waters (TTW), you cannot follow them. If pirates are captured, they are not prisoners of war; they are detainees who will, ultimately, stand trial. Therefore, all counter-piracy operations must be conducted within this mindset of constabulary work.

Acknowledging some of these constraints, the UN extended jurisdiction to the TTW of Somalia itself. In the counter-piracy resolutions, the UN allowed[5]

> ... States **co-operating with the TFG**[6] in the fight against piracy and armed robbery at sea off the coast of Somalia, for which advance notification has been provided by the TFG to the Secretary-General, [to]:
>
> (a)   Enter the **territorial waters of Somalia** for the purpose of repressing acts of piracy and armed robbery at sea, in a manner consistent with such action permitted on the high seas with respect to piracy under relevant international law...

The background to these resolutions is important because the TFG yielded sovereignty of their TTW to the international community, in respect of any piratical activity, so long as there continued to be co-operation.[7] Later, UNSCRs extended the ability for those arrested for armed robbery at sea within Somali TTW to be prosecuted in different, more suitable, jurisdictions. Thus, although operating within the territory of Somalia, foreign ships were able to freely navigate, inspect, arrest and transfer to other jurisdictions those suspected to be engaged in piratical acts.

Until they have been through the proper process of law, suspected pirates are just that—suspected. When they are arrested, their detention, trial and sentencing are all conducted accordingly. For European warships, this includes the rights and protections afforded by the ECHR.[8]

---

[5]UNSCR 1816 (2008).

[6]Transitional Federal Government.

[7]The most recent UNSCR on piracy (UNSCR 2246 (2015)) once again reaffirms the renewed consent of the Somali authorities, maintaining that this resolution does not establish customary international law in respect of any other states.

[8]ECHR (1950), European Convention of Human Rights, especially the rights not to be subject to inhumane and degrading treatment (Art 3), not to be discriminated against (Art 14), the right to a fair trial (Art 6) and the prohibition of collective expulsion (Protocol No.4). In addition, Art 19 of the Charter of Fundamental Rights of the EU (2000) provides: '1. Collective expulsions are prohibited.

The location of the subsequent trials and sentencing was therefore something that required a series of bilateral agreements with regional States. There have now been a number of successful criminal prosecutions of pirates, and there is ongoing work to develop regional capacity to combat piracy autonomously.

The piracy business model depends on the vulnerability of commercial ships and the ability of pirates to act with impunity. Although criminal networks operate ashore, the crimes of piracy and armed robbery at sea only take place on the water. Therefore, so long as one establishes sea control, piracy can be repressed even if the coastal State remains unstable. Such sea control has been achieved through merchant vessels carrying private armed security teams, sailing through the internationally recognised transit corridor, adopting best maritime practices and being supported by navies from across the world.

It has been a laborious process for contributing nations and organisations to set up the proper framework, and attempts to create a lasting legacy, in particular regional stability, continue to evolve. However, the result, for now, even without defeating the criminal networks that exist ashore, is the decline of piracy in the region.

3   Resolution 2240

On 9 October 2015, the UNSC adopted Resolution 2240, authorising Member States,

> ...acting nationally or through regional organisations that are engaged in the fight against migrant smuggling and human trafficking, to inspect **on the high seas** off the coast of Libya vessels that they have reasonable grounds to suspect are being used for migrant smuggling or human trafficking **from Libya**...

Whilst piracy was an international crime affecting freedom of navigation far away from the economies themselves, Resolution 2240 was triggered by the humanitarian disaster on the border of Europe where there is a special sensitivity towards the problem.

The business models for human trafficking and migrant smuggling at sea are different, and both have significant differences to the piracy model. Migrant smugglers are dependent on would-be migrants. They are facilitators, and so, in the absence of personnel willing to cross the Mediterranean, their business model falls apart. In contrast, those trafficking humans are able to generate their own business and are not dependent on a supply of volunteers. However, unlike piracy, in both cases the risk/reward analysis is not so closely linked to the actions taken at sea.

---

2. No one may be removed, expelled or extradited to a State where there is a serious risk that he or she would be subject to the death penalty, torture or other inhumane or degrading treatment or punishment.'

Both human trafficking and migrant smuggling at sea are criminalised within the Protocols to the Palermo Convention; thus, whilst they can be viewed as international crimes, they are not crimes of universal jurisdiction. The primacy of flag State jurisdiction remains in respect of any vessel on the high seas that is implicated in either crime. It is for that reason that the Resolution requires States to

...make good faith efforts to obtain the consent of the vessel's flag State.

The requirement to make efforts to obtain flag State consent is not a new formula for the UN to use. It has been used twice before with respect to crude oil smuggling (UNSCR 2146) and charcoal and small arms smuggling (UNSCR 2182).[9] In the case of charcoal and small arms, 6 h was seen by some nations as being the requisite period for a flag State to respond after which the requirement for 'good faith efforts' was satisfied. In the Indian Ocean, 6 h makes very little difference should a boarding eventually be conducted, whereas in the Mediterranean it may well be too late.

Whilst the definition of *good faith efforts* therefore remains a matter of debate, the important point is that the Resolution reaffirms that it is the flag State that has primary jurisdiction and that the 'good faith' derogation from international law should not be considered a violation or comment upon customary international law; if anything, it confirms it.

Nevertheless, the practical application is not so straightforward since, depending on the time of day, or day of the week, in which the consent is being sought, 4–6 h could be considered too short a time to try and gain said consent. There is therefore a balance to be struck between the respect for the jurisdictional primacy of the flag State on the one hand and the practicalities of conducting kinetic operations on the other. Whilst it is clear that the UNSC still intends in the first instance to defer to the flag State, it may be that in repeating this 'good faith efforts' formula, and leaving it to the troop-contributing nations to decide how that ought to be interpreted, the UNSC is generating a gradual erosion of what once was an absolute peacetime norm.

It will be noted as well that the Resolution narrows its scope to migrant smuggling and human trafficking *from Libya*, but it would be a mistake to say that the problem is limited to Libya alone. It exists across the North African coast flowing up from the south. Resolution 2240 does not deal with people departing from Syria, Egypt, Algeria or Tunisia, thus limiting the scope of application on the high seas. This is not necessarily a criticism; the Resolution had to be this narrow to exist in the first place, and one might argue that something is better than nothing, but it does place additional constraints on an already limited task.

Distinction needs also to be made between where and how military forces can operate. The Resolution

---

[9]Since the time of writing it has been used again in UNSCR 2292 (2016) concerning the prohibition on the trafficking of illegal arms into and out of Libya. Whilst this UNSCR does not resolve the problem, it is complementary to the author's view that it is the criminal, and in this case terrorist, networks that operate ashore in Libya and the MENA region that are the means by which this issue will be resolved.

> Calls on Member States…to **assist Libya, upon request**, in building needed capacity including to secure its borders and to prevent, investigate and prosecute acts of smuggling of migrants and human trafficking **through its territory and in its territorial sea**.

Resolution 2240 allows only that assistance be given to Libya upon its request. In other words, it does not give States the unfettered right to enter into or conduct operations within Libyan TTW or ashore. Unlike Somalia, it is not a question of co-operation; Libya has not requested such action.

Indeed, the political and security situation as it stands is so unstable that Libya cannot currently make such a request nor, as is discussed later, could the international community answer it. A further resolution would be required, extending the jurisdiction of the international community to the TTW and ashore. However, not only would this seriously impinge upon Libyan sovereignty; it would not necessarily have any significant effect on the criminality.

Consideration must be given to the disposal of any suspected traffickers or smugglers and who has jurisdiction over them. This is covered later in the article, but in terms of the contrast with Somalia, the point should be made that it is not simply a matter of sending the suspected criminals to a convenient regional State for processing. Flag State jurisdiction and territorial jurisdiction, rather than universal jurisdiction, are what dictate the onward destination of the suspected criminals.

Whilst there may be the political will to act, the legal finish that could be applied to counter-piracy operations does not translate to the challenges closer to home. There are challenges over jurisdiction, both with regard to Libyan territory and the flag State of ships and, as will be shown, human rights concerns over the disposal of suspected criminals, which limit operations far more than was the case in Somalia.

Finally, unlike piracy, it might be argued that the criminality described by the Resolution is somewhat anecdotal to the humanitarian perspective that has driven action in this region. In other words, whilst pirates themselves, rather than those taken hostage, drove the global response to piracy, the motivation to conduct the operation in the Mediterranean is not so much driven by the desire to suppress criminality (albeit that is a necessary task) as a desire to prevent dead migrants washing up on beaches. If this is the case, then some thought needs to be given to whether the priority in the Mediterranean is to save lives or to fight the criminals. Although not mutually exclusive, clarity of aim is central to defining success.

---

4 Human Trafficking vs Migrant Smuggling

As the Resolution points out, there is a clear distinction between migrant smuggling and human trafficking. However unfortunate is the plight of the migrants, legally when they take to the sea they do so consensually. In contrast, when humans are trafficked, they do not. That difference affects not only the nature of the crimes themselves but also the geography of where the criminality takes place.

There is also a difference in the nature of criminal gain; for migrant smugglers, the payment is up front and provided by the migrants, after which there is minimal interest in their welfare. When humans are trafficked, however, the benefit of their worth is only realised upon safe delivery to the buyer. The human element is the entire *raison d'etre* of the process, so great care is taken to ensure that they reach their destination in a marketable condition.

These distinctions mean two things. First, you are very unlikely to encounter the crime of human trafficking committed at sea.[10] If the traffickers even choose that method of transport to start with (as opposed to by land or air), it will not be on board a vessel that is likely to fall under the suspicion of a passing warship. That is not to say that their discovery is impossible, but it is rare.

Second, if a warship encounters migrants on the high seas, the migrants themselves will not be the criminals that the Resolution seeks to combat but a product of the criminal exploitation in need of protection. The known methodology of smugglers is not to accompany the migrants—they have no need to. They take the money; send the migrants to sea with a GPS, a chart and a radio; and instruct them to head for Europe and/or reach the high seas and radio for assistance. Discounts are offered to migrants with experience to act as helmsmen.

Although some smugglers do take to sea as well, it is as an escort to ensure that the migrants reach the high seas. In such cases, they operate in separate vessels that never leave the TTW, therefore remaining outside the jurisdictional reach of vessels on the high seas. In order to remain attractive, the smugglers offer the migrants some hope of survival, doing the bare minimum to ensure their safety, but beyond that there is very little connection between the smugglers and the migrants themselves.

For these reasons, a very different approach needs to be taken to each of these two forms of transnational crime and the way they are addressed.

5   Combatting Transnational Crime Under Resolution 2240

There is nothing unlawful about the presence of a boat of people on the high seas. The Migration Protocol[11] requires States that encounter vessels carrying potential migrants to 'ensure the safety and humane treatment of the persons on board'. If this occurs then, once rescued, those persons are brought to a place of safety, e.g. Italy. In that situation, insofar as they are legally brought onto the territory of a third State, they are not illegal immigrants, at first, but rescued persons. This leads to the counter-intuitive situation that the more ships placed on the high seas to combat illegal migration, the greater chance migrants have of successfully crossing the border into Europe. The migrants therefore take their chances, considerably emboldened by the fact that, should the weather or their vessel deteriorate, they have a chance of rescue.

---

[10]For further detail as to the patterns of human trafficking see the UNODC report on human trafficking (2016) exposes modern form of slavery.

[11]Protocol against the Smuggling of Migrants by Land, Sea and Air (2000).

Since it is only upon the illegal entry into foreign territory that the crime of illegal migration actually occurs, it is difficult to describe the criminality of those parties in Libya who never leave their own territory, and there is very little evidentially that can be held against the migrant smugglers on account of the boats discovered at sea—at best the seizure of mobile phones may assist in gathering intelligence of criminal networks but is unlikely to lead to prosecution.

In this sense, it would seem that only a land-based operation conducted either by the Libyan Government (akin to the efforts being made by the Turkish Government in the Aegean) or by foreign forces conducting constabulary operation on Libyan soil is the only way to remedy this.[12] The desperate plight of the would-be migrants means that there will be a constant demand for the services of these facilitators. But until the situation in Libya improves, such that there is sufficient stability to want to put troops into the country for such an operation, and the rule of law is re-established such that one can have faith in the judicial system that the suspected criminals are handed over to, such an operation cannot be conceived of.

The criminality of human trafficking, codified in the Trafficking Protocol,[13] is a little clearer since typically both the 'trafficker' and the 'trafficked' are simultaneously on board. In terms of the evidence available, it may be, for example, that the human 'cargo' do not appear on the manifest or that they are clearly being held against their will or that there is a criminal network as to their onward disposal. Proving the crime therefore becomes a little easier, but there remains the question of what to do with the people you discover.

The primacy of flag State jurisdiction means that if consent to board were granted (or good faith efforts were made to obtain it), and a human trafficker were to be discovered, unless he had the same nationality as that of the warship conducting the arrest, the jurisdiction over the suspected criminal would remain with the flag State of the vessel upon which he was discovered.

There may be some potential to develop the effectiveness of any task group set up to tackle such problems through the granting of standing consent by flag States in certain circumstances. This already exists, for example, in NATO's counterterrorism operation in the Mediterranean with respect to the ability to board ships suspected of terrorism-related activities. However, it is another step still for a nation not only to grant standing consent to board but also to arrest, detain and prosecute anyone found on board suspected of trafficking activity. Although the Trafficking Protocol encourages co-operation between states, such a yielding of sovereignty on a standing basis may be too great a demand for most nations.

---

[12]Indeed, Parliamentary Assembly of the Council of Europe (2011), states at paragraph 11: 'The Assembly also considers it essential that efforts be made to remedy the prime causes prompting desperate individuals to risk their lives by boarding boats bound for Europe. The Assembly calls on all member States to step up their efforts to promote peace, the rule of law and prosperity in the countries of origin of potential immigrants and asylum seekers.'

[13]Protocol to Prevent, Supress and Punish Trafficking in Persons, Especially Women and Children (2000).

Turning to the issue of human rights, the case of Hirsi Jamaa v Italy brought before the European Court of Human Rights[14] is informative. In May 2009, 11 Somali nationals and 13 Eritrean nationals were part of a group of about 200 individuals who left Libya aboard three vessels with the aim of reaching the Italian coast. On 6 May 2009, when the vessels were 35 nm south of Lampedusa, they were intercepted and transferred to Italian military ships, which returned them to Tripoli. During the voyage, the Italian authorities did not inform the migrants of their true destination, took no steps to identify them and confiscated all of their personal documents from them. Despite their objections, on arrival in Tripoli, the migrants were handed over to the Libyan authorities and forced to leave the Italian ships.

At a press conference on 7 May 2009, the Italian Minister for the Interior stated that the operation to intercept the vessels on the high seas and to push the migrants back to Libya was the consequence of the entry into force on 4 February 2009 of a bilateral agreement concluded with Libya, representing an important turning point in the fight against clandestine immigration.

The European Court of Human Rights came to a number of important conclusions, starting with the fundamental point that personnel taken on board warships on the high seas fall under the full and exclusive control of that warship.[15] From that flows the full protection of human rights that are equally applicable to migrants and smugglers alike, in particular, with respect to Libya in the above case, issues of non-refoulement.

The ECHR therefore applies not only wherever a detention operation involving the signatories takes place[16] but also in respect of any act carried out by a State vessel on the high seas where such a degree of control is exerted.[17] This means that not only would a detainee have to be treated in compliance with those rights on board, but it would further prohibit his transfer into the custody of a State where those rights were not protected.

If the flag State of the ship is one in which there is legitimate assurance that the suspected trafficker will receive a fair trial, the solution would be to deliver him to that State. If, however, such assurance does not exist, or cannot be accepted, as would be the case for most ships involved in this type of activity, then it would be more likely that the suspected criminal would have to be retained by the State of the arresting warship or released.

In addition, the victims would seek the warship's assistance, and, under the Trafficking Protocol, it would have to be rendered. This obliges the State responsible for the immediate care of the victims to provide housing; counselling and

---

[14]ECHR (2009)—Judgement, 23 February 2012.

[15]Ibid. The court followed the progression of case law from ECHR (1999) which talked of 'effective control' through to the then more recent judgement of ECHR (2007) which considered the extraterritorial application of the ECHR to, in that case, detention facilities.

[16]See Royal Courts of Justice (2015), 715 for a recent example of the extent of extra-territorial application of the ECHR.

[17]See ECHR (2009), letter of 15 July 2009 from Mr. Jacques Barrot, Vice-President of the European Commission.

information regarding their legal rights; medical, psychological and material assistance; and employment, educational and training opportunities.[18]

This has the potential to cast a political shadow over the operation, the practical result being that warships suspecting a vessel of human trafficking may do nothing beyond reporting their suspicions to the flag State of the ship and the port of destination.

6   Combatting Transnational Crime Under a Future Resolution

Should a further resolution be agreed upon by the UNSC, the crimes of migrant smuggling and human trafficking within Libyan territory would still fall under Libyan law.[19] Unless jurisdiction was entirely removed from Libya, it would be for Libya to define the nature of the criminality, trial and any eventual punishment.

In respect of migrant smuggling, by the time the potential migrants have left the Libyan shore, the criminal facilitators are long gone. Should warships start to operate in Libyan waters, the practice of escorting migrants would no doubt cease, such that the criminals would have to be combatted on land. Whilst humanitarian aid could be rendered at sea, it would not address the cause of the criminality, nor would it deter migrants seeking that method of transport.

Even ashore, there is nothing unlawful *per se* about accepting money in return for the use of a vessel. The criminality occurs when that contractual exchange is accompanied by the intent to facilitate illegal migration.

Thus, even if you were to arrest someone on Libyan soil accepting money and placing people on a boat, the extent to which you would be able to prove their *criminal intent* is extremely limited. These are not lorry drivers crossing borders with people hidden in the back; these are people charging extortionate rates to facilitate others in attempts to *smuggle themselves* into a foreign country.

That is not to say it is impossible; Article 6(1) of the Migration Protocol states:

Each State Party shall adopt such legislative and other measures as may be necessary to establish as criminal offences, when committed intentionally and in order to obtain, directly or indirectly, a financial or other material benefit:

(a)   The smuggling of migrants.

And Article 5(2) of the *Palermo* Convention states:

The knowledge, intent, aim, purpose or agreement referred to...**may be inferred from objective factual** circumstances.

---

[18]Protocol to Prevent, Supress and Punish Trafficking in Persons, Especially Women and Children (2000), Art.6 (Protection of victims of trafficking in persons).

[19]Note also the UNHCR Press release (2009a, b), stating *inter alia*, 'Libya has not signed the 1951 UN Refugee Convention, and does not have a functioning national asylum system'.

Other nations with more advanced jurisprudence concerning the facilitation of crime can incorporate this into their domestic laws, but insofar as these are crimes committed under Libyan jurisdiction, it is to their courts, their laws of evidence and their penal system that we must turn. This again raises the question posed by the requirement for compliance with the ECHR as to whether these individuals could in fact be handed over to the Libyan authorities at all.

The situation for human trafficking is similar, although unlike migrant smuggling, this is an operation that could potentially be conducted in Libyan waters where there would be shared jurisdiction between Libya and the flag State of the vessel.

Since the same concerns over Libyan justice and the ECHR would prevail, the consequent constraints about handing over the suspected trafficker would also apply. Given the flag State's shared jurisdiction of the vessel upon which the trafficker was arrested, they too could claim jurisdiction, but that raises the same concerns as to the suitability of the flag State to deal with these criminals discussed before.

It may be, as was the case in the context of armed robbery in Somali TTW, that a future UN resolution legitimises the transfer of suspected criminals to suitable regional States for prosecution. However, no such resolution currently exists, and the impact that it would have on the principle of flag State jurisdiction makes such a resolution unlikely.

There are therefore differing, but no less real, problems to conducting operations in Libyan waters or ashore that find their origins in the instability of Libya as a whole. If suspected criminals are arrested within Libyan jurisdiction, there is as yet no satisfactory way in which they can be processed, rendering any such operation impotent.

7   Conclusion

Although pirates originate on land, they can be neutralised at sea. Combined with it being a crime of universal jurisdiction, the legal and political framework to counter piracy is relatively straightforward. In contrast, there are myriad challenges posed by both trafficking and smuggling that cannot be solved by ships on the water.

Trafficking and smuggling are entirely different operations, where the crimes and the criminals operate geographically, temporally and materially distinctly from one another. The only common ground is that both originate from the land, and whilst the symptoms can be observed at sea, it is to the land that we must look for the cure.

Maritime forces can seek to protect the lives of those desperate individuals who risk everything in search of a better future, and they can help to build an intelligence picture in support of any coastal State seeking to suppress migration. But Libyan stability, such that the international community can have faith in the rule of law therein, is the only way to solve this humanitarian crisis.

References

Charter of Fundamental Rights of the EU (2000) (2000/C 364/01), http://www.europarl.europa.eu/charter/pdf/text_en.pdf. Accessed 27 Oct 2017

ECHR (1950) European convention of human rights, 4 November 1950, http://www.echr.coe.int/Documents/Convention_ENG.pdf. Accessed 28 Oct 2017

ECHR (1999) of Bancovic and others v Belgium, ECHR (52207/99), http://www.rulac.org/assets/downloads/ECtHR_Bankovic_Admissibility.pdf. Accessed 05 Sep 2017

ECHR (2007) of Al Skeini and others v The United Kingdom, ECHR (55721/07), http://www.refworld.org/pdfid/4e2545502.pdf. Accessed 05 Sep 2017

ECHR (2009) of Hirsi Jamaa and Others v. Italy (27765/09) – ECHR, http://hudoc.echr.coe.int/app/conversion/pdf/?library=ECHR&id=001-109231&filename=001-109231.pdf. Accessed 05 Sep 2017

ITLOS M/V 'Saiga' (No.2) (1999) Saint Vincent and the Grenadines v Guinea, ITLOS case No.2; 38 ILM 1323, 1355, https://www.itlos.org/cases/list-of-cases/case-no-2/. Accessed 05 Sep 2017

Parliamentary Assembly of the Council of Europe (2011) Resolution 1821 (21 June 2011), http://assembly.coe.int/nw/xml/XRef/Xref-XML2HTML-en.asp?fileid=18006&lang=en. Accessed 05 Sep 2017

Protocol against the Smuggling of Migrants by Land, Sea and Air (2000) supplementing the United Nations Convention against Transnational organised Crime (Migration Protocol), https://www.unodc.org/documents/southeastasiaandpacific/2011/04/som-indonesia/convention_smug_eng.pdf. Accessed 05 Sep 2017

Protocol to Prevent, Supress and Punish Trafficking in Persons, Especially Women and Children (2000) supplementing the United Nations Convention against Transnational Organised Crime (Trafficking Protocol), https://treaties.un.org/Pages/ViewDetails.aspx?src=IND&mtdsg_no=XVIII-12-a&chapter=18&lang=en. Accessed 05 Sep 2017

Royal Courts of Justice (2015) of Al-Saadoon and Others v. Secretary of State for Defence, [2015] EWHC (Admin) 715, https://www.judiciary.gov.uk/wp-content/uploads/2015/12/r-al-saadoon-v-secretary-of-state-for-defence-2015-ewhc-715-admin.pdf. Accessed 05 Sep 2017

UNCLOS (1982) United Nations Convention on the Law of the Sea, 1833 U.N.T.S. 397

UNHCR Press release (2009a) UNHCR deeply concerned over returns from Italy to Libya, 7 May 2009, http://www.unhcr.org/news/press/2009/5/4a02d4546/unhcr-deeply-concerned-returns-italy-libya.html. Accessed 28 Oct 2017

UNHCR Press release (7 May 2009b) http://www.unhcr.org/news/press/2009/5/4a02d4546/unhcr-deeply-concerned-returns-italy-libya.html. Accessed 05 Sep 2017

United Nations Convention against Transnational Organised Crime and the Protocols thereto (Palermo, 2000), https://www.unodc.org/documents/middleeastandnorthafrica/organised-crime/UNITED_NATIONS_CONVENTION_AGAINST_TRANSNATIONAL_ORGANIZED_CRIME_AND_THE_PROTOCOLS_THERETO.pdf. Accessed 05 Sep 2017

UNODC report on human trafficking (2016) http://www.unodc.org/documents/data-and-analysis/glotip/2016_Global_Report_on_Trafficking_in_Persons.pdf. Accessed 27 Oct 2017

UNSCR 1816 (2008) United Nations Security Council Resolution S/RES/1816 (2008), http://www.un.org/en/ga/search/view_doc.asp?symbol=S/RES/1816(2008). Accessed 05 Sep 2017

UNSCR 2246 (2015) United Nations Security Council Resolution, S/RES/2246 (2015), http://www.un.org/en/ga/search/view_doc.asp?symbol=S/RES/2246(2015). Accessed 05 Sep 2017

UNSCR 2292 (2016) United Nations Security Council Resolution, S/RES/2292 (2016), http://unscr.com/en/resolutions/2292. Accessed 28 Oct 2017

Oliver Clark is a U.K. barrister. Having studied for his first degree at Oxford, he joined the Royal Navy in 2006 where he commissioned as a logistics officer. He has served on board the destroyers HMS Liverpool and HMS Exeter, the LPH HMS Ocean, and the carriers HMS Illustrious and HMS Ark Royal. He has worked as the logistics officer for 814 NAS and as Flag Lieutenant to the First Sea Lord. He qualified as a barrister in 2014, which included time studying international law back at his old college, St Peter's, in Oxford. Having worked as a legal advisor at NATO's Maritime Command, specialising in international and maritime law, he is now working in the Tri-Service environment at the U.K.'s Joint Helicopter Command.

Part III

Law of Armed Conflict

Prize Law and Contraband in Modern Naval Warfare

Marcel Schulz

Abstract

Prize law and the law of contraband are based on the rules of peacetime public international law, especially peacetime law of the sea. The origin of prize and contraband laws is the Paris Declaration of 1856; however, they still are part of the modern humanitarian law and the law of armed conflict at sea. Many historical regulations have barely changed and remain valid today, with States showing no interest in changing them.

This chapter initially illuminates historical developments of this very unique and special aspect of naval warfare, which is the precondition for any understanding of modern rules. The Paris Declaration abolished privateering and established the distinction between the neutral and enemy characteristics of vessels as the legal basis for capture and seizure.

The second part of this chapter discusses how only civilian objects—vessels, aircraft and goods—may be subject to prize law and the law of contraband and details necessary definitions. It then focuses on conditions and different aspects of the right to visit, search and diversion that exists today. Lastly, the second part of the chapter outlines conditions for capture and seizure and the legal consequences of resistance against it.

The last section of the chapter addresses the issue of prize court proceedings.

While there may be uncertainties regarding some details, the chapter demonstrates that there is a general agreement on the core rules of prize law and law of contraband. They are in no way outdated but rather provide a very practicable framework.

M. Schulz (✉)
The Parliamentary Party of the German Social Democratic Party (SPD, Landtag) of the Federal German State of Brandenburg regarding, (Law and Economy), Potsdam 14467, Germany
e-mail: marcel.schulz.gm@gmx.de

J. Schildknecht et al. (eds.), *Operational Law in International Straits and Current Maritime Security Challenges*, Operational Maritime Law 1,
https://doi.org/10.1007/978-3-319-72718-9_12

1   Introduction

The law of the sea is one of the rather old components of public international law. It is due to the ability of the nations to sail the seas, that at least basic rules were needed governing this issue. This is why early elements of the law of the sea can be traced all the way back to ancient Greece.[1]

As a part of public international law, the law of the sea aims to bring the interests of the States to balance. The core principle of its peacetime law, the freedom of the seas, was primarily established as early as 1609 by Hugo Grotius in his work 'De mare librum'.[2] Today's peacetime law of the sea is meant to balance the right of all nations interested in the multiple use of the sea.[3] And of course there was and always will be an enormous interest of nations in the military use of the seas.[4] Even in time of peace, States are strongly devoted to jealously guarding their military strengths and interests. Indeed, the peacetime law of the sea pays due regard to a variety of military issues. For good reasons, the law of naval warfare, therefore, builds upon the peacetime law of the sea.[5]

One function of the law of naval warfare is to balance the freedom of the seas, as the core interests of the neutral States, against the interests of the respective belligerents. Out of the freedom of the seas derives in particular the right of neutrals to continue to conduct international trade. Belligerents, on the other hand, clearly have no interest to allow enemies any international trade with or aiding by anyone.[6] The law of naval warfare addresses this particular issue through its prize law and contraband branch.

While it has been determined that since World War II the issue of prize law has played only a minor role in the law of naval warfare,[7] States are, nevertheless, unwilling to give up these rights simply because they are not prominently discussed in legal literature. This article will, therefore, address the question of prize law and contraband in modern naval warfare as it is still a valid legal right of States at war.

2   Definition of Prize and Contraband

Regarding the law of war, the gaze, too often, turns towards the right to conduct belligerent acts and mere destruction. Indeed, regarding the law of armed conflict on land, there is no clear definition for the so-called economic warfare.[8] However,

---

[1]Vitzthum (2006), para 11–13.
[2]Heintschel von Heinegg (2014), para 6.
[3]Vitzthum (2006), para 6.
[4]Schulz (2014), pp. 103–104.
[5]Kraska (2015), p. 875.
[6]Kraska (2012), para 2.
[7]Heintschel von Heinegg (1995a), p. 493.
[8]Lowe and Tzanakopoulos (2013), para 1.

regarding the law of naval warfare, the 'economic warfare' has an extensive tradition. Economic warfare is a well-recognised part of the law of naval warfare, governed by its own unique regulations. Means and methods of economic warfare are blockade, visit and search, direction of a vessel's or airplane's course and the seizure and capture of vessels or airplanes and their cargo.[9]

The English word 'prize', as well as its French counterpart 'prise', or the German 'Prise', have their roots in the Latin word 'prehendere', which means 'to seize'. The origin of the term 'contraband' lies in the Latin words 'contra bannum', easily translated as 'against the ban'. The term 'prize law' by its origin, therefore, deals with various aspects of seizing, its preconditions and its consequences. The law of contraband on the other hand deals with the aspect of goods that are destined for a belligerent and could be used to support a belligerent's war effort.[10] Both are closely related and will be subjects of the following examination.

3   History[11]

In a very rudimentary form, the concept of neutrality can be traced back to the twelth century.[12] Hampering the concept of neutrality in the following centuries, however, was the overwhelming acceptance of privateering. From the sixteenth up to the nineteenth century, naval powers of that time recognised privateering as lawful. Private vessels, equipped as warships, were authorised by national governments to attack the government's enemies. The right was provided by issuing the so-called letter of marque. The privateer, due to his special status, was bound to conduct his actions in accordance with the law of naval warfare. He, therefore, had to limit his actions to the time of war. Since the concept of neutrality was known, neutral ships were not legitimate targets.[13] The crucial weakness of the concept of neutrality at that time was that privateers very well acted as part-time pirates to boost their income. The benefit for the governments laid in the possibility to deny responsibility in cases where a privateer violated the law of warfare.[14]

In respect of the development of the modern law of naval warfare, the Declaration Respecting Maritime Law of 1856 (Paris Declaration)[15] can, for good reasons, be identified as the beginning.[16] Before the Paris Declaration, privateering was widely recognised as lawful. The signatory States of the Paris Declaration were very well

---

[9]Heintschel von Heinegg (1995a), p. 482.

[10]Schaller (2015), para 1.

[11]Detailed on the history of prize law and with a variety of further sources Heintschel von Heinegg (1995b), pp. 2–4.

[12]Regarding the development of the law of naval warfare Wehberg (1915), pp. 15–18.

[13]Bederman (2009), paras 1–3.

[14]Bederman (2009), para 4.

[15]Paris Declaration (1856), pp. 89–90.

[16]Heintschel von Heinegg (1995b), p. 2.

aware of the fact '[t]hat maritime law, in time of war, has long been the subject of deplorable disputes'. Born from the wish to continue trade with the neutral Scandinavian States during the Crimean War between the allied France and Great Britain on the one side and Russia on the other, France and Great Britain declared in separate but coordinated declarations what can be considered an early regime of prize law and contraband, as well as the abolition of privateering. Even though the declarations were originally to be limited to the duration of the Crimean War (1853–1856), the Peace Congress of Paris finally adopted the Paris Declaration, stating that [. . .]

1. Privateering is, and remains, abolished;
2. The neutral flag covers enemy's goods, with the exception of contraband of war;
3. Neutral goods, with the exception of contraband of war, are not liable to capture under enemy's flag; [. . .][17]

At first, only seven States signed the declaration, but finally 51 States became signatories, including many major maritime powers of the time. Additionally, even major non-parties, such as the United States of America, complied with the stated provisions, which subsequently and undoubtedly acquired customary international law status.[18]

Later, in 1907, two Hague Conventions also covered prize law and contraband issues. The Hague Convention (VI) Relating to the Status of Enemy Merchant Ships at the Outbreak of Hostilities[19] was virtually not obeyed and can be regarded as obsolete.[20] The Hague Convention (XI) Relative to Certain Restrictions with Regard to the Exercise of the Right of Capture in Naval War[21] did not share this fate. In fact, the Hague Convention XI is, even today, partially used on a customary international law basis. Its scope of application thereby partially extended to aircraft.[22] The treaty mainly deals with three issues. Chapter I on postal correspondence did not develop customary international law character,[23] whereas chapter II, regarding the exemption from capture of certain vessels, and chapter III, providing for the treatment of crews of the enemy merchant ships, somewhat did.[24]

The London Conference, with its so-called London Declaration of 1909,[25] aimed to improve the protection of neutral merchant shipping.[26] The respective treaty never entered into force. Nevertheless, once again certain provisions were adopted by

---

[17]Roberts and Guelff (2000), p. 47.
[18]Roberts and Guelff (2000), p. 47.
[19]Hague VI (1907).
[20]Heintschel von Heinegg (1995a), p. 486.
[21]Hague XI (1907).
[22]Heintschel von Heinegg (1995a), pp. 485–486.
[23]Tucker (1957), pp. 90–91.
[24]Roberts and Guelff (2000), pp. 119–120.
[25]London Declaration (1909).
[26]Heintschel von Heinegg (1995a), p. 486.

some of the major nations of World War I (1914–1918)[27] and may still be regarded as customary international law today.[28] The regulations concerned are those overseeing the transfer of property, which, at that stage, did not come automatically with the seizure anymore but remain reserved for the decision of the judge of a prize court.[29]

In 1913, as a restatement of the law of naval warfare, the Oxford Manual was adopted by the Institut de Droit International.[30] Therein, especially the belligerents' rights to destroy seized enemy ships were heavily restricted. Article 104 Oxford Manual stated that '[b]elligerents are not permitted to destroy seized enemy ships, except in so far as they are subject to confiscation and because of exceptional necessity, that is, when the safety of the captor ship or the success of the war operations in which it is at that time engaged, demands it. Before the vessel is destroyed all persons on board must be placed in safety, and all the ship's papers and other documents which the parties interested consider relevant for the purpose of deciding on the validity of the capture must be taken on board the war-ship. The same rule shall hold, as far as possible, for the goods.' The obligation to secure the ship's papers and documents was established with good reason. According to Article 110 Oxford Manual, '[t]he legality and the regularity of the capture of enemy vessels and of the seizure of goods must be established before a prize court'. Eventually, Article 113 Oxford Manual recognised the right to compensation if the seizure of the ship or of the goods were not upheld by the prize court and thus recognises a liability for wrongful acts of the responsible States.

The practice during World War I (1914–1918) widely ignored the enumerated regulations.[31] The well-known catchword in this context is the so-called unrestricted submarine warfare. As one consequence of these events of World War I, the States focused on the legal restrictions of submarine warfare in the following time.[32] The most prominent outcome of this effort is the 1936 London Protocol.[33] In its core provision (Rule 2), it states that 'except in the case of persistent refusal to stop on being duly summoned, or of active resistance to visit or search, a warship, whether surface vessel or submarine, may not sink or render incapable of navigation a merchant vessel without having first placed passengers, crew and ship's papers in a place of safety'.

Despite all treaty regulations, the sinking of enemy merchant vessels without any prior warning or providing safety of crew or passengers was also common practice during World War II (1939–1945) by all parties of the war.[34] Germany waged this

---

[27]Kraska (2012), para 19.

[28]Fleck (2015), para 14.

[29]Heintschel von Heinegg (1995a), pp. 487–488.

[30]Ronzitti (2009), para 1.

[31]Heintschel von Heinegg (1995a), pp. 366–367.

[32]Heintschel von Heinegg (1995a), pp. 366–368.

[33]London Protocol (1936).

[34]Roach (2000), p. 70; Heintschel von Heinegg (1995a), p. 488.

measure as a reaction to the practice of the allied forces who advised their merchant vessels to report the position of German warships to the allied forces or even ram them. Regarding the judgment on Admiral Dönitz in the Nuremberg Tribunals, it was consequent but nonetheless remarkable that he therefore was not found guilty of committing war crimes.[35]

4   Contemporary Public International Law

Due to the close relation of today's peacetime law of the sea and the law of naval warfare, it comes close to an obligation to use the 1982 United Nations Convention on the Law of the Sea (UNCLOS)[36] as the starting point. The convention codifies the core peacetime law of the sea, widely reflecting customary international law, applied even by relevant non-parties of the Convention such as the greatest sea power at present, the United States of America.[37]

The law of naval warfare, by contrast, applies only if an armed conflict occurs. In comparison to the peacetime law, it has multiple sources, mostly, however, the customary international law,[38] which for the most part was codified in 1994 in the San Remo Manual on International Law Applicable to Armed Conflicts at Sea (San Remo Manual)[39] written by renowned experts on the law of the sea and humanitarian law. The law of naval warfare builds upon the peacetime law of the sea, which in the case of an armed conflict may be modified.[40] Since prize law and the law of contraband are part of the law of armed conflict, it has to be examined how both are situated in this described framework of the peacetime and wartime law of the sea.

4.1   Existence of an Armed Conflict

The application of the humanitarian law is a precondition for the application of prize law, just as it is for the law of contraband. Both are therefore only applicable if an armed conflict occurs.[41] This is today, and likely for the foreseeable future, applicable only in an armed conflict between (at least two) States. There are two specific reasons why there is no need to regard the option of an armed conflict between a State actor and a non-State party, which may under certain circumstances also trigger

---

[35]Ronzitti (2009), para 14.

[36]UNCLOS (1982).

[37]In detail addressing the issue which norms reflect customary international law see Harris (2004), pp. 382–384. If the author of this article refers to UNCLOS articles, he does so, recognising the customary international law character of the respective provisions.

[38]Bothe (2013), para 84.

[39]San Remo Manual (1995).

[40]Kraska (2015), p. 875.

[41]Extensively on the beginning and termination of an armed conflict Dinstein (2005), pp. 30–32.

the application of humanitarian law. First, there does not seem to be any non-State actor capable of exercising possible respective rights because there is simply a lack of means. Second, there is no written or customary law that extends the existing law of naval warfare, rights and duties between States to non-State actors. As stated in Rule 1 San Remo Manual, the parties of an armed conflict at sea are bound by the principles and rules of international humanitarian law from the moment armed force is used.[42]

4.2 Areas of Naval Warfare

The specifics of the element water lead to the question where the law of naval warfare is applicable.[43] Once again, the peacetime regulations of UNCLOS provide the basis. They define different rights and duties for the so-called land territory (Article 2 UNCLOS) and internal waters (Article 2 and Article 8), territorial sea (Article 2 ff. UNCLOS), contiguous zone (Article 33 UNCLOS), exclusive economic zone (Article 55 ff. UNCLOS) and the high seas (Article 86 ff. UNCLOS).

4.2.1 Land Territory and Internal Waters, Territorial Sea

The area of warfare indisputably extends past their sovereign land territory and the internal waters, including everything landwards of the States' baseline,[44] which generally is to be drawn according to Article 5 ff. UNCLOS. The sovereignty of a costal State according to Article 2 UNCLOS extends to the territorial sea, to the airspace over the territorial sea, as well as to its bed and subsoil. The width of the territorial sea is to be determined for each case individually under the regulations of Article 3 ff. UNCLOS.

If the territorial waters belong to States not part of the armed conflict, the belligerents have, due to the customary international law codified in Article 2 (4) of the Charter of the United Nations[45] and Article 1 of the Convention (XIII) Concerning the Rights and Duties of Neutral Powers in Naval War,[46] the duty to respect the sovereignty of the neutral State. Primarily, this means that belligerents must refrain from any acts of naval warfare within the territorial waters of neutral States and shall not infringe on their territorial integrity.[47] An exception is made if a neutral State grants one of the belligerents the right to operate maritime or other military bases on its territory.[48] This, however, negates the neutrality of the State altogether, and further effects of such action are not discussed here.

---

[42]Kleffner (2014), paras 1201–1203.

[43]Extensively on the area of an armed conflict at sea Heintschel von Heinegg (1995a), pp. 196–198.

[44]Heintschel von Heinegg (1995a), p. 213.

[45]UN Charter (1945).

[46]Hague XIII (1907).

[47]Heintschel von Heinegg (1995a), pp. 197–198.

[48]Heintschel von Heinegg (1995a), p. 198.

4.2.2   High Seas, Exclusive Economic Zone and Continental Shelf

Article 87 para. 1 UNCLOS contains a list of freedoms of the high seas. The most important ones comprised within the article are the freedoms of navigation and overflight. These also apply in the exclusive economic zone, whereas other freedoms of the high sea do not.[49] On the high seas, including exclusive economic zones, there are no local limitations that restrict where the belligerents conduct hostilities. Furthermore, belligerents are not limited to any kind of proclaimed exclusion zone,[50] even if those zones are used quite frequently in maritime practice.[51]

4.2.3   The Final Theatre of Naval Warfare

Components of the theatre of war are, as also laid down in Rule 10 San Remo Manual, the high seas and the land territory, the internal waters, the territorial sea, the exclusive economic zone, the continental shelf and, if existent, the archipelagic waters of belligerent States. Belligerent actions can be conducted in, on or over the respective parts of the sea or territory. The exclusive economic zone and the continental shelf of neutral States may be included in the theatre of war, leaving belligerent States with the obligation, according to Rule 34 San Remo Manual, to pay due regard for the rights and duties of the coastal State. Rule 12 San Remo Manual states the general rule that carrying out operations in areas where neutral States enjoy sovereign rights, jurisdiction or other rights under general international law, belligerents shall have due regard for the legitimate rights and duties of those neutral States.

With a look at the special status that neutral States enjoy, it must be stated that neutral States also carry their burden of duties. Most importantly, they have to refrain from any actions that would infringe their neutrality. Nevertheless, it is not to be forgotten that neutral States are free to join belligerents, which then, within the blink of an eye, would change their status.

4.3   Subject to Prize Law and the Law of Contraband

Having determined the preconditions, the question remains unanswered; what is subject to prize law and the law of contraband?

The peacetime law of the sea grants certain rights of control to warships and other State ships. Warships and State ships, for example, may, according to Articles 105, 110 and 111 UNCLOS, seize pirate ships and visit and pursue ships under certain conditions.[52] Even though there are some similarities between rights during war and peacetime, peacetime rights must not to be confused with the wartime prize law and law of contraband. The different rights have their origin in different sources

---

[49]Treves (2009), para 10.

[50]Dinstein (2010), pp. 227–229.

[51]On the various aspects of possible zones in naval warfare Heintschel von Heinegg (2015b).

[52]Regarding these aspects see Fink (2010), pp. 7–45.

of public international law and are applicable only to their respective fields of law. This chapter focuses on the mentioned wartime rights only.

By prize law, the capture and seizure of third parties' private property during an armed conflict is legal. So is the private property's subsequent transition into the property of the capturer, if certain preconditions are met, as will be examined later. Whereas enemy merchant ships are generally subject to prize at any time without preconditions, neutral merchant vessels are subject to prize only if they are transporting contraband.[53] The question what is to be categorised as contraband is, due to the inconsistent State practice, not easy to answer, thus one topic at a time.

4.3.1 Civilian Objects

Since prize law and the law of contraband only address civilian objects, there are some distinctions to be made.

Prize law is not applicable to legitimate military targets. Nevertheless, for the sake of distinction, 'legitimate military targets' must shortly be discussed. The definition of 'military target' in naval warfare corresponds with the humanitarian law definition of military target for the warfare on land. The definition of the Additional Protocol I (AP I) can be conveyed to the law of naval warfare as customary international law.[54] Military objectives are, according to AP I and as laid down also in Rule 40 San Remo Manual, limited to those objects that by their nature, location, purpose or use make an effective contribution to military action and whose total or partial destruction, capture or neutralization, in the circumstances ruling at the time, offer a definite military advantage. The destruction of such a target is principally lawful. Measures, such as seizure or course direction, against targets that lawfully can be sunk on sight are considered less intense measures than destruction and are therefore legal as a 'de minimum' measure. Thus, e.g., warships do not fall under prize law.[55] They are by definition legitimate military targets by purpose. They can therefore be attacked on sight or captured as booty of war[56] and, without any further measures, be used as a warship of the capturer.[57] However, the capturer has to fulfil the criteria of Article 29 UNCLOS regarding the captured ship. This will usually be done by reflagging the ship with its own flag and marking the ship with the respective warship marks.

The second distinction to be made is the one between booty of war and a prize. Subject to booty of war is any movable public property that belongs to the enemy State, even if it is of a non-military character. If such property is captured on the battlefield, the belligerent party whose forces seized it automatically acquires it, in accordance with customary international law.[58] Immune from capture is cultural

---

[53]Schaller (2015), para 3.

[54]Dinstein (2010), p. 89.

[55]Heintschel von Heinegg (1995a), pp. 275–277.

[56]Tucker (1957), pp. 104–105; Dinstein (2010), p. 247.

[57]Dinstein (2010), pp. 247–248.

[58]Dinstein (2010), pp. 247–248.

property due to Article 14 of the Convention for the Protection of Cultural Property in the Event of an Armed Conflict (Cultural Property Convention).[59]

The above mentioned raises the question: at what point is a vessel not to be considered a military target? In order for this to be determined, the civilian character of an object has to be defined, and the principle of distinction once again comes into play. The definition turns out to be a negative one: merchant ships, as a legal term, are to be distinguished from warships and State ships in international law.[60] Consequently, Rule 13 lit. h San Remo Manual states that a merchant vessel is a vessel, other than a warship, an auxiliary vessel or a State vessel, such as a customs or police vessel, which is engaged in commercial or private service. Merchant vessels therefore do not benefit from the immunity of the State that covers State ships in peacetime. In wartime, they remain civilian objects, as codified in Rule 41 sentence 2 San Remo Manual. In conclusion, neutral and even enemy merchant vessels are recognised as civilian objects and are therefore, in general, exempt from attack.[61]

4.3.2 Neutral or Enemy Character of Vessels and Aircraft

Neutral vessels are subject to prize law only in a few certain cases.[62] To generally be subject to prize, the merchant vessel or airplane has to be of enemy character. This is not always easy to determine. The determination is, however, crucial. Since a positive definition of neutral merchant vessels is not to be found, all merchant vessels that are not considered enemy may be considered neutral.[63] The first major clue to such an evaluation gives the flag State principle. It is generally accepted that the character of a ship is determined by the flag it flies. This rule is codified, inter alia, in Article 57 para. 1 of the 1909 London Declaration, as well as in the German ZdV 15/2, the Humanitarian Law in Armed Conflicts Manual[64] referring to the German Prize Ordinance of 1939 (German Prize Ordinance),[65] which established the flag State principle in its Article 6 para. 1 sentence 1.[66] In accordance with those regulations, Rule 112 San Remo Manual states that the fact that a merchant vessel is flying the flag of an enemy State or that a civilian aircraft bears the marks of an enemy State is conclusive evidence of its enemy character. The conditions under which States may grant the flag to merchant ships[67] will not be further discussed at this point due to the extensiveness of the topic.

According to Rule 113, the fact that a merchant vessel is flying the flag of a neutral State or a civilian aircraft bears the marks of a neutral State is prima facie

---

[59]Article 14 Cultural Property Convention (1954).

[60]Lagoni (2011), para 4.

[61]Dinstein (2010), p. 112.

[62]Heintschel von Heinegg (1995b), p. 33.

[63]Heintschel von Heinegg (1995b), p. 33.

[64]Bundesministerium der Verteidigung (2013), para. 1026; Heintschel von Heinegg (1995b), p. 6.

[65]Prisenordnung (1939).

[66]Heintschel von Heinegg (1995b), p. 6.

[67]Wolfrum (2006), para 30 ff.

evidence of its neutral character. However, the evidence can be rebutted. According to Article 6 para. 1 sentence 2 German Prize Ordinance, the nationality of the owner of the vessel will be the determining factor if the vessel is not entitled to fly the respective flag. This shows that the flag may be the major indication, but also only one of many. Rule 117 San Remo Manual indeed names registration, ownership, charter or other criteria also as possible clues of determination. The primary evidence of its lawful registration is given by the ship's papers.[68] In the context of a neutral or an enemy character of vessels, the possibility that shipowners may try to transfer ship registration to a neutral State flag to bypass the enemy character disadvantages is also of special note.

Before the outbreak of hostilities, the transfer of an enemy vessel to a neutral flag shall be valid according to Article 55 London Declaration unless it is proven that the transfer was made in order to evade the consequences to which an enemy vessel, as such, is exposed. Article 55, however, presumes that if the bill of sale is not on board a vessel, which has lost its belligerent nationality less than 60 days before the outbreak of hostilities, then the transfer is considered to be void. This presumption may be rebutted. According to the article, there is an absolute presumption that the transfer is valid, where it was effected more than 30 days before the outbreak of hostilities; if it is unconditional, complete and in conformity with the laws of the countries concerned; and if its effect is such that neither the control of nor the profits arising from the employment of the vessel remain in the same hands as before the transfer.[69]

After the outbreak of hostilities, the transfer of an enemy-flagged vessel to a flag of a neutral State is impossible and to be considered void unless, according to Article 56 London Declaration, it is proven that such transfer was not made in order to evade the consequences to which an enemy vessel, as such, is exposed. The presumption is absolute if the transfer has been made during a voyage or in a blockaded port, a right to repurchase or recover the vessel is reserved to the vendor or the requirements of the municipal law governing the right to fly the flag under which the vessel is sailing have not been fulfilled.[70] Here, the burden of proof shifts from the belligerent who has to take it in respect of transfers prior to the outbreak of the hostilities to the neutral in respect of transfers made subsequently.[71]

France incorporated Articles 55 and 56 of the London Declaration into its Article XIII of the Instructions of December 9, 1912.[72] Article 7 German Prize Ordinance is at least in part identical to Article 55. Despite these facts, it is important to note that the London Declaration never entered into force. And as Heintschel von Heinegg

---

[68]Heintschel von Heinegg (1995b), p. 10.

[69]Article 52 para. 1 and 2 Oxford Manual (1913) are almost equally-worded to Article 55 London Declaration (1909).

[70]Article 52 para. 3 Oxford Manual (1913) are almost equally-worded to Article 56 London Declaration (1909).

[71]Heintschel von Heinegg (1995b), p. 11.

[72]Heintschel von Heinegg (1995b), p. 12.

concluded, '[t]he provisions of the 1909 London Declaration which may be considered an attempt to compromise differences in state practice did not successfully contribute to the establishment of a generally accepted rule of international law'.[73] Indeed, the San Remo Manual does not include all respective norms. The German Humanitarian Law in Armed Conflicts Manual in its 2013 edition also supports this assumption. The Manual refers to some regulations of the London Declaration, which Germany accepts to be customary international law, including Article 57, however not Articles 55 and 56. Instead, the German Humanitarian Law in Armed Conflicts Manual continues to base its legal arguments on the German Prize Ordinance.[74] Hence, Articles 55 and 56 of the London Declaration may only be taken as a guideline.

Eventually, it has to be stated that the finding of the enemy character of a merchant vessel is to be made on a case-by-case decision. The flag state principle provides the principle that is amended in the case of suspicion. The special case of suspicion that occurs if the flag changed shortly before or after the outbreak of hostilities is addressed in Articles 55 and 56 London Declaration, which provide a guideline but, as of yet, do not represent customary international law.

4.3.3 Enemy or Neutral Character of Goods

The enemy character of cargo is even harder to evaluate than the enemy character of the vessel itself. The general rule ties the enemy or neutral character of the merchant vessel to the carried goods. In the absence of proof of a neutral character of goods found on board an enemy vessel,[75] they are, according to Article 59 London Declaration, presumed to be enemy goods. However, by the article's wording, the presumption made of the character of the goods is rebuttable. The burden of proof lies with the owner of the cargo.[76] This was applied by the prize courts during World Wars I and II.[77]

4.4 Right to Visit, Search and Diversion, Capture/Seizure

During an armed conflict, States have, under certain circumstances, the right to visit, search and divert as well as capture or seize and condemn merchant vessels. The following paragraphs examine the exact conditions and circumstances.

---

[73]Heintschel von Heinegg (1995b), p. 13.

[74]Bundesministerium der Verteidigung (2013), para 1027.

[75]According to Schaller (2015), para 19 '[t]he enemy or neutral character of goods carried on board an enemy merchant ship is determined by the enemy or neutral character of their owner'.

[76]Colombos (1963), para 774; Heintschel von Heinegg (1995b), p. 13.

[77]Heintschel von Heinegg (1995b), p. 13.

4.4.1   Entitlement to Exercise the Rights of Visit, Search and Diversion, Capture/Seizure and Condemnation

Rule 118 San Remo Manual states that belligerent warships and military aircraft have the right to visit and search merchant vessels outside neutral waters, as long as there are reasonable grounds for suspecting that they are subject to capture. Deduced from the States' sovereignty, the right is limited to the States' forces[78] and accepted as customary international law.[79]

The definition of warship—relevant in peacetime as well as wartime—is to be found in Article 29 UNCLOS. A warship is a ship belonging to the armed forces of a State bearing the external marks distinguishing its nationality, under the command of an officer [. . .], and manned by a crew that is under regular armed forces discipline. Based on the definition of warship, but adjusted with regard to the specifics of aircraft, military aircraft is by customary international law defined as any aircraft operated by the armed forces of a State bearing the military markings of that State, commanded by a member of the armed forces and controlled, manned or pre-programmed by a crew subject to regular armed forces discipline.[80] As a major difference, unmanned aerial vehicles are included in the definition of military aircraft, whereas unmanned naval vehicles are not (yet) accepted as warships.[81] Obviously, due to their nature, military airplanes have difficulties conducting visit and search operations. They therefore have to use diversion to port options. A similar issue may become virulent if unmanned naval vehicles one day are defined as warships. Military helicopters, by contrast, are accepted as military aircraft and, due to their ability to use (war)ships as their platform, are frequently used during boarding operations.

The spirit of prize law and the law of contraband is to enable the belligerent to verify the non-enemy character of the vessel or its cargo.[82] Merchant vessels—as they cannot deduce rights from their ship's flag State sovereignty—are not entitled to conduct visit and search or to attack. If they were to do so against public private vessels of the enemy, they would be considered pirates and treated accordingly.[83]

4.4.2   Visit, Search, Diversion

Regarding Rule 118 San Remo Manual, it stands out that the rule makes no difference between enemy or neutral merchant vessels. Indeed, there is no question that enemy vessels are also subject to visit and search even though enemy merchant vessels are prima facie subject to capture without a prior procedure of visit and search.[84]

---

[78]Oppenheim and Lauterpacht (1952), p. 467.

[79]Tucker (1957), p. 333; Oppenheim and Lauterpacht (1952), p. 848.

[80]Program on Humanitarian Policy and Conflict Research at Harvard University (2009), Rule 1 (x).

[81]Schulz (2014), pp. 115–116; different: von Schmeling (2014), pp. 242–243.

[82]Kraska (2012), para 6.

[83]Oppenheim and Lauterpacht (1952), p. 467.

[84]Colombos (1963), para 883; Heintschel von Heinegg (1995b), p. 17.

Rule 125 San Remo Manual has similar wording as seen in Rule 134 of the HPCR Manual on the International Law Applicable to Air and Missile Warfare, written by the legal experts of the Program on Humanitarian Policy and Conflict Research at Harvard University. Both manuals in the following respect codify customary international law: if, after interception for the purpose of verification of the aircraft's identity,[85] reasonable grounds for suspecting still exist that a civilian aircraft is subject to capture, belligerent military aircraft have the right to order the civilian aircraft to proceed, for visit and search, to a belligerent airfield. This belligerent airfield has to fulfil certain further conditions, e.g. that it is safe for the type of aircraft involved.[86] If those conditions cannot be met by the reachable airfields, diversion is the alternative.

As an alternative to visit and search, Rule 119 San Remo Manual offers the belligerent the opportunity to divert neutral merchant vessels from their declared destination. So does rule 126 lit b San Remo Manual regarding the diversion of civilian aircraft. In both cases, the master of the neutral merchant vessel or civilian aircraft has to explain his consent to be diverted. A belligerent using this option avoids the risk to let a neutral merchant vessel contribute to his enemy's war efforts and the effort attached to a visit and search operation. The neutral merchant vessel avoids the inconvenience of a visit and search and maybe even a subsequent capture. Thus, assuming the necessary approval of both parties involved, the norm solely codifies a win-win situation. Rule 126 lit a San Remo Manual denies the precondition of consent regarding enemy civilian aircraft.

Neutral merchant ships travelling alone are subject to visit and search in any case.[87] An exception from the general rule that neutral merchant ships are generally subject to visit and search is stated in Rule 120 San Remo Manual. According to the Manual, a neutral vessel is exempt from visit and search if it is bound for a neutral port and under the convoy of an accompanying neutral warship of the same nationality as that of the vessel or a neutral warship of a State with which the flag State of the merchant vessel has concluded an agreement providing for such convoy. It is, however, doubtful that the content of Rule 120 has already transformed into customary international law. There may be a tendency to exempt neutral merchant vessels under neutral convoy from search, which is due to the fact that respective norms are incorporated in a number of treaties such as Articles 61 and 62 London Declaration or Article 34 German Prize Ordinance. Nevertheless, beginning in 1916, Great Britain has supported the view that neutral merchant vessels under convoy are subject to the right of visit and search and therefore hampered the creation of public international law due to contrary state practice.[88] Rule 127 San Remo Manual

---

[85]Program on Humanitarian Policy and Conflict Research at Harvard University (2013), rule 134, para 1.

[86]Program on Humanitarian Policy and Conflict Research at Harvard University (2013), rule 134, para 2.

[87]Kraska (2012), para 6.

[88]Heintschel von Heinegg (1995b), p. 18.

provides a similar regulation adjusted to the specifics of aircraft. With a glance at the difficulties determining the character of the norm regarding naval vessels, a clear determination of the character of Rule 127 San Remo Manual cannot be expected.

If a visit and search at sea is impossible or unsafe, a belligerent may, according to Rule 121 San Remo Manual, divert the merchant vessel to an appropriate area or port in order to exercise the right of visit and search. Regarding the latest developments related to modern naval warfare, this regulation may very well gain in importance. Aircraft, submerged submarines and unmanned naval vehicles can be used to divert vessels but cannot conduct visit and search operations.[89] Emerged submarines are always in great danger of being targeted.[90] Staying close to a suspicious merchant vessel for a longer lapse of time increases the danger of attack also for 'normal' warships[91] since a major part of a warship's defence strategy is to constantly keep moving. Taking these considerations into account, it comes as no surprise that numerous states adopted the practice of diverting merchant vessels to port to detain and search them there.[92] Since the merchant vessel in this case is being diverted in order to be visited and searched in a safe place, the merchant ship is under the obligation to obey.[93]

4.4.3   Measures of Supervision

For neutral merchantmen, diversion and detention entail considerable financial losses.[94] The belligerent, on the other side, is confronted with the choice either to permit 'goods to enter neutral ports, part of which are certainly destined to find their way to enemy hands, or to impose rigid controls upon such commerce at risk of interfering on occasion with what is undeniably legitimate neutral trade'[95]. In addition, it should be mentioned that the execution of visit and search operations is extremely complex. It requires a tremendous amount of organization and continuous training of personal. It is therefore only consequent that the San Remo Manual provides measures of supervision in order to diminish the necessity of visit and search operations and their respective disadvantages on both sides. The most successful system to prevent conflicts between neutrals and belligerents was the implementation of the so-called Navicerts during World War I.[96] These certifications were handed out after an inspection of the cargo in port if the cargo was verified as permissible.[97] The system was even extended in World War II and expanded by the so-called Ship's Warrant. A ship's warrant was handed out to ships, whose owner or

---

[89]Schulz (2014), p. 114.

[90]Ronzitti (2009), para 14.

[91]Heintschel von Heinegg (1995b), p. 19.

[92]Heintschel von Heinegg (1995b), p. 20.

[93]Doswald-Beck (1995), p. 199.

[94]Doswald-Beck (1995), p. 200; Heintschel von Heinegg (1995b), p. 20.

[95]Tucker (1957), p. 280.

[96]Colombos (1963), para 898.

[97]Colombos (1963), para 782.

charterer concluded an agreement with the Ministry of War Transport in London, confirming not to carry contraband or to conduct any trade whatsoever that would support the enemy's war effort.[98] Eventually, these systems laid the basis for Rule 122 San Remo Manual stating that in order to avoid the necessity of visit and search, belligerent States may establish reasonable measures for the inspection of cargo of neutral merchant vessels and certification that a vessel is not carrying contraband. By now, systems of certifications are implemented in various military manuals.[99] Nevertheless, this does not guarantee for unimpeded passage since the certification does not prohibit a belligerent from conducting a visit and search operation. Also, certifications issued by one belligerent do not have any effect on the opposing side.[100] The question whether the submission to such measures of supervision could be regarded as an 'un-neutral' service by the opposing belligerent was rejected by the round table experts in Rule 123 San Remo Manual.[101] Germany followed this opinion in its latest Manual edition.[102] Similar certifications, the so-called Aircerts, have been introduced for civilian aircraft.[103] Rules 132 to 134 San Remo Manual regarding measures of supervision of aircraft correspond with those on naval vessels.

4.4.4 Resistance to Visit and Search

Neutral merchant vessels are under the legal obligation to accept visit and search measures.[104] If neutral merchant vessels nevertheless (try to) resist, they face legal consequences. Regarding these consequences, the possible measures of resistance are crucial.

A neutral merchant vessel's resistance by the use of force triggers the right of self-defence of the warship. Furthermore, forceful resistance as an act of hostility renders the neutral merchant vessel, according to Article 63 London Declaration, liable to capture,[105] which is accepted as customary international law.[106] The mere flight from visit and search by contrast does not render the neutral merchant vessel open to capture. Warships are entitled to employ sufficient force only to stop the merchant vessel.[107]

Contrary to the neutral merchant vessel, it is accepted in customary international law that enemy merchant vessels are under no obligation to submit to visit and search, which makes perfect sense due to the fact that visit and search are the first

---

[98]Colombos (1963), para 783.

[99]Doswald-Beck (1995), p. 200; Bundesministerium der Verteidigung (2013), para 1237.

[100]Doswald-Beck (1995), p. 200.

[101]Doswald-Beck (1995), p. 200; Schaller (2015), para 24.

[102]Bundesministerium der Verteidigung (2013), para 1237.

[103]Schaller (2015), para 24.

[104]Ipsen (2014), para 9.

[105]Bundesministerium der Verteidigung (2013), para 1236; Oppenheim and Lauterpacht (1952), p. 856.

[106]Oppenheim and Lauterpacht (1952), p. 856.

[107]Heintschel von Heinegg (1995b), p. 19.

steps towards capture.[108] An enemy vessel may refuse visit and search and defend itself against the attempt with any means.[109] If possible, it may even sink the attacker or capture it.[110] On the other side of the coin, enemy merchant vessels that continuously and deliberately resist have to accept the consequences of their resistance, which is condemnation of the vessel and cargo.[111] Furthermore, the vessel becomes a legitimate military target and may therefore be destroyed without any prior warning.[112]

4.4.5   Capture/Seizure of Enemy Vessels or Aircraft

As rule of customary international law, codified in Rules 135 and 138 sentence 1 San Remo Manual, enemy merchant vessels and goods on board such vessels may generally be captured outside neutral waters[113] and enemy civilian aircraft outside neutral airspace as codified in Rules 141, 144 sentence 1 San Remo Manual by taking them as a prize for adjudication. Visit and search are not preconditions of a lawful capture.[114] The capture is finally complete when the vessel is under the control of the capturer.[115]

No exception is made for enemy merchant vessels that are surprised by the outbreak of hostilities in a belligerent port.[116] Indeed, in numerous cases, States granted belligerent merchant vessels a period of grace to leave their ports.[117] Nevertheless, a large number of States failed to ratify the codification of respective regulations in the Hague Convention (VI) Relating to the Status of Enemy Merchant Ships at the Outbreak of Hostilities.[118] Other major powers attached reservations or denounced the Convention before the outbreak of World War II.[119] Regarding this practice, it is obvious that the States remain on the position that they may grant enemy merchant vessels a period of grace to leave their ports but do not have to.[120] The case of vessels leaving one port in peacetime and entering another after the outbreak of hostilities without knowing may be, given today's possibilities of receiving information, regarded as obsolete.

According to Rule 136 San Remo Manual, which matches or is very similar to a variety of (draft) treaty provisions, certain enemy vessels still are exempt from

---

[108]Colombos (1963), para 884.

[109]Oppenheim and Lauterpacht (1952), p. 467.

[110]Colombos (1963), para 884.

[111]Heintschel von Heinegg (1995b), p. 18.

[112]Bundesministerium der Verteidigung (2013), paras 1029–1030.

[113]Doswald-Beck (1995), p. 205.

[114]Kraska (2012), para 21.

[115]Colombos (1963), para 903; Kraska (2012), para 26.

[116]Different: Bundesministerium der Verteidigung (2013), para 1028.

[117]With examples Oppenheim and Lauterpacht (1952), pp. 478–479.

[118]Hague VI (1907).

[119]Heintschel von Heinegg (1995b), p. 29.

[120]Rowson (1947), pp. 167–168.

capture. Those vessels have to refrain, however, from taking part in the hostilities.[121] In the case of any kind of participation, Rule 137 San Remo Manual constitutes the exception of the exception and re-subjects them to capture. In any other cases, the following vessels are exempt from capture:

- hospital ships[122] and small craft used for coastal rescue operations;[123]
- other medical transports,[124] as long as they are needed for the wounded, sick and shipwrecked on board;
- vessels granted safe conduct by agreement between belligerent parties, including cartel vessels[125] [. . .] and vessels engaged in humanitarian missions [. . .];
- vessels engaged in transporting cultural property under special protection;[126]
- vessels charged with religious, non-military scientific or philanthropic missions,[127] as long as they are not vessels collecting scientific data of likely military applications;
- small coastal fishing vessels and small boats engaged in local coastal trade,[128] although they are subject to the regulations of a belligerent naval commander operating in the area; and
- vessels designed or adapted exclusively for responding to pollution incidents in the marine environment when actually engaged in such activities.

As already mentioned above, and still applicable today, no general rule of exception exists for enemy mail boats.[129] Regarding enemy aircraft, there are corresponding rules exempting medical aircraft and aircraft granted safe conduct by agreement between the parties to the conflict from capture. However, although the above-enumerated vessels are exempt from capture, the inspection and search of the vessels, including hospital ships,[130] is still lawful.

Rule 138 San Remo Manual on the possibility of diversion according to military circumstances constitutes a proposal for progressive development by the round table experts.[131] The alternative to the capture of enemy merchant vessels in Rule 138 sentence 2 San Remo Manual is merely of declaratory nature. The enemy

---

[121]Heintschel von Heinegg (1995b), p. 30.

[122]Article 22, para 1 Geneva Convention II (1949); Oppenheim and Lauterpacht (1952), p. 479 f.

[123]Article 27, para 1 Geneva Convention II (1949); Heintschel von Heinegg (1995b), p. 31.

[124]Kraska (2012), para 33.

[125]Colombos (1963), para 660; Oppenheim and Lauterpacht (1952), p. 542.

[126]Article 14 Cultural Property Convention (1954); Heintschel von Heinegg (1995b), p. 30.

[127]Article 4 Hague XI (1907); Oppenheim and Lauterpacht (1952), pp. 476–477.

[128]Article 3, para. 1 Hague XI (1907); Oppenheim and Lauterpacht (1952), pp. 477–478.

[129]As already mentioned above: extensively on postal correspondence Tucker (1957), pp. 90–92; Oppenheim and Lauterpacht (1952), p. 480.

[130]Article 31, para. 1 Geneva Convention II (1949); de Oliveira Godinho (2009), para 18; Doswald-Beck (1995), p. 208.

[131]Doswald-Beck (1995), p. 209.

merchant vessel's diversion from its declared destination—if previously visited and searched and found liable to capture—is a voluntary refrain from the right of lawful capture.

As an exceptional measure, Rules 139 and 140 San Remo Manual grant the right to destroy—and sink—a captured enemy merchant vessel. This is only when military circumstances preclude taking or sending such a vessel for adjudication as an enemy prize. Once the property is transferred, the vessel is at the capturer's disposal anyway. Yet a precondition for the transfer is the decision of the responsible prize court. Leaving the choice between destruction and adjudication to the belligerent would undermine this principle.[132] Paying due regard to the exceptional character, some further criteria must be met, which according to Rule 139 San Remo Manual are the following:

- the safety of passengers and crew must be provided for;
- documents and papers relating to the prize are to be safeguarded; and
- personal effects of the passengers and crew must be saved, if feasible.

Taking the safety of the passengers seriously, ship's lifeboats are generally not regarded as a place of safety, except if land is close or another vessel will be able to take the passengers on board. The destruction of enemy passenger liners carrying only civilian passengers is for obvious reasons prohibited under all circumstances. If the capture of passenger vessels cannot be completed, diversion is the only permitted alternative. Looking at the codification in Rule 140 San Remo Manual and its broad implementation in State practice,[133] the tendency to allow destruction in nearly every case[134] did not gain acceptance. Rather, the exceptions have to be kept as narrow as possible.[135]

4.4.6 Capture/Seizure of Cargo on Board of Enemy Vessels or Aircraft

It was already stated in the Paris Declaration, and is still accepted today, that on board of enemy vessels neutral goods generally remain free from capture[136]—despite the fact that their determination as neutral may be difficult, as was explained above. The exceptions from the principle are goods that are contraband in character or goods that are found on board a vessel that is actively resisting visit and search or

---

[132]Oppenheim and Lauterpacht (1952), p. 487.

[133]Kraska (2012), para. 21; excluding enemy passenger vessels carrying only civilian passengers form destruction Bundesministerium der Verteidigung (2013), para 1040.

[134]Heintschel von Heinegg (1995b), p. 26 refers to state practice and the legal writing examples in Oppenheim and Lauterpacht (1952), p. 487.

[135]Heintschel von Heinegg (1995b), p. 26; Oppenheim and Lauterpacht (1952), p. 487; Colombos (1963), para 909 f.; Kraska (2012), para 24.

[136]Today see e.g. Bundesministerium der Verteidigung (2013), para 1035.

trying to breach a blockade.[137] Since these are the conditions under which also neutral vessels become liable to capture, the details may be discussed later.

In general, enemy goods are subject to capture. As some vessels are under special protection, even so are a variety of goods. Misleading is that the San Remo Manual lists protected goods only in its section VI under the headline 'capture of neutral merchant vessels and goods'. The Manual does not mention that also certain enemy goods are protected, such as the following:

- equipment exclusively intended for the treatment of wounded and sick members of armed forces or for the prevention of disease, provided that the particulars regarding their voyage have been notified to the adverse power and approved by the latter;[138]
- cultural property;[139]
- consignments of medical and hospital stores and objects necessary for religious worship intended only for civilians and consignments of essential foodstuffs, clothing and tonics intended for children under 15, expectant mothers and maternity cases;[140]
- consignments of foodstuffs, medical supplies and clothing, if the whole or part of the population of an occupied territory is inadequately supplied, as long as the consignments are in compliance with the conditions laid down by the occupying power;[141]
- instruments and other materials essential for the performance of the duties of relief societies;[142] and
- postal correspondence and information material of and for national Information Bureau for prisoners of war and a Central Prisoners of War Information Agency.[143]

Included in the protections are also the personal belongings of the crew and passengers of the captured vessel.[144] The protected status of postal correspondence cannot be regarded as customary international law. In fact, the State practice of World Wars I and II suggests that the belligerents are not willing to exempt postal correspondence from the application of contraband.[145]

---

[137] Heintschel von Heinegg (1995b), p. 32.

[138] Article 38, para 1 Geneva Covention II (1949); Article 29, para 1 London Declaration (1909).

[139] Article 14 Cultural Property Convention (1954).

[140] Article 23 Geneva Convention IV(1949).

[141] Article 59 Geneva Convention IV (1949); Heintschel von Heinegg (1995b), p. 32.

[142] Heintschel von Heinegg (1995b), p. 32.

[143] Articles 74 and 122 ff. Geneva Convention III (1949).

[144] Article 29, para 2 London Declaration (1909); Colombos (1963), para 685.

[145] Scheuner (1962a), p. 200.

4.4.7 Capture/Seizure of Neutral Vessels or Aircraft

Principally, neutral vessels are free from seizure, capture and destruction.[146] Under certain circumstances, they may, however, be liable to capture. This is if the neutral vessel

- carries contraband,[147]
- performs un-neutral service,[148]
- refuses and actively resists to visit and search,[149] or
- breaches a blockade and/or attempts respective breaches.[150]

Except one (see *supra* lit. e), all listed possible preconditions for the right to capture according to Rule 146 San Remo Manual (see *supra* lits. a–d, f) may be summed up under the above-named four options. Corresponding rules also exist for neutral civilian aircraft.[151] None of the enumerated activities, however, are a violation of international law. When performing these activities, the private neutral merchantmen become liable to the belligerents' right to prevent them from rendering assistance to the enemy.[152] The right to capture may therefore be considered as a legal consequence of a lawful action.

Regarding the consequences of the resistance to visit and search, reference may be made to the respective section above. With respect to attempts to and the breach of blockade, this topic is a sufficient content for another contribution and will therefore not be discussed in further detail.[153]

Rule 146 lit e San Remo Manual must be seen as critical. The principle of freedom of navigation continues to apply in wartime. The Commentary on the San Remo Manual now states: 'in the immediate area of naval operations, for example, in the vicinity of naval units, belligerents' security interests outweigh the freedom of navigation of neutral merchant shipping. If neutral merchant vessels do not comply with such orders they may be presumed to have enemy character or hostile intent and may thus be treated as if they were enemy ships, provided the orders were not given arbitrarily.'[154] However, the San Remo Manual itself in its Rule 105 clarifies that a belligerent cannot be absolved of its duties under international humanitarian law by establishing zones that might adversely affect the legitimate uses of defined areas of the sea. The exclusion of neutral shipping from the immediate area of operation

---

[146]Heintschel von Heinegg (1995b), p. 33; Doswald-Beck (1995), p. 213.

[147]Tucker (1957), p. 253; Rule 146 lit. a San Remo Manual (1995).

[148]Tucker (1957), p. 253; Rule 146 lit. b, c and d San Remo Manual (1995).

[149]Heintschel von Heinegg (1995b), p. 33.

[150]Tucker (1957), p. 253; Rule 146 lit. f San Remo Manual (1995).

[151]Rule 153 to 155 applying rules 148 to 150 also to neutral civilian aircraft.

[152]Tucker (1957), pp. 252–253, regarding contraband Doswald-Beck (1995), p. 201.

[153]Giving a substantial overview on subject: Heintschel von Heinegg (2015a).

[154]Doswald-Beck (1995), p. 202.

would indeed significantly lower possible hostile contacts.[155] Nevertheless, the mere presence of a vessel or aircraft within a declared zone does not automatically qualify it as hostile, and only in very unusual cases does it lead to the evaluation of the contact as legitimate military target.[156] Free-fire zones must not be allowed under any circumstances.[157] Indeed, the crucial issue is one of self-defence,[158] and the respective threshold may very well be lowered within a declared zone or the known area of operations, but some safeties must remain in place.

Considering the mentioned categories above, only the carrying of contraband and the performance of un-neutral service still require further examination.

4.4.7.1 Carriage of Contraband

The most important categories rendering neutral merchant vessels liable to capture is the carrying of contraband. The term contraband was primarily dealt with in the London Declaration.[159] As often, the devil is in the details.

Traditionally, a distinction was made between absolute and conditional contraband.[160] This distinction can be traced back to Grotius.[161] Later, Article 22 London Declaration enumerated certain items that without notice may be treated as contraband of war. Other items enumerated in Article 24 London Declaration that are susceptible to use in war, as well as for purposes of peace, constitute conditional contraband. Articles 27 to 29 London Declaration eventually established a third category of so-called free goods that may not be declared contraband of war. It did, however, not turn into customary international law.[162] Article 30 London Declaration endorsed the so-called doctrine of 'continuous voyage'.[163] Accordingly, absolute contraband is liable to capture if it is shown to be destined to a territory belonging to or occupied by the enemy or to the armed forces of the enemy. Doing so, it is immaterial whether the carriage of goods is direct or entails transhipment or a subsequent transport by land. Finally decisive, thereafter, shall be only the destination.[164] Conditional contraband according to Article 33 London Declaration generally is liable to capture only if it is shown to be destined for the use of armed forces or of a government department of the enemy State. Article 35 London Declaration then states that it is, however, only liable to capture when found on board a vessel bound for territory belonging to or occupied by the enemy or for the armed forces of the enemy, not when it is to be discharged in an intervening neutral

---

[155]O'Connell (1984), p. 1109.
[156]Heintschel von Heinegg (2015b), para 48.
[157]Dinstein (2010), p. 228.
[158]O'Connell (1984), p. 1110.
[159]Schaller (2015), para 7.
[160]Schaller (2015), para 11.
[161]Colombos (1963), para 760.
[162]Schaller (2015), para 11.
[163]Schaller (2015), para 14.
[164]Heintschel von Heinegg (1995b), p. 43.

port. Although the concept of contraband was applied by the belligerents during both world wars, the States' practice on contraband is anything but uniform.[165] Indeed, the belligerents soon stretched the scope of application of the rules designed to apply for absolute contraband to extend over the categories that, by the London Declaration, were classified as conditional contraband.[166] The British Government issued not less than 15 contraband lists during World War I. Whereas the first lists of August 1914 nearly matched the standards of the London Declaration, the latest list included 248 items categorised as absolute and conditional contraband.[167] Other major belligerents of the war, including France and Germany, followed suit.[168] Raw materials, foodstuffs, fuels of any kind, as well as money and gold, were declared absolute contraband.[169] Hall therefore set up the theory 'that the articles composing it [contraband] must vary with the circumstances of particular cases [. . .]. There can be no question that many articles, of use alike in peace and war, may occasionally be as essential to the prosecution of hostilities as are arms themselves; and the ultimate basis of the prohibition of arms is that they are essential.'[170] Regarding the State practice, it comes as no surprise that Hall's assumption found approval in legal literature.[171]

Today, contraband can be defined according to Rule 148 San Remo Manual, which in this respect clearly codifies customary international law. Contraband thereafter is defined as goods that are ultimately destined for territory under the control of the enemy and that may be susceptible for use in armed conflict.[172] According to Rule 149 San Remo Manual, publishing a contraband list is a mandatory precondition for the right of capture to apply. Thereby, the contraband list may vary according to the particular circumstances of the armed conflict but shall be reasonably specific. And indeed, parties to an armed conflict usually supply contraband lists to one another and to neutral States, enumerating what they consider to be contraband. With respect to the majority of captureable goods, the rule may be regarded as codification of customary international law.[173] Nevertheless, the commentary on the San Remo Manual acknowledges views in favour of the right to capture munitions without mentioning them in a contraband list, as long as they are obviously intended for military use.[174] It is therefore difficult to decide with certainty

---

[165]Scheuner (1962b), p. 291; Colombos (1963), para 760; Schaller (2015), para 9.

[166]Colombos (1963), para 776; giving an broad overview regarding the different practice Heintschel von Heinegg (1995b), p. 43 f.

[167]Colombos (1963), para 776.

[168]Heintschel von Heinegg (1995b), p. 44.

[169]Scheuner (1962b), p. 291.

[170]Hall and Higgins (1924), p. 781.

[171]Colombos (1963), para 776; Heintschel von Heinegg (1995b), p. 44.

[172]Colombos (1963), para 760; Tucker (1957), p. 263.

[173]Schaller (2015), para 16.

[174]Doswald-Beck (1995), p. 216.

whether Rule 149 has been established as 'customary international law or whether it merely reflects a long-standing factual tradition'.[175]

Goods, as it is stated in Rule 150 San Remo Manual, not on the belligerent's contraband list are so-called free goods. Those goods are not subject to capture. According to Rule 150, as a minimum, 'free goods', including so-called truly free goods,[176] are as follows:

- religious objects;
- articles intended exclusively for the treatment of the wounded and sick and for the prevention of disease;
- clothing, bedding, essential foodstuffs and means of shelter for the civilian population (for women and children in particular), as long as no serious reason is given to believe that such goods will be diverted to other purposes or that a definite military advantage would accrue to the enemy by their substitution for enemy goods that would thereby become available for military purposes; and
- items destined for prisoners of war, including individual parcels and collective relief shipments containing food, clothing, educational, cultural and recreational articles.

Also exempt from capture are the following:

- goods otherwise specifically exempted from capture by international treaty or by special arrangement between belligerents; and
- other goods not susceptible for use in armed conflict.

Since it is, under international law, up to the belligerents to exempt certain goods by bi- or multilateral treaty or agreement, this regulation seems to be a mere declaratory statement. Regarding goods not susceptible for use in armed conflict, there is no need for capture since the purpose of the right to capture is to prevent the rendering of any kind of assistance or support to the enemy. The question that arises here again is which goods are surely not susceptible for use in armed conflict. It once again has to be answered with due respect to Hall's assumption that the evaluation 'must vary with the circumstances of particular cases'.

4.4.7.2 Un-neutral Service

With respect to the performance of un-neutral service, at first the term itself has to be defined. Indeed, the States' practice with regard to un-neutral service and its consequences cannot be regarded as uniform.[177] Well established are the rights of belligerents to prevent neutral merchant vessels from transporting belligerent troops,

---

[175]Schaller (2015), para 16.
[176]Doswald-Beck (1995), p. 217.
[177]Schramm (1913), pp. 251–253.

as well as from transmitting information for the belligerent's opponent.[178] The enumeration of Rule 146 lits. b and c San Remo Manual presents examples that may be regarded as un-neutral, naming the transport of belligerent troops (lit. b) or the operation directly under enemy control, orders, charter, employment or direction (lit. c), though not in support of the belligerent's military operations at sea. A similar general distinction was previously conducted in Article 46 London Declaration. Nevertheless, taking into account the different possible intensities of un-neutral service—meaning in particular the effect on the respective belligerent's war effort—a more sophisticated distinction of un-neutral service and its respective legal consequences seems appropriate, despite the difficulties in State practice.

Due to their highest possible support of the belligerent's war effort, vessels directly participating in the military operations of a belligerent, vessels acting in any capacity as a naval or military auxiliary to a belligerent's armed forces and vessels travelling under convoy of a belligerent warship render neutral vessels in any case liable to capture. Furthermore, if necessary, they may be attacked and sunk on sight, which is only logical since they perform the same acts as warships and must therefore share their fate.[179]

The intensity of the contribution to the belligerent's war effort by operating directly under the control, orders, charter, employment or direction of a belligerent government is less intense than in the preceding category. Therefore, those contributions do not render vessels liable to destruction. Regarding their performance, which is the one of an enemy merchant vessel, it justifies a liability to capture and the same treatment as enemy merchant vessels.[180] Vessels carrying enemy persons or dispatches are liable to capture,[181] whereby on the details there again is only an uncertain State practice.[182]

The acceptance of Ship's Warrant or Navicert is not regarded as un-neutral service, as stated in Rule 123 San Remo Manual and explained above.[183]

4.4.7.3 Consequences of the Exceptional Liability to Capture of Neutral Vessels or Aircraft

The capture of a neutral merchant vessel is exercised by taking the respective vessel as prize for adjudication,[184] codified in Rule 146 sentence 2 San Remo Manual.

Again, for certain cases, an exceptional right is granted for the destruction of captured neutral merchant vessels. Rule 151 San Remo Manual does so; it is almost equally worded as Rule 139, which codifies the exceptional right of the destruction

---

[178]Heintschel von Heinegg (1995b), p. 37.

[179]Tucker (1957), pp. 329–330.

[180]Tucker (1957), p. 322.

[181]Oppenheim and Lauterpacht (1952), pp. 833–835; Schramm (1913), pp. 251–253.

[182]Going into the details regarding the mentioned uncertain state practice Tucker (1957), pp. 325–327.

[183]Different: Heintschel von Heinegg (1995b), p. 40.

[184]Heintschel von Heinegg (1995b), p. 34.

of enemy vessels in very limited cases. Rule 151 para. 2 San Remo Manual establishes further restrictions. The destruction should not be ordered without there being complete certainty that the captured vessel can be neither sent into a belligerent port nor diverted nor properly released. Furthermore, a vessel may not be destroyed for carrying contraband unless the contraband, reckoned either by value, weight, volume or freight, forms more than half the cargo. Nevertheless, as an exceptional measure, the destruction according to customary international law is legitimate. Once finally destroyed, the destruction is subject to adjudication by the competent prize court.[185]

Similarities also exist between Rule 140 San Remo Manual on enemy passenger vessels and Rule 152 on the destruction of captured neutral passenger vessels. Rule 152 codifies the prohibition of the destruction of captured neutral passenger vessels carrying civilian passengers at sea. The specification that the vessel, for the safety of the passengers, shall be diverted to port to complete capture indicates that the possibilities for a proper evacuation of all passengers at sea are evaluated in general as insufficient. This is only consequent in view of the fact that warships are rather unsuitable to take a considerable number of passengers on board and to transfer them to safety. However, after the disembarkation of the passengers to a place of safety, the destruction is not prohibited.[186]

4.4.8 Capture/Seizure of Cargo on Board of Neutral Vessels and Aircraft

Goods on board neutral merchant vessels are, according to Rule 147 San Remo Manual, subject to capture only if they are contraband. This rule was constituted in the 1856 Paris Declaration declaring that '[t]he neutral flag covers enemy's goods, with the exception of contraband of war'. No question arises in the case of contraband as discussed extensively above.[187] This implies that, in principle, all other goods on board neutral merchant vessels are exempt from capture. A crucial exception, however, is the fate of the cargo tied in a way to the character of the transporting vessel. Regarding the forcible resisting against visit and search by a neutral merchant vessel, the State practice is not uniform. Whereas British prize courts take a clear position in generally condemning respective cargo regardless of its contraband character, American prize courts do not always do so.[188] The German Prize Ordinance, according to Articles 12 and 37 para. 2, declares neutral cargo, regardless of its contraband character, only subject to condemnation if it belongs to the master or owner of the vessel.

---

[185]Doswald-Beckl (1995), p. 219.

[186]Doswald-Beck (1995), p. 219.

[187]The question here lies in the exact definition of the term contraband.

[188]Heintschel von Heinegg (1995b), p. 41.

4.5   Prize Court Proceedings

If the belligerents have successfully finished a capture or seizure, it does not, however, constitute the end of the related proceedings. If, under certain preconditions, the destruction of the prize may be lawful without previously presenting the case to a prize court, this, however, does not constitute an exception to the principle that a prize court proceeding is required. In fact, the destruction is, as extensively discussed above, firstly, only an exceptional measure; secondly, tied to very narrow preconditions; and thirdly, subject to an adjudication by a prize court.

4.5.1   The General Rule of Prize Court Proceedings

After the successful capture, the concerned merchant vessel and its goods generally have to be transferred to a port.[189] The master and crew can assist the capturer in navigating the prize into port, but they may not be compelled to do so.[190] Taking into account the factors influencing maritime operations such as time, distance, weather, and security and safety matters, a good argument can be made that the master of the captor has certain discretion in selecting the prize court.[191] Regarding the weight of the interference with freedom of navigation, the duration of search, diversion or detention must, on the other, side be kept as short as possible.[192] Comparable rules must be applied on aircraft paying due regard to their specifics.

The lawful capture does not necessarily lead to condemnation by the prize court, and the lawfulness of the capture does not depend upon later condemnation.[193] By customary international law, the transfer of private to state property in prize law cases has to be subject to a proper trial.[194] Hence, it requires a prize court decision for the property to eventually pass from the private owner to the capturer.[195]

Prize courts may be established on the sovereign territory of the capturing State or his allies. They may also be established on board of a warship of the capturer or his allies within the territory of the capturer or his allies. Not conclusively solved is the question whether prize courts may be established on board warships on the high seas. Colombos sees no objections against such prize courts.[196] It is, however, to be taken into consideration that the sovereignty of a State over its land territory and territorial waters is genuine, whereas warships, as artificial platforms, only derive their sovereignty from their respective State. It is therefore at least arguable that prize courts on board of warships cannot provide a comparable legitimacy on the high seas

---

[189]Colombos (1963), para 925.

[190]Tucker (1957), p. 347.

[191]In favour of a wide discretion Kraska (2012), para 9; more restrictive Tucker (1957), p. 348.

[192]Heintschel von Heinegg (1995b), p. 22; Colombos (1963), para 893.

[193]Tucker (1957), p. 346.

[194]Colombos (1963), para 925; Scheuner (1962a), p. 201.

[195]Oppenheim and Lauterpacht (1952), pp. 474–475; Kraska (2012), para 26; Tucker (1957), p. 347.

[196]Colombos (1963), para 926.

as prize courts can on land or in territorial waters. There is complete agreement that prize courts may not be established on neutral territory or within neutral territorial waters.[197] Despite the fact that prize courts could be legitimately established, none has been established under national law in recent times,[198] owing to lack of necessity.

A characteristic of the prize courts is that they are national courts applying international prize law and national law.[199] States, consequently, have established prize courts in very different ways. Some States integrated their prize courts within their regular judicial system, some established administrative tribunals and others created independent prize courts.[200] The applied international law may be codified in national legislation or reflected in authority and jurisdiction, as long as they are in accordance with international law.[201] The court has to investigate the circumstances of the capture and, based on the evidence, has to decide whether there is sufficient cause for the final condemnation of the vessel, its cargo or both.[202]

The fact that national prize court proceedings are subject to national legislation and proceedings is its core criticism.[203] Thus, it comes as no surprise that proposals for the creation of an international prize court were made in the eighteenth century.[204] They found their manifestation in the Hague Convention (XII) Relative to the Creation of an International Prize Court.[205] The international prize court would have been a court of appeal against judgments of the national prize courts.[206] An international prize court, however, was for several reasons never established.[207]

Remarkably, the authority of the prize court does not dissolve with the end of the armed conflict. In fact, prize courts are authorised to handle all prize law matters related to the hostilities until these matters are finally solved.[208] Looking at peace treaties, it is at the liberty of States to include regulations that touch issues of prize law practice of the previous war, as it, e. g., happened in Article 440 of the Treaty of Versailles.[209,210] Thereby, such treaties and the respective regulations today would

---

[197]Colombos (1963), para 927.

[198]Roach (2015), para 24.

[199]Schramm (1913), p. 368.

[200]Schramm (1913), pp. 370–371; Kraska (2012), para 9.

[201]Kraska (2012), para 9.

[202]Tucker (1957), pp. 347–348.

[203]Colombos (1963), para 961.

[204]Schindler and Toman (2004), p. 1093.

[205]Hague XII (1907).

[206]Schindler and Toman (2004), p. 1093.

[207]Roach (2015), para 24.

[208]Colombos (1963), para 688; Schramm (1913), p. 379.

[209]Treaty of Versailles (1919).

[210]Giving an overview how different peace treaties dealt with the matter previous prize court decisions Colombos (1963), para 689.

be subject to the Vienna Convention on the Law of Treaties[211] and especially subject to the regulations of section 2 on the invalidity of treaties.[212]

4.5.2 Consequences of Improper Exercise of Rights

Release of the supposed prize is the consequence, if the evidence presented to the prize court is not found to be sufficient to justify condemnation. If at the moment of the capture the capturer had adequate reasons to conclude that he would be entitled to capture, he is nevertheless not liable to claims for cost or damages. If the capturer had no sufficient suspicion and the capture is then found unlawful, then the capturer is liable for the respective claims.[213] If the duration of search, diversion or detention is longer than necessary, the interference in the voyage of a ship was unnecessary, or the diversion of the ship was unjustified, the prize court has to award damages.[214] A claim for damages, however, cannot be based solely on the mere suffering of inconvenience.[215]

If for any reason the capturer does not submit the case to the court, the private owner can demand the prize court to bring about a final decision. If the capturer does not promote the trial, the court is furthermore, on request of the claimant, entitled to order the release of the property and its surrender.[216] The same goes for captors who intentionally choose to bring proceedings to a prize court of which it is known that it does not pay due regard to the vessel owners' and cargo shippers' right to appear in defence of their property.[217]

5   Concluding Remarks

The roots of prize law and the law of contraband have been explained and their development shown. The core rules of prize law, identified to be customary international law, date as far back as the Paris Declaration of 1856.

Within an armed conflict, which is a precondition for the application of prize law, only civilian vessels or aircraft can be subject to prize law. This crucial distinction, if vessels or aircraft are of neutral or enemy character, usually is made on the basis of the flag that the ship flies or the marks that the aircraft carries. Flying the enemy flag is conclusive evidence of a vessel's enemy character. Regarding vessels flying neutral flags, the prima facie evidence of its neutral character can be rebutted. The ship's registration, ownership, charter or other criteria may be additional evidence. On the issue of the invalidity of the transfer of the flag shortly before the outbreak of

---

[211]Vienna Convention on the Law of Treaties (1969).

[212]On the customary law status of this section of the treaty Kohen and Heathcote (2011), p. 1017.

[213]Tucker (1957), p. 346.

[214]Colombos (1963), para 893; Heintschel von Heinegg (1995b), p. 22.

[215]Heintschel von Heinegg (1995b), p. 22; Colombos (1963), para 893 f.

[216]Colombos (1963), para 925.

[217]Kraska (2012), para 9.

hostilities, a set customary international law does not yet exist; however, very strong tendencies are recognizable. In terms of the character of the goods on board, it is generally tied to the character of the vessel or aircraft, but this distinction remains rebuttable.

Only warships and military aircraft are entitled to conduct visit and search operations and capture of enemy and neutral merchant vessels or civilian aircraft outside neutral waters. It is a tendency, rather than a rule of customary international law, to exempt neutral vessels or aircraft under convoy of neutral warships or military aircraft. Under certain conditions, a diversion of the merchant vessel is possible. In certain cases, due to safety reasons regarding civilian passengers and crew, diversion, in order to conduct the visit and search operation at a safe place, remains the only lawful option. As for aircraft, due to their operational nature, they cannot be visited and searched in flight, and therefore they must be diverted to an airfield for the procedure to be executed.

Regarding measures to reduce the necessity of visit and search operations for the belligerents and to reduce the interference with neutral shipping and air traffic for neutrals, the so-called Navicerts or Aircerts and the so-called Ship's Warrant have shown to be effective. Nevertheless, they do not guarantee unimpeded passage, and certifications issued by one belligerent do not have any effect on the opposing side.

Enemy vessels, aircraft and goods on board such vessels and aircraft may generally be captured outside neutral waters or airspace. Some enemy vessels and goods are nevertheless exempt from capture, either by conventional or customary international law, due to the fact that they serve special functions.

Neutral vessels and aircraft and goods on board such vessels or aircraft are principally immune from capture. They become, however, liable to capture if they carry contraband, perform un-neutral service, refuse and actively resist to visit and search, breach a blockade or attempt respective breaches. The definition of 'contraband' today is, according to Rule 148 San Remo Manual and accepted in customary international law, 'goods which are ultimately destined for territory under the control of the enemy and which may be susceptible for use in armed conflict'. The practice to distribute contraband lists to each other and to neutral States enumerating what the belligerents consider to be contraband, as seen in World Wars I and II, is accepted as customary international law. Considering the fact that contraband lists may vary according to the particular circumstances of the armed conflict, they shall, according to Rule 149 San Remo Manual, be reasonably specific. This 'shall', however, highlight how broad the definition of contraband can be. Except for arms and munitions, there is still no agreement on what articles constitute contraband.

The prize proceedings are concluded only by the adjudication of the respective prize court. It requires its decision for the private neutral or enemy property to eventually pass to the capturer. Not even an exceptional destruction of the prize before the prize court's decision hinders the prize court to eventually decide if the capture was legal at the time of capture.

In conclusion, it can be stated that a general agreement on the above-mentioned core rules of prize law and law of contraband exists; however, there remains some debate as to the specific details. Nevertheless, these core rules are sufficient to govern the legal issue and to provide a practicable framework of international law.

References

Bederman DJ (2009) Privateering. In: Wolfrum R (ed) Max Planck encyclopedia of public international law. OUP, Oxford

Bothe M (2013) Friedenssicherung und Kriegsrecht. In: Vitzthum W, Proelß A (eds) Völkerrecht. De Gruyter, Berlin, pp 639–740

Bundesministerium der Verteidigung (2013) Zentrale Dienstvorschrift (ZDv) 15/2 - Humanitäres Völkerrecht in bewaffneten Konflikten – Handbuch. Bundesministerium der Verteidigung, Berlin

Colombos CJ (1963) Internationales Seerecht, German edn. C.H. Beck, München

Cultural Property Convention (1954) Convention for the Protection of Cultural Property in the Event of an Armed Conflict, adopted May 14th 1954, 249 UNTS 240

de Oliveira Godinho F (2009) Hospital ships. In: Wolfrum R (ed) Max Planck encyclopedia of public international law. OUP, Oxford

Dinstein Y (2005) War, aggression and self-defence, 4th edn. CUP, Cambridge

Dinstein Y (2010) The conduct of hostilities under the law of international armed conflict, 2nd edn. CUP, Cambridge

Doswald-Beck L (ed) (1995) Commentary on the San Remo manual on international law applicable to armed conflicts at Sea. Cambridge University Press, Cambridge

Fink MD (2010) The right of visit for warships: some challenges in applying the law of maritime interdiction on the high seas. Mil Law Law War Rev 49:7–45

Fleck D (2015) London Naval Conference (1908–1909). In: Wolfrum R (ed) Max Planck encyclopedia of public international law. OUP, Oxford

Geneva Convention II (1949) for the Amelioration of the Condition of the Wounded, Sick and Shipwrecked Members of the Armed Forces at Sea, adopted August 12th 1949, 75 UNTS 31

Geneva Convention III (1949) Relative to the treatment of prisoners of war, adopted August 12th 1949, 75 UNTS 135

Geneva Convention IV (1949) Relative to the protection of civilian persons in time of war, adopted August 12th 1949, 75 UNTS 287

Hague VI (1907) Hague Convention (VI.) Relating to the status of enemy merchant ships at the outbreak of hostilities, adopted October 18th 1907, 2 AJIL, Supplement: Official Documents (1908)

Hague XI (1907) Hague Convention (XI.) Relative to certain restrictions with regard to the exercise of the right of capture in Naval War, adopted October 18th 1907, 2 AJIL, Supplement: Official Documents (1908)

Hague XII (1907) Hague Convention (XII.) Relative to the creation of an International Prize Court, adopted October 18th 1907, 2 AJIL, supplement: official documents (1908), pp 174–202

Hague XIII (1907) Hague Convention (XIII.) Concerning the rights and duties of neutral powers in Naval War, adopted October 18th 1907, 2 AJIL, supplement: official documents (1908), pp 202–216

Hall WE, Higgins AP (eds) (1924) A treatise on international law, 8th edn. Clarendon Press, Oxford

Harris DJ (2004) Cases and materials on international law. Sweet & Maxwell, London

Heintschel von Heinegg W (1995a) Seekriegsrecht und Neutralität im Seekrieg. Duncker & Humblot, Berlin

Heintschel von Heinegg W (ed) (1995b) Visit, search, diversion and capture. In: Bochumer Schriften zur Friedenssicherung und zum Humanitären Völkerrecht, vol 24. UVB Universitätsverlag Dr. N. Brockmeyer, Bochum

Heintschel von Heinegg W (2014) Internationales öffentliches Seerecht (Seevölkerrecht). In: Ipsen K (ed) Völkerrecht. C.H. Beck, München, pp 861–928

Heintschel von Heinegg W (2015a) Blockade. In: Wolfrum R (ed) Max Planck encyclopedia of public international law. OUP, Oxford

Heintschel von Heinegg W (2015b) War zones. In: Wolfrum R (ed) Max Planck encyclopedia of public international law. OUP, Oxford

Ipsen K (2014) Bewaffneter Konflikt und Neutralität. In: Ipsen K (ed) Völkerrecht. C.H. Beck, München, pp 1175–1258

Kleffner JK (2014) Scope of application of international humanitarian law. In: Fleck D (ed) The handbook of international humanitarian law. OUP, Oxford

Kohen M, Heathcote S (2011) Article 42 convention of 1969. In: Corten O, Klein P (eds) The Vienna convention on the law of treaties – a commentary. Oxford University Press, Oxford, pp 1015–1028

Kraska J (2012) Prize law. In: Wolfrum R (ed) Max Planck encyclopedia of public international law. OUP, Oxford

Kraska J (2015) Military operations. In: Rothwell DR, Elferink AGO, Scott KN, Stephens T (eds) The Oxford handbook of the law of the sea. OUP, Oxford, pp 866–887

Lagoni R (2011) Merchant ship. In: Wolfrum R (ed) Max Planck encyclopedia of public international law. OUP, Oxford

London Declaration (1909) Declaration concerning the Laws of Naval Warfare, signed February 26th 1909, 3 AJIL, Supplement: Official Documents (1909), pp 179–220

London Protocol (1936) adopted November 6th 1936, 31 AJIL, Supplement: Official Documents (1937), pp 137–139

Lowe I, Tzanakopoulos A (2013) Economic warfare. In: Wolfrum R (ed) Max Planck encyclopedia of public international law. OUP, Oxford

O'Connell DP (1984) In: Shearer IA (ed) The international law of the sea, vol 2. Oxford, Clarendon Press

Oppenheim L, Lauterpacht H (1952) International law, vol II, 7th edn. Longmans, Green & Co., London

Oxford Manual (1913) Manual of the laws of Naval War. Oxford, 9 August 1913, https://ihl-databases.icrc.org/ihl/INTRO/265?OpenDocument. Accessed 27 Oct 2017

Paris Declaration (1856) Declaration respecting maritime law, adopted April 16th 1856, 1 AJIL, Supplement: Official Documents (1907)

Prisenordnung (1939) Deutsche Prisenordnung vom 28.08.1939, Reichsgesetzblatt 1939 I, p 1585. http://www.u-boote-online.de/krieg/prisenordnung/priseno/inhalt.php. Accessed 27 Oct 2017

Program on Humanitarian Policy and Conflict Research at Harvard University (2009) HPCR manual on the international law applicable to air and missile warfare

Program on Humanitarian Policy and Conflict Research at Harvard University (2013) Commentary on the HPCR manual on the international law applicable to air and missile warfare. CUP, New York

Roach JA (2000) The law of naval warfare at the turn of two centuries. Am J Int Law 94:64–77

Roach JA (2015) Neutrality in naval warfare. In: Wolfrum R (ed) Max Planck encyclopedia of public international law. OUP, Oxford

Roberts A, Guelff R (eds) (2000) Documents on the law of war

Ronzitti N (2009) Naval warfare. In: Wolfrum R (ed) Max Planck encyclopedia of public international law. OUP, Oxford

Rowson WD (1947) Prize law during the Second World War. Br Year B Int Law 24:160–215

San Remo Manual on International Law Applicable to Armed Conflicts at Sea (1995) Available on the Homepage of the ICRC: https://www.icrc.org/ihl/INTRO/560?OpenDocument, latest visit July 10th, 2017

Schaller C (2015) Contraband. In: Wolfrum R (ed) Max Planck encyclopedia of public international law. OUP, Oxford

Scheuner (1962a) Beuterecht im Seekrieg. In: Schlochauer H-J (ed) Wörterbuch des Völkerrechts, vol 1, 2nd edn. De Gruyter, Berlin, pp 199–201

Scheuner (1962b) Konterbandrecht. In: Schlochauer H-J (ed) Wörterbuch des Völkerrechts, vol 2, 2nd edn. De Gruyter, Berlin, p 291

Schindler D, Toman J (eds) (2004) The laws of armed conflicts. Brill-Nijhoff, Leiden

Schramm (1913) Das Prisenrecht in seiner neuesten Gestalt. Ernst Siegfried Mittler und Sohn, Berlin

Schulz M (2014) Autonomie zur See. In: Frau R (ed) Drohnen und das Recht. Mohr Siebeck, Tübingen, pp 103–118

Treaty of Versailles (1919) Treaty of Peace with Germany, adopted June 28th 1919, 1 ATS 1, https://www.loc.gov/law/help/us-treaties/bevans/m-ust000002-0043.pdf. Accessed 27 Oct 2017

Treves T (2009) High seas. In: Wolfrum R (ed) Max Planck encyclopedia of public international law. OUP, Oxford

Tucker RW (1957) The law of war and neutrality at sea. US Government Printing Office, Washington, DC

UN Charter (1945) Charter of the United Nations, adopted June 26th 1945, UN Conference on International Organization Doc., vol XV (1945), p 335

UNCLOS (1982) United Nations Convention on the Law of the Sea, adopted December 10th 1982, 1833 UNTS 3

Vienna Convention on the Law of Treaties (1969) Adopted May 23rd 1969, 1155 UNTS 331, https://treaties.un.org/doc/publication/unts/volume%201155/volume-1155-i-18232-english.pdf. Accessed 27 Oct 2017

Vitzthum W (2006) Kapitel 1. Begriff, Geschichte und Rechtsquellen des Seerechts. In: Vitzthum W (ed) Handbuch des Seerechts. C.H. Beck, München

von Schmeling E (2014) Rechtsprobleme des Einsatzes von unbemannten 'Kriegsschiffen'. Neue Zeitschrift für Wehrrecht 56:235–254

Wehberg H (1915) Das Seekriegsrecht. In: Stier-Somlo (ed) Handbuch des Völkerrechts, vol 6. Kohlhammer, Stuttgart

Wolfrum R (2006) Kapitel 4. Hohe See und Tiefseeboden (Gebiet). In: Vitzthum W (ed) Handbuch des Seerechts. C.H. Beck, München

Marcel Schulz studied law at the European University Viadrina in Frankfurt (Oder), Germany, and at the University of Essex in Colchester, England. He focused his studies on Public International Law, especially on Humanitarian Law, the Law of the Sea and the Law of the European Union. From 2012 to 2015, he worked as research assistant for the Chair of Public Law, especially Public International Law, at the European University Viadrina. During his legal clerkship, Schulz, inter alia, worked for the Committee of Foreign Affairs of the German Federal Parliament (Deutscher Bundestag) and the Federal Ministry of Defence. Since September 2015, he has been a political adviser of the parliamentary group of the German Social Democratic Party (SPD) at the legislative assembly of the Federal German State of Brandenburg.

The Right of Visit of Foreign-Flagged Vessels on the High Seas in Non-international Armed Conflict

Martin Fink

Abstract

This chapter presents three theories on the use of the right of visit during non-international armed conflicts. The belligerent right of visit and search, which is part of the laws of naval warfare, applies only in international armed conflict. Current conflicts are, however, more often non-international in character. Viewed within this context, the non-existence of a right of visit during a non-international armed conflict may present itself as a legal gap in the operational need for States to board foreign-flagged vessels. The three theories could serve as a departure for discussion whether there may be sufficient legal grounds to apply the right of visit in a non-international armed conflict.

1   Introduction

It is often opined that most of today's armed conflicts have the character of a non-international armed conflict (NIAC). The law applicable to NIACs will regulate military operations undertaken in such conflicts. When applied to the maritime dimension, one interesting legal point that comes to the fore is the view that the laws of naval warfare do not apply in non-international armed conflict.[1] In particular, this means that the belligerent right of visit and search cannot be used during a NIAC. From an operational point of view, this is unfortunate because the ability to visit a foreign-flagged vessel without requesting beforehand consent of the flag State

---

[1]Heintschel von Heinegg (2015), p. 375.

M. Fink (✉)
Royal Netherlands Navy, University of Amsterdam, Amsterdam, Netherlands
e-mail: finkmd@hotmail.com

This is a U.S. government work and its text is not subject to copyright protection in the United States; however, its text may be subject to foreign copyright protection 2018
J. Schildknecht et al. (eds.), *Operational Law in International Straits and Current Maritime Security Challenges*, Operational Maritime Law 1,
https://doi.org/10.1007/978-3-319-72718-9_13

is a powerful legal instrument in the toolbox of belligerent States. In the recent past, practice, such as the naval operations conducted within the context of Operation *Enduring Freedom* (OEF) and Operation *Active Endeavour* (OAE), has grappled with this issue of non-existence of a belligerent right of visit and search in NIACs. This has led to different *modus operandi* by warships of participating States with regard to visit and search during these operations.[2]

Within general international law, there are different legal possibilities that would allow for boarding a foreign-flagged vessel during a NIAC outside the legal regime of the laws of armed conflict. Examples are (*ad hoc*) flag state consent, international agreements and UN Security Council resolutions that adopt such authority. All of these examples, however, depend on another party or institution to consent with or allow the boarding of foreign-flagged vessels. In the last decade, some thoughts may have also developed on the right of visit based on the law of self-defence and within the context of the law of armed conflict. But they are not fully developed. By way of food for thought on this issue, this chapter briefly presents three theories on the right of visit during non-international armed conflict that are based on either the *ius in bello* or the *ius ad bellum*.

2   Three Theories for Ship Boarding During a NIAC

Of the three theories that will be noted here, one theory is argued from the context of the *ius in bello*. The two other theories are argued within the context of the law of self-defence. The emergence of the latter two theories has in the first place been made possible due to the evolution of the scope of the law of self-defence. In the traditional sense, an armed attack from a State against another State can trigger the right of a State to defend itself. In the State's reaction against such attack, the use of force use can fulfil the conditions of an international armed conflict. Subsequently, the belligerent right of visit and search applies to the conflict. In the context of a non-international armed conflict, the right to invoke the right of self-defence is firstly premised on the view that an armed attack can also be initiated by a non-State actor. This view has gained much recognition, in particular after the practice of using self-defence as a legal basis after the 9–11 attacks and subsequently for military operations in Afghanistan and during the 2006 conflict between Israel and Hezbollah in Lebanon.[3] This helped support the view that a NIAC could exist not only between a State and non-State actors on its own territory, but also between a State and non-State actors that are on another territory. Accepting this view, and also fulfilling the conditions to consider that the use of force as a reaction to the armed attack by a non-State actor would amount to a non-international armed conflict, leads to the view that armed conflict can be waged against non-State actors outside of one's own State. In the maritime dimension during a NIAC, there are, however, no rules that

---

[2]Fink (2016), pp. 213–218.
[3]Amongst these scholars are Gill, Dinstein and Bethlehem.

regulate the boarding of vessels on the high seas. This leads to the second point of discussion in the evolution of self-defence, namely the debate on the geographical scope of self-defence. In the same vein, the debate can be moved into the maritime dimension in which it will be a discussion between the geographical scope of self-defence and the exclusive jurisdiction of a flag State over its vessels. In sum, the evolution of the law of self-defence has given more room to argue the existence of a right of visit of foreign-flagged vessels during a non-international armed conflict. In the next paragraphs, I will briefly point out these arguments by means of three theories.

2.1   Theory One: Self-Defence As a Basis for a Single-Action Ship Boarding

The first theory argues that self-defence can be a legal basis for so-called single-action ship boarding. This is in fact often argued in the context of self-defence against vessels that carry weapons of mass destruction (WMD).[4] Essentially, two legal discussions are important in this context. The first is that the situation would have to fulfil the conditions of anticipatory self-defence in order for a State to react to it with military means.[5] Here, the main debate on whether or not the conditions are fulfilled lies with the interpretation of imminence, which in this context is seen as a question of the gravity of the danger rather than a temporal question of when the act will occur. Proponents of this view support the 'last window of opportunity' standard: the situation of the threat that comes from the vessel is considered to be grave enough in terms of the scale and effects of the damage that will occur should it materialise, and the State must act or else it would lose its last window of opportunity.[6] As Guilfoyle notes, 'The critical justification for pre-empting WMD is that attack's potential scale, not its temporal imminence'.[7] Based on the practice of cases with regard to the use of anticipatory self-defence, Tabori-Szabo warns in this respect that signals of a trend indeed exist with regard to altering the temporal dimension, but that this opinion is still a minority-opinion.[8]

The second legal discussion in this context is the tension between self-defence and the exclusive jurisdiction of the flag State over its vessel. This discussion is premised on the basis that the use of the vessel by a non-State actor is not attributable to the flag State and that, under those circumstances, self-defence can still be invoked. With regard to this tension between self-defence and exclusive jurisdiction, proponents take the view that self-defence is neither dependent on the will of others, nor is it geographically limited. In this discussion of balancing the right of self-

---

[4]See e.g. Walker (2009), pp. 347–410 and Hodgkinson (2007).

[5]The well-known *Caroline*-criteria: the danger must be instant, overwhelming, leaving no choice for other means and no moment for deliberation.

[6]Akande and Lieflander (2013), p. 565.

[7]Guilfoyle (2005), p. 758.

[8]Tabori-Szabo (2011), p. 198.

defence and exclusive sovereignty, scholars have given support to the view that the right of self-defence can be invoked against a non-State actor within the territory of another State when the State is unwilling and/or unable to deal with the non-State actor that is within its territory.[9] By analogy, for the maritime dimension, it could, therefore, be argued that when a flag State is unwilling and/or unable to deal with non-State actors or a threatening situation against a State that flows from the presence of WMD on board, invoking self-defence does not breach the exclusive jurisdiction of the flag State. If one would subscribe to this theory, it means that self-defence (once all the conditions are fulfilled) can be another exception to the exclusive jurisdiction of the flag State. In the context of a NIAC it must, however, be underlined that although there might be a non-international armed conflict ongoing between a State and a non-State actor that is based on a *ius ad bellum* perspective of an initial armed attack by the non-State actor, the legal basis of self-defence to board a particular vessel is a separate weighing of conditions of self-defence in a particular case and is not based on the self-defence that was initially invoked against the non-State actor. In other words, this argumentation does not rely on whether or not a situation of armed conflict exists, but is based on the question whether a situation on board a foreign-flagged vessel can be considered as an imminent armed attack against which a State can invoke the right of self-defence.

2.2   Theory Two: A Self-Defence Right of Visit

The second theory also argues a right to board a foreign-flagged vessel by a belligerent warship during a non-international armed conflict from the perspective of self-defence. When the evolving right of self-defence against non-State actors opens the possibility of acting against them on the territory of another State, for the maritime dimension it seems counterintuitive to say that no right of visit would be available to counter seaborne (threats of) attacks. The difference between the first theory and the second theory is that the second theory uses the original initial self-defence to argue the existence of a right of visit, which under the circumstances might be necessary and proportionate. This theory, in other words, proposes a right of visit of foreign-flagged vessels, should a non-international armed conflict exist, based on the view that this would be a proportionate and necessary action against the non-State opponent. In order to balance the proportionality against the exclusive jurisdiction of the flag State, limitations to such a right of visit would be to restrict this right only to vessels that fly the flag of the State in which the non-State actor is active. Moreover, and for the same reason of proportionality and necessity, the vessel would have to be under a substantial level of control of the non-State actor. This theory is also not meant to allow for a right of visit and search that seeks to inspect neutral vessels for which reasonable suspicion exists of transporting

---

[9]See e.g. Bethlehem (2012) and Schmitt (2013).

non-State opponents or its means. Rather, it is limited to situation in which it is clear that non-State opponents are using the vessel for its own purpose.

This theory comes close, or may have the same thought process, to a theory that is noted by Professor Heintschel von Heinegg. Based on the practice of the French–Algerian War and the Gaza conflict, he opines that a right of visit in a NIAC might exist when the parameters of the original right of visit during an IAC are adjusted with the following conditions: (1) it must be vital to the security interests of the State, (2) there are reasonable grounds for believing that the foreign vessels are engaged in activities jeopardising those security interests (e.g., by supplying the non-State party with arms) and (3) the measures are undertaken in close proximity to the conflict area.[10] Interestingly, he states that the legal basis for this is not the *ius in bello* applicable to international armed conflicts, but the right of self-defence. He states: 'Rather, the legal basis is found in the right of self-defense or in the customary right of self-preservation in -order to protect the territorial and political integrity of the State. This right is equally exercisable in an international or non-international armed conflict.'[11] As will be explained below, the difference, however, of Heintschel von Heinegg's view and the theory posed here is the different purpose of the visit. Be that as it may, it still has broadly the same legal argumentation.

2.3 Theory Three: The Vessel As Military Objective

The third and last theory in search of legal arguments to visit and search a vessel within the context of a NIAC is a view that centralises the vessel as a military objective. As opposed to the other two theories, this theory is derived from the *ius in bello* rather than the *ius ad bellum*. A vessel can be used as a means of transportation for non-State actors or its instruments (such as WMD). The vessel is then, for instance, driven by the original crew that is not part of the organised armed group and may not even know that its passengers are members of an organised armed group. Another possibility, however, is that the vessel is under complete control of the non-State actor and is solely used for the latter's purposes. Arguably, in this case, the vessel becomes a military objective, which can be targeted within the limitations of the law of targeting of the laws of armed conflict. When it can be targeted, as a lesser means the vessel can also be captured, which would involve the boarding of the vessel in order to take over control of the vessel and persons.

The conditions of an object becoming a military objective do not concern itself with the legal ownership of the object. Still, the question of whether targeting or taking control over the vessel as military objective would in one way or another be a wrongful act against the flag State. First, it is argued that this is not the case because a state of necessity is reached in which the State has invoked the right of self-defence and, when the criteria for non-international armed conflict are met, a State can

---

[10]Heintschel von Heinegg (2012).

[11]Heintschel von Heinegg (2012), pp. 226–227.

lawfully target its opponents. The situation of self-defence will take away the wrongfulness of the act. Second, one can additionally argue that when the vessel is completely taken over by the non-State actor and has now become *de facto* a military means for the non-State actors, it might, arguably, loose its link with the flag State. In that respect, the flag State might also argue that it has stopped being responsible for the vessel. The perspective, therefore, shifts from a vessel that carries non-State actors to non-State actors that have basically confiscated a vessel from the State to put it completely to its use.

3 Purpose of a NIAC Visit

Important to note is that, in the three theories put forward, the purpose for boarding a foreign-flagged vessel is different from the primary purpose of why the belligerent right of visit and search exists in an international armed conflict. In the latter perspective, the legal means exists, simply said, to pursue economic warfare against an opponent. In the traditional sense, the belligerent right of visit and search is meant to be a means for the purpose of enforcing the rules on prize, such as the capture of contraband that is destined for the enemy. Quite differently, the theories mentioned above apply the means of a right of visit to be able to act against a non-State actor or it instruments, such as WMD, or the vessel as a military objective. In other words, the right of visit in a NIAC might be used directly to be able to act against the opponent. Remotely, it may possibly resemble an implied right of the belligerent in an international armed conflict to board an *enemy* merchant vessel in order to capture it.

Taken this different purpose to the right of visit in non-international armed conflict, it might not be wholly appropriate to start from the point of view to question whether the existing belligerent right of visit and search in an international armed conflict should directly apply to a non-international armed conflict, as they are incomparable in purpose. If one would accept one of these three theories to be legally sufficient grounds to board a foreign-flagged vessel during a NIAC, the scope of the right in terms of who can be boarded and under what circumstances a boarding can take place can be different from the IAC right of visit and search. The traditional belligerent right of visit and search is a balancing act between neutral rights and belligerent rights in order to weaken the opponent's economic power. In the theories presented here, it may be the same balancing act but for a different purpose, which may cause a different outcome than transposing the IAC balance directly to a NIAC.

4 Advantages

As noted, the first two theories have moved the issue of boarding foreign-flagged vessels away from being something that is within a legal regime and situated them into the realm of a legal basis. In view of modern conflict, this view has its operational advantages. Firstly, it circumvents the operationally challenging issue of flag State consent to board a foreign-flagged vessel. Within the context of high seas ship boarding, it would mean that, if the stringent conditions of self-defence are met and a flag State is unable or unwilling to act against the non-State actor, the vessel can be boarded in self-defence. Secondly, an other advantage of connecting the right to board to the *ius ad bellum* instead of the *ius in bello* is that it bypasses the question of whether the law of naval warfare applies in non-international armed conflict or against non-State actors. To take the example of Afghanistan, it is widely viewed that the conflict situation in Afghanistan changed after the Taliban had been brought to a fall and the *Loya Jirga* was convened in June 2002. First, many commentators view that the status of the armed conflict changed from that point onwards from an international armed conflict to a non-international armed conflict.[12] When the right to board another vessel is based on self-defence rather than on the belligerent right of visit and search, the change of status of the conflict is irrelevant.

5 Concerns

Concerns, however, also exist. A first legal concern of the theories that are based on self-defence is that it blurs the distinction between the basic system of international law and the use force, namely the distinction between the *ius ad bellum* and *ius in bello*. In this context, Geoffrey Corn has noted a debate on the so-called 'third tier', in which the conditions of self-defence are used as a third legal regime, next to IHRL and LOAC.[13] In this approach, the law of self-defence provides both a basis *and* a legal regime for and during military operations. The law of self-defence not only is used to determine whether force *can* be used, but also provides the scope of authorities during the actions itself. In the context of this contribution, this would mean that the boarding and subsequent actions, such as the application of force, are conducted under the conditions of the law of self-defence (proportionality, necessity, immediacy). Corn, who is a fervent opponent of this view, has noted that proponents of the third tier can avoid assessing the nature of hostilities and how they implicate *ius in bello* applicability.[14] This is, obviously, a convenient argument in current-day conflict and fits neatly in the view that WMD can be stopped and seized on board a foreign-flagged vessel based on self-defence. A second concern is that self-defence, in particular in the second theory, is stretched to fill gaps that should, in fact, be discussed from a perspective of the *ius in bello*. Possible overstretching of the *ius ad bellum* to let it spill over in the *ius in bello* area may be limited by setting strict conditions to the right, as, for instance, Heintschel von Heinegg has already noted.

---

[12]See e.g. Pejic (2007), p. 345.
[13]Corn (2012).
[14]Corn (2012), p. 73.

6 Concluding Remarks

There is not an awful lot of thought put into in the fact that modern conflict has moved to non-international in nature and what it may result to in the maritime dimension, in particular with regard to the effectiveness of naval forces against non-State actors. Obviously, this discussion starts with an operational need for naval forces to be able to undertake visits on the high seas during non-international armed conflict. Until so far, practice in naval operations against Al Qaida during operation *Enduring Freedom* has given us one example where such a need for a right of visit in a NIAC was both felt and exercised. Further examples of a possible need only exist in theory, such as the discussion on how to deal with WMD on a foreign-flagged vessel. At this point in time, no specific right of visit for warships exists in the law of armed conflict applicable to non-international armed conflict.

This article has noted three theories that argue possible avenues for a right of visit in a NIAC from *ius ad bellum* and *ius in bello* perspectives. It has also noted the advantages and concerns of these theories. I am not an outspoken proponent of any of these theories, and they are not presented here to persuade that such a right actually exists based on the arguments given to support the theories. It may even be that the arguments presented are, in fact, legally unsound. But I am conscious of the possible need for naval forces to board foreign-flagged vessels on the high seas during a non-international armed conflict. Recent conflicts such as in Libya, Yemen and Lebanon have or have had the tendency of being non-international in character and include a maritime dimension to the conflict. It is not wholly inconceivable that States will be confronted by a non-State actor that can also find its way to the sea. It seems to me, therefore, that it merits to put some thought into this subject. The three presented theories could serve as a start of a legal debate on this subject.

References

Akande D, Lieflander T (2013) Clarifying necessity, imminence and proportionality in the law of self-defence. Am J Int Law 107:364–570

Bethlehem D (2012) Self-defense against an imminent or actual armed attack by non-state actors. Am J Int Law 106:769–777

Corn G (2012) Self-defense targeting: blurring the line between the ius ad bellum and the ius in bello. In: Watkin K, Norris A (eds) Noninternational armed conflict in the twenty first century, International Law Studies, vol 88. US Naval War College, Newport, RI, pp 57–92

Fink MD (2016) Maritime Interception and the law of naval operations, (PhD, commercial version is forthcoming)

Guilfoyle D (2005) The proliferation security initiative: interdicting vessels in international waters to prevent the spread of weapons of mass destruction. Melb Univ Law Rev 29:734–764

Heintschel von Heinegg W (2012) Methods and means of naval warfare in non-international armed conflicts. In: Watkin K, Norris A (eds) Noninternational armed conflict in the twenty first century, International Law Studies, vol 88. US Naval War College, Newport, RI, pp 211–236

Heintschel von Heinegg W (2015) The law of military operations at sea. In: Gill TD, Fleck D (eds) The handbook of international law of military operations, 2nd edn. Oxford University Press, Oxford, pp 375–418

Hodgkinson SL (2007) Challenges to maritime interception operations in the war on terror: bridging the gap. Am Univ Int Law Rev 22:583–670

Pejic J (2007) Unlawful/enemy combatants: interpretations and consequences. In: Schmitt MN, Pejic J (eds) International law and armed conflict: exploring the faultlines. Martinus Nijhoff Publisher, Boston, pp 335–355

Schmitt MN (2013) Extraterritorial lethal targeting: deconstructing the logic of international law. Columb J Transnl Law 52:79–114

Tabori-Szabo K (2011) Anticipatory action and self-defence. Essence and limits under international law. Asser Press

Walker GK (2009) Self-defense, the law of armed conflict and port security. S C J Int Law Bus 5 (2):347–410

Martin Fink is a Commander in the Royal Netherlands Navy. He has served in several national and international legal postings as a military legal advisor, amongst which were the Netherlands Maritime Force (NLMARFOR) and NATO Joint Force Command Naples, and has had a brief spell at the Netherlands Ministry of Defence. He has been on several operational tours as a legal advisor, among which were Iraq, Afghanistan and South Sudan. He has been a lecturer of international law at the Netherlands Defence Academy and is a researcher at the University of Amsterdam, at the Amsterdam Centre of International Law (ACIL), and holds a doctor iuris at the same University.

Occupation of Sea Territory: Requirements for Military Authority and a Comparison to Art. 43 of the Hague Convention IV

Tassilo Singer

Abstract

The law of occupation is codified solely with a view to land territory in Hague Convention IV and Geneva Convention IV. It can be argued, however, that the law of occupation can also be applied to the sea. This requires a simultaneous occupation of the adjacent land territory and sufficient capability of the occupying power to enforce its authority at sea in the form of effective control. The article discusses the legal basis for such an application of the rules of occupation to the sea, as well as requirements for military authority in the maritime domain. The article also points out several peculiarities of the adaption for the sea territory concerning the rights and duties of the occupying power, such as the duty to guarantee freedom of communications. The legal challenges, which remain due to indefinite terms or wide margins of appreciation, do, however, prove the need for a careful adaption.

1 Legal Basis and Scope: Law of Occupation and Sea Territory

Belligerent occupation of territory is neither a novelty nor a legal regime of past imperialism or colonialism. Occupation is rather a necessary element in the cycle of armed conflict and ongoing hostilities, the restoration of peace and order, and finally the reinstatement of a local government. Dinstein describes the beginning of an occupation: "Once combat stabilizes along fixed lines, not coinciding with the

T. Singer (✉)
University of Passau, Passau, Germany
e-mail: tassilo.singer@gmx.de

J. Schildknecht et al. (eds.), *Operational Law in International Straits and Current Maritime Security Challenges*, Operational Maritime Law 1,
https://doi.org/10.1007/978-3-319-72718-9_14

255

original international frontiers, the cross-border areas seized and effectively controlled by a Belligerent Party are deemed to be subject to belligerent occupation."[1]
The law of (belligerent) occupation belongs to the realm of international humanitarian law or law of armed conflict.[2]

The law of occupation has a Janus-faced function. On the one hand, it affords the
occupying power the legal authority to ensure its own safety by all necessary
measures, with a special focus on the protection of its armed forces against insur-
gency. On the other hand, it demands from the occupying power to unfold the
authority to protect the civilian population and maintain the basic legal structure and
order in the occupied territories.[3] Moreover, the relevant international law has to
determine the relationship between the occupying force, the local population and the
ousted government.[4]

Generally, the lawfulness of the occupation regime does not depend on the *jus ad
bellum*.[5] However, the legal consequences of an occupation can be grave in view of
the jus ad bellum as an occupation could be considered as aggression.[6] An occupation can be considered as a violation of the prohibition of the use of force and could
grant the right to self-defense to the occupied state.

The military authority in the occupied territory somehow has to balance these
often contravening interests.[7] At the same time, the existence of (a certain) military
authority itself over a territory is the constituting factor for the implementation of the
law of occupation. As an occupation is usually particularly directed to land territory,
the discussion mostly encompasses the legal rules onshore. However, the present
study will focus on the requirements of military authority over occupied sea territory
and describe the scope and limits of rights and duties of the occupying power.

1.1   Legal Basis

The legal sources for the law of occupation are primarily the Hague Regulations
from 1899 (Section III—Art. 42 ff.), which were revised and annexed to the Hague
Convention (IV) from 1907[8] and the provisions of the Geneva Convention (IV) from
1949[9] (Section III—Art.47 ff.), hereinafter GN IV.[10] In contrast to the Hague

---

[1]Dinstein (2009), p. 1.

[2]Benvenisti (2009), para. 20.

[3]Compare Articles 42 through 56, HR (1899), and Hague Convention IV (1907).

[4]Benvenisti (2009), para. 1.

[5]Benvenisti (2009), para. 20.

[6]Art. 3 lit. a UN Definition of Aggression (1974).

[7]Benvenisti (2009), para. 27: *"creates a tension with its authority and obligation to ensure public
order and civil life as elaborated in the previous sections"*.

[8]See note 4.

[9]Geneva Convention (IV) (1949).

[10]Dinstein (2009), pp. 4–5.

Regulations, the focus of the Geneva Conventions is to enhance the protection of the civilian population in occupied territories. According to Art. 154 of GC IV, the Convention is supplementary to the Hague Regulations,[11] so the Hague Regulations will form the major part of the analysis. Also, there are some rules on the occupation of territory[12] in Additional Protocol I to the Geneva Conventions.[13] The applicability of these rules, however, depends on whether the relevant state is bound to the protocol[14] or if the rule is considered as customary international law.[15] However, the rules of AP I have only limited relevance for the analysis of military authority over occupied sea territory as they mostly transfer regular protection standards from the law in international armed conflict to the law of occupation. Finally, the ICJ found in its Israeli Wall Advisory Opinion that human rights law might be applicable in some situations exclusively or parallel to humanitarian law[16] too. However, those situations are seldom, as international humanitarian law is considered, viewed as *lex specialis* by the ICJ.[17] Therefore, human rights law can be considered helpful where IHL is unclear or contains legal loopholes.[18] Concerning the requirements and content of military authority, though, human rights law can only form a supplementary protection for the civilian population next to GC IV. As an additional source, the Oxford Manual of 1913 can be referred to, as it mentions the occupation of maritime territory, despite the manual not being concluded as an international treaty and not considered as customary international law.[19]

1.2   Scope and Applicability of the Law of Occupation

As a precondition for the analysis of military authority over occupied sea territory, the scope of the mentioned legal sources and their applicability to sea territory has to be determined.

1.2.1   The Hague Convention (IV) and the Hague Regulations

According to Art. 2 Hague Convention (IV), the Hague Convention and its annex (the Hague Regulations) apply only between contracting powers and only if all the belligerents are parties to the Convention. The law of occupation deriving from the

---

[11]ICJ (2004), para. 89; Dinstein (2009), p. 6.

[12]Compare: Art. 3(b) AP I (1949) see note 14; Art. 5 (4) AP I (1949); Art. 43 AP I (1949); Art. 44 AP I (1949); Art. 45 (3) AP I (1949); Art. 73 AP I (1949).

[13]AP I (1949).

[14]Dinstein (2009), pp. 7–8.

[15]Compare: Henckaerts and Doswald-Beck (2005).

[16]ICJ (2004), para. 109.

[17]Ibid.

[18]Gasser and Dörmann (2013), p. 265.

[19]Manual of the Laws of Naval War (1913): Source of the Text: Ronzitti (1988), Commentary by Verri, pp. 329–340; Dinstein (2009), pp. 47–48.

Hague Regulations (HR) by now is viewed as customary international law, though.[20]

The rules for military authority over the (occupied) territory of a hostile state are incorporated in Arts. 42–56 HR. The prerequisite for their applicability is set out in Art. 42. It provides that a territory is occupied when it is placed under the authority of the hostile army.

The applicability of the Hague Regulations on sea territory could be doubted for several reasons. From a positivistic position, the title of the Hague Regulations is "Respecting the Law and Customs of War on Land." Hence, it seems most likely that an application on occupation at sea originally had not been in the interest of the contracting parties. As the Hague Regulations form the main corpus of the law of occupation, at least in view of the military authority and rights of the occupying power, the core of the law of occupation would not be applicable to sea territory. The same applies to the customary law, which is derived from the statements of the Hague Rules.

For a legally clear result, one has to differentiate between two topics. Firstly, the question is whether the rules of the Hague Regulations can apply to sea at all and whether a direct application of the HR is possible. Secondly, it has to be determined if an occupation of sea can happen independently from an occupation ashore or if an occupation ashore is an indispensable prerequisite for an occupation over a sea area.

The wording of the specific rules of the HR seems to confirm the positivistic line of argument. At no point does the HR make reference of sea territory in view of the law of occupation; instead, solely the occupation of territory is mentioned. The word "sea" is referred to only once in Art. 53 (2) HR concerning the seizure of certain appliances.[21] One could conclude that if the HR should have been applicable to the occupation of a sea territory too, the word "sea" would have been inserted far more often, especially as sea situations seem to have been envisaged by the authors of the HR. On the other hand, you could argue that, as at least a sea issue is mentioned, the occupation of sea had been accepted already as a possible variation of an occupation.

Furthermore, one can consider the overall context of the rules governing occupation and military authority over territory in the HR. Therein, one can identify three main fields of rules: firstly, rules that govern the rights of the occupant and the administration and maintenance of public order; secondly, rules that provide for the protection of the population and its property; thirdly, rules regarding state property and natural resources. So the main focus of these rules seems to be directed at circumstances that can only appear and be governed ashore. Only in a few situations, and provided the occupying power has the necessary capabilities, do the rules of the Hague Regulations seem to be applicable, e.g. for the usufruct of the belongings and national resources of the occupied state (fish or seabed resources).

---

[20]Trial of the Major War Criminals (1945); ICJ (2004), para. 89; For a more detailed proof compare: Dinstein (2009), p. 5.

[21]Art. 53 (2) HR (1899): "All appliances, whether on land, at sea, or in the air, adapted for the transmission of news or for the transport of persons or things, exclusive of cases governed by naval law, depots of arms and, generally, all kinds of munitions of war, may be seized, even if they belong to private individuals, but must be restored and compensation fixed when peace is made."

Nevertheless, from a legal perspective, it seems unsatisfactory that the rules governing military authority should only apply and end at the coastline, even if the whole administration and governing authority of the original state has been expelled from the area and cannot exercise any control over the sea anymore. The sea thereby would become a legal gray area, wherein no state authority at all exists. The word "territory" in the Hague Regulations could also be understood in a broader sense, encompassing also sea territory. Territory can be every area, be it land or water, to which the territorial sovereignty of a state extends.[22] Sea territory, which belongs and is subject solely to the sovereignty of a state, is called "territorial waters" or "territorial sea." This is accepted as customary international law[23] and can be deduced from Art. 1 Convention on the Territorial Sea and the Contiguous Zone[24] and can also be found in Art. 2 UNCLOS.[25]

Still, it has to be noted that the sovereignty of a state remains unaffected by an occupation. No sovereignty is transferred to an occupying power (prohibition of annexation), and the former state retains the title to the territory de jure.[26]

It would seem irrational and artificial to have a legal framework, which starts to apply as soon as the territorial control of a state has been broken[27] and which is aimed to encompass everyone within that area of replaced control, but to differentiate within the former sovereign area ashore and at sea. This could lead to a factually uncontrolled area. Hence, one can interpret the word territory in Section III of the HR as encompassing also the territorial waters of the occupied state.

Also, as the possible seizure of appliances "at sea" and "submarine cables" are mentioned,[28] in the Regulations one could argue that the contracting parties were in favor of an extension of the law of occupation and thought it obvious that the HR are also applicable to an occupation of sea territory.

This line of argument can be supported by a systematic argument on a larger scale: there is also the Hague Convention (XIII),[29] which deals with duties of neutral powers in naval war. However, this convention does not mention the situation of an occupation at all, even if there are some legally problematic situations conceivable, such as the question whether an occupant is entitled to search a neutral ship in the territorial sea of an occupied state or if the visit of an occupied port violates the law of neutrality. Hence, one could conclude that the failure to address neutral naval powers' responsibilities with regard to an occupant indicates that there was no need

---

[22]ICJ (1986), Merits, para. 212; Epping (2014), p. 52.

[23]Yalem (1960), pp. 210–211.

[24]Convention on the Territorial Sea and the Contiguous Zone (1958).

[25]UNCLOS (1982).

[26]Dinstein (2009), p. 49; UK Manual (2004), para. 11.9–11.10; Gasser and Dörmann (2013), pp. 274–275.

[27]Gasser and Dörmann (2013), pp. 277–278.

[28]Arts. 53, 54 Hague Regulations.

[29]Hague Convention XIII (1907).

to include any rules governing the occupation of sea territory as these rules were considered included in Hague Convention (IV).

Furthermore, the Manual of the Laws of Naval War of 1913[30] explicitly determines in Art. 88 that an "Occupation of maritime territory, that is of gulfs, bays, roadsteads, ports and territorial waters, exists only when there is an (simultaneous) occupation of continental territory. The occupation, in that case, is subject to the laws and usages of war on land."[31] Hence, this text clearly supports the applicability of the Hague Convention IV to occupation of sea territory.[32] This position also was taken into account by the US and UK during the occupation of Iraq 2003.[33]

The purpose of military authority facilitates that view too. As explained before, the rules for military authority, especially Art. 43 of the Hague Regulations, shall protect the civilian population and life and impose the duty on the occupying power to restore and maintain public order. If this duty did not apply to sea territory, there would be a factually ungoverned, anarchistic zone, wherein the occupying force would not be obliged to care for the rights of the civilian population (e.g., fishery or security). However, this is absolutely in contrast to the purpose to protect the population and its livelihood. Especially in a situation of occupation, the population is rather in need of protection; wherefore, the law of occupation has been formed.

In contrast, the wording "land" seems to impose a heavy constraint and therefore could contradict a direct application of the HR. However, the strong arguments[34] in favor of an application of the law of occupation to sea territory prevail, especially as the historical discussion moved in the same direction. The situation is also comparable to an occupation at shore as the territorial sovereignty of the former state would de facto (however in this case not de jure)[35] not extend anymore to sea territory. A legal regulation for sea territory is required because otherwise a legal gray area would exist concerning this territory. In conclusion, the Hague Regulations have to be applied directly to occupied sea territory despite the wording. But, as most of the rules concern rights and duties that can mostly only be exercised ashore, one has to interpret the rules accordingly and adapt the legal content to an occupation of territory at sea.

With regard to the second question, it might be questionable if an occupation at sea can be established without an occupation of land territory.[36] First of all, the status of territorial sea as sovereign territory is linked to the adjacent land territory

---

[30]Manual of the Laws of Naval War (1913).

[31]Source of the Treaty Text: Ronzitti (1988), p. 317.

[32]Verri in Ronzitti (1988) (see note 20), p. 337.

[33]Kelly (2003), pp. 127–165.

[34]More skeptically: Benvenisti (2012), p. 55.

[35]Dinstein (2009), p. 49.

[36]Compare: ICRC (2012), p. 50: APPENDIX 3—Agenda & Guiding Questions: "Can military presence outside the boundaries of the territory concerned over its airspace or in its territorial waters or a combination of thereof, be considered effective control?".

(compare Art. 5 UNCLOS). A separate legal status for sea territory without respecting the (sovereign) status of the land territory therefore does not make sense.[37] Also, if sea territory could be occupied separately, most of the rules of the HR would have to be modified as they are regulating situations that practically happen on land or depend on land situations. It can be doubted in practice if an effective control, as required for military authority according to Art. 42 HR, can be established without controlling a beachhead ashore. Finally, the Oxford Manual of 1913 explicitly states in its Art. 88 that an occupation at sea is only possible with a coinciding occupation onshore.[38] Hence, the legal problem was recognized before, and the found solution was identical to the suggestion here. Therefore, an occupation at sea requires that all of the legal prerequisites prevail both onshore and at sea (= nexus between land and sea occupation), and in case no occupation onshore is effectively in place, no occupation over the correlating sea territory is legally possible.[39]

1.2.2 Geneva Convention Relative to the Protection of Civilian Persons in Time of War (GC IV)

The Fourth Geneva Convention is applicable according to its Art. 2 in international armed conflicts, meaning any armed conflict that arises between two or more of the High Contracting Parties, even if the state of war is not recognized by one of them. Furthermore, the convention applies to all cases of partial or total occupation of the territory of a High Contracting Party, even if the occupation meets no armed resistance. GC IV is considered as customary international law,[40] too, and thereby not depending on the signatory status of a party. Compared to the Hague Regulations, the wording of the convention is not restricted to land territory. In addition, GC IV does not differentiate at all between different types of territory as it shall be applicable in every situation of an international armed conflict to provide comprehensive protection. Hence, it seems clear that the mentioned (occupied) territory in Art. 2 GC IV encompasses sea territory as well. Thus, the supplementary rules for the protection of civilians of GC IV are directly applicable to the occupation of sea territory.

1.2.3 Additional Protocol I (AP I)

The scope of application of Additional Protocol I to the Geneva Conventions matches the scope of GC IV as it refers in Arts. 1, 3 AP I to Common Art. 2 GC I-IV. Some of the articles of the Additional Protocol are viewed as customary international law too.[41] Therefore, an international armed conflict has to prevail in the relevant territory. Additionally, the wording of Art. 3 lit. b AP I clearly extends the applicability of its rules until the termination of an occupation. As there is no

---

[37]Compare also the general principle: "the land dominates the sea": ICJ (1969), para. 96.

[38]Manual of the Laws of Naval War (1913), p. 317.

[39]Compare: Dinstein (2009), p. 47.

[40]Geneva Convention (IV) (1949) is universally ratified, see United Nations Treaty Collection 973.

[41]Henckaerts (2005) pp. 177, 187–188.

limitation to land territory, the applicability of AP I to the occupation of sea territory is legally possible and does not pose a problem.

1.2.4 Human Rights Law

Finally, also human rights law can apply during an occupation. The law of occupation is considered an own legal regime and forms a part of international humanitarian law. Therefore, human rights law can only be applicable in addition to and so long as the matter is not regulated specifically (*lex specialis*) by the law of occupation.[42] Human rights law in general is widely considered applicable during armed conflicts. However, most of its rules can be derogated if the life of the nation is in danger and if certain conditions are prevailing.[43]

In cases of occupation, human rights[44] would have to be applied extraterritorially, meaning that the relevant state has to exercise effective control or jurisdiction in the territory.[45] The relationship between these preconditions and the requirements of military authority therein might be decisive.[46] However, one has to be aware that some countries, e.g. the USA and Israel, do not accept the general applicability of human rights treaties in occupied territories.[47] Alternatively, the occupying state could be bound by local human rights law, as well, if it exists as part of the "laws in force in the country" according to Art. 43 HR.

Nevertheless, the legal content of military authority is solely regulated in the law of occupation in the Hague Regulations and GC IV. The legal debate about the extraterritorial application of human rights during an occupation shall stay aside in this analysis as it is of little relevance for the requirements of military authority over occupied sea territory.

1.2.5 UN Security Council Resolutions

The UN Security Council, as legal authority under Chapter VII, can impose additional duties/obligations on the occupant or award specific authority to the occupant.[48] The best example forms Resolution 1483 from 2003,[49] governing the occupation of Iraq by the USA and the UK. This resolution confirms the contemporary applicability of the law of occupation[50] and lays out the legal framework of the

---

[42]Compare the lex specialis rule, given by the ICJ (findings) in its ICJ (2004), Advisory Opinion, paras. 106, 109; UNSCR 1483 (2003); Benvenisti (2003), pp. 862–863.
[43]Art. 4 ICCPR; ICJ (2004), para. 127; Sassoli (2005), p. 666; Manual for Law of Armed Conflict of the German Armed Forces (Hereinafter German Manual) (2013), paras. 105, 595.
[44]Compare to the extraterritorial application: Dennis (2005).
[45]Compare, ECHR (1999); ECHR (2007), paras. 123–124, 136–137: Concerning also the question if human rights can be "divided and tailored".
[46]ECHR (1996), para. 52; ICRC (2012), pp. 39–40, 137–139.
[47]Benvenisti (2009), para. 13.
[48]Benvenisti (2009), para. 18.
[49]UNSCR 1483 (2003).
[50]Benvenisti (2003), pp. 861–862.

occupation, especially reinforcing the concept of debellatio (no sovereign title is acquired by the occupant), the applicability of international human rights law, the need for an effective administration, and the usufruct rule for the benefit of the inhabitants of the occupied areas concerning Iraqi oil. Security Council resolutions can also generate new rules for an occupation, such as the introduction of a monitoring process performed by the "Special Representative for Iraq," the International Advisory and Monitoring Board, and public accountants.[51]

2 Military Authority: Requirements and Application to Sea Territory

According to Art. 42 (1) HR, a "territory is considered occupied when it is actually placed under the authority of the hostile army." Therefore, as the authority depends on the armed forces and the occupation is performed by a hostile army, "authority" has to be understood as "military authority." The title "military authority" of Section III of the Hague Regulations also underlines the feature "military." Furthermore, Art. 42 HR is viewed as customary international law.[52]

2.1 Meaning of Military Authority

Military authority in the context of occupation means the effective control over a part or the whole of the enemy territory, achieved by armed forces of the occupying state. As stated before, military authority is the central element of the law of occupation. Still, the term is not mentioned in GC IV and AP I and thereby underlines the supplementary role of GC IV and AP I for the law of occupation and especially for the present research objective of military authority over sea territory. Only if military authority exists can an occupation be obtained and the law of occupation apply, according to Art. 42 HR.[53]

2.2 Requirements and Scope

2.2.1 Requirements

The law of occupation shall apply as soon as the occupying power has assumed the control over a territory and the national authorities no longer have control over the territory. Thereby, a turning point situation exists out of which the occupying power is considered more suitable by law to exercise authority over a territory and its

---

[51]Benvenisti (2003), pp. 861–864; UNSCR 1483 (2003), paras. 4, 5, 8, 12, 20.

[52]Benvenisti (2012), p. 44.

[53]Gasser and Dörmann (2013), pp. 268–270.

inhabitants. So the occupying armed forces must have the capabilities to enforce its authority over the civilian population in the occupied territories.[54]

Based on an interpretation of Art. 42, in conjunction with Art. 43 HR,[55] two conditions must be fulfilled for military authority to exist[56]: first, the original government is unable to exercise its authority in the relevant area as a consequence of the hostilities.[57] The opinions on the second requirement, however, are divided. Either it is required that the occupying army has actually substituted its own authority for that of the expelled government.[58] According to this view, the occupant has to exercise the former state's authority in effect, for example basic governmental functions with a view to the territory or the population. This would imply that an army, which is solely in place in the territory but does not exercise authority vis-á-vis the population, does not occupy that territory in the legal sense.[59] In this case, the Hague Regulations would not apply and the occupied state and its forces would not have to obey its rules.[60]

Some deemed it sufficient that the occupant has only potential control, meaning that it just has to be in a position to substitute its own authority for that of the former government.[61] Therefore, an occupant does not have to actually substitute and enforce its authority but be in the area and just be able (have the capabilities) to do so. This position lowers the degree and effectivity of military authority that has to be exercised during a military campaign in enemy territory to constitute an occupation in the legal sense. Accordingly, an occupying force cannot claim that there is no occupation when there is no military authority exercised in actuality and therefore claim that it is not bound to the HR. This interpretation prevents the occupant from circumventing the HR by own behavior. Instead, the occupant would automatically be obliged by law as soon as the effective control of a territory is achieved. Also, the (authentic) French text seems to suggest that the power of the occupant is a de facto capability, not a legal authority, as both Art. 42 and Art. 43 speak of "de fait."[62] As otherwise the occupant could evade certain duties,[63] especially vis-à-vis the civilian population, the requirement of a potential control seems far more preferable. This would enhance the duties of the occupying power vis-á-vis the population and foster

---

[54]Gasser and Dörmann (2013), pp. 268–269.

[55]ICRC (2012), p. 38.

[56]Gasser and Dörmann (2013), p. 269; Compare the test in the UK Manual (2004), p. 275 f. para. 11.3.

[57]UK Manual (2004), p. 275, para. 11.3; Benvenisti (2009), para. 5.

[58]ICJ (2005), paras. 173.

[59]Benvenisti (2009), para. 5.

[60]Benvenisti (2009), para. 4.

[61]ICTY (2003), para. 217; Israel Supreme Court (2008), para. 11; US Tribunal of Nuremberg (1949), pp. 55–56; Manual of Military Law of War on Land (1958), para. 503; UK Manual (2004), p. 275, para. 11.3; German Manual (2013), p. 80, para. 527; Benvenisti (2012), pp. 47–48; Benvenisti (2009), para. 5; Roberts (1985), pp. 300–301.

[62]ICRC (2012), pp. 37–38.

[63]Roberts (2009), para. 5.

its protection. This view can be supported by the ratio of the development of the law of occupation by the introduction of GC IV and AP I and its aim to strengthen the protection of civilians during an occupation. A legal loophole based on arbitrary avoidance of the necessary actual control is clearly contravening this purpose. Hence, it is sufficient for the establishment of military authority in view of the applicability of the law of occupation as soon as the occupying powers have the potential control over the relevant area.[64] However, the authority of the former territorial sovereign has to be suppressed and replaced by the occupying power, which has to have "a sufficient force present"[65] in the occupied territory, in any case.[66]

2.2.2 Effective Control in the Context of Belligerent Occupation

As military authority is measured by the existence of control, the criterion of effective control is decisive for the existence of an occupation.[67] To determine the existence of effective control, Ferraro suggests an effective control test, which consists of three cumulative requirements: the unconsented presence of foreign armed forces (1), the ability of the foreign forces to exercise authority over the territory concerned in lieu of the local sovereign, (2) and the related inability of the latter to exert its authority over the territory (3).[68] However, those requirements are still too imprecise to enable a clear and transferrable decision of whether or not effective control prevails. In the ICTY Naletilic Decision, the court provides more detailed guidelines for the determination of whether or not the occupation has been established.[69] Hereto, the "occupying power must be in position to substitute its own authority for that of the occupied authorities, which must have been rendered incapable of functioning publicly; the enemy's forces have surrendered, been defeated or withdrawn. In this respect, battle areas may not be considered as occupied territory. However, sporadic local resistance, even successful, does not affect the reality of occupation; the occupying power has a sufficient force present, or the capacity to send troops within a reasonable time to make the authority of the occupying power felt; a temporary administration has been established over the territory and the occupying power has issued and enforced directions to the civilian population."[70] Benvenisti seems to affirm the ICTY's criteria but concentrates more on the occupying forces: the occupying force must have the ability to send detachments within a reasonable time, to perform its authority within the occupied area. The number of troops necessary to maintain an effective occupation depends on multiple factors, such as the disposition of the inhabitants, the number and

---

[64]Compare: German Manual (2013), para. 527.

[65]ICTY (2003), para. 217.

[66]Ferraro (2012), p. 144; Compare also Lieber Code (1863) Section 1, para. 1 Sentence 2.

[67]Ferraro (2012), pp. 139–140.

[68]Ferraro (2012), p. 142.

[69]ICTY (2003), para. 217; Discussed in: Ferraro (2012), pp. 141–142.

[70]ICTY (2003), para. 217.

distribution of the population, and the nature of the terrain. Nonpersisting resistance, even if sometimes successful, does not render an occupation ineffective. However, if a territory is lost again to the enemy and the occupying power has to recapture that area and regain its control, no occupation prevails during that time. It is not required that the occupying forces are continuously present in all places at any time.[71] For example, it is sufficient if troops are stationed at strategic points of the territory.[72] Nevertheless, it is imperative for an occupation of land territory that there are at least troops on the ground in the relevant area.[73]

Concerning the measureable physical presence of troops of the occupying state, it is essential for effective control that the occupying power has at least sufficient capabilities to extend its control in a noticeable way over the territory and its inhabitants.[74] Of course, strong presence of troops on the ground extending over the whole, relevant area is the best indicator for effective control. However, the establishment of an administration and the execution of directions and rulings toward the population also provide significant evidence for effective control.[75] Effective control does not have to be absolute, denying any resistance against the occupying forces. In any case, a formal declaration of occupation is neither required nor constitutive and does not poses any legal value in view of the law of occupation,[76] even if it might prove useful for future interaction with the population.[77] In the end, the conclusion that the preconditions of an occupation are prevailing at the relevant times in the relevant area always depends upon a factual case-by-case analysis.[78] It has to be admitted, though, that the requirements for assuming control by a foreign army are not fully determined.[79]

2.2.3 Scope and Limits of Military Authority

According to Art. 42 (2) HR, "the occupation extends locally only to the territory where such authority has been established and can be exercised," and thereby effective control has been established.[80] If the control over a part of the territory is still embattled or lost by the occupying power, there is no occupation prevailing in this area and the law of occupation does not apply so long as effective control is not

---

[71]Benvenisti (2009), para. 8; Ferraro (2012), pp. 145–146.

[72]Gasser and Dörmann (2013), p. 269.

[73]Dinstein (2009), p. 44; ICRC (2012), APPENDIX 3, Agenda, p. 17.

[74]ICTY (2003), para. 217; Compare also: UK Manual (2004), p. 275, para. 11.2, p. 277, para. 11.6; German Manual (2013), para. 527; Gasser and Dörmann (2013), pp. 268–269.

[75]German Manual (2013), para. 527; UK Manual (2004), p. 276, para. 11.3.2.

[76]UK Manual (2004), p. 276, para. 11.4; Benvenisti (2009), para. 9.

[77]UK Manual (2004), p. 276, para. 11.4.1.

[78]Benvenisti (2009), para. 8; ICTY (2003), para. 218.

[79]Benvenisti (2009), para. 33.

[80]HR (1899), Art. 42 (1); UK Manual (2004), pp. 275, 277, paras. 11.3, 11.5.

gained or regained by the occupant.[81] The moment when an area is considered occupied is a "question of fact."[82]

Additionally, it has been suggested that the rules for occupation must already be observed as far as possible during a march-through and even on the battlefield.[83] The exact moment when military authority is established is often unclear, however, especially as the existence of potential control is controversial and might often be disputed.[84] Military authority is considered to exist definitely, as soon as the administration of the occupied area is established and the inhabitants become subject to the rule of the occupying forces.[85]

Nevertheless, the status of occupation has a temporary character[86] and, as a generally transitory legal regime, has to end at some point. From a legal point of view, it remains unclear whether an occupation ends at a specific time or if it is a gradual process,[87] as Art. 3 lit. (b) AP I might suggest.[88] Deduced from Arts. 42 and 43 HR, an occupation generally ends when the occupying army lacks the necessary control, and thus the required military authority is or is rendered unable to perform its duties according to Art. 43 HR for a continuous amount of time.[89] The protection of the civilian population, however, does not end merely because of the absence of control of the occupying force; compare Art. 47 GC IV, Art. 3 lit. b AP I. Also, the cessation of hostilities does not necessarily lead to the end of the state of occupation.[90]

2.3   Transfer and Scope of Military Authority Over Sea Territory

2.3.1   Authority and Effective Control Over Sea Territory

The decisive question is if and how the previous parameters for military authority can be transferred to an occupation of sea territory. As stated in the first chapter, the law of occupation generally can be applied either directly or analogous to an occupation of sea territory. Also, Art. 88 of the Oxford Manual proposes that the rules determining the occupation onshore have to be transferred to the occupation of

---

[81]Gasser and Dörmann (2013), pp. 268–269, 272–273; UK Manual (2004), pp. 275–276, para. 11.2, 11.3.2; German Manual (2013), para. 528.

[82]LOAC Deskbook (2015), p. 119.

[83]Roberts (1985), p. 256; Gasser and Dörmann (2013), pp. 273–274.

[84]ICRC (2012), APPENDIX 3, Agenda & Guiding Questions, p. 16.

[85]Roberts (1985), pp. 256–257; Gasser and Dörmann (2013), pp. 268–270.

[86]Benvenisti (2009), para. 21; Pictet (1958), p. 275.

[87]ICTY (2003), paras. 219–222.

[88]Roberts (1985), paras. 2, 6, 56.

[89]Compare Roberts (2009), paras. 20; 25; 35–43; UK Manual (2004), p. 277, paras. 11.7–11.8; ICTY (2003), para. 218.

[90]Gasser and Dörmann (2013), pp. 280–281; Art. 6 para. 3 S.1 GC IV; LOAC Deskbook (2015), p. 121.

maritime (i.e., sea) territory.[91] So the requirements of Art. 42 HR have to be met. However, each rule has to be interpreted in every single case, and therefore the requirements for military authority deriving from Art. 42 HR have to be adapted to the peculiarities of sea territory.

As stated in the chapter before, the former government must be unable to exercise its authority and the occupying forces must have substituted their own authority in the occupied territory. The occupying force thereby must have gained control over the area. This does not mean that the occupying forces have to be continuously present in all places at any time.[92]

Yet the occupant must have a sufficient force present, or at least the capacity to send detachments within a reasonable time to perform its authority, within the occupied area. The amount of troops, which are required to maintain an effective occupation, depends on multiple factors, such as the distribution of the population and the nature of the terrain.

However, it might be questioned if military presence of naval forces alone in the territorial waters can be viewed as adequate to reach the necessary level of effective control.[93] As the Oxford Manual states, an occupation of territorial sea and thereby the ability to effectively control territorial water were deemed sufficient already in 1913. Since the rules for land occupation have to be transferred to sea and boots on the ground are considered sufficient for an occupation onshore,[94] the physical presence of naval forces is also viewed as a sufficient military presence at sea. Taking into account the current developments in technology and naval warfare providing more range, tools, and options, effective control of occupied sea territory is a fortiori technically possible. In contrast, according to the prevailing opinion, military presence in the air alone cannot be considered sufficient.[95]

The factors for the extent and the limits to the existence of military authority, such as nonpersisting resistance or the loss of occupied territory to the former government, are the same on land and therefore can be transferred directly to sea territory. Nevertheless, as explained already in the first chapter, an occupation at sea requires, according to Art. 88 Oxford Manual, a correlating, simultaneously existing occupation onshore (continental), in addition to the regular legal prerequisites. If a land occupation is in force, the necessary military authority has to be established at sea in order to form an effective sea occupation.

In case the hostile state does still control sea territory next to the occupied area and has naval forces available, it could threaten the occupied area. If the former state can enter and exit the area easily and without being inhibited by the occupant, it is questionable if the occupant has reached sufficient control for an occupation of this

---

[91]Dinstein (2009), p. 47.

[92]Compare: Dinstein (2009), p. 44; ICTY (2003), para. 217.

[93]ICRC (2012), pp. 17–18, 50.

[94]ICRC (2012), p. 17; Ferraro (2012), pp. 143–147.

[95]ICRC (2012), pp. 17, 50; Gasser and Dörmann (2013), p. 268; Ferraro (2012), pp. 143, 145; Dinstein (2009), p. 48; Frau and Singer (2015), p. 88.

sea territory. In such a case, it could be argued that the territory is still contested as the occupant is not able to solely exercise authority in the area.[96] Derived from the rules for a land occupation, it is absolutely sufficient that the occupying naval forces can reach the intruder in a reasonable time,[97] expel or destroy it, and thereby defend the occupied territory.

Another possibility to specify the meaning of effective control in the sea context could be a comparison to other forms of domination over maritime areas like war zones or blockades. Regardless of doubts to the lawfulness, maritime war zones or total exclusion zones in state practice do not have a legal parameter on the degree, effectiveness, or necessity of control in common[98] and therefore are unsuitable. In contrast, one of the mandatory requirements of a blockade is effectiveness.[99] This means that either the blockaded areas have to be totally cut off from imports or exports because of the control of the blockading force or at least that there is a high probability that entries and exits are recognized and prevented. If a blockade is not effective, all measures that have been taken with regard to the blockade are unlawful.[100] The same applies if the blockade is discriminatory or does not apply impartially.[101] Hence, the rules for the effectiveness of the control are rather strict (in comparison to the determined parameters for effective control of sea territory) and leave little room for interpretation. However, there remain serious doubts of whether or not the rules for a blockade can be transferred directly to an occupation. In contrast to an occupation, which extends depending on the range of the military authority of the occupant to the whole area of a territorial sea, a blockade constitutes merely a line, which may not be crossed. In particular, it is not the exclusive purpose of an occupation to prevent all external intrusions into an area or close an area for everyone as a blockade. An occupation takes an area of sea territory in possession, controls that area, and tries to defend it outward against other belligerents, both within its borders and against intrusion from the land. It does not have to prohibit everyone, encompassing indiscriminately also neutral ships, to enter this area even if it may do so. Therefore, the standard of the effectivity of the control as required for a blockade cannot be transferred to an occupation of sea territory.

Furthermore, one could think of a comparison to the laying of mines and the connected duties of the minelaying state. The minelaying state thereby is restricted, especially by rules protecting the rights of neutral states. However, there is no rule that encompasses a standard for the effectiveness of any duties in this context. Particularly, the rule that minelaying states have to pay due regard to the legitimate

---

[96]Compare: Gasser and Dörmann (2013), pp. 272–273; Dinstein (2009), pp. 44–45.

[97]ICTY (2003), para. 217; Benvenisti (2009), para. 8.

[98]San Remo Manual (1995), pp. 181 ff. Ronzitti (1988), pp. 10, 40, 73.

[99]Compare San Remo Manual (1995), para. 95, Explanations, pp. 181–183; Ronzitti (1988), pp. 72–73.

[100]German Manual (2013), para. 1063; Commander's Handbook (2007), para. 7.7.2.3; Frau and Singer (2015), p. 88.

[101]Commander's Handbook (2007), para. 7.7.2.4; Frau and Singer (2015), p. 89.

uses of the high seas cannot be interpreted in a way that it includes a standard for the effectivity of the measures. In fact, the due regard obligation can be understood as awarding the minelaying state a margin of appreciation.[102] This wider understanding includes a variety of measures to enable the legitimate use of the high seas and does not determine a lower or a higher degree. The telos of the rule is to enable the use of the high sea without fixing the methods to reach it. Thereby, no precise standard can be found, and the rule cannot serve as a standard for effectivity.

Concluding, the naval forces of the hostile state have to be expelled from the territorial waters, which are planned to be occupied. Also, the occupying naval forces have to take over the authority over the relevant sea territory. Applying the determined parameters, the occupying naval forces have to provide or station sufficient capabilities in the occupied area to be in a position to actually control the sea territory. The occupant thereby has to be able to deploy naval forces in a reasonable time to every point of the occupied sea territory. Therefore, it is generally not sufficient for the naval forces of the occupant to only break any resistance of the former authority and then leave the maritime territory or patrol the area without setting up an administration.[103]

There is no fixed amount or type of troops or ships that are necessary to assure these capabilities as it depends on various factors as population and its common habits, traffic, and nature in this area. The existence of an occupation has to be determined on a case-by-case basis.[104]

Concerning the legal characteristics of sea territory, other factors become relevant, which have not been recognized in the HR, GC IV, and AP I. Examples for legal peculiarities, which might have to be observed by the occupant, are the right to innocent passage[105] or if the territorial sea contains international straits or archipelagic waters (status sui generis),[106] which have to be secured, kept open,[107] and the traffic regulated by the state authority.[108] The transferability of general rights and duties from the former state to the occupying state will be discussed in detail later.

In order to control a sea territory in an adequate way, the occupant has to monitor its occupied maritime territories to a certain and reasonable extent because the occupant has to be able to react in an adequate time to border violations and possible attempts to recapture or contest the occupied sea territories. Otherwise, the occupant could not deny the entrance or exit of hostile ships in a commonly expectable

---

[102]Compare: San Remo Manual (1995), para. 88 and explanations p. 173, para. 88.2 and 88.3.

[103]UK Manual (2004), p. 276, para. 11.3.2.

[104]Benvenisti (2009), para. 8.

[105]Although the innocent passage of warships is sometimes controversial during armed conflict: compare San Remo Manual (1995), paras. 31, 32, and Explanations at p. 108 f. Generalizing the right to close its own territorial sea: pp. 104 f. para. 26.3.

[106]Heintschel von Heinegg (2014), pp. 891, 894–895.

[107]Compare San Remo Manual (1995), paras. 26–27, Explanations at pp. 104–105, para. 26.3.

[108]Compare Arts. 17, 21–22, 24, 25, 45, 52–53, UNCLOS (1982), (Innocent Passage), Arts. 38, 41, 42, 44, 54 UNCLOS (1982) (International Straits and Transit Passage).

amount of time and therefore would not be considered as effectively controlling the occupied area. Mining of some parts of the occupied area might prove useful but has to be undertaken with due regard to the legal restrictions.[109]

The requirement to monitor does not impose an excessive threshold. Surveillance and border control could also be performed by UAV[110] and UMV[111] systems, which are advantageous due to their long endurance and their sensor and communication capabilities.[112] As soon as unmanned technologies become a common tool to dominate territory, the required level of control could rise accordingly. Therefore, if a state owns unmanned aerial or maritime systems, it might have the duty to make use of unmanned technology in a certain ("sufficient" or "adequate") manner to set up its control and to uphold the occupation over the sea territory.[113] Some even assert that Art. 42 could be reinterpreted and the effective control can be maintained solely by unmanned systems as the projection of military power beyond the boundaries of occupied territory would be considered sufficient.[114] However, the use of unmanned technologies alone is not sufficient to establish and maintain effective control as it cannot fully substitute the required military presence of human soldiers in the occupied area.[115]

In other cases of status change of areas such as blockades, minefields, and eventually zones,[116] the state that exercises the measure should notify every neutral (flag) state that might be affected. Accordingly, you can deduce that an occupant should notify neutral states as soon as an occupation of a sea area has been established.

2.3.2 Scope

Finally, the scope of the military authority has to be transferred to occupied sea territory. In addition to the necessary occupation of the adjacent land territory, the expansion of the authority on sea territory is required. According to Art. 88 Oxford Manual, maritime territory is defined as consisting of gulfs, bays, ports, and territorial waters. But what are the outer limits of an occupied sea territory? The territorial waters generally extend up to 12 nm, according to Art. 3 UNCLOS and based on

---

[109]San Remo Manual (1995), paras. 80–92 and explanations pp. 168–176.

[110]Unmanned Aerial Vehicle.

[111]Unmanned Maritime Vehicle in a broader sense, encompassing also unmanned underwater vehicles.

[112]Schmitt (2012), pp. 598–601; Schmitt and Thurnher (2013), pp. 247, 250.

[113]Compare in contrast to the law of occupation: Frau and Singer (2015), pp. 84–85.

[114]Compare the discussion at: Ferraro (2012), p. 143.

[115]Compare: Ferraro (2012), pp. 145–146.

[116]Compare: Hague Convention VIII (1907), Art. 3; San Remo Manual (1995), para. 83 and explanations p. 172, para. 93 and explanations p. 177, para. 106 lit. (e) and explanations pp. 181–183.

customary international law,[117] and its outer limits are determined according to customary international law and Art. 4 f. UNCLOS. So the question remains if the borders of the occupied territorial sea (width) have to be identical to the occupied land territory, or can they be extended (funnel shaped) depending solely on the military authority? This would be the case if the naval forces are able to conquer and control more of the sea territory than the land forces are able to control of the land territory. Because an occupation of sea territory depends on a simultaneous occupation onshore, it can be deduced that the occupied land territory is defining for the occupation of sea territory. Also, as the requirements of effective control (in the sense of potential control, not actual and persistent control) are less strict, the range and scope of the occupied territory would not be clear as there is no continuous presence of forces necessary at the borders of the area. Therefore, a strict determination and limitation of the borders of the occupied sea territory is required. Moreover, it would be very difficult to prove the control of a differing area and its other borders in practice except for stationing troops everywhere, where the border should be. Hence, the borders of the adjacent territory[118] are decisive for the limits of the occupied sea territory and are drawn like the delimitation of regular territorial sea beginning and ending at the limits of the occupied land territory.

Furthermore, the question arises as to whether the military authority only includes the territorial sea during an occupation or if it can extend to the contiguous zone or even the exclusive economic zone.[119] Article 88 Oxford Manual only refers to the territorial waters, not mentioning the contiguous zone and the exclusive economic zone.[120] However, the Oxford Manual was an older approach to codify the existing and undisputed law of naval warfare until 1913. Even the exact delimitation of the territorial sea was disputed for a long period of time. The international treaties,[121] which refer to and establish the contiguous zone and the EEZ in UNCLOS, also were concluded considerably later.[122] Therefore, the Manual could not encompass any statement on the contiguous zone and the EEZ, or probably it did not want to as the opinions on those were diverging by then.

The purpose of the contiguous zone and the EEZ is not to grant sovereignty over that area to a state but to admit certain rights on that area and, in the case of the EEZ, its resources.[123] If an occupation is established, the law of occupation determines

---

[117]San Remo Manual (1995), Explanations p. 94, para 14.2; Heintschel von Heinegg (2014), p. 878.

[118]Compare Verri in Ronzitti (1988), p. 337.

[119]Abbreviated in the Following as: EEZ.

[120]Source of the Text: Ronzitti (1988), p. 317.

[121]Convention on the Territorial Sea and the Contiguous Zone (1958); Convention on the High Seas (1958); UNCLOS (1982).

[122]However consider the earlier recognition of the contiguous zone in customary international law, Heintschel von Heinegg (2014), p. 864.

[123]Compare Art. 24 Convention on the Territorial Sea and the Contiguous Zone (1958); Art. 33 and Art. 55, 56 UNCLOS (1982); Heintschel von Heinegg (2014), p. 895.

that the occupant shall take over the "de-facto authority" over the relevant area[124] with certain jurisdictional and administrative rights and duties deriving from international law.[125] One could also argue that, as the contiguous zone derives from and is linked to the territorial sea, it would be inconsistent to treat it differently from the occupation of territorial sea. Further on, the law of occupation entitles the occupant to measures that are related to the physical control of the area.[126] The rights and duties that are linked to the authority over the contiguous zone and the EEZ are mostly of a nature that requires physical control. As you have to deny any transfer of sovereignty to the occupant,[127] the temporary performance (de facto) of sovereign rights by the occupant is not prohibited and, with a view to the rights and duties of Art. 43 HR, even required.

The wording of the rules on the contiguous zone and EEZ also supports this as Art. 33 UNCLOS and Art. 24 Convention on the Territorial Sea mention the "exercise (of) control" and Art. 55 UNCLOS refers to "rights and jurisdiction of the coastal State." Consequently, the rights connected with the adjacent contiguous zone and the EEZ can be transferred to the occupant during the occupation, as well, under the condition that it is able to exercise control in those areas.

Furthermore, if one excludes the contiguous zone and the EEZ from the scope of the rights and duties of the occupant, one would create a similar legal gray area as argued before. This would mean that there would not be any control of the exploitation of natural resources in the zones if the former state's authority has been expelled. However, this might harm the inhabitants of the area (for example, fishermen) and thereby is in contrast to the legal purpose of the law of occupation and the duty to protect the resources against damage and theft, according to Art. 43, 44 HR.[128]

Concerning the requirements of control in the EEZ, one could also argue that the necessary control over these zones can only be established if infrastructure like an oil platform exists there and if these are under the control of the occupant. This would concentrate the rights and duties only on the exploitation of natural resources and deny the rights and duties in cases where there are no such structures available. Furthermore, there is no legal reason why the possible military authority over the EEZ has to be restricted in contrast to the fairly loose threshold (potential control and reaction in a reasonable time) for control in territorial waters by simultaneously endangering the rights and ownership over natural resources by the former state (the former state keeps the sovereign title over the resources) and the welfare of the population in the occupied area.

Hence, the contiguous zone and the EEZ can be controlled and thus come under the military authority of the occupant if the occupying forces are able to extend and

---

[124]Gasser and Dörmann (2013), pp. 274–275.

[125]Dinstein (2009), pp. 46, 49; Compare German Manual (2013), para. 530.

[126]Gasser and Dörmann (2013), p. 275.

[127]Dinstein (2009), pp. 49–51.

[128]ICJ (2005), para. 248; Benvenisti (2003), p. 870.

exercise their control in these areas in the same manner as in occupied territorial waters. The control, however, has to be restricted to the rights of the coastal state and may not be viewed as territorial rights. It is also argued by some that the same applies to the continental shelf regarding the rights to exploit resources as the legal basis is comparable[129] and derives from the land territory.[130]

Finally, the beginning and the end of an occupation of the aforementioned sea areas do not pose any special problems, and the developed parameter for land territory can be transferred directly.

In conclusion, when control of a sea area is possible, the occupying power has to have all capabilities that are necessary to exercise the rights and duties deriving from the HR, GC IV and AP I, which can be adapted and applied to an occupation of sea territory.

3   Rights and Duties of the Occupying Power: Reference and Transfer of Art. 43 of Hague Convention IV

3.1   Art. 43 of Hague Convention IV

As soon as an occupation is established, the occupant shall take all the measures in his power to restore, and ensure, as far as possible, public order and safety while respecting, unless absolutely prevented, the laws in force in the country according to Art. 43 HR. Article 43 is recognized as customary international law.[131] On the one hand, it implies the (quite extensive) right of the occupant to exercise authority in any possible way ("all measures") and in a second step simultaneously restricts these rights by committing the occupant to respect (besides its additional duties under international law) the existing local laws. However, this restriction is loosened again by the exception that there might be circumstances in which the occupant can also derogate from these legal rules ("unless absolutely prevented").

The general aim of Art. 43 HR is to entitle the occupying power to fight any unrest in the chaotic circumstances during the period of occupation with all feasible methods and means and thereby to protect the local population.[132] However, Art. 43 HR can also be interpreted as preferring the interests of the occupant (and the former government) to the interests of the inhabitants.[133] In order to reach these objectives, Art. 43 HR contains two elements, which "are closely interrelated"[134]: the executive and the legislative components. These follow from the duty to establish

---

[129]UNCLOS (1982), Art. 77.

[130]Dinstein (2009), p. 47 f. Compare UNCLOS (1982), Art. 76.

[131]Trial of the Major War Criminals (1945), pp. 248–249; ICJ (2004), paras. 89, 124; Sassoli (2005), pp. 662–663; Benvenisti (2012), p. 69.

[132]Dinstein (2009), p. 92.

[133]Benvenisti (2009), para. 24.

[134]Sassoli (2005), p. 663.

and guarantee public order and safety. The legislative element is a consequence of the rule of (limited) continuity of the laws in force.[135]

3.1.1 Public Order and Life

The "the duty to restore and ensure public order and safety" requires the occupant to adopt all "available, lawful and proportionate"[136] measures to tackle dangers to these legally protected rights. However, it is not necessary (by law) that these acts are successful.[137] With regard to the authentic French text, the terms "public order" and "safety" have to be understood as "public order" and "life." Therefore, they have a broader scope than public safety (which is implied already in the term "public order").[138] Besides the reestablishment of public order, the civilian population has to be protected "from a meaningful decline in orderly life,"[139] and thereby the social life and the welfare of the inhabitants have to be maintained by the occupying forces.[140] In respect of the duty to stabilize the economic and social circumstances, the occupying power can take actions to influence and promote the economy of the occupied territory.[141] Article 43 HR has to be viewed as a general clause in relation to the maintenance of civil life.[142] The exact legal content of civil life is specified in the provisions of Arts. 44–56 HR and is supplemented by Arts. 50–52, 54–62 GC IV and Arts. 63 f. 69 AP I.

It is not required to set up a special administrative body, and it is appropriate to administer the occupied territory by ordinary troops.[143] The measures to advance public order can either be shaped as police operations or as military operations, depending on the demands of the current situation. However, the legal framework is different in military operations as mainly international humanitarian law applies. In contrast, national law, and possibly international human rights law (disputed),[144] has to be observed for police operations. Also, the aims, the directions, and the objects of military and police operations may differ widely.[145]

---

[135]Compare Benvenisti (2009), paras. 22–26, 27–28; Sassoli (2005), p. 663.

[136]Sassoli (2005), p. 664.

[137]Dinstein (2009), p. 92; Sassoli (2005), pp. 664–665.

[138]Dinstein (2009), pp. 89, 91–93; Benvenisti (2009), para. 22; Sassoli (2005), pp. 663–664.

[139]Dinstein (2009), pp. 91–92.

[140]Sassoli (2005), pp. 663–664.

[141]Dinstein (2009), pp. 93–94.

[142]Compare: Sassoli (2005), p. 664.

[143]Dinstein (2009), pp. 55–56.

[144]Sassoli (2005), p. 666.

[145]Sassoli (2005), pp. 665–666.

3.1.2 Legislation and the Existing Legal System

As provided in Art. 43 HR, the existing national legal system generally has to be preserved and the constitution may not be changed.[146] If this restriction is viewed as absolute, it would not even be possible to change the legal system of a former dictatorship, which deprived most of the population of any basic rights. Consequently, the occupant could not fulfill its duties in terms of public life. This tension between the authority and obligation of the occupant[147] can be dissolved by relying on the wording of Art. 43 HR "unless absolutely prevented." This could be interpreted as allowing to change or suspend the law (only) if it is required for the occupant to fulfill its duties.[148] However, the exact meaning remains unclear.[149] The exception also could be understood as being restrictive, allowing only for limited legal changes. Nevertheless, due to an abstract form, it enables a certain degree of flexibility.[150] Hence, Art. 43 HR sometimes is used to justify far-reaching legislative powers, but in other cases the legislation was very restrictive referring to a conservative interpretation of the wording.[151] Mostly, the term "unless absolutely prevented" is understood to mean that the local laws can be suspended, changed, or overruled. This is considered to be the case when the internal legal system is inappropriate or insufficient to restore and maintain public order and the legal system itself is the root of public unrest, for example if the system discriminates certain groups of the population by restricting their admission to professions and public offices (sectarian systems). Next to reasons of maintaining public order, also the welfare of the population and the "exigencies" of armed conflict are viewed as lawful exceptions for altering and adapting the local legal system.[152] Furthermore, this interpretation is supported by the wording of Art. 64 GC IV, which clarifies that the occupying power is entitled to alter those provisions "which are essential to enable (...) to fulfil its obligations."[153] Some even extend the meaning of "unless and absolutely prevented" to "necessity"[154] or simply requiring a "sufficient justification." This possible expansion of authority has to be considered in the assessment of the intervention in Iraq in the last decade and other "transformative" occupations.[155]

Presupposing that the legal conditions for legislative actions of the occupant are given, the practical question arises as to whether and how legislative acts can be

---

[146]German Manual (2013), para. 569; UK Manual (2004), p. 278; Compare also: Sassoli (2005), pp. 671–672.

[147]Benvenisti (2009), para. 27.

[148]Benvenisti (2009), para. 27.

[149]Sassoli (2005), p. 663.

[150]Sassoli (2005), pp. 668, 663.

[151]Sassoli (2005), p. 673.

[152]UK Manual (2004), pp. 283–284, para. 11.25; German Manual (2013), paras. 544–545.

[153]Compare the discussion about the scope (exclusively penal laws or any laws): Sassoli (2005), pp. 669–670; Benvenisti (2009), para. 27.

[154]LOAC Deskbook (2015), p. 122.

[155]Compare Benvenisti (2009), para. 28; Sassoli (2005), pp. 673–674; Dinstein (1978), p. 112.

performed by the occupying military forces. The core competencies of a military generally are not directed at legislation. However, during an invasion and especially at the beginning of an occupation, it cannot be excluded that the military in the first instance has to enact certain laws to restore and maintain the public order. The legislative duties can have a broad range and be very technical, e.g. if there is a need for changes to the constitution of a state or if particular legal areas are affected like the law of the sea. Furthermore, the legal changes or adaptions should respect the social-cultural peculiarities of the occupied country to foster the acceptance of the new rules in the population, which makes it even more complicated. The demand for and the density of the legislative actions will rise and fall gradually, depending on the range and duration of the occupation. Consequently, there is a need for specialized legal experts in the military, who are experienced in legislative and executive procedures (concerning the latter, the legislation can and will extend also to administrative issues). The organizational structure and the competences of such a legislative mission have to be determined in every single case and depend on the mandate, the legal basis, and the respective (political) goal of the occupation. It is also possible, especially if an occupation lasts for a longer period, that legislative actions will be performed by civilian experts or by a mixed civilian-military team. An occupation established by an international military coalition can render legislative processes more difficult due to higher coordination efforts but also ease the burden of the individual countries by shared capabilities.

As a result (of these findings), it is recommended that NATO and each of its member states build up and maintain a staff of legal personnel and executives who are able to initiate and coordinate legislative procedures during an occupation. This duty derives from the international obligation to teach international humanitarian law as the law of occupation forms an irremovable part of IHL. The Allied Command Transformation Staff Element Europe (ACT SEE) Legal Office might be a suitable institution for this project. Besides the saving of costs and capabilities in the single nations, the alliance is the best level to settle such a program because herein a unified framework for states from different legal systems and thereby a unified approach can be developed. Also, the experiences in legislation gathered during past occupations can be combined and made available to all member states. The CLAMO website can be cited as a suitable example for a file-sharing platform for operational law materiel.[156] If a single member state is in need of expert knowledge on legislative procedures during an occupation, the state can resort to the NATO capabilities.

As accompanying measures, concepts for legislative actions during an occupation period should be researched and developed. Those concepts should contain patterns of rules and associated explanations for (the most) frequent needs for legislation (e.g., security and police, customs and taxes, corruption, basic administration) and should be structured like a modular system with generic ROE comparable to those of NATO document MC 362/1. To build up this database, the existing LAWFAS

---

[156]See CLAMO-Webpage: https://www.jagcnet.army.mil/CLAMO.

System[157] might be a useful tool. Thereby, a framework and respective postwar ROE for the military forces could be easily established during a mission. With resort to the data pool, the occupying forces can act straightforward and still retain the flexibility to decide in the single case.

The duty to restore and ensure law and order also contains the rights and obligations of the occupied state vis-à-vis its neighbors and other third state. This can both be treaty law or customary international law.[158] The territorial scope of international obligations of the former state depends on the content of its provisions. Some treaties and the rules included therein are connected and linked to territorial peculiarities or even single areas, e.g. the governance of river traffic or the sharing of common water resources.[159] If a provision is inextricably bound to a physical or territorial feature or area and this particular area is under the control of the occupant, international obligations have to be applied to the occupant. This obligation is not restricted to the neighbor countries but extends to all international obligations if they are directed to a certain area, which is occupied.[160] Thus, the occupant will be bound by these rules as he is the de facto authority in the concerned area, holds control over the relevant matter, and is obliged to respect the existing legal system and order, wherein international obligations are included. The occupant can also enact new treaties with third states to fulfill its obligations deriving from Art. 43 HR, especially to foster the welfare or well-being of the population.[161] Nevertheless, the occupant is not entitled to conclude international treaties, which bind the inhabitants beyond the period of occupation.[162]

Besides respect for the existing law, the occupant is obliged to ensure the applicable human rights standards in the occupied territory.[163] However, the occupant can also refuse to apply certain derogable human rights for reasons of public order and to the extent required by the circumstances and without violating other international obligations.[164]

Finally, the duty to restore and maintain public order in the aforementioned sense also includes the right of the occupant to suppress any military opposition by force in the occupied territories, be it by the former state or be it by local rebels or insurgents. Article 43 HR cannot be interpreted as restricting or preventing the occupant from fighting any threats or dangers to its own occupying forces. Therefore, the occupant is entitled to enact relevant legislation in order to foster its own military interests as well.[165]

---

[157]NATO LAWFAS System: compare Baquerizo Lozano (2015).

[158]LOAC Deskbook (2015), p. 122.

[159]Benvenisti (2012), pp. 83–84; Benvenisti (2003), pp. 868, 870.

[160]Benvenisti (2003), p. 870.

[161]Benvenisti (2012), pp. 83–86; ICJ (1971), paras. 122, 125.

[162]Benvenisti (2003), p. 868.

[163]UK Manual (2004), p. 282, para. 11.19; Compare: ECHR (1999), paras. 57, 80.

[164]Sassoli (2005), pp. 666–667.

[165]Sassoli (2005), pp. 673–674; Compare also: German Manual (2013), paras. 544–545.

During the occupation, the applicability of GC IV is restricted by Art. 6 (3) GC IV to one year. However, this restriction itself is considered void due to the contravening wording of Art. 3 lit. b AP I.[166] Despite this, the ICJ upheld the one-year rule in its Wall Advisory Opinion.[167] Yet many states, for example the USA and Israel, do not adhere to this rule (Art. 6 (3) GC IV) in practice.[168] As the character of an occupation is limited temporarily and is transitional, also the changes of the law have to be restricted accordingly until the end of the occupation.[169]

In contrast to the rules governing an occupation in the HR, the rules of GC IV are directed specifically to the local population and its needs. Due to the historic developments that underlie GC IV, the competences with a view to the authority of the occupant were increased parallel to its growing duties in relation to the inhabitants, especially to ensure civil life. Hence, the aforementioned restrictions on the legislation have been relaxed, in particular to authorize the occupant to foster and enact human rights obligations in the occupied areas.[170] Furthermore, Art. 29 GC IV specifies that the occupying power is responsible for the treatment of protected persons also by its agents. This rule was further refined in the Loizidou judgment, in which the ECHR stated that it makes no difference if the control is exercised by the armed forces or subordinate local agents.[171] Finally, some rules of GC IV are applicable[172] before the occupant establishes the necessary authority in the occupied areas (during the invasion) and when the territory is still embattled or the occupant is losing control over the occupied territory.[173]

The legal interaction between Art. 43 HR and the rules of GC IV and thereby the legal status quo can be concluded as follows: Art. 43 HR contains a basic framework for the authority and the rights and duties of the occupant. However, this framework was considered insufficient, especially with regard to the interests of the local population. Therefore, supplementary rules were developed and included in the "younger" GC IV, which specify and (further) extend the legal rights and duties focusing on a better and intensified protection of the interests of the inhabitants of the occupied area. In contemporary law, therefore, the establishment of an effective administration is a central element of the duties of the occupant.[174]

---

[166]LOAC Deskbook (2015), p. 121.

[167]ICJ (2004), para. 125.

[168]Benvenisti (2009), para. 26; Gasser and Dörmann (2013), pp. 280–281.

[169]Sassoli (2005), p. 673; Gasser and Dörmann (2013), pp. 280–281.

[170]Benvenisti (2009), paras. 23–25.

[171]ECHR (1996), Merits, para. 52, 56 f. Dinstein (2009), pp. 57–58.

[172]Such as "other provisions of international humanitarian law": Art. 27–34 Geneva Convention IV (1949); for the "General protection of populations against certain consequences of war": Art. 13–26 Geneva Convention IV (1949); Besides the occupant is obliged to respect the fundamental guarantees according to Art. 75 AP I (1949), which is viewed as customary international law.

[173]Gasser and Dörmann (2013), pp. 273–274.

[174]Compare UNSCR 1483 (2003), para. 4.

As stated before, the occupant acquires neither sovereignty nor sovereign rights over the occupied area. However, the occupying forces can, and must, exercise provisional and temporary control and thus may perform certain rights of the former state (de facto authority) during its absence.[175]

If the occupant fails to restore and maintain the public order, the occupant can be held responsible.[176] Admittedly, a belligerent occupation might pose problems to the occupant with regard to the fulfillment of all rights and duties due to the ongoing armed conflict, the local resistance against the occupying forces, or lack of capacity. The law provides exceptions and limits to these duties. The wording of Art. 43 HR ("take all the measures in his power") can be interpreted in the sense that the duties of the occupant can be restricted by its means. Also, according to Art. 43 HR, the obligations "to restore and ensure" reach only "as far as possible." They extend only as far as the relevant capabilities of the occupying nation are available[177] or the level of security allows.[178] Basically, Article 43 HR is held rather general and does not determine precisely which exact measures can be taken.[179] Another legal argument can be found in the exception "unless absolutely prevented" of Art. 43 HR. However, this exception has to be seen with a view to the possible legal activity of the occupant.[180] In that sense, if security reasons or military necessity requires the occupying forces to do so, (local) legal rules can be temporarily suspended.[181]

This raises the question, however, what is meant precisely by the wording "in his power." Does the occupant have to use all of its remaining forces, especially troops from its homeland, to fulfill the obligations of the law of occupation, or does the occupant retain some sort of discretionary power on how many troops it wants to use? A maximum obligation to use all of his forces seems arbitrary, though. The law is vague on that point, and the wording "in his powers" cannot be interpreted to use every possible man and weapon, especially as there is no state practice in that relation. It would be contradictory to demand a potential control and a relative presence of soldiers (to reach every point of the occupied territory) to establish military authority on the one hand and on the other hand to require a much higher (ultimate) degree of forces to be present to fulfill the obligations deriving from exactly that military authority. Besides this legal caveat, such a high burden to employ the maximum of forces would not meet the consent of the international community and would harm the observance of the law.

The obligations with a view to security do not require total crime prevention. It is necessary, however, that the occupant fights pillages, marauding gangs, and other

---

[175]Dinstein (2009), p. 49; Gasser and Dörmann (2013), pp. 274–275; LOAC Deskbook (2015), p. 120.

[176]Benvenisti (2009), para. 22; ICJ (2005), paras. 178–180 and 245.

[177]Compare also: German Manual (2013), p. 81, para. 531.

[178]Dinstein (2009), pp. 91–92; Sassoli (2004), p. 4.

[179]Dinstein (2009), p. 93; Compare also Art. 27 Geneva Convention IV (1949).

[180]Benvenisti (2012), pp. 90–91.

[181]Compare, Dinstein (2009), pp. 91–92.

serious erosions of security.[182] Hence, the military can only be obliged to create such an acceptable level of security that police forces could guarantee public order. As a minimal threshold, the occupying forces have to have enough forces present to potentially control the occupied territory. Minor rumors, which erupt due to too little troops or control, cannot trigger the responsibility of the occupant as they do not affect legally the existence of the occupation itself.[183] However, due to its obligation for the security of the population, the occupant has to insert sufficient forces to restore public order again as soon as it gains knowledge from the decrease of security and it can be commonly expected under the prevailing circumstances.

Therefore, it seems more reasonable to apply an equal standard to both the required military authority and the necessary amount of forces that have to be employed. Thereby, the law of occupation is kept consistently, and no unrealistic standard is imposed on the occupant. If the general security and public order drop too low, the occupant will have the duty to send more troops, to maintain the occupation, and to sustain the capability to fulfill its duties.

Also, if there are limited capacities of the occupant, the question arises if there are different priorities of the various obligations and duties. Especially, it could be necessary to distinguish between the obligations from the law of occupation and general obligations deriving from international law and treaties. The law of occupation itself does not rank the rules. Nevertheless, the rights and duties of the law of occupation, which are connected to the security interests of the occupant and the population, have to have the highest priority. This can be deduced from Art. 43 HR and the purpose of the law of occupation, to balance the interests of the occupant and the population. You cannot prioritize the interests of the occupant before the obligations with a view to the population because the aim of GC IV—to additionally foster the rights of the population—would be ignored. Due to the general *lex specialis* rule, the obligations deriving from the law of occupation are on a higher rank than obligations, which are deduced from (general) international law, especially international treaties. The duties of the occupant, with a view to security and the population, are always superior. Consequently, also obligations from international law that are connected or in a direct relation to obligations of the law of occupation have to be preferred before obligations that only have an indirect connection or only have an effect on the fulfillment of an occupation obligation.

3.2   Transfer and Adaption of Art. 43 Over Occupied Sea Territory

As the occupation of sea territory is considered legal, the requirements for its establishment have to be fulfilled (effective control). Consequently, the legal content of Art. 43 HR as a general clause and also the aforementioned specific rights and duties have to be transferred, adapted, and observed in an occupied sea territory, the

---

[182]ICJ (2005), para. 248.

[183]Benvenisti (2009), para. 8; Ferraro (2012), pp. 145–146.

contiguous zone, and the EEZ. Concerning the specific rights and duties, it is necessary to decide on the applicability of each rule in the relevant "sea-situation" to avoid a legal gray area on the one hand and to limit the application of the law to situations where it can be applied without overstretching its legal purpose on the other hand. For example, the rules on relief, medical and food supplies can be transferred quite easily on sea situations as a duty to enable the deliverance via the sea territory, while the rules for taxes or forced recruitment seem dysfunctional or inconvenient. In contrast, another example is the rule of Art. 54 HR for submarine cables between the occupied territory and neutral states that applies directly to situations at sea.

It has to be borne in mind that most of the administrative rights and duties of the occupant usually will be exercised ashore, even if the scope of the rules affects the sea territory.

When transferred to sea territory, the general clause of Art. 43 HR provides that the occupying power shall restore and maintain public life and security within the sea territory and the adjacent zones. This means that the occupant has to develop and keep a certain level of administration and control, such as coast guard, customs, or fisheries control. This especially encompasses the duties of the Rescue Coordination Center (RCC) if the occupying state is a member to the SAR Convention.[184] Deriving from the rule to ensure that "necessary arrangements are made for the provision of adequate search and rescue services for persons in distress at sea round their coasts,"[185] the occupant has to take over the part of the former state with a view to an RCC. The occupant may regulate the access to the occupied ports, as originally the territorial state is entitled to do so.[186] The range of these rights and duties depends on the status quo of the original state and is limited by the existing national laws governing these matters. However, Art. 43 HR provides that the occupying forces may restrict their administration or the original status quo afloat due to security issues or military necessity.

Furthermore, the occupant is entitled to maintain order and security also, with a view to its own security needs. Therefore, the occupying forces may also lay mines in the occupied sea territory. However, the international law concerning mines and its restrictions on their use must still be observed.[187]

Besides the regular duties to administer the occupied area, it is argued that these duties also include the international legal obligations of the former state, which logically can be transferred to the occupant.[188] This is of particular interest in the context of sea territory as there are several international obligations that concern third states.

---

[184]SAR Convention (1979).

[185]Compare: SAR Convention (1979), Annex, Chapter 2. Organization, 2.1.1.

[186]ICJ (1986), para. 213.

[187]Compare, San Remo Manual (1995), pp. 25–26, especially para. 85.

[188]Benvenisti (2012), pp. 83–84; Benvenisti (2003), p. 870.

Hence, when the original state is expelled from the sea territory, all of its international obligations that are connected to the relevant area have to be met by the occupant.[189] With a view to sea territory, the adjacent contiguous zone and the EEZ, especially the area-bound rights, become relevant, such as transit and passage rights concluded as the "freedoms of communications and maritime commerce" and bilateral fishing agreements with access rights.[190]

Therefore, if the occupant is the de facto authority in these areas, the occupying forces are obliged, inter alia, to allow innocent passage in the territorial sea (Arts. 17 ff. UNCLOS), through archipelagic waters (Art. 52 UNCLOS) and transit passage through international straits according to Arts. 37 ff., 45 UNCLOS. Accordingly, the occupant has to guarantee certain rights, as, for example, provided in Arts. 24, 44 UNCLOS. On the other hand, the occupant is entitled to regulate the use of these rights to the same extent as the original state, compare Arts. 21, 25, 41, 42, 53, 56, 60, 62 (2) UNCLOS. In the contiguous zone, the occupying forces may assume the rights of the original state pursuant to Art. 33 UNCLOS. In the EEZ, the occupant is particularly bound by Arts. 56 (2), 58, 61 UNCLOS.[191] If there are no or only insufficient legal rules governing the sea territory, the occupant may develop legal rules and legislate for the benefit of the population or for its own security needs.[192]

Speaking in general terms, the occupant has to enable the international sea traffic through the occupied territories and zones and therefore has to keep former routes open. As discussed with a view to the duties from Art. 43 HR, the obligations from the freedoms of communications and of maritime commerce can be restricted too. They extend only as far as the relevant capabilities of the occupying nation are available or the level of security allows, according to Art. 43 HR.

Besides the usage for transit, traffic, or trade, the occupied sea territory and EEZ also may contain oil, gas, or other resources. Resources are an important element for the public life and the benefit of the inhabitants, at least as a mean of financing the maintenance of state institutions. Therefore, Art. 43 HR also contains the duty to protect resources in the adjacent zones and the territorial sea.[193] If the occupying power wants to continue to exploit resources, it must comply with the *lex specialis* rule of Art. 55 HR (rule of usufruct) for immovable resources such as oil. The occupying power is thereby limited to public property. However, it may utilize the product or proceeds for its own needs to uphold the occupation or for the good of the inhabitants.[194] The occupant may also use mining facilities and—concerning sea

---

[189]LOAC Deskbook (2015), p. 122.

[190]ICJ (1986), para. 214; Klein (2011), p. 32, note 58.

[191]Compare: ICJ (1986), paras. 213–214; Concerning the different rights and duties: Heintschel von Heinegg (2014), pp. 882–885, 889–890, 894–895, 896–897, 908–910.

[192]Dinstein (2009), pp. 109, 112–113, 115–116; Sassoli (2005), pp. 673–678.

[193]Benvenisti (2012), pp. 81–82; Benvenisti (2003), p. 870. ICJ (2005), paras. 245, 248.

[194]Benvenisti (2012), pp. 81–82; Benvenisti (2009), paras. 30–31.

territory—existing oil platforms on an average and usual level and amount.[195] Besides the use of existing facilities, the occupant has also the duty to keep such institutions intact and running, but only if the use and exploitation contribute to the occupant's security needs or the benefit of the inhabitants.[196] However, it is very controversial if the occupant may build new oil or gas platforms in occupied territories and exploit subjacent oil fields for its own benefits.[197] This can be assessed more generously if the value of the newly exploited resources is utilized for the benefit of the population.[198]

As mentioned before, the occupant eventually could not have enough capabilities to fulfill all of its obligations at the same time. There might be a situation in which the duties directly drawn from the law of occupation (maintenance of security) conflict with other obligations from international law like the duty to enable safe passage.

A possible hierarchy of obligations, however, must respect the following legal principles. The occupant becomes obliged by international law and international treaties as part of the legal system of the former state. According to Art. 43 HR, this system has to be maintained by the occupant. Article 43 HR thereby represents an opening clause for other international law. Also, the purpose of the law of occupation is to balance and protect the security of the occupying forces and certain rights and the well-being of the population. Obligations deriving from international law and treaties, such as UNCLOS, firstly are directed at the interests of the former state (relationship to third states) and not at the well-being of the population. In case the occupant has to prioritize between security for the inhabitants or for its own forces and security for third states deduced from international obligations, the occupant is committed by the law of occupation to prefer the rights and the benefit of the local population and its occupying forces.

Hence, it can be deduced that the obligations deriving from the law of occupation have priority over the obligations of other international laws. If obligations of legal systems other than the law of occupation are competing due to low capabilities, the obligations have to be preferred that are directly related to or in connection of the aforementioned goods, the general security, the interests of the occupying forces, and the well-being of the population. Obligations without a connection to the goods of the law of occupation are of lower importance than the mentioned obligations.

Accordingly, the occupant has to utilize its available capabilities, firstly, to foster the rights and duties deriving from the law of occupation, especially from Art. 43 HR. Secondly, the occupant has to fulfill all of the duties that do not directly originate from the law of occupation but are somehow related to the rights and duties

---

[195]Dinstein (2009), p. 215; UK Manual (2004), p. 303, para. 11.86; However prohibition of pillage: ICJ (2005), paras. 244–245; Benvenisti (2009), para. 30.
[196]Benvenisti (2012), pp. 81–82, 264–265; Benvenisti (2003), p. 863 f. UK Manual (2004), p. 303, para. 11.86.
[197]Compare also UNCLOS (1982), Art. 60.
[198]Dinstein (2009), p. 216.

of the law of occupation. A good example would be the enforcement and control of fishery, if fishery is a common source of food for the population of the occupied area. The freedoms of communication and maritime commerce could also constitute such obligations as due to intact commerce the welfare of the population ("public life") is maintained. However, the welfare of the population is of less importance in comparison to any food- or medicine-related obligation, if those are of uttermost importance for the well-being of the population.

In any case, the occupant shall try to fulfill all of its duties to avoid any damages to third states. The minimum level of capabilities, which have to be made available by the occupant, is the level of potential control needed for the establishment of an occupation. If no potential control can be established at sea, consequently the former state retains the obligations relating to the freedoms of communications and of maritime commerce. There is no legal duty to send additional ships to the occupied area (for example, from the navy at home), except for the maintenance of the needed military authority. Also, the duties in connection with sea traffic contain an amount of control that mostly is identical to the required potential control. Therefore, if there is no sufficient control of an international strait, for example, it is likely that the required military authority does not prevail, and consequently also no occupation of that area exists.

If a duty like enabling transit passage cannot be fulfilled by the occupying forces (as they are absolutely prevented as long as their capabilities are bound), the occupant shall at least notify the international community and the concerned states. This duty could be deduced for the territorial sea from the Corfu Channel case.[199] It is comparable to situations at sea as a blockade or the establishment of a minefield because the (total) restriction of the use of an international strait or innocent passage also poses a danger to neutral shipping. The wording in the Corfu Channel case with a view to the duty to "notify for the benefit of shipping in general" speaks of "such obligations," encompassing that there are duties to notify in various situations of danger.[200] Also, some consider the duty to notify to be a rule of customary international law.[201] In any case, it must be observed that any measure or regulation taken by the occupant in this context is restricted until the end of the occupation and may not last beyond that time period based on the law of occupation.[202]

Finally, the rules for legislation in occupied territories as an abstract matter can be exercised concerning sea territory. The mentioned limits ("unless absolutely prevented") and the derogation of local law for the benefit of the population or security apply identically.

---

[199]ICJ (1949), pp. 22, 35.

[200]ICJ (1949), p. 22.

[201]Murphy (2012), p. 129; Critically: McIntyre (2006), pp. 162–163.

[202]Benvenisti (2003), p. 871.

4 Conclusion

The occupation of the territorial sea and its adjacent zones encompasses several challenges to the existing law of occupation. Despite being highly relevant, as the example of the Iraq occupation and the question on the use of the Iraqi offshore facilities has shown, these issues have not been discussed in depth before. It has been found that the existing law and the general rules are applicable to an occupation over the territorial sea and its adjacent zones. The Hague Regulations can be applied directly. The general requirement for military authority as of Art. 42 HR is the effective control of the occupant, which has to be understood in a broad sense and as the potential control over the whole occupied area. This concept can be transferred without constraints to those sea areas but has to be adapted to the peculiarities at sea. Nevertheless, it is obligatory that a certain amount of military force is present in the occupied sea territory. Based on the historical findings of the Oxford Manual, an occupation of sea territory requires a parallel occupation of the adjacent land territory. The extent of the occupied land territory is also defining for the geographical range of the occupied sea territory. The end of an occupation and other legal restrictions such as the duration of acts and changes can be transferred identically. The rights and duties that are conferred to the occupant as a legal consequence include different challenges to the occupying powers than those ashore. On the one hand, Art. 43 HR as a general clause assigns also international obligations to the occupant, especially with a view to the law of the sea and the freedom of communications and maritime commerce. On the other hand, some of the specific rights of the HR might not be applicable to the circumstances at sea. In any case, the occupant is entitled to limit certain rights and duties. These exceptions can be based on security needs and military necessity and the own capability of the occupying forces. Nevertheless, the public order, security, and life always have to be restored and/or maintained for the benefit of the inhabitants.

In the end, the law of occupation and the connected rights and duties are always imposed on the occupant *de lege lata* as soon as the legal requirements are met. The exceptions to these duties are based not on the will of the occupant but on the objective realities and the factual capacities and possibilities. Especially as rights of third countries can be affected, like the freedoms of communication and maritime commerce, the occupant is obliged to enable and maintain the legal standard, as far as possible, in occupied sea territory by its military authority.

References

Books and Articles

Baquerizo Lozano V (2015) Introducing LAWFAS. In: NATO Legal Gazette, Issue 36, November 2015, pp 9–10 at http://www.act.nato.int/images/stories/media/doclibrary/legal_gazette_36.pdf. Accessed 24 Oct 2017

Benvenisti E (2003) Water conflicts during the occupation of Iraq. Am J Int Law 97(4):860–872

Benvenisti E (2009) Occupation, belligerent. In: Max Planck encyclopedia of public international law.   http://opil.ouplaw.com/view/10.1093/law:epil/9780199231690/law-9780199231690-e359?rskey=XYOEli&result=1&prd=EPIL. Accessed 19 June 2017

Benvenisti E (2012) The international law of occupation, 2nd edn. Oxford University Press, Oxford

Center for Law and Military Operations. CLAMO Website: https://www.jagcnet.army.mil/CLAMO. Accessed 19 June 2017

Commander's Handbook (2007) US Commander's handbook on the law of Naval operations. NWP 1-14M, July 2007

Dennis MJ (2005) Application of human rights treaties extraterritorially in times of armed conflict and military occupation. Am J Int Law 99:119–141. https://doi.org/10.2307/3246094

Dinstein Y (1978) The international law of belligerent occupation and human rights. Israel YB Hum Rts 8:104–143

Dinstein Y (2009) The international law of belligerent occupation. Cambridge University Press, Cambridge

Epping V (2014) In: Ipsen (ed) Völkerrecht, 6th edn. C.H. Beck, München

Ferraro T (2012) Determining the beginning and end of an occupation under international humanitarian law. Int Rev Red Cross 94(885):133–163

Frau R, Singer T (2015) Schiffe versenken – Seeblockaden, neutrale Schifffahrt und das Völkerrecht. In: Brake M (ed) Maritime Sicherheit – Moderne Piraterie. Peter Lang, Frankfurt a Main, pp 81–98

Gasser H-P, Dörmann K (2013) Protection of the civilian population. In: Fleck (ed) The handbook of international humanitarian law, 3rd edn. Oxford University Press, Oxford, pp 231–320

German Manual (2013) Manual for law of armed conflict of the German armed forces

Heintschel von Heinegg W (2014) In: Ipsen (ed) Völkerrecht, 6th edn. C.H. Beck, München

Henckaerts J-M (2005) Study on customary international humanitarian law: a contribution to the understanding and respect for the rule of law in armed conflict. Int Rev Red Cross 87 (857):175–212

Henckaerts J-M, Doswald-Beck L (eds) (2005) Customary international humanitarian law, volume I: rules. Cambridge University Press, Cambridge

ICRC (2012) Occupation and other forms of administration of foreign territory, Expert Meeting, Report prepared and edited by Tristan Ferraro

Kelly M (2003) Iraq and the law of occupation: new tests for an old law. Yearb Int Humanitarian Law 6:127–165

Klein N (2011) Maritime security and the law of the sea. Oxford University Press, Oxford

LOAC Deskbook (2015) US army, law of armed conflict deskbook, international and operational law department, 5th edn

Manual for Law of Armed Conflict of the German Armed Forces, ZDv 15/2 (2013)

Manual of Military Law of War on Land (1958) United Kingdom, Part III

Manual of the Laws of Naval War (1913) Oxford, 9. August 1913

McIntyre O (2006) The role of customary rules and principles of international environmental law in the protection of shared international freshwater resources. Nat Resour J 46(1):1–57

Murphy S (2012) Principles of international law, 2nd edn. West Academic Publishing, St. Paul, Minnesota

Pictet J (ed) (1958) Commentary to the IV Geneva Convention IV relative to the protection of civilian persons in time of war. ICRC, Geneva

Roberts A (1985) What is military occupation? Br Yearb Int Law 55:249–305

Roberts A (2009) Occupation, military, termination of. In: Max Planck encyclopedia of public international   law.   http://opil.ouplaw.com/view/10.1093/law:epil/9780199231690/law-9780199231690-e1927?rskey=uKZKd5&result=1&prd=EPIL. Accessed 19 June 2017

Ronzitti N (1988) The law of naval warfare, a collection of agreements and documents with commentaries. Martinus Nijhoff Publishers, Dordrecht

San Remo Manual (1995) In: Doswald-Beck L (ed) San Remo Manual on international law applicable to armed conflicts at sea. Cambridge University Press, Cambridge

Sassoli M (2004) Article 43 of the Hague regulations and peace operations in the twenty-first century. Background Paper prepared for Informal High-Level Expert Meeting on Current Challenges to International Humanitarian Law, Cambridge, June 25–27, 2004

Sassoli M (2005) Legislation and maintenance of public order and civil life by occupying powers. Eur J Int Law 16(4):661–694

Schmitt M (2012) Unmanned combat aircraft systems and international humanitarian law: simplifying the oft benighted debate. Boston Univ Int Law J 30:595–619

Schmitt M, Thurnher J (2013) "Out of the Loop": autonomous weapon systems and the law of armed conflict. Harv Natl Secur J 4:231–281

UK Manual (2004) The joint service manual of the law of armed conflict, JSP 383

Yalem R (1960) The international status of the territorial sea. Vill Law Rev 5:206–214

Judgments and Court Decisions

ECHR (1996) Case of Loizidou v Turkey, App. No 15318/89, ECHR 1996-VI

ECHR (1999) Bankovic v Belgium, App no 52207/99, ECHR 2001-XII, para 75

ECHR (2007) Al Skeini v United Kingdom, App no 55721/07, ECHR 2011

ICJ (1949) Corfu Channel Case, Judgment of April 9th, 1949 ICJ Rep. 4

ICJ (1969) North Sea Continental Shelf Cases (Judgment), ICJ Rep. 3

ICJ (1971) Legal Consequences of the Continued Presence of South Africa in Namibia, Advisory Opinion, ICJ Rep. 16

ICJ (1986) Case Concerning Military and Paramilitary Activities in and against Nicaragua (Merits), ICJ Rep. 14

ICJ (2004) Legal consequences of the construction of a wall in the occupied Palestinian Territory, ICJ Rep.136, 2004, 43 ILM 1009, 1034-5 (2004)

ICJ (2005) Armed Activities on the Territory of the Congo, ICJ Rep. 168

ICTY (2003) Prosecutor v. Naletilic et al., Trial Chamber, see: http://www.icty.org/case/naletilic_martinovic/4. Accessed 24 Oct 2017

Israel Supreme Court (2008) Tzemel Adv v Minister of Defence and Commander of the Antzar Camp, 1983 & A and B v State of Israel

Trial of the Major War Criminals (1945) International Military Tribunal in Nuremberg, published in 41 AJIL (1947) 172, 248–249

US Tribunal of Nuremberg (1949) Von List case, Law Reports of Trial of War Criminals, Vol VIII, 1949

Treaties and Resolutions

AP I (1949) Protocol (No. I) additional to the Geneva Conventions of 12 Aug 1949 relating to the protection of victims of International armed conflicts, 8 June 1977, 1125 UNTS 3

Convention on the High Seas (1958) 450 UNTS 11

Convention on the Territorial Sea and the Contiguous Zone (1958) 29 Apr 1958, 516 UNTS 205

Geneva Convention (IV) (1949) Relative to the Protection of Civilian Persons in Time of War, 12 Aug. 1949, 75 UNTS 287

Hague Convention (IV) respecting the Laws and Customs of War on Land and its annex: regulations concerning the Laws and Customs of War on Land, The Hague, 18 October 1907

Hague Convention VIII (1907) Relative to the laying of automatic submarine contact mines. The Hague, 18 October 1907, 36 Stat. 2332

Hague Convention XIII (1907) Concerning the rights and duties of neutral powers in naval war, The Hague, 18 October 1907, 36 Stat. 2415

HR (1899) Hague Regulations Respecting the Laws and Customs of War on Land, Annexed to Hague Convention II, 1899, and Hague Convention IV, 1907, 36 Stat. 2277

Lieber Code (1863) Instructions for the Government of Armies of the United States in the Field, 24 April 1863, at http://avalon.law.yale.edu/19th_century/lieber.asp. Accessed 24 Oct 2017, also in D. Schindler and J. Toman (1988) The Laws of Armed Conflicts. Martinus Nihjoff Publishers, p 3–23

SAR Convention (1979) International convention on maritime search and rescue, 1405 UNTS 23489, entered into force 22 June 1985, A revised Annex to the SAR Convention entered into force in January 2000 and a further revision has been adopted 2004 (MSC 78/26/Add.1)

UN Definition of Aggression (1974) United Nations General Assembly, Res 3314 [XXIX] [14 December 1974] GAOR 29th Session Supp 31 vol 1, 142

United Nations Treaty Collection UNTC I-973., https://treaties.un.org/pages/showDetails.aspx?objid=0800000280158b1a. Accessed 24 Oct 2017

UNCLOS (1982) United Nations Convention on the Law of the Sea, 10 Dec 1982, 1833 UNTS 3, No. 31363

UNSCR 1483 (2003) United Nations Security Council Resolution, 22 May 2003, 42 ILM 1016 (2003)

Tassilo Singer was research associate and lecturer at the University of Passau (2012–2013; 2015–2017) and at the European University Viadrina (2013–2015). Apart from this, he has been guest lecturer at different universities in Europe and gave presentations at various conferences and workshops in Europe. He has published several works in the field of international law and in particular concerning the *ius ad bellum* and the law of armed conflict. His most recent publication is "Update to Revolving 2.0: The Extension of the Period for Direct Participation in Hostilities Due to Autonomous Cyber Weapons," which has been published as a peer review paper for the NATO Cycon 2017.

Since Oct. 2013, he has been a Ph.D. candidate under the auspices of Prof. Wolff Heintschel von Heinegg, and finished his thesis with the working title "Dehumanization of Warfare—Challenges for International Law" in Sept. 2017.

His current research focus is on modern weapon technologies such as unmanned systems, autonomy, and cyber warfare, with view to international law.